LIVING IN THE SHADE OF
ISLAM

Living in the shade of Islam

İsmail Büyükçelebi

The Light

New Jersey
2005

Published by The Light, Inc.
26 Worlds Fair Dr. Suite C
Somerset, New Jersey, 08873, USA

www.thelightpublishing.com

Library of Congress Cataloging-in-Publication Data

Büyükçelebi, Ismail, 1948-
    Living in the shade of Islam / Ismail Buyukcelebi
    Translated by Ali Unal.-- 1st ed.
    p. cm.
    Includes index.
    ISBN 1932099867
    1. Islam--Doctrines. 2. Islam--Essence, genius, nature. I. Title.
BP165.5.B89 2005
297.2--dc22
2005002595

Printed by
Çağlayan A.Ş., Izmir - Turkey
March 2005

TABLE OF CONTENTS

is no changing God's creation. That is the right religion, but most people know it not. (30:30)

Islam seeks to unite us with the vast domain of being, and strives to create an absolute unity between us and the universe. We are the most essential partner in the Realm of Existence, and each Muslim is the co-religionist of all creatures:

> What, do they desire another religion than God's, while to Him has surrendered whosoever is in the heavens and Earth, willingly or unwillingly, and to Him they shall be returned? (3:83)

> Have you not seen how all who are in the heavens and in Earth, the sun, moon, stars and mountains, trees and beasts, and many of humanity prostrate to God? (22:18)

THE UNIVERSAL MESSAGE

While constant change is observed in nature, there is an underlying aspect of permanence in everything. For instance, a seed germinates underground and grows into a tree without the laws of germination and growth changing. Likewise the essential character of humanity and human life with all its vital, indispensable necessities, regardless of any external material or other changes in our lifestyles, as well as their impact upon our lives and environment, have remained unchanged since the creation of Adam and Eve. All of us share certain general conditions of life and value: we are born, mature, marry, have children, and die; we have some degree of will and common desires; we share certain values, such as honesty, kindness, justice, courage, and so on.

Thus all Prophets sent by God were sent with the same message. Each created being naturally depends upon his or her Creator. Only the Creator is Self-Existent, unique and single, and not composite, subject to change, or contained by time or space. Belief in such a Divine Being constitutes the primary foundation of the Divine religion preached by all Prophets. Its other pillars are belief in the Resurrection, all Prophets without distinction, angels, Divine Scriptures, and Divine Destiny (including human free will).

Those who do not use their free will to discipline themselves face the danger of enslavement by their passions. Such a lack of self-discipline causes us to wrong others, for the goal of such behavior is to satisfy our desires. Since the Divine religion does not allow such wrongdoing, those who pursue it try to corrupt religion in order to justify their whims and fancies. This causes disorder, oppression, unending conflict, and destruction. God wills mercy for His creation, not oppression or injustice, and that its members live in peace so that justice prevails. However, history relates that the followers of earlier Prophets split into opposing factions and tampered with the religion to serve their preferences or interests.

All previous Prophets were sent to restore the Divine religion to its original purity by purging the innovations and deviations added by its adherents. This is why Prophet Muhammad was sent after Jesus to preach the same pillars of faith. God revealed to him the Qur'an, which contains the eternal principles for our individual and collective life. Since God decrees that the Qur'an is absolutely and permanently preserved, the Prophet is the last Messenger.

Islam honors the religious experience of those who came before its revelation, because Islam confirms and completes what is true in those religions. Given this, Muslims say that Prophet Abraham and all other Prophets were *muslim*. Such an outlook explains why Islamic civilization, from its very beginnings, was and remains tolerant, plural, and inclusive. It has always been this way, except for the rarest of exceptions.

Islam says that God's universal providence would be denied if Prophets were raised for one nation only and if other nations had no Prophets. The Qur'an states that God is the Lord and Sustainer of all worlds. He did not discriminate among nations when sending His Revelation, and so Muslims must not distinguish between any of His Messengers:

> The Messenger (Muhammad) believes in what was sent down to him from his Lord. Each believer believes in God and His angels, His Books, and His Messengers. We make no distinction between any of His Messengers. They say: "We hear and obey.

> Our Lord, grant us Your forgiveness. Unto You is the home-coming." (2:285)

Islam is the consummation of all religions. By accepting the Prophets and Scriptures of all nations, Islam affirms God's Unity and universal providence, as well as the universality of religious experience. Muslims are true followers of all Prophets, including Abraham, Moses, and Jesus.

Muslims reject the term *Muhammadanism*, for they do not worship Muhammad. To understand Islam as its adherents do, such words as *Muhammadan* or *Muhammadanism* need to be dropped. Muhammad never claimed to be more than a man who received revelations from God. He did not make Islam; he simply received it.

ISLAM DOES NOT ACCEPT CONTRADICTIONS

Tawhid implies the equality and unity of all people in their relation with God, and thus indicates homogeneity, equality, and the unity of human origin. Humanness is the one element ingrained in the nature of all individuals. People of different social strata were not created by separate deities with varying levels of power, for this would violate *tawhid* by allowing possible disparity in their essential nature and erecting insuperable barriers between them. The same God created everyone, and so all people have the same fundamental essence: *O humanity, be conscious of your Lord, Who created you of a single soul* (4:1).

Given this, Islam rejects legal, physical, class, social, political, racial, national, territorial, genetic, or even economic factors. *Tawhid* means considering humanity as a unity and working to eliminate all efforts at division based upon such factors as color, social status, occupation, education, geography, religion, and ideology. All such divisions are reconcilable only by replacing *tawhid* with *shirk* (dualism, trinitarianism, or polytheism).

The Qur'an declares:

> O humanity, We created you from one (pair) of a man and a woman and formed you into peoples and tribes to know each other (not to take pride in your color or race, or claim superiority due to your color, race, or socioeconomic status). (49:13)

In fact, the noblest person in God's sight is the one who is most God-conscious. The Prophet is reported to have said: "Your Lord is One. You are from Adam and Adam is from dust. An Arab is not superior to a non-Arab, nor a white person over a black person, except for his or her piety and righteousness." (I. Hanbal, *Musnad*, 5:411)

This belief in human unity is the corollary of God's Unity. The same God created and nourishes all people, regardless of race, color, creed, and culture. Thus everyone is His servant, and those most dear to Him are His best servants. The Prophet is reported to have said:

> God says to His servants on the Day of Reckoning: "You did-n't visit me when I was sick." They reply: "How could I visit You, since You are the Lord of creation?" God says: "Don't you remember that My servant so-and-so fell sick and you didn't visit him (or her)? If you had, you would have found Me with him (or her). You didn't give Me food when I asked you for it." They ask: "How could we give You food, since You are the Lord of creation?" God says: "Don't you remember My servant so-and-so who asked you for food but you refused. If you had done so, you would have found Me with him (or her)." God says: "You didn't give Me water when I asked you." They ask: "How could we give You water, since You are the Lord of cre-ation?" God retorts: "Don't you remember My servant so-and-so who asked you for water but you refused? If you had done so, you would have found Me with him (or her)."

The Prophet informs us that a prostitute entered a road lead-ing to Paradise and deserved it because she gave water to a thirsty dog out of compassion, whereas another woman entered a road leading to Hell because she let a cat die of hunger. (Bukhari, "Anbiya," 54.) This is Islam, with its arms wide open to all crea-tures, regions, and ages.

Despite all these facts and centuries of close contact with oth-er cultures and its many similarities with Judaism and Christianity, Islam remains somehow alien and "other." Having played a sig-nificant part in the colonized Muslim world's struggle to throw off its colonial masters and resume its rightful place in the world,

Islam inevitably became associated in the popular mind with politics and ideology. More recently, it has become associated with backwardness and anti-Western feelings as Muslims strive to rediscover their spiritual and cultural heritage and to live accordingly. And many people, always ready for simplistic answers to and explanations of an impossibly complex issue, latch on to such obvious associations and "truths" and probe no further.

This book seeks to present Islam's true face and make it known in a summarized form with most of its aspects: its essentials of faith, principles and ways of worshipping God, morality, and rules ordering human life and relations between people.

CHAPTER ONE

The Meaning of Religion and
a General Outline of Islam

THE MEANING OF RELIGION AND A GENERAL OUTLINE OF ISLAM

R eligion comes from either *relegere* ("to read" or "to pursue together," as well as "legible" and "intelligent") or, much more likely and generally accepted, from *relegare* ("to tie back" or "to bind fast"). Hence a religious person used to mean a monk tied by his vows. *Ligament* and *ligature* also come from this root. For Romans, it meant being tied back, staying connected with ancestral customs and beliefs, or a kind of loyalty. For Christians, the word originally meant being tied back or connected to God.

The corresponding Arabic word is *din*, which literally means restoring one's rights, obedience, adopting as a way of life, being in debt, calling to account, managing, rewarding or punishing, serving, and lending. Muslim theologians describe *din* as the set of principles revealed by God through His Prophets and Messengers, and the set that humanity should follow, of its own free will, to acquire happiness in both worlds.

The concept of religion may be viewed from two perspectives: the human or the Divine. Monotheists take religion to be God-revealed principles, values, and commandments, and so do not refer to humanity when explaining religion's origin. In contrast, modern Western and Westernized people under the influence of scientific materialism say that humanity created religion and then used anthropology, sociology, and psychology to explain it away.

The common denominator in the Western "scientific" analysis of religion is that it is a human invention designed either to project repressed desires or weaknesses or the result of individual or collective efforts to systematize a community's beliefs and rites.

RELIGION IN THE QUR'AN

The Qur'an uses *din*, usually translated as "religion," in different contexts with various meanings. The most important and common of these are the collection of moral, spiritual, and worldly principles, system, and way of conduct (33:5, 40:26); judging, rewarding, punishing (1:4, 51:6, 82:18-19); way, law, constitution (12:76); servanthood and obedience (16:52); and peace and order (8:39).

With Islam, God completed the religion He revealed and chose for humanity: *This day I have perfected your religion for you, completed My Favor upon you, and have chosen for you Islam as your religion* (5:3). Literally, Islam means "submission, peace, and salvation." In its most fundamental aspect, Islam is epitomized in the most frequently recited of all Qur'anic phrases, the *Basmala* – In the name of God, the Merciful (*al-Rahman*), the Compassionate (*al-Rahim*). Both words are related to *rahma* (mercy and compassion). God manifests Himself via His absolute, all-inclusive Mercy and Compassion, and Islam is founded upon that affirmation. The Qur'an calls Prophet Muhammad's mission *a mercy for all the worlds* (21:107).

Islam with Its Basic Features

Islam is distinguished from other religions by several characteristics, among them are the following:

Monotheism

Islam is uncompromisingly monotheistic, for its theology begins and ends with God's Unity (*tawhid*). Given this, the universe is seen as an integral whole of interrelated and cooperative parts in which a splendid coordination, harmony, and order are displayed throughout the universe and within each living organism. This harmony and order come from the Unity of the One Who created them and Who is absolute, without partner, peer, or like. It is God Who has created the universe with whatever is in it and administers it. What we deduce from the operation of the universe and call "natural laws" are, in fact, God's regular ways of creating things and events and administering the universe. From this perspective, the universe, which is governed by God and obeys Him, is literally *muslim* – submitted to God. Thus its operations are orderly and harmonious.

Humanity

The quality of being human comes from our immaterial and spiritual aspects, not from our natural and material aspects. The spirit and intellect do not originate in the physical body; rather, the spirit uses the body, and only life gives the body any meaning.

A fruit tree's future life is encapsulated in its seed, and a tree is worth only as much as the value of the fruit it yields. In the same way, each person's life-history is recorded and is of value only in proportion to the number of good deeds done and the level of virtue attained. Again, just as a tree increases by means of the seeds in its fruit, we prosper by our good deeds, the weight and consequence of which one day will be revealed to us.

We have three principal drives: desire, anger, and intellect. We desire or lust after the opposite sex, and love our children and worldly possessions. We direct our anger at what stands in our way, and by using it can defend ourselves. Our intellect enables us to make the right decisions. The Creator does not restrain these drives, but rather requires us to seek perfection through self-discipline so that we do not misuse them. If they remain undisciplined, immorality, illicit sexual relationships, and prohibited livelihoods, tyranny, injustice, deception, falsehood, and other vices will appear in individuals and throughout society. In addition, humanity could not help but ask these vital questions since its appearance on Earth: Who am I? Where do I come from? What is my final destination? What does death demand from me? Who is my guide on this journey, beginning from clay and passing through the stages of a sperm-drop, a blood-clot, and a lump of flesh, another creation where the spirit is breathed into my body, and finally reaching the grave and through there to the Hereafter?

It is in all of these questions that the essential problem of human life lies, and our individual and collective happiness requires being able to give the correct answer to the vital questions mentioned, as well as in disciplining our faculties so that we may produce a harmonious peaceful individual and social life. Since it is not possible for the human intellect to totally comprehend where true human happiness lies in both this world and the next, humanity needs a universal intellect, a guidance from beyond human reason and experience, to whose authority all may assent freely. That guidance is the religion revealed and perfected by God through His Prophets.

Prophets

All Prophets came with the same essentials of belief: belief in God's Existence and Unity, the world's final destruction, Resurrection and Judgment, Prophethood and all Prophets without distinction, all Divine Scriptures, angels, and Divine Destiny and Decree (including human free will). They called people to worship the One God, preached and promoted moral virtue, and condemned vice. Differences in particular rules and injunctions were connected with the existing economic and political relationships. Thus to be a Muslim means believing in all of the Prophets and the original previous Scriptures.

A Prophet, one purified of sin and vice and having a deep relation with God, guides people to truth and sets a perfect example for them to follow. Such people have the following essential characteristics: absolute and complete truthfulness, trustworthiness, communication of the Divine Message; the highest intellectual capacity, wisdom, and profound insight; sinlessness; and no mental or physical defects. Just as the sun attracts planets by the invisible force of gravitation, Prophets attract people by the force of their profound relation with God, certain miracles, and the sheer nobility of their person, purpose, and character.

Islam honors the religious experience of those who came before its revelation, because Islam confirms and completes what is true in those religions. Given this, Muslims say that Prophet Abraham and all other Prophets were *muslim*. Such an outlook explains why Islamic civilization, from its very beginnings, was and remains tolerant, plural, and inclusive. It has always been this way, except for the rarest of exceptions.

Belief

Belief, the essence of religion, is far more than a simple affirmation based upon imitation. Rather, it has degrees and stages of expansion or development, just as a tree's seed gradually is transformed into a fully grown, fruit-bearing tree. Belief contains so many truths pertaining to God and the universe's realities that the most perfect human science, knowledge, and virtue is belief in and knowledge of God originating in belief based upon argument and investigation. Those who attain the degree of "certainty of belief coming from direct observation of the truths on which belief is based" can study the universe as a kind of Divine Scripture.

The Qur'an, the universe, and humanity are three manifestations of one truth. In principle, therefore, there can be no contradiction or incompatibility between Qur'anic truths (issuing from the Divine Attribute of Speech) and truths derived from the objective study of its counterpart, the created universe (from the Divine Attributes of Power and Will). An Islamic civilization true to its authentic, original impulse contains no contradiction between science (the objective study of the natural world) and religion (the personal and collective effort to seek God's good pleasure). True belief is not based on blind imitation, but rather appeals to our reason and heart and combines reason's affirmation and the heart's inward experience and submission. As Said Nursi reminds us:

> Belief in God is creation's highest aim and most sublime result, and humanity's most exalted rank is knowledge of Him. The most radiant happiness and sweetest bounty for jinn and humanity is love of God contained within knowledge of God. The human spirit's purest joy and the human heart's sheerest delight is spiritual ecstasy contained within love of God. All true happiness, pure joy, sweet bounties, and unclouded pleasures are contained within knowledge and love of God.[1]

Worship

Belief engenders different kinds of worship, such as responding to explicit injunctions (e.g., the prescribed prayers, fasting, alms-giving, and pilgrimage) and obeying prohibitions (e.g., avoiding all intoxicants, gambling, usury, killing, oppression, usurpation, deception, and unlawful sexual relationships). Those seeking to strengthen their belief and attain higher ranks of perfection should be careful of their heart's and intellect's "acts" (e.g., contemplation, reflection, invocation, recitation of God's Names, self-criticism, perseverance, patience, thankfulness, self-discipline, and perfect reliance upon God). Moral virtues are the fruits of religious life. As Prophet Muhammad said: "I have been sent to perfect good morals." (Tabarani, *Mu'jam al-Awsat*, 7:74.)

Universal Moral Virtues

As mentioned just above, Islam encourages such virtues as honesty, love, compassion, generosity, altruism, truthfulness, trustworthiness, and helpfulness, and refraining from all vices such as lying, ostentation, and deception. These are essentially reflections of our true nature. Created by the One, Who is All-Wise, All-Generous, All-Compassionate, every person has an innate inclination toward these virtues. Therefore they are confirmed and established by Islam, which was revealed by God through His Prophets to show humanity how to resolve all of its psychological and social problems.

Collective Life

By means of belief and worship, as well as its intellectual, moral, and spiritual principles, Islam educates us in the best possible way. In addition, it uses its socioeconomic principles to establish an ideal society free of dissension, corruption, deception, oppression, anarchy, and terror, one that allows everyone to obtain happiness both in this world and the next.

The life of religion and serving God accepts right, not force, as the point of support in social life. It proclaims that the aim of individual and collective life is to attain virtue and God's approval instead of realizing selfish interests, and mutual assistance instead of conflict. It seeks the internal and external unity of communities through ties of religion, profession, and country, not through racism and negative nationalism. It works to erect a barrier against

worldly desires and encourages us to strive for perfection by urging the soul to pursue sublime goals. Right calls for unity, virtue brings solidarity, and mutual assistance means helping each other. Religion secures brotherhood, sisterhood, and attraction. Self-discipline and urging the soul to virtue brings happiness in this world and the next.

God's Two Kinds of Laws

God has established two kinds of laws: the religious rules (issuing from His Attribute of Speech and governing our religious life) and the so-called laws of nature (issuing from His Attribute of Will and governing creation and life). The reward or punishment for following or ignoring them is given at different times. Reward and punishment for obeying or disobeying the former usually comes in the next life, while for the latter, in this life.

The Qur'an constantly draws our attention to natural phenomena, the subject matter of science, and urges us to study them. In the first 5 centuries of Islam, Muslims united science and religion, intellect and heart, and material and spiritual. Later on, however, in addition to losing the lead in science due to their negligence of the Divine laws of nature, they no longer practiced Islam's religious rules. This is why they have fallen into a wretched state behind the powers equipped with science and technology. So their salvation requires following both kinds of laws.

WE NEED GOD AND RELIGION MORE THAN EVER BEFORE

Although modern technology has blinded us to some fundamental human limitations so that we consider ourselves omnipotent, self-sufficient, and self-existing or possessors of unlimited power, in reality we are weak, frail, needy, and destitute. Although we cannot create a leaf or a gnat, or even a molecule of water, our entrapment by modern technology's spell makes us loathe to admit this. We are content to ascribe all natural events, from sunrise and sunset to the movements of atoms, to nominal natural laws that function without our intervention. Even our bodies work independently of us, for we cannot prevent ourselves from sleeping,

becoming hungry or thirsty, or dying at the hands of a micro-
scopic creature.

We always are accompanied by sorrows arising from past misfortunes and by worries about the future. Fear, love, and expectations are inseparable from our existence, while such things as
youth and beauty, of which we are very fond, leave without saying "good-bye." We greatly fear and are overwhelmed unexpectedly by misfortune, old age, and death. Countless requirements
must be maintained if we are to go on living, yet we have total
control over none of them. We may be injured, accidents may end
our hopes, and disease and unexpected events always threaten and
block our way to happiness. We endure earthquakes, storms, floods,
fires, and other natural catastrophes. Both the vast variety of phenomena and our awareness of our own frailty make our own weakness and helplessness quite clear.

Despite our claims of dominating nature and conquering
space, we have more need of religion than our ancestors ever did.
We may not be worshipping fetishes as they did, such as trees,
animals, rivers, fire, rain, and heavenly bodies, but, according to
Erich Fromm, millions of us have our own fetishes: national heroes,
movie stars, politicians, sports figures, musicians, and many, many
others.

Furthermore, millions of us practice such modern religions
as transcendental meditation, necromancy, Satanism, and spirit
worship in the hope of satisfying that which cannot be satisfied
with scientific and technological advancements. Others seek fulfillment in stadiums, nightclubs, casinos, jobs, and trade unions.
They transform such places into places of devotion because they
cannot suppress their need to worship. Inevitably, those who do
not believe in and worship the One God become the slaves of
numerous deities.

RELIGION

Since its appearance on Earth, humanity has found true peace and happiness in religion. As it is impossible to talk of morality and virtue where people do not practice the true religion, it is also difficult to imagine real happiness, for morality and virtue originate in a good, clear conscience. Religion is what makes one's conscience good and clear, for it is a connection between humanity and God.

৯৯ ৯৬

Religion is the best school, a most blessed institution founded to inculcate in people good moral qualities. It is open to everyone, from the youngest to the oldest, and only those who attend it attain peace, satisfaction, and freedom. Those without religion, by contrast, cannot save themselves from losing everything, including their true identity.

৯৯ ৯৬

Religion is the collection of Divine principles that guide people to what is good and right, not by force but by appealing to their free will. All principles that secure our spiritual and material progress, and thereby our happiness in both worlds, are found in religion.

৯৯ ৯৬

Religion means recognizing God in His absolute and transcendental Oneness; acquiring spiritual purity by acting in His way; arranging relationships in His name and according to His commandments, and feeling a profound interest in and love for all creation on His account.

৯৯ ৯৬

Sooner or later, those who do not recognize religion will come to despise such high values as chastity, patriotism, and love of humanity.

৯৯ ৯৬

Immorality is a disease caused by the absence of religion, and anarchy is a product of the same lack.

৯৯ ৯৬

Do atheists, who devote their lives to attacking, not have some obligation to demonstrate the benefits, if any, and the good consequences, if any, of atheism?

Religion and science are two faces of a single truth. Religion guides us to the true path leading to happiness. Science, when understood and used properly, is like a torch that provides us with a light to follow the same path.

෨ ෬

All the beautiful "flowers" of laudable virtues are grown in the "gardens" of religion, as are the most illustrious "fruits" of the tree of creation, such as Prophets, saints, and scholars of high achievement. Although atheists deliberately ignore them, regardless of how hard they try they will be unable to remove them from the hearts of people and the pages of books.

෨ ෬

Nothing in true religion is contrary to sound thinking, common sense, and knowledge. Therefore true religion cannot be criticized from any rational point of view. Those who do not accept religion either are devoid of sound thinking and reasoning or have a wrong conception of knowledge and science.

෨ ෬

Religion is an inexhaustible and blessed source that lays the foundation of true civilization. It is through religion that we are elevated so high in spirit and feelings that we make contact with metaphysical worlds, where we are "fed" to full satisfaction with all kinds of beauty, virtue, and goodness. Virtues are to be sought in the practice of religion. It rarely happens that an atheist has laudable virtues, or that a religious person has none.

෨ ෬

Men and women attain true humanity by means of religion, which distinguishes them from animals. For atheists, there is no difference between human beings and animals.

෨ ෬

Religion is the way established by God, while atheism is the way of Satan. This is why the struggle between religion and atheism has existed since the time of Adam and will continue until the Last Day.

(M. Fethullah Gülen, *Pearls of Wisdom*, The Light, Inc., 2005.)

CHAPTER TWO

The Essentials of the Islamic Faith

THE ESSENTIALS OF THE ISLAMIC FAITH

All Prophets came with the same essentials of faith, which are also Essentials of the Islamic Faith: belief in God's Existence and Unity, the world's final destruction, Resurrection and Judgment, Prophethood and all Prophets without distinction, all Divine Scriptures, angels, and Divine Destiny and Decree (including human free will).

 I.   God's Existence, Oneness, and Attributes
 II. The Invisible Realm of Existence
 III. Divine Decree and Destiny, and Human Free Will
 IV. The Resurrection and the Afterlife Qur'anic Arguments for the Resurrection
 V.   Divine Books and the Qur'an
 VI. Prophethood and Prophet Muhammad

I. GOD'S EXISTENCE, ONENESS, AND ATTRIBUTES

The existence of God is too evident to need any arguments. Some saintly scholars even have stated that God is more manifest than any other being, but that those who lack insight cannot see Him. Others have said that He is concealed from direct perception because of the intensity of His Self-manifestation.

Knowledge of God

God Almighty should be considered from five perspectives. One is His "Essence" as Divine Being (*Zat*), which only He can know. The Messenger says: "Do not reflect upon God's 'Essence'; instead, reflect upon His creation." (Abu Nu'aym, *Hilyat al-Awliya'*, 6:67.) God has no partners, likes, or resemblance, as indicated in: *There is nothing like Him* (42:11). The second perspective is His Essential, "Innate" Qualities as being God, which are the Attributes' source.

The third perspective is His Attributes, which are of three kinds: Essential Attributes (e.g., Existence, Having No Beginning, Eternal Permanence, Being Unlike the Created, Self-Subsistence, Absolute Oneness); Positive Attributes (e.g., Life, Knowledge, Power, Speech, Will, Hearing, Seeing, Creating); and innumerable "Negative" Attributes, summed up as "God is absolutely free from any defect and shortcoming."

The Attributes are the sources of the Names: Life gives rise to the All-Living, Knowledge to the All-Knowing, and Power to the All-Powerful. The Names are the sources of the acts: giving life has its source in the All-Living, and knowing everything down to the smallest thing originates in the All-Knowing. God is "known" by His acts, Names, and Attributes. Whatever exists in the universe, in the material and immaterial worlds, is the result of the Names' and Attributes' manifestations: Universal and individual provision points to His Name the All-Providing, and the All-Healing is the source of remedies and patient recovery. Philosophy has its source in Wisdom, and so on. The acts, Names, and Attributes are the "links" between God and the created, or the "reflectors" with which to have knowledge of God.

Although we try to know or recognize God by His acts, Names, and Attributes, we must not think of Him in terms of associating likeness or comparison unto Him, for nothing resembles Him. He is absolutely One, Single, and totally different from all that exists or has the potential to exist. In this sense, His Oneness is not in terms of number. He also has Unity and relations with the created. To have some knowledge of Him through His acts, Names, and Attributes, some comparisons are permissible. This is pointed to in: *For God is the highest comparison* (16:60).

Some of God's Names

In order to make Himself known, God Almighty mentions Himself with some Names or Titles, some of which are as follows:

- *Al-Rahman:* The All-Merciful (One Who has mercy for all His creation and provides for them their sustenance).
- *Al-Rahim:* The All-Compassionate (especially toward His believing servants).

- *Al-Fard:* The Absolutely Independent One.
- *Al-Ahad:* The All-Unique, Peerless.
- *Al-Hayy:* The All-Living (One Who has no beginning and no end, Who lives and does not die).
- *Al-Qayyum:* The Self-Subsistent (Who takes care of and maintains His creation).
- *Al-'Adl:* The All-Just.
- *Al-Samad:* The Self-Sufficient (Who needs no one and Whom everyone else needs).
- *Al-Quddus:* The All-Holy (and One Who keeps the universe clean).
- *Al-Haqq:* The Truth (One Who always says, does, and orders the truth and establishes it, and in Whose decrees and acts there is nothing false, meaningless, and useless).
- *Al-Hakim:* The All-Wise (having absolute wisdom in All His decrees and acts).
- *Al-'Alim:* The All-Knowing (One Who knows all that is hidden from us and all that is known to us).
- *Al-Sami':* The All-Hearing.
- *Al-Basir:* The All-Seeing (One Who witnesses all things and events).
- *Al-Qadir:* The All-Powerful (Who has absolute power over all things).
- *Al-Razzaq:* The All-Providing.
- *Al-'Azim:* The All-Mighty.
- *Al-Kabir:* The All-Great.
- *Al-Khaliq:* The Creator.
- *Al-Mawla:* The Guardian (One Who owns, guards, and supports His creatures, and Who provides victory and protection to those who do what He has commanded and avoid what He has forbidden).
- *Al-'Aliy:* The All-High (One Who is High above everyone in His power and status).
- *Al-'Aziz:* The All-Honored and Triumphant with irresistible might.
- *Al-'Afuw:* The One Who overlooks and pardons His servants' sins and faults.
- *Al-Hafiz:* The All-Protecting.
- *Al-Halim:* The All-Clement (One Who is forbearing, mild, and gentle. He is patient and does not rush to punish His servants for their sins).
- *Al-Ghafur:* The One who forgives the sins and mistakes of His servants.
- *Al-Karim:* The All-Generous (One Who is noble, generous, and gracious).

- *Al-Wadud:* The All-Loving.
- *Al-Wahhab:* The One Who bestows mercy and success upon His creation.
- *Al-Nasir:* The All-Helping (and One Who gives victory to His believing servants).
- *Al-Ra'uf:* The All-Pitying.
- *Al-Shakur:* The One Who rewards His servants for their good deeds much more than they deserve.
- *Al-Tawwab:* The One Who enables His servants to turn to Him in repentance and accepts their sincere repentance.

Tawhid (God's Oneness)

First, the most fundamental and important teaching of Prophet Muhammad, upon him be God's peace and blessings, is belief in the Oneness or Unity of God. This is expressed in the primary kalima of Islam as: "There is no deity but God" (*La ilaha illa'llah*). This phrase is the bedrock of Islam, its foundation and its essence.

All religions revealed to the Prophets have the same essence. Over time, however, the original message was misinterpreted, mixed with superstition, and degenerated into magical practices and meaningless rituals. The conception of God, the very core of religion, was debased by anthropomorphism, deifying angels, associating others with God, and considering Prophets or godly people as incarnations.

Prophet Muhammad, upon him be God's peace and blessings, rejected such theological trends and restored the conception of God as the only Creator, Sustainer, and Master of all creation to its pristine purity. Thus, as John Davenport puts it:

> Among many excellencies of which the Qur'an may justly boast are two eminently conspicuous: the one being the tone of awe and reverence which it always observes when speaking of, or referring to, the Deity, to Whom it never attributes human frailties and passions; the other the total absence throughout it of all impure, immoral and indecent ideas, expressions, narratives, etc., blemishes, which, it is much to be regretted, of too frequent occurrence in the Jewish scriptures.[1]

Tawhid is the highest conception of Godhead, the knowledge of which God has sent to humanity throughout history by means of His Prophets. This was the knowledge with which Adam was sent down to Earth; the same knowledge that God revealed to Noah, Abraham, Moses, and Jesus, God's blessings be upon them all; and which Muhammad, upon him be God's peace and blessings, brought to humanity. It is knowledge, pure and absolute, without the least shade of ignorance. It dispels all the clouds of ignorance and illuminates the horizon with the light of reality.

But who can create and control this majestic universe? Only He can do so Who is Master of all; Who is Infinite and Eternal; Who is All-Powerful, All-Wise, Omnipotent and Omniscient; Who is All-Knowing and All-Seeing. He must have supreme authority over all that exists in the universe. He must possess limitless powers, must be Lord of the universe and all that it contains, must be free from every flaw and weakness, and none may have the power to interfere with His work. Only such a Being can be the Creator, the Controller and the Governor of the universe.

Moreover, it is essential that all of these Divine Attributes and powers must be vested in One Being. It is impossible for two or more personalities having equal powers and attributes to coexist, for they would be bound to collide. Therefore, there must be one and only one Supreme Being having control over all others. You cannot think of two governors for the same province or two supreme commanders of the army!

Similarly, the distribution of these powers among different deities, so that, for instance, one of them is all-knowing, the other all-providing, and still another life-giver, and each having an independent domain, is also unthinkable. The universe is an indivisible whole, and each such deity would be dependent upon others in carrying out its task. A lack of coordination would be bound to occur. And if this happened, the world would fall to pieces. These attributes are also non-transferable. It is not possible that a certain attribute might be present in a certain deity at one time and at another time be found in another deity. A divine being who is incapable of remaining alive himself cannot give life to others. The one who cannot protect his own divine power cannot be suited to govern the vast limitless universe.

The Meaning of the *Kalima al-Tawhid*

In Arabic, *ilah* means "one who is worshipped," in other words a being that, on account of its greatness and power, is considered worthy of worship, to be bowed to in humility and submission. The concept *ilah* also includes the possession of infinite power, conveys the sense that others are dependent upon it, and that it is not dependent upon anyone else. The word *ilah* also carries a sense of concealment and mystery. The Persian word *khuda*, as well as *deva* in Hindi and *god* in English, have similar connotations. Other languages also contain words with a similar meaning.

On the other hand, the word *Allah*, which we tend to render in English as *God*, is the essential personal name of God. *La ilaha illa'llah* literally means: "There is no ilah other than the One Great Being known by the name Allah." It means that the universe contains no being worthy of worship other than Allah, that we should bow in submission and adoration only to Him, that He is the only Being possessing all power, that we are in need of His favor, and that we are all obliged to seek His help. He is concealed from our senses, and our intellect cannot perceive what He is.

The One true God is a reflection of Islam's unique concept of God. To a Muslim, God is the Almighty, Creator and Sustainer of the universe, Who is similar to nothing and nothing is comparable to Him. When the Prophet's contemporaries asked him about God, He revealed *Surat al-Ikhlas*, which is considered the essence of unity or the motto of monotheism, as follows:

> In the name of God, the All-Merciful, the All-Compassionate. Say (O Muhammad): He is God, the One, Unique. God is the Self-Sufficient (Who needs no one and Whom everyone else needs). He has not begotten, nor has been begotten, and there is none equal to Him. (112:1-4)

The Creator must be of a different nature from the things created, because if He is of the same nature as they are, He will be temporal and will therefore need a maker. It follows that nothing is like Him. If the Maker is not temporal, He must be eternal. But if He is eternal, He cannot be caused. If nothing apart from Him causes Him to continue to exist, He must be Self-Sufficient and Self-Subsistent. If He does not depend upon anything for the continuance of His own Existence, this Existence can have no end. The Creator is therefore eternal and everlasting: "He is the First and the Last."

He is Self-Sufficient and Self-Subsistent or, to use a Qur'anic term, *as-Samad* and *al-Qayyum*. The Creator does not create only in the sense of bringing things into being, for He also preserves them, takes them out of existence, and is the ultimate cause of whatever happens to them.

'Ali Ibn Abi Talib is reported to have said:

> He is Being but not through the phenomenon of coming into being. He exists but not from non-existence. He is with everything but not by physical nearness. He is different from everything but not by physical separation. He acts but without the accompaniment of movements and instruments. He is the One, only such that there is none with whom He keeps company or whom He misses in his absence.[2]

Islam rejects characterizing God in any human form or depicting Him as favoring certain individuals or nations on the basis of wealth, power, or race. He created human beings as equals. They may distinguish themselves and obtain His favor only through virtue and piety.

Literally, *tawhid* means "unification" (making something one) or "asserting oneness." It comes from the Arabic verb *wahhada* (to unite, unify, or consolidate). However, when used in reference to God, it means realizing and maintaining God's Unity in all of our actions that directly or indirectly relate to Him. It is the belief that God is One, without partner in His dominion and His actions, without similitude in His Essence and Attributes, and without rival in His Divinity and in worship. These three categories are commonly referred to by the following titles: *Tawhid ar-Rububiya* ("Maintaining the Unity of Lordship"), *Tawhid al-Asma' was-Sifat* ("Maintaining the Unity of God's Names and

Attributes"), and *Tawhid al-'Ibada* ("Maintaining the Unity of God's Worship").

Tawhid al-Rububiya is based upon the fundamental concept that God alone caused all things to exist when there was nothing, He sustains and maintains creation without any need from it or for it, and He is the sole Lord of the universe and its inhabitants without any real challenge to His sovereignty. In Arabic, the word used to describe this quality is *Rububiya*, which is derived from the root *Rabb* (Lord). According to this category, since God is the only real power in existence, it is He Who has given all things the power to move and to change. Nothing happens in creation except what He allows to happen. In recognition of this reality, Prophet Muhammad, upon him be God's peace and blessings, often would repeat the exclamatory phrase *La hawla wa la quwwata illa bi'llah* (There is neither strength, nor power, save with God).

Tawhid al-Asma' wal-Sifat has four aspects. In order to maintain the unity of God's Names and Attributes in the first aspect, God must be referred to according to how He and His Prophet have described Him and called Him. The second aspect involves referring to God as He has referred to Himself, without giving Him any new names or attributes. In the third aspect, God is referred to without giving Him the attributes of His creation. For example, He cannot be said to rest or sleep, for this would give Him some of the attributes belonging to His creation. Nor can He be portrayed as "repenting" for His "bad thoughts," for this is what people do after they realize their errors. The attributes of hearing and seeing are among human attributes, but are without comparison in their perfection when attributed to the Divine Being. In other words, God does not need eyes and ears to possess these attributes. The fourth aspect requires that no person can be given the attributes of God in their perfection.

In spite of the wide implications of the first two categories, firm belief in them alone is not sufficient to fulfill the Islamic requirements of *tawhid*. *Tawhid al-Rububiya* and *Tawhid al-Asma' wal-Sifat* must be accompanied by their complement, *Tawhid al-'Ibada*, in order for *tawhid* to be considered complete according to Islam. It requires that all forms of worship must be directed only to God, because He alone deserves worship and can grant benefit to created beings as a result of His worship. Furthermore, there is no need for any intermediary between humanity and God. God emphasized the importance of directing worship to Him alone by pointing out that this was the main purpose for creating jinn and humanity, and the essence of the Message brought by all Prophets.

Consequently, the gravest sin is *shirk* (the worship of others instead of God or along with God). In *Surat al-Fatiha*, which every Muslim recites in his or her prayers at least 17 times daily, verse four reads: *You alone do we worship and from You alone do we seek help*, a clear statement that all forms of worship should be directed only to the One Who can respond: God.

The study of *tawhid* cannot be considered complete without a careful analysis of its opposite: *shirk*. *Shirk* literally means partnership, sharing, or associating. In Islamic terms, however, it refers to assigning partners to God in whatever form it may take.

Kinds of Associating Partners with God (*Shirk*)

One may associate partners with God in His *Rububiya*, *Asma wal-Sifat*, and *Ibada*.

Shirk in al-Rububiya

This kind of shirk refers either to the belief that others share in God's Lordship over creation as His equal or near equal, or that there exists no Lord over creation at all. In the first case, *shirk* by association, this means that a main God or Supreme Being over creation is recognized; however His dominion is shared by lesser deities, spirits, mortals, heavenly bodies, or earthly objects. According to Islam, all such systems are polytheistic. In the second case, *shirk* by negation, the various philosophies and ideologies almost amount to an explicit or implicit denial of God's Existence. For example, pantheism and monism fall into this category.

Shirk in al-Asma' wal-Sifat

This includes both the common pagan practice of giving God the attributes of His creation as well as the act of giving created beings God's Names and Attributes in their absolute meaning particular to God. In the first case, *shirk* by humanization, God is given the form and qualities of human beings and animals. Due to humanity's superiority over animals, the human form is more commonly used by idolaters to represent God in creation. Consequently, the image of the Creator is often painted, molded, or carved in the shape of human beings possessing the physical features of those who worship them. In the second case, *shirk* by deification, created beings or things are given or claim God's Names or His Attributes in their absolute meaning particular to God.

Shirk in al-'Ibada

This means to direct acts of worship to other than God, and to seek the reward for worship from the creation instead of the Creator. This category also has two main aspects, as follows:

AL-SHIRK AL-AKBAR (MAJOR SHIRK). This occurs when any act of worship is directed to that which is not God. It represents the most obvious form of idolatry, which God sent all Prophets to call upon humanity to abandon. This concept is supported by: *Surely We have sent to every nation a Messenger ordering, worship God and avoid Taghut* (false gods) (16:36).

Taghut actually means anything that demands worship and is worshipped along with God or instead of God. Much emphasis has been placed on such evil, for it contradicts the very purpose of creation as expressed in God's statement: *I have not created jinn or humanity except to worship Me* (51:56).

Major *shirk* represents the greatest act of rebellion against the Lord of the Universe, and is thus the ultimate sin that virtually cancels all of a person's good deeds and guarantees its perpetrator eternal damnation in Hell. Consequently, false religion is based primarily upon this type of *shirk*. All human-made systems in one way or another invite their followers to the worship of creation.

AL-SHIRK AL-ASGHAR (MINOR SHIRK). God's Messenger said: "The thing I fear for you the most is *al-shirk al-asghar(minor shirk)*." The Companions asked: "O Messenger of God, what is minor *shirk*?"

He replied: "Showing off (*al-riya'*), for God will say on the Day of Resurrection when people are receiving their rewards: 'Go to those for whom you were showing off in the material world and see if you can find any reward from them.'" He also declared: "O people, beware of secret *shirk!*" The people asked: "O Messenger of God, what is secret *shirk?*" He replied: "When a person gets up to pray and strives to beautify his prayer because people are looking at him, that is secret *shirk*." (al-Daylami, *al-Firdaws*, 2:376)

DIVINE LOVE AS THE REASON BEHIND EXISTENCE[3]

There is an inseparable relation between God, nature, and humanity. Nature and humanity are two "books" written with different material but having the same meaning. The reason behind their existence is Divine Love.

Suppose a kind, compassionate, and generous person wills to feed some very poor, hungry, and destitute people. So, he prepares a banquet on his fine ship and watches them from above while they eat. You may understand how much of their grateful enjoyment and happiness they can express only by giving thanks and praising that noble and generous person so that he is pleased and exhilarated.

In the same way, the All-Merciful and Compassionate One has spread out a vast food-laden table on Earth's face and causes Earth to travel in the space with all of its inhabitants. He feeds them from the food on this table and invites those of His servants who are infinitely hungry and destitute to Paradise's everlasting gardens. He prepares each garden as if it were a magnificent table laid out with all kinds of food and drink, which are of pure pleasure and delight. Consider the pleasure and happiness that the above-mentioned person feels at his guests' enjoyment, although he is not the true owner of what he offers, and then compare it with the indescribable sacred love and pleasure felt by the All-Merciful One.

Consider another example. If a skillful technician invents something that works as intended, he or she is pleased and says: "What wonders God has willed." The Majestic Maker invented the vast universe. He made Earth (in general) and each creature in it (in particular), especially our head, in such a way that science should be lost in admiration. Each creature displays the expected results to the utmost degree and in a very beautiful way. Their obedience to God's laws for the universe's creation and operation, which comprise their worship, glorification, and specific praise and exaltation of Him, as well as the attainment of Divine purposes for their lives, please Him to a degree beyond our comprehension.

Or, say a just judge receives great pleasure from doing and establishing justice, and becomes extremely happy when he or she can restore the rights of the oppressed against the oppressor. Compare with this the sacred meanings arising from the reality that the Absolutely Just Ruler, the Majestic Overwhelming One, gives all creatures the right of existence. He gives animate beings the right of life, protects and maintains their existence and lives against aggression, restores all rights in the universe, acts with absolute justice, and will judge humanity and jinn in the Hereafter and establish absolute justice.

As in the examples above, each Divine Name contains many sorts of beauty, grace, and perfection, as well as many levels of love, pride, honor, and grandeur. This is why some exacting scholars, who manifest the Divine Name the All-Loving, have concluded: "The essence of the universe is love. All creatures move with the motive of love. All laws of attraction, rapture, and gravity originate in love." One of them even said:

> *With love the spheres are intoxicated,*
> *angels are intoxicated, and so are stars.*
> *The heavens, the sun, the moon,*
> *and Earth are intoxicated.*
> *Intoxicated are the elements and plants*
> *and trees and human beings.*
> *All animate beings are intoxicated,*
> *and so are all atoms of creation.*

Every creature is intoxicated, according to its capacity, with the "wine" of Divine love. People love those who are kind to them, as well as true perfection and transcendent beauty. They also love those who are kind to those whom they love and for whom they have mercy. Given this, we can understand that the Majestic and Beautiful, the Most Beloved of Perfection, in each of Whose Names are innumerable treasuries of kindness, Who makes all those whom we love happy with His favors and is the source of countless perfections and levels of beauty and grace, is worthy of infinite love and the creation's intoxication with His love. This is why some who have manifested the Divine Name the All-Loving have said: "We do not even want Paradise. A gleam of the Divine Love is eternally sufficient for us," and why, as Prophet Muhammad said: "A single minute spent in beholding the Divine Beauty in Paradise excels all the bounties of Paradise.

So, perfect love and all perfections attained through love are possible within the spheres of the universal manifestations of Divine Names upon beings as a whole (Unity) and the spheres of their particular manifestations upon individuals (Oneness or Uniqueness). Any perfections imagined outside of those spheres are false.

THE REASON BEHIND THE EVENTS IN THE UNIVERSE

If someone enthusiastically performs a natural or social duty, an observer may infer two reasons for doing so: the ultimate cause (what can be obtained from doing so) and the motive or necessary cause (one's yearning to do it and subsequent enjoyment in doing it). For example, eating when hungry gives some satisfaction [necessary cause], while food nourishes the body [ultimate cause].

Likewise, the existence of the universe and the incessant, amazing activity in it are caused by two kinds of Divine Names and for two comprehensive purposes or results. The first purpose and cause is that God's Beautiful Names manifest themselves in countless ways and kinds. This causes multiplicity in creation. Further, the Divine Names manifest themselves incessantly and seek to display their works continuously. This causes the Book of the Universe, with all of its "sentences, words, and letters" to be renewed constantly. Each part of this Book, which is the manifestation of the Divine Names, is a sign or indication of the Sacred Divine Essence so that conscious living beings can know Him.

The second cause or purpose is that every creature is active because it yearns for and takes pleasure in activity. Activity itself is a pleasure. Likewise God, the Necessarily Existent Being and in conformity with His essential independence of creation and absolute perfection, feels infinite sacred affection and love. Such affection and love cause an infinite sacred enthusiasm, which engenders a limitless sacred joy that, in turn, is the source of infinite sacred pleasure. Due to this pleasure special to His Divine "Essence," God has infinite compassion. In turn, this compassion causes His creatures to attain their relative perfection by enabling them to realize their full potential. His creatures' perfection and the pleasure they find in attaining it pleases God so much that His infinite sacred pleasure requires the whirl of creation.

However, the followers of materialistic philosophy and secular natural sciences, unaware of this delicate Divine Wisdom, attribute such activity, which displays perfect knowledge, wisdom, and insight, to unconscious nature, blind coincidence, and causality. This causes them to fall into the dark pits of misguidance.

II. THE INVISIBLE REALM OF EXISTENCE[4]

Belief in the invisible realm of existence and the beings inhabiting it is another essential of Islamic faith. Since our sensory powers are limited, it is not wise to deny outright the existence of realms beyond our senses. Also, we know so little about existence that what we do know is considerably less than what we do not. Our sciences are still in their "childhood," and the future will witness dazzling scientific discoveries and developments.

Sciences are supported by theories and develop through trial-and-error investigation of those theories. Numerous "established" facts were once considered false, and many other "established" facts are now known to be incorrect. We accept unquestionably, and without any scientific basis, the existence of many things. Since the beginning of time, most people have believed in the existence of the spirit and angels, jinn and Satan. So, it would seem to be more scientific to allow their existence in theory and then investigate it. Denying their existence is unscientific, insofar as such a judgment or conclusion must be based on concrete proof. No one can prove and therefore scientifically claim the non-existence of the invisible realm of existence.

Many physical qualities, such as heat and cold, and such abstract qualities as beauty and charm, and feelings of joy, sorrow, and love, can be experienced directly and measured to some degree. Materialists attribute these to some biochemical processes in the brain, and some scientists (like psychologists and psychiatrists) still try to explain them by natural or physical laws. However, our non-physical side (namely, our feelings, beliefs, potentialities, desires, and so on that vary enormously from individual to individual, although everyone has the same material elements) is too profound to be explained by physics, chemistry, or biology.

Angels and Other Invisible Beings

Angels are purely spirit beings that stand for the purely good aspect in existence, while Satan and his descendants represent the purely evil aspect. God is One and Infinite, without opposite. All other beings and existents have an opposite. Since we have two opposite aspects in our nature, one inclined toward good and the other toward evil, angels represent this good aspect while Satan represents the evil one. Angels invite us to our purely spiritual or "angelic" aspect, while Satan tries to seduce us through tempting us to do evil. The resulting struggle in each individual, and in the universe as a whole, has been ongoing since the beginning of existence. Everyone feels a stimulus toward good and evil at the same time. The former comes from the angels or our unpolluted spirit; the latter comes from Satan collaborating with our carnal self, which represents our animal aspect.

We accept the existence of natural laws and forces unquestionably, and even go so far as to attribute to them all phenomena in the universe. We ascribe a tiny seed's growth into a huge, elaborate tree to the law of germination and growth in that seed, and the universe's incredible balance to the laws of gravitation and repulsion. But we ignore the absolute will, knowledge, power, and wisdom necessary for the universe's very existence, operation, and balance. The One Who has absolute Will, Knowledge, Power, and Wisdom has such powerful invisible beings as winds or gales, and others much more powerful than natural forces or laws. These beings are angels.

In addition to religious scholars, almost all Muslim philosophers and even all Oriental philosophers agree on the existence of angels and all kinds of spirit beings, despite differences in naming them. All Prophets, numbering 124,000 in reliable religious sources, unanimously report the existence of angels, spirit beings, jinn, and Satan. All saints and religious scholars agree on this invisible realm's existence. We hardly need to say that two specialists in a matter are preferable to thousands of non-specialists. In addition, it is an established fact that once a matter is confirmed by two people, its denial by thousands carries no weight. Furthermore, all people of religion and followers of almost all religions unanimously accept the existence of these beings.

All Divine Scriptures record the existence of spirit beings and the human spirit, and the story of Satan and his intrigues to seduce us exist in all of them. Above all, can one doubt the report of the Qur'an and the testimony and experiences of Prophet Muhammad, upon him be peace and blessings? The proofs of the Qur'an's Divine authorship, Prophethood's mission, and the Prophethood of Muhammad and all other Prophets, upon them be peace, also prove the invisible realm's existence and thus the existence of the spirit, angels, jinn, and Satan.

The best and most rational way of establishing the existence of such beings is expounded by Islam, described by the Qur'an, and was seen by the Prophet, upon him be peace and blessings, during his Ascension through the heavens. The Qur'an explains the meaning of angelic existence so reasonably that anyone can understand it. It relates that we are a community responsible for carrying out the Divine Commandments issuing from the Divine Attribute of Speech, and that angels are a community whose "working class" carries out the Divine Laws of nature issuing from the Attribute of Will. They are God's honored servants who do whatever He commands. The existence of angels and other spirit beings can be established by proving the existence of an individual angel, because denying them amounts to denying the species. Thus, accepting the individual requires accepting the species.

A consensus has formed, especially among followers of religions, that there have always been some who can see and converse with angels, jinn, Satan, and other spirit beings. Therefore, we can conclude that religious belief in the existence of such beings is based on the experiences which the Prophets and other godly persons have had with them. Such accounts have been narrated by reliable sources.

The Characteristics of Angels

Angels are created from "light," not the light that we know, but light in its more refined and subtle form, which we call *nur*. The Arabic word for angel is *malak*. According to its root form, *malak* means "messenger," "deputy," "envoy," "superintendent," and "powerful one." The root meaning also implies descent from a high place. Angels are beings who build relations between the meta-cosmic world and the material one, convey God's commands, direct the acts and lives of beings (with God's permission), and represent their worship in their own realms.

Having refined or subtle bodies of *nur* (light), angels move very rapidly and permeate or penetrate all realms of existence. They place themselves in our eyelids or in the bodies of other beings to observe God's works through our or their eyes. They also descend into the hearts of Prophets and saintly people to bring them inspiration. Such inspirations are usually from God, but sometimes they may be from angels.

Some animals, like honeybees, act according to Divine inspiration, although science asserts that all animals are directed by impulses. But science cannot explain what an impulse is and how it occurs. Scientists are trying to discover how migrating birds find their way, and how young eels hatched in the ocean find their way to the rivers of Europe, which is their native water. Even if we attribute this to information coded in their DNA, this information is assuredly from God, Who knows everything, controls the universe, and assigns angels to direct the lives of such creatures.

Everything that exists, either as an individual or as a species, has a collective identity and performs a unique, universal function. Each flower displays a superlative design and symmetry and recites, in the tongue of its being, the Names of the Creator manifested on it; the entire Earth performs a universal duty of glorification as though it were a single flower; and the heavens praise and glorify the Majestic Maker of the universe through their suns, moons, and stars. Even inert material bodies, although outwardly inanimate and unconscious, perform a vital function in praising God. Angels represent these immaterial bodies in the world of the inner dimensions of things, and express their praise. In return, these immaterial bodies are the angels' representatives, dwellings, and mosques in this world.

There are various classes of angels. One class is engaged in constant worship; another worships by working. These working angels have functions that resemble human occupations, like shepherds or farmers. In other words, Earth's surface is like a general farm, and an appointed angel oversees all of its animal species by the command of the All-Majestic Creator, by His permission and Power, and for His sake.

Earth's surface is also an arable field where all plants are sown. Another angel is appointed to oversee all of them in the Name of Almighty God and by His Power. Lower ranking angels worship and glorify Almighty God by supervising particular plant species. Archangel Michael, upon him be peace, is the head of all these angels.

Angels who function as shepherds or farmers bear no resemblance to human shepherds or farmers, for their supervision is purely for God's sake, in His Name, and by His Power and command. They observe the manifestations of God's Lordship in the species they are assigned to supervise, study the manifestations of Divine Power and Mercy in it, communicate Divine commands to it through some sort of inspiration, and somehow arrange its voluntary actions.

Their supervision of plants, in particular, consists of representing in the angelic tongue the plants' glorification in the tongue of their being. In other words, they proclaim in the angelic tongue the praises and exaltations that all plants offer to the Majestic Creator through their lives. These angels also regulate and employ the plants' faculties correctly and direct them toward certain ends. Angels perform such services through their partial willpower and a kind of worship and adoration. They do not originate or create their acts, for everything bears a stamp particular to the Creator of all things, meaning that only God creates. In short, whatever angels do is worship, and it is therefore not like the ordinary acts of human beings.

The Majestic Maker of this huge palace of creation employs four kinds or classes of laborers: angels and other spirit beings; inanimate things and vegetable creations, which are quite important servants of God working without wages; animals, which serve unconsciously in return for a small wage of food and pleasure; and humanity, which works in awareness of the Majestic Creator's purposes. Men and women learn from everything, and supervise lower-ranking servants in return for wages in the form of rewards here and in the Hereafter.

The first class consists of angels. These beings are never promoted for what they do, for each has a fixed, determined rank and receives a particular pleasure from the work itself, as well as a radiance from worship. That is, their reward is found in their service. Just as we are nourished by and derive pleasure from air and water, as well as light and food, angels are nourished by and receive pleasure from the lights of remembrance and glorification, worship and knowledge, and love of God. Since they are created of light in its more refined and subtle form, light sustains them. Even fragrant scents, which are close to light, are a sort of enjoyable nourishment for them. Indeed, pure spirits take pleasure in sweet scents.

From their jobs performed at the command of the One Whom they worship, their actions for His sake, their service rendered in His Name, their supervision through His view, their honor gained through connection with Him, their "refreshment" found in studying His Kingdom's material and immaterial dimensions, and their satisfaction in observing His Grace and Majesty's manifestations, angels receive such elevated bliss that we cannot even begin to comprehend it. In addition, only they can perceive this bliss.

Angels do not sin or disobey, for they do not have an evil-commanding soul that must be resisted. They have fixed stations, and so are neither promoted nor abased. They are also free of such negative qualities as envy, rancor, and enmity, and from all lusts and animal appetites found in human beings and jinn. They have no gender, do not eat or drink, and do not feel hunger, thirst, or tiredness. Praise, worship, recitation of God's Names, and glorification of Him are their nourishment, as are light and sweet fragrances.

Besides those deputed to represent and supervise various species on Earth and present their worship to God, there are four Archangels and other angels having special nearness to God. There are other groups of angels known as *Mala'-i A'la* (the Highest Council), *Nadiy-i A'la* (the Highest Assembly), and *Rafiq-i A'la* (the Highest Company), as well as angels appointed to Paradise and Hell. Angels who record a person's deeds are called *Kiramun Katibun* (the Noble Recorders), and, as stated in a *hadith*, 360 angels are responsible for each believer's life. They guard their charges, especially during infancy and old age, pray for them, and ask God to forgive them. Other angels help believers during times of war, attend assemblies that praise and glorify God, as well as study meetings held for God's sake and to benefit people.

God Almighty is powerful over everything. Even though He can guard everyone by Himself, He may appoint angels to guard His servants. To earn such a guardianship and the company of angels, one has to willingly do what is good and establish a close relation with God Almighty. One must have strong belief in God and all other pillars of faith, never abandon regular worship and prayer, lead a disciplined life, and refrain from forbidden things or sinful acts.

Belief in angels has many benefits. For example, it provides us with some sort of peace and removes our loneliness. The inspiration breathed by angels exhilarates us, enlightens us intellectually, and opens new horizons of knowledge and thought. Awareness of the continuous company of angels also helps us abstain from sin and improper behavior.

The Characteristics of Jinn

The word *jinn* literally means something hidden or veiled from sight. As mentioned earlier, jinn are a species of invisible beings. A short Qur'anic chapter is named for them, and in it we learn that a band of jinn listened to Prophet Muhammad, upon him be peace and blessings, and some became believers (72:1-2, 11).

From this, we understand that jinn are conscious beings charged with Divine obligations. They were created before Adam and Eve and were responsible for cultivating and improving the world. Although God later superseded them with us, He did not exempt them from religious obligations.

The Qur'an states that jinn are created from smokeless fire (55:15). In another verse, it clarifies that this fire is scorching and penetrates as deep as the inner part of the body (15:27).

Like angels, jinn move extremely fast and are not bound by the time and space constraints within which we normally move. However, since the spirit is more active and faster than jinn, a person who lives at the level of the spirit's life and who can transcend what we know as limits of matter and the confines of time and space, can be quicker and more active than them. For example, the Qur'an relates that when Prophet Solomon asked those around him who could bring the throne of the Queen of Sheba (Yemen), one jinn answered that he could bring it before the meeting ended and Prophet Solomon stood up. However, a man with a special knowledge from God replied: "I can bring it to you quicker than the blink of an eye," and he did so (27:38-40).

Nothing is difficult for God Almighty. It is as easy for Him to create the universe as it is for Him to create a tiny particle. He has provided human beings, jinn, and angels with the power and strength appropriate for their functions or duties. As He uses angels to supervise the movements of celestial bodies, He allows humanity to rule Earth, dominate matter, build civilizations, and produce technology.

Power and strength are not limited to the physical world, nor are they proportional to bodily size. We see that immaterial things are far more powerful than huge physical entities. For example, our memory is far more spacious and comprehensive than a large room. Our hands can touch a very near object, but our eyes can travel long distances in an instant, and our imagination can transcend time and space all at once. Winds can uproot trees and demolish large buildings. A young, thin plant shoot can split rocks and reach the sunlight. The power of energy, whose existence is known through its effect, is apparent to everybody. All of this shows that something's power is not proportional to its physical size; rather, the immaterial world dominates the physical world, and immaterial entities are far more powerful than material ones.

Angels and Jinn in This World

Angels and jinn can assume a form and appear in this world in the shape of any being. Here, we observe movement from the visible to the invisible: water evaporates and disappears into the atmosphere, solid matter becomes a liquid or a gas (steam), and matter becomes energy (nuclear fission). Likewise, we observe movement from the invisible to the visible: gases become fluids, evaporated water becomes rain (as well as snow or hail), and energy becomes matter. Similarly, intangible thoughts and meanings in our minds can appear in the tangible form of letters and words in essays and books.

In an analogous way, such invisible beings as angels, jinn, and other spirit entities are clothed in some material substance, such as air or ether, and then become visible. According to Imam Shibli, if God wills, He allows them to assume a form when they utter any of His Names, for this functions like a key or a visa enabling them to assume a form and become visible in this world. If they try to do so without God's permission, by relying upon their own abilities, they are torn into pieces and perish.

When Gabriel came to Prophet Muhammad, upon him be peace and blessings, with Revelation or God's Messages, he rarely appeared in his original form. Rather, he usually came as a warrior, a traveler, or a Companion named Dihya. Once he came as a traveler dressed in white and, in order to instruct the Companions in religion, asked the Prophet such questions as: What is belief? What is Islam? What is *ihsan* (perfect goodness or excellence or perfection of virtue)? When is the Day of Judgment?

Jinn also can appear as snakes, scorpions, cattle, donkeys, birds, and other animals. When the Prophet, upon him be peace and blessings, took the oath of allegiance from them in the valley of Batn al-Nakhla, he wanted them to appear to his community either in their own form or in other agreeable forms, not in the forms of such harmful animals as dogs and scorpions. He warned his community: "When you see any vermin in your house, tell it three times: 'For God's sake, leave this place,' for it may be a friendly jinn. If it does not leave, it is not a jinn."

The jinn who gave allegiance to God's Messenger promised him: "If your community recites the *Basmala* (In the Name of God, the All-Merciful, the All-Compassionate) before anything they do and cover their dishes, we will not touch their food or their drink." Another Tradition says: "[After you relieve yourselves] do not clean yourselves with bones and dried pieces of dung, for bones are among the foods of your jinn brothers." (Bukhari, Wudu', 4:21, 156)

Jinn and Human Beings

Some people have an innate ability to go into a trance and contact beings from the invisible realms of existence. However, it should not be forgotten that whether these are angels or jinn, invisible beings have their own conditions of life and are bound to certain limits and principles. For this reason, one who gets in touch with jinn should be careful, for one may easily fall under their influence and become their plaything.

Sins and uncleanliness invite the influence of evil spirits and unbelieving jinn. People of a susceptible nature, those who tend to be melancholy, and those who lead a dissipated and undisci-plined life are their primary targets. Evil spirits usually reside in places for dumping garbage or other dirty places, public baths, and bathrooms.

Jinn can penetrate a body even deeper than X-rays. They can reach into a being's veins and the central points of the brain. They seem to be like lasers, which are used in everything from com-puters to nuclear weaponry, from medicine to communication and police investigations, and to removing obstructions in our veins and arteries. So, when we consider that Satan and all jinn are cre-ated from a smokeless fire that penetrates deep into the body, like radiation or radioactive energy, we can understand the meaning of the Prophetic Tradition: "Satan moves where the blood moves." (Bukhari, "Ahkam," 21; Ibn Maja, "Siyam," 65.)

Although science does not yet accept the existence of invis-ible beings and restricts itself to the material world, we think it is worth considering the possibility that evil spirits play some part in such mental illnesses as schizophrenia. We constantly hear of cases that those who suffer from mental illness, epilepsy, or even cancer recover by reciting certain prayers. Such cases are serious and significant, and should not be denied or dismissed by attributing them to "suggestion" or "auto-suggestion." When science breaks the thick shell in which it has confined itself and accepts the existence of the metaphysical realm and the influence of metaphysical forces, its practitioners will be able to remove many obstructions, make far greater advances, and make fewer mistakes.

The Qur'an states that God bestowed upon the House of Abraham the Scripture, Wisdom, and a mighty kingdom (4:54). This mighty kingdom manifested itself most brilliantly through the Prophets David and Solomon, upon them be peace. Prophet Solomon ruled not only a part of humanity, but also jinn and dev-ils, birds and winds: *God subdued unto him devils, some of whom dove for pearls and did other work* (21:82). Solomon had armies of jinn and birds, and he employed jinn in many jobs: *They made for him what he willed: synagogues, fortresses, basins like wells and boilers built into the ground* (34:13); and: *Wind was also subdued to him; its morning course was a month's journey and the evening course also a month's journey* (34:12).

Satan and His Whispering

The jinn we know as Satan was created from (some sort of) fire. Before his obedience and sincerity were tested through Adam, he had been in the company of angels, acting and worshipping as they did. Unlike angels, however, who cannot rebel against God (66:6), Satan (called Iblis prior to his test) was free to choose his own path of conduct. When God tested him and the angels by commanding them to prostrate before Adam, the seeds of his self-conceit and disobedience blossomed and swallowed him. He replied in his vanity: *"I am better than him. You created me from fire, while You created him from clay"* (38:76).

Satan was created for important purposes. Since God has free will, He also gave us free will so that we could know good from evil and choose between them. In addition, God gave us great potentials. It is our development of these potentials and the struggle to choose between good and evil that cause us to experience a constant battle in our inner world. Just as God sends hawks upon sparrows so that the latter will develop their potential to escape, He created Satan and allowed him to tempt us so that our resistance to temptation will raise us spiritually and strengthen our willpower. Just as hunger stimulates human beings and animals to further exertion and discovery of new ways to be satisfied, and fear inspires new defenses, so Satan's temptations cause us to develop our potentials and guard against sin.

There is an infinitely long line of spiritual evolution between the ranks of the greatest Prophets and saints down to those of people like Pharaoh and Nimrod. Therefore, it cannot be claimed that the creation of Satan is evil. Although Satan is evil and serves various important purposes, God's creation involves the whole universe and should be understood in relation to the results, not only with respect to the acts themselves. Whatever God does or creates is good and beautiful in itself or in its effects. For example, rain and fire are very useful. But they also can cause great harm when abused. Therefore, one cannot claim that the creation of water and fire is not totally good. It is the same with the creation of Satan. His main purpose is to cause us to develop our potential, strengthen our willpower by resisting his temptations, and then rise to higher spiritual ranks.

Evil thoughts, fancies, and ideas that occur to us involuntarily are usually the result of Satan's whispering. Like a battery's two poles, there are two central points or poles in the human heart (by "heart" we mean the seat or center of spiritual intellect). One receives angelic inspiration, and the other is vulnerable to Satan's whispering.

When believers deepen their belief and devotion, and if they are scrupulous and delicate in feeling, Satan attacks them from different directions. He does not busy himself with those who follow him voluntarily and indulge in all that is transitory, but usually seeks out those sincere, devout believers trying to rise to higher spiritual ranks. He whispers new, original ideas to sinful unbelievers in the name of unbelief, and teaches them how to struggle against true religion and those who follow it.

Satan does everything he can to seduce us. He approaches us from the left and tries, working on our animal aspect and our feelings and faculties, to lead us into all sorts of sin and evil. When he approaches us from the front, he causes us to despair of our future, whispers that the Day of Judgment will never come, and that whatever religion says about the Hereafter is mere fiction. He also suggests that religion is outdated and obsolete, and thus of no use for those who are living now or who will live in the future. When he comes upon us from behind, he tries to make us deny Prophethood and other essentials of belief, like God's Existence and Unity, Divine Scriptures and angels. Through his whispers and suggestions, Satan tries to sever completely our contact with religion and lead us into sin.

Satan approaches devout, practicing believers from their right to tempt them to ego and pride in their virtues and good deeds. He whispers that they are wonderful believers, and gradually causes them to fall through self-conceit and the desire to be praised for their good deeds. This is a perilous temptation for believers, and so they must be incessantly alert to Satan's coming upon them from their right.

In fact, Qur'an 4:76 tells us that the guile of Satan is ever feeble. It resembles a cobweb that appears while you are walking between two walls. It does not cause you to stop, and you should not give it any importance. He suggests or whispers and presents sinful acts in a "falsely ornamented wrapper," so believers must never accept his "gifts."

To free ourselves from Satan's evil suggestions, we should remove ourselves from the attractive fields of Satan and sin. Heedlessness and neglect of worship are invitations to Satan's "arrows." The Qur'an declares: *Whose sight is dim to the remembrance of the All-Merciful, We assign unto him a devil who becomes his comrade* (43:36). Remembrance of the All-Merciful, noble or sacred phenomena, and a devout religious life protect us from Satan's attacks. Again, the Qur'an advises:

> If a suggestion from Satan occurs to you, seek refuge in God. He is All-Hearing, All-Knowing. Those who fear God and ward off (evil), when a passing notion from Satan troubles them, they remember, and behold! they see. (7:200-1)

Satan sometimes tries to tempt us through obscene scenes. He causes us to obsess over illicit pleasures. On such occasions, we should try to persuade ourselves that any illicit pleasure will result in fits of remorse and may endanger our afterlife or even our mortal life. We should not forget that the life of this world is but a passing plaything, a comforting illusion, and that the true life is that of the Hereafter.

Spells and Sorcery

Those who deny spells and sorcery do so either because they do not believe in anything related to metaphysics or what they suppose to be connected with religion, or because they are unaware of realities beyond the physical realm.

Most of us have heard of or even seen many such cases. As the Prophet, upon him be peace and blessings, declared that the evil eye is an undeniable fact, sorcery is also an undeniable reality. The Qur'an speaks about (and severely condemns) the sorcery practiced to cause a rift between spouses. According to the Qur'an and Islam, sorcery and casting spells are as sinful as unbelief.

While breaking a spell is a good, meritorious deed, it must not be adopted and practiced as a profession. Although our Prophet, upon him be peace and blessings, met with jinn, preached Islam to them, and took their allegiance, he never explained how to contact them or how to cast or break a spell. However, he taught how jinn approach us and seek to control us, how we can protect ourselves against their evil, and how to ward off and be saved from the evil eye.

The safest way to protect ourselves against evil spirits is to have a strong loyalty to God and His Messenger, upon him be peace and blessings. This requires following the principles of Islam strictly. In addition, we should never give up praying, for prayer is a weapon against hostility, protects us from harm, and helps us to attain our goals. Prayer does not mean to ignore and neglect material means in attaining goals. Rather, applying them is included in prayer. As we pray for ourselves, we also must request those who we believe to be near to God to pray for us. The Companions frequently asked the Prophet to pray for them.

Some people go to exorcists. Although a few people might know how to drive out evil spirits, such activity is usually quite dangerous, for most exorcists deceive people. Also, an exorcist must be very careful about his or her religious obligations, refrain from sin, and be an upright person who knows how to exorcise somebody.

Believers should not go to those psychiatrists or doctors who restrict themselves to the narrow confines of matter. Materialist psychiatrists who do not believe in the spirit and spirit beings may advise patients suffering from spiritual dissatisfaction or possessed by evil spirits to indulge themselves in pleasure and amusement. This is like advising a thirsty person to quench his or her thirst with salty sea water.

God's Messenger, upon him be peace and blessings, mentioned that special prayers should be recited to protect oneself against the evils of Satan and other unbelieving jinn. The Verse of the Throne (2:255) is one of them. We also read that: *If a stimulus from Satan occurs to you, seek refuge in God immediately* (41:36). That is, say: "I seek refuge in God from Satan, the accursed."

As reported by 'A'isha, the Mother of Believers and one of the Prophet's wives, God's Messenger recited the *suras al-Falaq* and *al-Nas* three times every morning and evening, and then breathed into his joined palms and rubbed them against the parts of his body he could reach. (Bukhari, "Da'awat," 11.) He also recited three times every morning and evening: "In the Name of God, Whom nothing on Earth and in heaven can give harm as against His Name. He is the All-Hearing, the All-Knowing." (Tirmidhi, "Da'awat," 13.) This recitation and the following one are among the prayers advised for protection against paralysis: "I seek refuge in all of God's words from all devils and vermin and from all evil eyes."

Imam al-Ghazzali advises us to protect ourselves against spells, charms, and evil spirits by reciting: "In the Name of God, the All-Merciful, the All-Compassionate" once, "God is the Greatest" 10 times, *The magician will not be successful wherever he appears* (20:69), and *from the evil of blowers upon knots* (113:4). Another imam advises us to recite these two verses 19 times after each sip of liquid (e.g., water, tea, or soup).

III. DIVINE DECREE AND DESTINY, AND HUMAN FREE WILL[5]

The Qur'anic word translated as "destiny" is *qadar*. In its derivations, this word also means "determination," "giving a certain measure and shape," "dividing," and "judging." Muslim scholars of Islam define it as "Divine measure," "determination," and "judgment in the creation of things."

In one sense, Decree and Destiny mean the same thing. In another sense, however, Destiny means to predetermine or preordain, while Decree means to execute or put into effect. To be more precise, Destiny means that everything that exists, from subatomic particles to the universe as a whole, is known by God Almighty. His Knowledge includes all space and time, while He Himself is absolutely free of both of them. Everything exists in

His Knowledge, and He assigns to each a certain shape, life span, function or mission, and certain characteristics.

Consider the following analogy: Authors have full and exact knowledge of the book they will write, and arrange its chapters, sections, paragraphs, sentences, and words before writing it. In this sense, Destiny is almost identical with Divine Knowledge, or is a title of Divine Knowledge. Thus it is also called the "Supreme Preserved Tablet" (or the "Manifest Record"). Destiny also means that God makes everything according to a certain, particular measure and in exact balance:

> God knows what every female bears and what the wombs absorb and what they grow. And everything with Him is measured. (13:8)

> The sun and the moon are made punctual according to a calculation. The stars and the trees adore, in subservience to Him. And the sky He has uplifted; and He has set the balance, that you exceed not the balance, but observe the balance strictly, nor fall short thereof. (55:5-9)

The universe's exact measure and balance, order and harmony, as well as that of all it contains, clearly show that everything is determined and measured, created and governed by God Almighty. Therefore, Divine Destiny exists. Such assertions as determinism, which is upheld by many people and even some Marxists, to explain such an obvious universal order and operation are tacit admissions of Destiny. But we have to clarify one point here: According to Islam, absolute determinism cannot be used in the context of human action.

All seeds, measured and proportioned forms, and the universe's extraordinary order and harmony, which has continued for billions of years without any interruption or deviation, demonstrates that everything occurs according to God Almighty's absolute determination. Each seed or ovum is like a case formed by Divine Power into which Divine Destiny inserts the future life-history of a plant or a living being. Divine Power employs atoms or particles, according to the measure established by Divine Destiny, to transform each seed into a specific plant, and each fertilized ovum into a specific living being. This means that the future life-history of these entities, as well as the principles governing their lives, are prerecorded in the seed or the fertilized ovum as determining factors and processes.

Plants and living beings are formed from the same basic materials. However, there is an almost infinite variety between species and individuals. Plants and living beings grow from the same constituent basic elements, and display great harmony and proportion. And yet there is such abundant diversity that we are forced to conclude that each entity receives a specific form and measure. This specific form and measure is established by Divine Destiny.

Belief in Destiny Is One of the Essentials of Faith

Our self-conceit and weak devotion leads us to attribute our accomplishments and good deeds to ourselves and to feel proud of ourselves. But the Qur'an explicitly states: *God creates you and what you do* (37:96), meaning that Divine Compassion demands good deeds and the Power of the Lord creates them. If we analyze our lives, eventually we realize and admit that God directs us to good acts and usually prevents us from doing what is wrong.

In addition, by endowing us with sufficient capacity, power, and means to accomplish many things, He makes it possible for us to realize many accomplishments and good deeds. As God guides us to good deeds and causes us to will and then do them, the real cause of our good deeds is Divine Will. We can "own" our good deeds only through faith, sincere devotion, praying to be deserving of them, consciously believing in the need to do them, and being pleased with what God has ordained. Given this, there is no reason for us to boast or be proud of our good deeds and accomplishments; rather, we should remain always humble and thankful to God.

On the other hand, we like to deny responsibility for our sins and misdeeds by ascribing them to Destiny. But since God neither likes nor approves of any sin or wrong act, all such deeds clearly belong to us and are committed by acting upon our free will. God

allows sins and gives them external forms, for if He did not our
free will would be pointless. Sins are the result of a decision on our
part, through our free will, to sin. God calls and guides us to good
deeds, even inspires them within us, but free will enables us to disobey our Creator. Therefore, we "own" our sins and misdeeds.

In short, because we have free will and are enjoined to follow religious obligations and refrain from sin and wrong deeds,
we cannot ascribe our sins to God. Divine Destiny exists so that
believers do not take pride in their "own" good deeds, instead
of thanking God for them. We have free will so that the rebellious carnal self does not escape the consequences of its sins.

A second, important point is that we usually complain about
past events and misfortunes. Even worse, we sometimes despair
and abandon ourselves to a dissolute lifestyle, and might even
begin to complain against God. However, Destiny allows us to
relate past events and misfortunes to it so that we can receive
relief, security, and consolation. So, whatever happened in the
past should be considered in the light of Destiny; what is to come,
as well as sins and questions of responsibility, should be referred
to human free will. In this way, the extremes of fatalism (*jabr*) and
denying Destiny's role in human actions (*i'tizal*, the view of the
Mu'tazila) is reconciled.

Divine Decree and Destiny in Relation to Divine Will

God registers everything in His Knowledge in a record containing each thing's particular characteristics, life span, provision, time
and place of birth and death, and all of its words and actions. All
of this takes place by Divine Will, for it is through Divine Will that
every thing and event, whether in the realm of Divine Knowledge
or in this world, is known and given a certain course or direction.
Nothing exists beyond the scope of the Divine Will.

For example, an embryo faces innumerable alternatives:
whether it will be a live being, whether it will exist or not, when
and where it will be born and die, and how long it will live, to
mention just a few. All beings are completely unique in com-
plexion and countenance, character, likes and dislikes, and so on,

although they are formed from the same basic elements. A particle of food entering a body, whether an embryo or fully developed, also faces countless alternatives as to its final destination. If a single particle destined for the right eye's pupil were to go to the right ear, this might result in an anomaly.

Thus, the all-encompassing Divine Will orders everything according to a miraculously calculated plan, and is responsible for the universe's miraculous order and harmony. No leaf falls and no seed germinates unless God wills it to do so.

Our relation with Divine Will differs from that of other beings, for only we (and the jinn) have the power of choice; in other words, free will. Based on His knowledge of how we will act and speak, God Almighty has recorded all details of our life. As He is not bound by the human, and therefore artificial, division of time into past, present, and future, what we consider "predetermination" exists in relation to us, not to God Himself. For Him, predetermination means His eternal knowledge of our acts.

In sum: Divine Will dominates creation, and nothing can exist or happen beyond Its scope. It is also responsible for the universe's miraculous order and harmony, and every thing and event is given a specific direction and characteristics. However, the existence of Divine Will does not mean that we do not have free will.

Destiny and Human Free Will

We feel remorse when we do something wrong. We beg God's forgiveness for our sins. If we trouble or harm someone, we ask that person to excuse us. These actions show that we choose to act in a particular way. If we could not choose our actions and were compelled to do them by a superior power, why should we feel remorse and seek forgiveness for anything?

Obviously, we choose to move our hands, speak, or stand up to go somewhere. Nothing compels us to do or not to do something. We decide to read a book, watch television, or pray to God. We are not forced to do any of these things. We hesitate, reason, compare, assess, choose, and then decide to do something. For example, if our friends invite us to go somewhere or do something, we first hesitate, compare, and then decide whether we will accompany them or not. We repeat this very process maybe 100 times a day before deciding to do or say something.

When we are wronged, we sometimes go to court to sue the one who wronged us. The court does not ascribe the wrong done to a compelling superior power like Destiny, and neither do we. The one accused does not excuse himself or herself by blaming that power. Virtuous and wicked people, those who are promoted to high social ranks and those who waste their time, those who are rewarded for their good acts or success and those who are punished for their crimes – all of this proves that each of us has free will.

Our free will is not visible and does not have material existence. However, such factors do not render its existence impossible. Everyone has two (physical) eyes, but we also can see with our third (spiritual) eye. We use the former to see things in this world; we use the latter to see things beyond events and this world. Our free will is like our third eye, which you may call insight. It is an inclination or inner force by which we prefer and decide.

Humanity wills and God creates. A project or a building's plan has no value or use unless you start to construct the building according to it, so that it becomes visible and serves many purposes. Our free will resembles that plan, for we decide and act according to it, and God creates our actions as a result of our decisions. Creation and acting or doing something are different things. God's creation means that He gives actual existence to our choices and actions in this world. Without God's creation, we can do nothing.

To illuminate a magnificent palace, we must install a lighting system. However, the palace cannot be illuminated until we flick the switch that turns on the lights. Until we do so, the palace will remain dark. Similarly, each man and woman is a magnificent palace of God. We are illuminated by belief in God, Who has supplied us with the necessary lighting system: intellect, reason, sense, and the abilities to learn, compare, and prefer.

Nature and events, as well as Divinely revealed religions, are like the source of electricity that illuminates this Divine palace of the human individual. If we do not use our free will to flick the switch, however, we will remain in darkness. Turning on the light means petitioning God to illuminate us with belief. In a manner befitting a servant at his or her lord's door, we must petition the Lord of the Universe to illuminate us and so make us a "king" in the universe. When we do this, the Lord of the Universe treats us in a way befitting Himself, and promotes us to the rank of kingship over other realms of creation.

God takes our free will into account when dealing with us and our acts, for He uses it to create our deeds. Thus we are never victims of Destiny or wronged by Fate. However insignificant our free will is when compared with God's creative acts, it is still the cause of our deeds. God makes large things out of minute particles, and creates many important results from simple means. For example, He makes a huge pine tree from a tiny seed, and uses our inclinations or free choice to prepare our eternal happiness or punishment.

To better understand our part and that of our willpower in our acts and accomplishments, consider the food we consume. Without soil and water, air and the sun's heat, none of which we can produce or create despite our advanced technology, we would have no food. We cannot produce a single seed of corn. We did not create our body and establish its relationship with food; we cannot even control a single part of our body. For example, if we had to wind our heart like a clock at a fixed time every morning, how long would we survive?

Obviously, almost all parts of the whole complex and harmonious universe, which is like a most developed organism, work together according to the most delicate measures to produce a single morsel of food. Thus, the price of a single morsel is almost as much as the price of the whole universe. How can we possibly pay such a price, when our part in producing that morsel is utterly negligible, consisting of no more than our own effort?

Can we ever thank God enough for even a morsel of food? If only a picture of grapes were shown to us, could all of us work together and produce it? No. God nourishes us with His bounty, asking in return very little. For example, if He told us to perform 1,000 *rak'at*s (units) of prayer for a bushel of wheat, we would have to do so. If He sent a raindrop in return for one *rak'at*, we would have to spend our whole lives praying. If you were left in the scorching heat of a desert, would you not give anything for a single glass of water?

In sum: Almost everything we have is given to us for practically nothing, and our part in the bounty we enjoy here is therefore quite negligible. Similarly, our free will is equally negligible when compared with what God Almighty creates from our use of it. Despite our free will's weakness and our own inability to really understand its true nature, God creates our actions according to the choices and decisions we make through it.

Divine Will and Human Free Will

- Divine Destiny, also called Divine determination and arrangement, dominates the universe but does not cancel our free will.
- Since God is beyond time and space, everything is included in His Knowledge, and He encompasses past, present and future as a single undivided point. For example: When you are in a room, your view is restricted to the room. But if you look from a higher point, you see the whole city. As you rise higher and higher, your vision continues to broaden. Earth, when seen from the moon, appears to be a small blue marble. It is the same with time. So, God encompasses all time and space as a single, undivided point, in which past, present, and future are united.
- Since all time and space are included in God's Knowledge as a single point, God recorded everything that will happen until the Day of Judgment. Angels use this record to prepare a smaller record for each individual.
- We do not do something because God recorded it; God knew beforehand that we would do it and so recorded it.
- There are not two destinies: one for the cause; one for the effect. Destiny is one and relates to the cause and the effect simultaneously. Our free will (our acts) is included in Destiny.
- God guides us to good things and actions, and allows and advises us to use our willpower for good. In return, He promises us eternal happiness in Paradise.

- We have free will, although we contribute almost nothing to our good acts. Our free will, if not used properly, can destroy us. Therefore we should use it to benefit ourselves by praying to God so that we may enjoy the blessings of Paradise, a fruit of the chain of good deeds, and attain eternal happiness. Furthermore, we should always seek God's forgiveness so that we might refrain from evil and be saved from the torments of Hell, a fruit of the accursed chain of evil deeds. Prayer and trusting in God greatly strengthen our inclination toward good, and repentance and seeking God's forgiveness greatly weaken, even destroy, our inclination toward evil and transgression.

IV. THE RESURRECTION AND THE AFTERLIFE

Qur'anic Arguments for the Resurrection

Although scientific findings like the second law of thermodynamics show that existence is on the way to destruction, even a collision of two planets could destroy the universe. Existence is an extremely delicately calculated organism, a system with parts subtly dependent upon each other. A human body is made up of about more than sixty trillion cells. As a single deformed, cancerous cell can kill the entire body, any serious deformation anywhere in the universe also could "kill" it. Our death sometimes comes unexpectedly and without any visible, diagnosed reason. Do we know whether or not the universe might "die" all of a sudden, unexpectedly, from a "disease" or a "heart attack"? Maybe our old world has terminal cancer because we abuse it so.

God's universal acts point to the Resurrection. The Qur'an argues for the Resurrection. To impress upon the human heart the wonder of what the Almighty will accomplish in the Hereafter, and to prepare the human mind to accept and understand it, the Qur'an presents the wonder of what He accomplishes here. It gives examples of God's comprehensive acts in the macro-cosmos and, at times, presents His overall disposal of the macro-, normo-, and micro-cosmoses (the universe, humanity, and atoms, respectively).

The first origination of the universe and humanity indicate their "second origination." The Qur'an presents the phenomenon of the universe's creation, which it defines as the *first origination* (56:62), while describing the raising of the dead as the *second origination* (53:47), to prove the Resurrection. It also directs our attention to our own origin, arguing:

> You see how you progressed – from a drop of sperm to a drop of blood, to a blood clot suspended on the wall of the womb, from a suspended blood clot to a formless lump of flesh, and from a formless lump of flesh to human form – how, then, can you deny your second creation? It is just the same as the first, or even easier [for God to accomplish]. (22:5; 23:13-16)

The Qur'an makes analogies between the Resurrection and His deeds in this world. It sometimes alludes to the deeds God will perform in the future and in the Hereafter in such a way that we are convinced of them by drawing analogies to what we observe here. It also shows similar events here and makes comparisons between them and the Resurrection.

The Qur'an likens the universe to a book unfolded. At the end of time, its destruction will be as easy for God as rolling up a scroll. As He unfolded it at the beginning, He will roll it up and, manifesting His absolute Power without any material cause, will re-create it in a much better and different form:

> On that day We shall roll up the heavens like a scroll rolled up for books. As We originated the first creation, so We shall bring it forth again. It is a promise (binding) upon Us. Truly We shall fulfill it (as We promised it). (21:104)

The Qur'an likens the Resurrection to reviving Earth in spring following its death in winter, and mentions how God disposes of atoms and molecules while creating us in stages. Nature experiences death in winter, but spring revives the soil. Dried-out pieces of wood blossom and yield leaves and fruits similar – but not identical – to those that existed in previous years. Innumerable seeds that fell into soil in the previous autumn now begin to germinate and grow into different plants without confusion. God's raising the dead on the Day of Judgment will be like this:

> Among His signs is that you see the soil dry and barren; and
> when We send down rain upon it, it stirs to life and swells. Surely
> God Who gives the dead soil life will raise the dead also to life.
> Indeed, He has power over all things. (41:39)

and:

> Look at the prints of God's Mercy: how He gives life to the soil
> after its death. Lo! He verily is the Reviver of the dead (in the
> same way), and He is able to do all things. (30:50)

Especially in *sura*s 81, 82, and 84, the All-Mighty alludes to
the Resurrection, as well as the vast revolutions and Lordly deeds
that shall take place at that time, in images that we can relate, by
analogy, to what we see here – scenes that we have witnessed in
autumn or spring – and then, with awe in our hearts, accept what
the intellect might otherwise refuse. As giving even the general
meaning of these three *sura*s would take a great deal of time, let's
take one verse: *When the pages are spread out* (81:10). This implies
that during the Resurrection, everyone's deeds will be revealed on
a written page.

At first, this strikes one as strange and incomprehensible.
But as the 81st *sura* indicates, just as the renewal of spring par-
allels another resurrection, "spreading out the pages" has a very
clear parallel. Every fruit-bearing tree and flowering plant has its
own properties, functions, and deeds. It worships according to
its glorification of God, which is how it manifests His Names.
Its deeds and life record are inscribed in each seed that will
emerge next spring. With the tongue of shape and form, these
new trees or flowers offer an eloquent exposition of the life and
deeds of the original tree or flower, and through their branches,
twigs, leaves, blossoms, and fruits spread out the page of its deeds.
He Who says: *When the pages are spread out* is the same Being Who
achieves these feats in a very wise, prudent, efficient, and subtle
way, as dictated by His Names the All-Wise, All-Preserving, All-
Sustaining and Training, and All-Subtle.

In its many verses, the Qur'an warns us that we were not
created with no goals and so can do whatever we want. We are

responsible beings, and whatever we do is recorded. Our creation from a drop of fluid through several stages, the utmost care shown to our creation and the importance attached to us, demonstrate that we have great responsibilities. We will be called to account for whatever we do in this world, which will take place in another world. In addition, our creation through stages is a manifest evidence for God's Power, Who is also able to raise the dead to life.

General Arguments for the Resurrection

A close analysis of the universe's functioning shows that two opposed elements are found everywhere, are deep-rooted, and result in good and evil, benefit and harm, perfection and defect, light and darkness, guidance and misguidance, belief and unbelief, obedience and rebellion, and fear and love. The resulting continual conflict of opposites causes enough incessant alteration and transformation to produce the elements of a new world. These opposed elements eventually will lead to eternity and materialize as Paradise and Hell. The eternal world will be made up of this transitory world's essential elements, which then will be given permanence.

Paradise and Hell are the two opposite fruits growing on the tree of creation's two branches, the two results of the chain of creation, the two cisterns being filled by the two streams of things and events, and two poles to which beings flow in waves. They are the places where Divine Grace and Divine Wrath manifest themselves, and will be full of inhabitants when Divine Power shakes up the universe.

In this world, oppressors depart with their oppressive power intact and the oppressed are still humiliated. Such wrongs will be brought before the Supreme Tribunal, for God would be unjust and imperfect if He allowed them to be ignored. Indeed, God sometimes punishes the guilty in this world. The suffering endured by previous disobedient and rebellious peoples teaches us that everyone is subject to whatever correction God Almighty's Splendor and Majesty chooses to apply. So, as declared in: *Keep apart on this day, O you criminals* (36:59), God's absolute Justice requires that He separate the good from the wicked in the Hereafter and treat each group accordingly.

Our place among creation is unique, for in ourselves we contain some aspect of all that exists in the universe. Our mental and spiritual faculties represent angelic and other spiritual worlds, such as that of symbols or immaterial forms. But because of our inborn capacity to learn and our possession of free will, we can excel even the angels. Our physical or biological being represents plants and animals. Although contained in time and space, our spiritual faculties and such other powers as imagination allow us to transcend them. Despite our unique and priceless worth when compared with other members of creation, some of us die at birth and others when we are still quite young. In addition, we long for eternity and desire eternal life, and some of our senses or feelings are satisfied with nothing less. If we could choose between eternal life with severe hardship during this life and eternal nonexistence after a short luxurious life, probably we would choose the former, maybe even to the extent of preferring eternal existence in Hell to eternal nonexistence. God, the All-Merciful and All-Wise, did not condemn us to eternal nonexistence or implant within us the desire for eternity so that we would suffer while trying to fulfill an impossible, yet heart-felt, desire. So Divine Wisdom requires the existence of an eternal world.

This world cannot judge an individual's actual worth. Although we have a small physical body, our mental and spiritual faculties allow us to embrace the whole universe. Our acts are not restricted only to this world, and therefore cannot be bound by time and space. Our nature is so universal that even the first man's acts affects the last man's life and character and all of existence. Restricting human beings to a physical entity, a very short life span, and a limited part of space, as materialists do, shows a complete misunderstanding and lack of appreciation for what each human being really is.

This world's scales cannot weigh the intellectual and spiritual value of Prophets and their achievements, or the destruction caused by such monsters as Pharaoh, Hitler, and Stalin. Nor can they weigh the true value of sincere belief and moral qualities. What is the proper reward for a martyr who has sacrificed everything for the sake of God, of others, or for such universal human values as justice and truthfulness; or for a believing scientist whose dedicated research results in an invention that benefits all people until the Last Day?

Only the scales of the other world, which weigh an atom's weight of good and evil, can weigh such deeds accurately:

> We set up a just balance for the Day of Resurrection. Thus, no soul will be treated unjustly. Even though it be the weight of one mustard seed, We shall bring it forth to be weighed; and Our reckoning will suffice. (21:47)

Even if nothing required the Resurrection, the sole necessity of weighing our deeds would require an infinitely just and sensitive balance to be established.

Although God does whatever He wills, none of His acts are without purpose. Based on this fact, His universal Wisdom requires the Resurrection. If it did not, we would have to answer the following questions: Is it conceivable that the Majestic Being, Who manifests the Sovereignty of His being Lord via the universe's inclusive and perfect order and purposiveness, justice and balance, would not reward believers who seek His protection as Lord and Sovereign, believe in His Wisdom and Justice, and obey them through worship? Would He allow those who deny His Wisdom and Justice, rebel against or ignore Him, to remain unpunished? As this impermanent world contains scarcely a thousandth part of His Wisdom and Justice with respect to humanity, most unbelievers depart unpunished and most believers unrewarded. Thus, God's Justice is necessarily deferred to a Supreme Tribunal, where we will be rewarded or punished in full.

In short, we were created for universal purposes. This is even stated in the Qur'an:

> Did you reckon that We only created you in vain, and that to Us you would not be returned? So, exalted is God (from exerting Himself in what is vain), the Sovereign, the Truth. There is no god but He; Lord of the Noble Throne. (23:115-16)

We were not created for mere play or sport, nor is our eternal nonexistence in the grave our ultimate destiny. Rather, we were created for an eternal life prepared for us by all of our actions and for an eternal world full of eternal beauty and blessing (Paradise) or evil and wickedness (Hell).

Divine Mercy and Munificence Require the Resurrection

God's Mercy and Munificence are, of course, eternal. An Eternal One manifests Himself eternally and requires the existence of eternal beings. His eternal Mercy and Munificence demand eternal manifestation and therefore eternal beings on whom He can confer eternal bounties. But our world is only temporary, and millions of living creatures die in it each day. What does this indicate? It indicates this world's final and complete death.

This world cannot receive the comprehensive manifestation of Divine Names and Attributes. Nor can living beings, who experience great hardship in maintaining themselves. For example, we cannot satisfy all our desires and appetites. Our youth, beauty, and strength, upon which we set our hearts, leave without a word and cause us great sorrow. Also, we have to exert ourselves even to obtain a cluster of grapes. If we were denied eternal nourishment after having tasted it, would this not be an insult and a mockery, a source of great pain? For a blessing to be real, it must be constant. Without an eternal life in which we can satisfy our desires eternally, all of God Almighty's bounties bestowed upon us would change into pain and sorrow. Therefore, after He completely destroys this world, God will transform it into an eternal one that can receive the comprehensive manifestations of His Mercy and Munificence without obstruction, one in which we can satisfy all our desires eternally.

Divine Pity and Caring Require the Resurrection

Divine Pity and Caring heal wounds and wounded hearts and feelings, cause a patient to recover, end the pangs of separation, and change pain and sorrow into joy and pleasure. They help human beings and animals throughout their lives, especially before and right after birth. Their mothers' wombs are well-protected homes in which they are nourished directly without any effort on their part.

After birth, Divine Pity and Caring provide them with breast-milk, the best possible food, and their parents' feelings of pity and caring. All of these are a single manifestation of Divine Pity and Caring.

Although Divine Pity and Caring encompass the whole universe, in this world we encounter wounds, hurt feelings, incurable illness, hunger, thirst, and poverty. Why? As above, the answer is that this world cannot receive the comprehensive manifestation of Divine Pity and Caring. Our inability to receive these manifestations, as well as our injustice to others and abuse of our innate abilities, intervenes between beings and the manifestations of Divine Pity and Caring. Above all, death is the fate of all living beings; only belief in another, eternal world can stop the sorrow it arouses in our hearts.

Divine Justice and Honor Require the Resurrection

God's Names and Attributes are all absolute and eternal. Therefore He is absolutely and eternally Merciful, Relenting, and Forgiving, as well as absolutely and eternally Mighty, Just, and Dignified. Although His Mercy embraces all things (7:156), some people commit such great crimes and sins (e.g., like unbelief and associating partners with God) that they can receive their full punishment only in another world. Besides, despite His Divine declaration that whoever kills a human being unjustly, it is as if he (or she) has killed all humanity (5:32), especially in a world like today's where "might is right" is the rule, thousands of innocent people are killed almost every day, and many others are wronged and deprived of their basic human rights. Even worse, a great many of the most abominable, atrocious sins and injustices go unpunished.

Death does not discriminate between the oppressed and the oppressors, the innocent and the guilty, the sinless and the sinful. This can only mean that while minor sins may or may not be punished in this world, major sins like unbelief, associating partners with God, murder, and oppression are referred to the Supreme Tribunal in the Hereafter, where God will rule on them with absolute Justice.

Divine Grace and Generosity Require the Resurrection

We are provided with whatever we need for almost nothing. The more necessary for life an item is, the more abundant and cheaper it is in nature. Our most pressing need is air, which we receive free of charge. Then comes water, which is almost free. God sends both of these from His infinite Mercy, and we make absolutely no contribution. Then come heat and light, which we receive from the sun for nothing. When we look at the rest of the bounties God provides, we see that they are extremely cheap. And yet we still demand that He perform a miracle so that we might believe in Him! Our effort to procure these blessings is minuscule when compared to how they were produced. However, if these bounties or blessings were only temporary and imperfect, our fear of death would change them into poison.

Thanks to God's being eternal, He will provide for us eternal and ever-better forms of bounties through His Names and Attributes, free of charge. As these blessings will be eternal, they will not become a source of pain engendered by our fear of death. For believers, He transforms death into a changing of worlds, a discharge from worldly duty, an invitation to the eternal abode He has prepared for them, and a passport to go to that abode.

Divine Beauty Requires the Resurrection

Listen to the birds singing on a spring morning, the murmur of a brook flowing through green fields or deep valleys. Look at the beauty of spectacular green plains and trees in blossom. Watch the sun rise or set, the full moon on a cloudless, clear night. All of these, and many more things that God Almighty presents to our senses, are but a single gleam of His absolute and eternal Beauty manifested through many veils. By observing such manifestations, through which He makes Himself known, we are enraptured.

Temporary blessings leave unbearable pain in our heart when they disappear. If spring came only once, we would sigh over it until we died. So, a true blessing must out of necessity be eternal. In this world, the Eternally Beautiful One shows us only shadows of His Beauty so that our desire to see Its eternal and perfect manifestation will be aroused. Moreover, somehow He will allow us to see Him in Paradise in a manner free of any qualitative and quantitative measure or dimension: *On that day there will be shining faces, gazing upon their Lord* (75:22-23).

The Relation between Things and Humanity Indicates the Resurrection

There is a basic relation between humanity and this world. We are born into an amiable environment and equipped with the required senses. We have feelings like compassion and pity, caring and love, for there are many things in the world to which we can apply them. We feel hunger and thirst, cold and heat. Fortunately, these feelings can be satisfied with that which was prepared before or with only a slight exertion on our part.

Take an apple, for example. Its color and beauty appeal to our eyes and our sense of beauty. Its taste addresses itself to our sense of taste, and its vitamins nourish our bodies. Despite our need of its nutriments, we might refuse to eat it if it were ugly and tasteless, and thereby deprive ourselves of its nourishment. This, as well as many other "natural" facts, shows that One with infinite Knowledge and Power created us and prepared a suitable environment for us. He knows all of our needs, capacities, and qualities, just as He knows "nature" down to its smallest building blocks.

Another example is reproduction, which depends upon mutual love and attraction between a man and a woman. If our Creator had not placed in each of us a love for and an attraction toward the opposite sex, if He had not allowed us to enjoy the process of reproduction, and if He had not ingrained in us a great love and caring for the resulting children, we would never have reproduced.

Death ends all pleasure and makes everything as if it had never been. Given this, if there were no Resurrection our life would be meaningless, leaving behind only suffering and pain. However, this world is a shadowy miniature of the other, eternal one. The bounties God bestows here are only examples of their eternal and much better forms in the eternal world, and are displayed here to encourage us to act in order to deserve them:

Give glad tidings to those who believe and do good deeds. For them there will be Gardens beneath which rivers flow. Every time they are served with the fruits therein, they will say: "This is what was given to us aforetime." They shall be given in perfect semblance. And there will be pure spouses for them, and they will abide there forever. (2:25)

Recording and Preservation Point to the Resurrection

Nothing disappears completely from this world. While our every word and act is recorded and preserved, why should we not be able to grasp that God records all of humanity's words and deeds in a way that is as yet unknown to us? Advances in science and technology constantly provide new evidence for the Existence and Unity of God and affirm, together with the Divine origin of the Qur'an, the truth of Islamic beliefs. The Qur'an declared centuries ago that:

> We shall show them Our signs in the outer world and within themselves until it will be manifest to them that (the Qur'an) is the truth. Does not your Lord suffice, since He is witness over all things? (41:53)

If people sincerely search for the truth and can "see" it as it is, and are not blinded by prejudice, ignorance, and worldly ambition and desire, every new scientific advance displays the truth of the Qur'an. We see that God enfolds everything in small things like seeds. For example, each human being is enfolded in a sperm or in his or her 46 chromosomes. If we had 44 or 48 chromosomes, we would be something completely different. Similarly, when we die and disappear into the soil, our most essential part (our soul) does not disappear, for God will use it to rebuild us on the Day of Resurrection. God preserves everything, and so nothing can disappear forever. For example, a plant that dies in autumn or winter continues to live in innumerable memories as well as in its seeds that will bring it back in an almost identical form next spring.

Just as God preserves things in their seeds, He somehow preserves sounds and voices, as well as appearances and sights, to display them in another world. Maybe one day these sounds and sights will be discovered.

Divine Power Establishes the Resurrection

Consider an atom. How it is formed and maintains its relationships with other atoms are astounding miracles. Creating a solar system or an atom, both of which resemble each other due to their orbiting bodies, and then regulating their movements and establishing their relationships are equally easy for God. Similarly, a cell is like an autonomous government. It has its own departments, each of which is interrelated with others and ruled by a center, as well as a "ministry of finance" that manages its income and expenditure. It is as if each cell was as smart as the smartest person on the planet. Besides, there are very close and substantial relations between these cells, all of which are ruled by a center: the brain.

These are only a few examples of the Creator's Power. Everything is equally easy for Him. Creating and administering the universe is as easy as creating and administering an atom; all of humanity, the most knowledgeable and conscious of all beings, could not create one atom even if all of us joined together to do so. So, if the absolutely Powerful One says He will destroy the universe and rebuild it in a different form, He will do so. God does not lie and is without defect, and so His promises can be believed. As stated in the Qur'an:

> The Day of Final Decision and Judgment is a fixed time, a day when the Trumpet is blown, and you come in multitudes, and the heaven is opened and becomes as gates. (78:17-19)

Instances of Death and Revival Indicate the Resurrection

An overall death, except for a certain region in the world, and revival is repeated every year. In winter, a white "shroud" covers the soil, whose yearly life cycle ends in autumn. Nature has already turned pale and shows fewer traces of life. The shell has fallen in and, ultimately, trees become like lifeless, hard bones; grass has rotted away and flowers have withered; migrating birds have left; and insects and reptiles have disappeared.

Winter, which is only temporary, is followed by a general revival. Warm weather causes trees to begin to bud and, wearing their finery, present themselves to the Eternal Witness. The soil swells, and grass and flowers start to bloom everywhere. Seeds that fell into the ground during the previous autumn have germinated and, having annihilated themselves, are transformed into new forms of life. Migrating birds return, and the planet hosts countless insects and reptiles. In short, with all its splendor and finery, nature appears before us.

God created the world and humanity when nothing of either thing existed. He brought our body's building-blocks together from soil, air, and water, and made them into a conscious, intelligent being. Is there any doubt that the person who made a machine can tear it apart and then reassemble it, or that an army commander can gather his dispersed soldiers through a trumpet-call?

Similarly, while reconstructing the world, God Almighty will gather our atoms and grant them a higher, eternal form of life:

> Say: "Travel in the land and see how He originated creation, then God brings forth the later growth. Assuredly, God is able to do all things." (29:20)

> Look at the imprints of God's mercy (in creation), how He gives life to the earth after its death. He surely is the reviver of the dead (in the same way), and He is able to do all things. (30:50)

The Benefits of Belief in the Resurrection

After belief in God, belief in the Resurrection has the primary place in securing a peaceful social order. Why should those who do not believe that they will be called to account strive to live an honest, upright life? But those of us who are convinced that God will one day call us to account in the other world certainly try to live a disciplined and upright life. The Qur'an declares:

> In whatever affair you may be, and whichever part of the Qur'an you recite, and whatever deed you do, We are witness over you

> when you are deeply engrossed therein. Not an atom's weight
> in Earth and in the heaven escapes your Lord, nor is there any-
> thing smaller or greater, but it is in a Manifest Book. (10:61)

Whatever we do is recorded by the angels appointed for that task. In addition, God fully knows and is fully aware of all our deeds, intentions, thoughts, and imaginings. Those who live in full consciousness of this fact will find true peace and happiness in both worlds; a family and community composed of such individuals would feel that they were living in Paradise.

Belief in the Resurrection prevents young people from wasting their lives in transitory and trivial things, and gives hope to the elderly who each day are moving closer to the grave. It also helps children endure the death of loved ones. Children who believe that they will be reunited with their deceased loved ones in a far better world find true consolation in the Resurrection. Everyone, regardless of age, gender, and any other artificial human-devised difference, needs belief in the Resurrection as much as they need air, water, and bread.

As this belief leads one to a life of peace, intellectuals who seek public peace and security should emphasize it. Those who are convinced of what the Qur'an declares – *Whoever does an atom's weight of good shall see it, and whoever does an atom's weight of evil shall see it* (99:7-8) – live a responsible life, and a community composed of such people finds true peace and happiness. When this belief is inculcated in the hearts of young people, they will no longer be a harmful element in society, but rather will seek to serve their nation and humanity.

Children are very sensitive and delicate. Extremely susceptible to misfortune, they also are easily affected by what happens to them and their families. When they lose a family member or become orphans, their world becomes dark and they fall into deep distress and despair. What else other than belief in the Resurrection and reunion with loved ones who have emigrated to the other world can compensate for the loss of parents, brothers and sisters, and friends? Children will find true consolation only when they are convinced that their beloved ones have flown to Paradise, and that they will be reunited with them.

As for the elderly, how can you compensate for their past years, their childhood and youth that have been left behind? How can you console them for the loss of their loved ones who preceded them in death? How can you remove from their hearts the fear of death and the grave, to which they are drawing closer day by day? How can you make them forget death, which they feel so deeply? Will more and newer worldly pleasures console them? Only convincing them that the grave, which seems to them like an open-mouthed dragon just waiting to devour them, is really a door to another and much better world, or simply a lovely waiting room opening onto that world, can compensate and console them for such losses.

Our free will, which we use to direct our life, gives us a unique position among all creatures. Free will is the manifestation of Divine Mercy and, if used properly, will cause us to be rewarded with the fruits of Mercy. Belief in the Resurrection is a most important and compelling factor urging us to use our free will properly and not to wrong or harm others.

Belief in the Resurrection also consoles the sick. A believer who suffers from an incurable illness thinks: "I am dying; no one can prolong my life. Everyone must die. Fortunately, I am going to a place (Paradise) where I will recover my health and youth and enjoy them forever." Secure in this knowledge, all beloved servants of God, Prophets and saints, welcome death with a smile. The Last Prophet, Prophet Muhammad, upon him be peace and blessings, said during his final minutes of life: "O God, I desire the eternal company in the eternal world." (Bukhari, "Marda," 19.)

The world is a mixture of good and evil, right and wrong, beauty and ugliness, and oppressors and oppressed. Many instances of wrong (appear to) go unnoticed, and numerous wronged people cannot recover their rights. Only belief in being resurrected in another world of absolute justice consoles the wronged and oppressed, and dissuades them from trying to avenge themselves. Similarly, those stricken with affliction and misfortune find consolation in the Resurrection, because they believe that whatever befalls them purifies them, and that anything lost in a catastrophe will be restored in the Hereafter as a blessing of the Hereafter, just as if they had given these items as alms.

Belief in the Resurrection changes a house into a garden of Paradise. Belief in the Resurrection reminds people of their familial responsibilities, and as they implement these duties, an atmosphere of mutual love, affection, and respect will begin to pervade the house.

This belief leads spouses to deepen their love and respect for each other. Love based on physical beauty is temporary and of little value, for it usually disappears shortly after marriage. But if the spouses believe that their marriage will continue eternally in the other world where they will be eternally young and beautiful, their love for each other will remain even though they gradually become old and lose their physical beauty.

Such a belief-based family life makes its members feel that they are already living in Paradise. Similarly, if a country orders itself according to this same belief, its inhabitants would enjoy a life far better than what Plato imagined in his *Republic* or al-Farabi (Alpharabios) in his *al-Madinat al-Fadila* (The Virtuous City). It would be like Madina in the time of the Prophet, upon him be peace and blessings, or the Muslim lands under the rule of 'Umar, may God be pleased with him.

Is Death Something To Fear?

The grave can be represented in three ways, for there are three types of people. For believers, it is the door to a more beautiful world. For those who admit the next life but live a misguided, dissipated life, it is the door to solitary imprisonment and an eternal jail that will separate them from their loved ones. Since they believe and confirm but do not live according to their belief, that is exactly how they will be punished. For unbelievers and the misguided who do not believe in the Hereafter, it is the door to "execution." Since they believe death to be an execution without resurrection, they will be punished in both the grave and the other world.

Death may come at any time, for its appointed hour is unknown. In the face of such an awesomely threatening reality,

we urgently search for a way to avoid punishment and imprisonment, for a way to change the grave into a door opening onto a
permanent world of light and eternal happiness. Death will be experienced in these three ways, as has been reported by 124,000 truthful reporters – the Prophets. Their reports have been confirmed
by millions of saints relying upon their discernment, vision, and
intuition. Also, innumerable truth-seeking scholars have proved
it rationally with their decisive proofs at the level of "certainty
depending on established knowledge." Both groups agree that
only belief in and obedience to God can save one from punishment
and imprisonment, and make the grave a way to eternal happiness.

If only one reliable reporter warned that a particular way
carried a 1 percent risk of death, people would be so afraid that
they would avoid it. But countless truthful, authoritative reporters
– Prophets, saints, and truth-seeking scholars – have provided proof
of their truth and warn us that misguidance and dissipation carry
a 100 percent risk of death followed by punishment. In contrast,
belief and worship change the grave into a door opening onto
an eternal treasury, a palace of lasting happiness. If we, especially those of us claiming to be Muslims, do not truly believe and
worship in the face of such a mighty warning, how will we overcome our anxieties while waiting to die, even if we were given
the rule of the whole world and enjoyed all of its pleasures?

Seeing old age, illness, misfortune, and numerous instances of
death everywhere reopens our pain and reminds us of death. Even
if the misguided and dissolute people appear to enjoy all kinds of
pleasure and delight, they most certainly are in a hellish state of
spiritual torment. However, a profound stupor of heedlessness
makes them temporarily insensible to it.

Obedient believers experience the grave as the door to an
eternal treasury and endless happiness. Since they have a "belief
coupon," a priceless ticket from the allocations of Destiny, they
always expect the call "come and collect your ticket" with a profound pleasure and spiritual delight. If this pleasure could assume
the material form of a seed, it would grow into a private paradise.
But those who abandon this great delight and pleasure to indulge

the drives of their appetites, who choose temporary and illicit pleasures that will give them great pain, fall far below the status of humanity.

So, those of you addicted to worldly pleasure and troubled about your future even while you struggle to secure it and your lives, if you want pleasure and delight, happiness and ease in this world, be content with what is religiously lawful. You must have understood by now that each forbidden pleasure contains a thousand pains. If future events, say 50 years from now, were shown in the theater, the dissolute would be horrified and disgusted with themselves. Those who wish to be eternally happy in both worlds should follow the Prophet's instruction on the firm ground of belief.

Eschatology in Islam

The main aspects of Islamic eschatology are similar to the Judeo-Christian tradition. Since they were derived from the same source and so originate from Divine Revelation, many common points can be found: for example, the invasion of the world shortly before the end of time by the barbarous Gog and Magog (Ya'juj and Ma'juj) tribes, the appearance of Dajjal (the Anti-Christ) and then a Messiah and/or Mahdi who will bring justice and order after global chaos, a global apostasy just before the world's destruction, Doomsday, Resurrection, the Supreme Judgment, the Bridge (*Sirat*), and Paradise and Hell as the final abode of conscious beings.

In this chapter, beginning with the "last things" before the world's overall destruction, we will summarize the events and stations of the Hereafter. Before analyzing this, it is necessary to explain the language of the main Islamic religious literature.

The Language of the Divine Books and the Prophetic Traditions

The Qur'an decrees: *There is not a thing wet and dry but it is in a manifest Book* (6:59). The Qur'an contains everything, but not to the same degree, in the form of seeds, nuclei, summaries, principles, or signs. Things are explicit, implicit, allusive, vague, or suggestive. Each form is used to meet the Qur'an's purposes and the context's requirements.

The Qur'an pursues four main purposes: To expose and establish in human minds and hearts God's Existence and Unity, Prophethood, bodily resurrection, and the worship of God and justice. To realize its purposes, the Qur'an draws our attention to God's acts in the universe, His matchless art displayed through creation, the manifestations of His Names and Attributes, and the magnificent, perfect order and harmony in existence. It explains how to worship and please the Creator, makes frequent mention of the other life, and explains how we can gain eternal happiness and be saved from eternal punishment. It mentions certain historical events, and lays down the rules of personal and social good conduct and morality as well as the principles of a happy, harmonious social life. It also gives news of important future events, especially those that will happen before the end of time. These have a prominent place in both the Qur'an and the Prophetic sayings.

The Qur'an is the last Divine Book and Prophet Muhammad is the final Prophet. Thus, both address all times, places, and levels of understanding. As the vast majority of people always have an "average" level of understanding, the Qur'an and the Prophet use the appropriate style and language to guide them to the truth and the Qur'an's basic purposes. Thus symbols, metaphors, allegories, comparisons, and parables requiring interpretation are quite common. Those who are well-versed in knowledge (3:7) know how to approach and benefit from the Qur'an and the Prophetic Traditions.

Another reason why the Qur'an does not concentrate on future events explicitly is that the point of religion is to examine and test the individual so that elevated and base spirits may be distinguished. Just as raw materials are fired to separate diamonds and coal, as well as gold and soil, Divine obligations test conscious beings and make them compete so that the precious "ore" in the "mine" of human potential may be separated from the "dross."

Since the Qur'an was sent to perfect humanity through trial in this abode of testing and competition, it can only allude to future events that everyone will witness one day, and only opens the door to reason to a degree that proves its argument.

If it mentioned them explicitly, the test would be meaningless. If the truth of Divine injunctions and Qur'anic and Prophetic predictions were clearly evident, everyone would have to affirm them, thereby rendering our God-given mental and spiritual faculties meaningless.

After this note, we may continue with brief mention of the last things:

The Last Things

THE *DAJJAL* (ANTICHRIST). God's Messenger, upon him be peace and blessings, mentioned two Antichrists: the Dajjal, who will appear in the non-Muslim world, and the Sufyan, who will appear in the Muslim world. Both beings are the greatest of all the Dajjals and Sufyans to appear in the world after the Messenger. Islamic sources report from the Messenger that more than 30 Dajjals will appear after him, and that the one or ones to emerge before the end of time will be the most harmful and destructive.

Another important point to stress is that the narrations of such beings are not exclusively about their persons. Rather, they are about their ideologies and committees, and the systems they will establish in all aspects of life. There are many reports from Prophet Muhammad, upon him be peace and blessings, about the Antichrist, with different degrees of authenticity according to the principles of Hadith science. We will mention some of them with the explanations of Bediüzzaman Said Nursi in his books *Mektubat* (The Letters) and *Şualar* (The Rays):

- "The hands of the Sufyan will be holed," meaning that the Sufyan will be a prodigal one and encourage prodigality and dissipation.
- "A terrible person will appear before the end of time. When he gets up one morning, he will find that on his forehead is inscribed: This is an infidel." This means that the Sufyan will be an apostate and, in imitation of unbelievers, will compel people to be dressed after the style of the non-Muslim world.
- "The dictators to appear before the end of time, including especially the Dajjal and Sufyan, will have a false Paradise and

Hell." This means that during their time, people will be addicted to amusement and worldly pleasures and the income disparity among social classes will increase. As a result, there will be rebellions against governments. Therefore, the places of pleasure and amusement, jails, and similar places of torture will stand side by side.

- "Before the end of time, there will be almost no people who worship God and mention His Names as an act of worship." This means that the places in which God is worshipped and His Names are mentioned will be closed, and that the number of believing worshippers will decrease considerably. Another meaning is that just before the world's destruction, God will take the believers' souls and the world will be destroyed upon the unbelievers' heads.

- "Certain terrible persons will emerge before the end of time, such as the Dajjal, and claim divinity and make people prostrate to them." This means that such persons will derive their force mostly from atheistic and materialistic trends and suppose themselves to have godly power. Their statutes will be built, and people will be forced to bow before them as a way of adoration.

- "The dissipation and dissension to appear before the end of time will be so widespread and powerful that no one will be able to control his or her carnal self against them." This means the dissipated life will seduce too many people, and that they will indulge in it willingly. The frightening dimensions of the dissipation and pleasure-addiction that the Dajjal will cause at this time have caused almost all Muslims, upon the Prophet's order, to take refuge in God for 14 centuries.

- "The Sufyan will be a knowledgeable one and fascinate many scholars." This means that although devoid of such means of power and reliance as kingdom, tribe, wealth, and courage, the Sufyan will gain authority due to his intriguing capacity and political genius. He bans religious education. Mostly because of their attachment to this life, many religious scholars and educationists will support him and his regime.

- "The first day of the Dajjal is equal to a year, his second day to a month, his third day to a week, and his fourth day to an ordinary day." This miraculous Prophetic tradition means that the Dajjal will appear in the north and proceed toward the south. As we know, in the places near the North Pole a whole year consists of a day and night, each of which lasts 6 ordinary months. Coming toward the south, there are places where a day lasts 3 months, a month, and a week, respectively.

  Another meaning is that both the Dajjal and the Sufyan will have four periods of rule: in the first period (one year) they will cause such destruction that normally could occur only in 300 years. During the second period, the destruction they will cause each year will be equal to 30 years' worth of destruction by others, and in one year of their third period they will cause 7 years' worth of destruction. Their fourth period will be normalized.

- "When the Dajjal appears, everyone will hear him. He will have an extraordinary mount and travel throughout the world within 40 days." This means that the Dajjal will appear when the means of communication and transportation develop to such an extent that an event happening in one part of the world will be heard in other parts, and that traveling throughout the world within around 40 days is possible.

GOG AND MAGOG. According to Qur'an 18:94-98 and 21:96, these are two barbarous tribes living in eastern Asia. Once before, a world-conqueror known in the Qur'an as Dhu'l-Qarnayn went as far as their lands and, to protect neighboring peoples from their attacks, built a formidable wall. When the time comes, they will surmount this wall and invade the civilized world.

The Mongols, who invaded the Muslim world and went as far as central Europe, were considered as Gog and Magog by the Muslims and Christians of that time. Having mentioned this interpretation, Said Nursi adds that a new invasion will come from the same direction. According to certain Prophetic Traditions, such great wars will break out that almost nine-tenths of humanity will perish.

THE MAHDI AND THE MESSIAH. This is perhaps the most important element of the last things. Both Jews and Christians expect a Messiah toward the end of time, and regard his coming as the sign of the final, worldwide triumph for each.

Islamic sources mention both individuals. Shi'a Muslims give particular importance to the Mahdi, who they say is named Muhammad. He is the twelfth (and last) Imam of a series that began with 'Ali ibn Abi Talib, the Prophet's cousin and fourth caliph. The Mahdi disappeared when he was 74 years old, and will reappear when the world is full of injustice to restore justice.

The majority of Muslims regard the Mahdi as one who will come toward the end of time, when the Muslim world is defeated and all Islamic principles are under comprehensive attack. Together with the Messiah, the Mahdi will defend the principles of Islam against atheistic and materialistic trends and revive the religious life. He will end the dominion of both the Dajjal and the Sufyan.

According to certain contemporary thinkers and scholars, including Said Nursi, the Mahdi is not a single person but rather the name of a global Islamic revival. It has three periods, each of which will be represented by a person and his group. Its leaders will be well-versed in religious sciences, have the highest moral standards, know the sociopolitical and economic conditions of their times, and be equipped with the necessary qualities of leadership. Together with his followers, the leader of the first period will defend Islamic principles against materialistic trends and expose them in an appropriate way. In the second period, the revived Islamic principles will gain ascendancy in many parts of the world, and Islamic life will experience a significant revival. The third period will see the global revival of religious life.

The third period most probably will follow the invasion of Gog and Magog, which will interrupt the second period. Christianity, according to the relevant Islamic sources, will be freed from its borrowings from certain ancient religions and philosophies and draw closer to Islam. Christianity and Islam will cooperate to repel the attacks of Gog and Magog and free the world from their invasion.

Sciences will realize their full development. Cities will be built in the sky, and it will be easy to travel there. Probably as a result of developments in genetics, one pomegranate will suffice for as many as 20 people, and its rind will provide shade for them. Wheat produced in a small house balcony will be enough to feed a family for a year.

We will elaborate the Messianic mission attributed to Jesus in Islamic sources after the end of this section under a separate title.

THE FINAL, WORLDWIDE APOSTASY AND THE WORLD'S DESTRUCTION. The unprecedented developments in science and technology will cause humanity to believe that it has so much knowledge and power that an authority above itself is no longer required or necessary. This will lead people to rebel against Heaven and indulge in debauchery to the extent that a worldwide apostasy will take place. Few believers will be left, and the unbelieving, rebellious forces will destroy the Ka'ba. This will mark the end of the world. God Almighty will gently take the souls of the believers.[6] According to Said Nursi, as the result of a probable collision of a heavenly body with Earth, the latter will begin to rotate in the opposite direction and the sun will rise in the west. This is the final sign of the world's destruction. Some Qur'anic verses which describe this destruction are as follows:

> When the sun is folded up; when the stars fall, losing their luster; when the mountains are moved; when the ten-month pregnant camels are abandoned; when the wild beasts are herded together; and when the seas are set boiling. . . (81:1-6)

> When the sky is rent asunder, when the planets are dispersed, when the oceans are poured forth, and when the graves are overturned, each soul will know what it has sent forward and what it has kept back. (82:1-5)

> When Earth is shaken with its (final) earthquake, and Earth yields up its burdens, and humanity says: "What is the matter with it?" That day it will proclaim its tidings, because your Master inspired it. That day humanity will come forth in scattered groups to be shown its deeds. Whoever does an atom's weight of good shall see it then, and whoever does an atom's weight of ill shall see it then. (99:1-8)

The Messianic Mission Attributed to Jesus
Christ toward the End of Time

Some of the first converts to Islam were subjected to severe persecution in Makka. They bore them patiently and never thought
of retaliation, as the Qur'an ordered Prophet Muhammad to call
unbelievers to the way of God with wisdom and fair preaching,
advised him to repel evil with what was better, and to respond
to his enemies' sins and faults with forbearance and forgiveness.
Makkan intolerance eventually compelled the local Muslims to
abandon their homes and property and emigrate to Madina, where
they could live according to their beliefs and where Islam's full social
and legal dimensions could evolve in peace.

But the Makkans' hostility continued, and in Madina the
Muslims became targets of new conspiracies. Although the native
Madinan believers (the Ansar) willingly shared everything with the
Emigrants (the Muhajirun), all suffered privations. In such strained
circumstances, God Almighty allowed them to fight their enemies,
for they had been wronged and driven from their homes unjustly (22:39).

The Battle of Badr (624) was the first major confrontation of
the Muslims and the enemy forces. Although outnumbered, the
believers won a great victory. If we do not accept the opinions of
some Qur'anic interpreters that *Sura Muhammad*, which contains
regulations on how to treat prisoners of war, was revealed before
Surat al-Anfal, no Divine commandment had been revealed
about how captives should be treated. The Muslims did not even
know whether they should kill the enemy on the battlefield or
take them as prisoners. After the battle, the Prophet consulted, as
he always did where there was no specific Divine commandment,
with his Companions on this issue.

Abu Bakr said: "O God's Messenger, they are your people.
Even though they did you and the believers great wrong, you will
win their hearts and cause their guidance if you forgive them and
please them." But 'Umar said: "O God's Messenger, they are the
leading figures of Makka. If we kill them, unbelief will no longer
be able to recover to oppose us. So give to each Muslim his clos-

est kin. Hand 'Aqil over to his brother 'Ali to kill. And his son, 'Abd al-Rahman, to Abu Bakr, and .... [so on]."

God's Messenger turned to Abu Bakr and said: "O Abu Bakr, you are like Prophet Abraham, who said: *He who follows me is of me, and he who disobeys me – but You are indeed Oft-Forgiving, Most Compassionate* (14:36). You are also like Jesus, who said: If *You punish them, they are Your servants. If You forgive them, You are the All-Honored with irresistible might, the All-Wise*" (5:118).

Then he turned to 'Umar and said: "O 'Umar, you are like Noah, who said: *O my Lord! Leave not even a single unbeliever on Earth!* (71:26). You are also like Moses, who said (of Pharaoh and his chieftains): *Our Lord, destroy their riches and harden their hearts so that they will not believe until they see the painful chastisement*" (10:88). (Ibn Hanbal, *Musnad*, 1:383.)

Moses, Jesus, and Muhammad

Islam, as the last, universal form of the Divine religion, orders its followers to believe in all of the Prophets. Thus being a Muslim also means being a follower of Jesus, Moses, and all other Prophets.

The Qur'an declares:

> The Messenger believes in what has been revealed to him by his Lord, and so do the believers. They all believe in God and His angels, His Scriptures, and His Messengers: "We make no distinction between any of His Messengers" – and they say: "We hear and obey. Grant us Your forgiveness, our Lord. To You is the journeying." (2:285)

As historical conditions required that the messages of all previous Prophets be restricted to a certain people and period, certain principles were stressed in those messages. Also, God bestowed special favors upon each Prophet and community according to the dictates of the time.

For example, Adam was favored with knowledge of the Names, the keys to all branches of knowledge; Noah was endowed with steadfastness and perseverance; Abraham was honored with intimate friendship with God and being the father of numerous Prophets; Moses was given the ability to administer and was exalted by being

God's direct addressee; and Jesus was distinguished with patience, tolerance, and compassion. All Prophets have some share in the praiseworthy qualities mentioned, but each one surpasses, on account of his mission, the others in one or more of those qualities.

When Moses was raised as a Prophet, the Israelites were leading a wretched existence under the Egyptian Pharaohs. Due to the Pharaohs' despotic rule and oppression, slavery had become ingrained in the Israelites' souls and was now part of their character. To reform them, to equip them with such lofty feelings and values as freedom and independence, and to rebuild their character and thereby free them from subservience to the Pharaohs, Moses came with a message containing stern and rigid rules. This is why the Book given to him was called Torah (Law). Given that his mission required that he be a somewhat stern and unyielding reformer and educator, it was natural for him to pray in reference to Pharaoh and his chieftains: *Our Lord, destroy their riches and harden their hearts so that they will not believe until they see the painful chastisement* (10:88).

Jesus came at a time when the Israelites had abandoned themselves to worldly pleasure and led a materialistic life. In the Qur'an, we read that:

> O you who believe! Many priests and anchorites in falsehood devour the wealth of people and hinder (them) from the Way of God. And there are those who hoard gold and silver and spend it not in the Way of God. Announce to them a most grievous chastisement. (9:34)

and that these same people exploited religion for worldly gain:

> You see many of them vying in sin and enmity and how they consume what is unlawful. Evil is the thing they have been doing. Why do the masters and rabbis not forbid them to utter sin and to consume the unlawful? Evil is the thing they have been doing. (5:62-63)

The Gospels relate a similar sentiment attributed to Jesus:

> You snakes, how can you say good things when you are evil, for the mouth speaks of what has filled the heart. A good person

brings good things out of his or her treasure of good things; a bad person brings bad things out of his or her treasure of bad things. (Matthew 12:34-35)

Take care! Be on your guard against the yeast of the Pharisees and Sadducees. The teachers of the law and the Pharisees are the authorized interpreters of Moses' Law. So you must obey and follow everything they tell you to do. Do not, however, imitate their actions, because they do not practice what they preach. They tie onto people's backs loads that are heavy and hard to carry, yet they are not willing to lift even a finger to help them carry those loads. They do everything so that people will see them ... They love the best places at feasts and the reserved seats in the synagogues. They love to be greeted with respect in the marketplaces and to have people call them "Teacher" ... How terrible for you, teachers of the Law and the Pharisees. You hypocrites ... You give to God one-tenth of the seasoning herbs, such as mint, dill, and cumin, but neglect to obey the really important teachings of the Law, such as justice, mercy, and honesty. You should practice these without neglecting the others. (Matthew, chapters 23, 13, and 12)

When Jesus was sent to the Israelites, the spirit of the True Religion had dwindled away and the religion itself had been reduced to a device for its exponents to rob the common people. So before proceeding to put the Law into effect, Jesus concentrated on belief, justice, mercy, humility, peace, love, repentance for one's sins, seeking God's forgiveness, helping others, purity of heart and intention, and sincerity:

Happy are those who know they are spiritually poor, for the kingdom of heaven belongs to them. Happy are those who mourn, for God will comfort them. Happy are those who are humble, for they will receive what God has promised. Happy are those whose greatest desire is to do what God requires, for God will satisfy them fully. Happy are those who are merciful to others, for God will be merciful to them. Happy are the poor in heart, for they will see God. (Matthew 5:3-10)

Prophet Muhammad has all of the qualities mentioned above, except that of being the father of Prophets. In addition, because of his mission's universality he is like Moses (he is a warner, established a Law, and fought his enemies) and Jesus (a bringer of good news who preached mercy, forgiveness, helping others, altruism, humility, sincerity, purity of intention, and moral values of the highest degree). Remember that the Qur'an declares that God sent Prophet Muhammad as a mercy for the whole of creation (21:107).

Islam presents God, before all other Attributes and Names, as the All-Merciful and All-Compassionate. By doing this, it indicates that He mainly manifests Himself as the All-Merciful and All-Compassionate, and that His wrath and punishment are shown when attracted by the individual's own unforgivable sins and wrongdoing. But God, the All-Forgiving, forgives most of His servants' sins: *Whatever misfortune befalls you is for what your own hands have earned, and for many (of them) He grants forgiveness* (42:30).

Prophet Muhammad had the mission of both Moses and Jesus. The historical episode mentioned at the article's beginning shows that Abu Bakr represented more the mission of Jesus and that 'Umar represented more the mission of Moses. Since Islam must prevail until the end of time, there may be occasions when its followers are required to act, according to circumstances, sometimes as Moses and sometimes as Jesus.

Islam and Jesus Christ's Messianic Mission

The reliable Books of Tradition contain many sayings of Prophet Muhammad that Jesus will return to this world before the end of time and observe the Muslim law. Although such Traditions have been interpreted in different ways, they can be interpreted as meaning that, before the end of time, Islam must manifest itself mostly in the dimension represented by Jesus. In other words, the main aspects of his Prophethood must be given prominence in preaching Islam. These aspects are the following:

- Jesus always traveled. He never stayed in one place, but preached his message on the move. Those who preach Islam must travel or emigrate.
- They must be the repentants, worshippers, travelers (in devotion to the cause of Islam and to convey it), those who bow and

prostrate (to God only), command good and forbid evil, and observe God's limits. For them there is good news (9:112).

- Mercy, love, and forgiveness had the first place. Jesus brought good news. Therefore, those who dedicate themselves to the cause of Islam must emphasize these characteristics and, never forgetting that Prophet Muhammad was sent as a mercy for all the worlds and the whole of existence, must convey good news to every place and call people to the way of God with wisdom and fair exhortation. They must never repel others.

The world today needs peace more than at any time in history. Most of our problems arise from excessive worldliness, scientific materialism, and the ruthless exploitation of nature. Everyone talks so much about the danger of war and environmental pollution that peace and ecology are the most fashionable words on people's tongues. But the same people wish to remove those problems through further conquest and domination of nature.

The problem lies in rebelling against heaven and in destroying the equilibrium between humanity and nature. This condition is a result of modern materialism's conception of and corrupt attitude toward humanity and nature. Most people are reluctant to perceive that peace within human societies and with nature is possible only through peace with the spiritual order. To be at peace with Earth, one must be at peace with the spiritual dimension of one's existence. This is possible only by being at peace with heaven.

In the Qur'an, Jesus introduces himself as follows:

> I am indeed a servant of God ... He has commanded me to pray and give alms as long as I live. He has made me dutiful to my mother, and has not made me oppressive, wicked. (19:30-32)

From the viewpoint of Jesus' promised messianic mission, this means that children will not obey their parents. Thus those who spread Islam in our age must strive to show due respect to their parents and elders, in addition to performing their prayers correctly and helping the poor and needy. The Qur'an enjoins:

> Your Lord has decreed that you worship none but Him, and that you show kindness to your parents. If either or both of

them attain old age with you, (show no sign of impatience, and) do not even say "uff" to them, nor rebuke them, but speak kind words to them. (17:23)

One of Jesus' miracles was healing the sick and reviving the dead with God's permission. In other words, respect for life was very important in his message. The Qur'an attaches the same degree of importance to life: *One who kills another wrongly is regarded as having killed humanity; one who saves a life is regarded as having saved humanity* (5:32). Those dedicated to the cause of Islam must attach the utmost importance to life and try to prevent wars, find cures for illnesses, and know that reviving a person spiritually is more important than healing diseases. The Qur'an declares: *O you who believe! Respond to God and the Messenger, when the Messenger calls you to that which will give you life* (8:24).

Death and the Spirit after Death[7]

People have an intrinsic feeling of eternity. They feel imprisoned in the narrow confines of this world and always yearn for eternity. Whoever hearkens to their conscious nature will hear it pronouncing eternity over and over again. Even the whole universe cannot compensate them for their "hunger" for eternal life, for which they were created. Humanity's natural inclination toward eternal happiness comes from an objective reality: the existence of eternal life and the human desire for it.

What Is Death?

The body is an instrument of the spirit, which governs and controls all of its members, cells, and minute particles. When the appointed hour comes, any illness or failure in the body's functions means an invitation to 'Azra'il, the Angel of Death. In reality, God causes people to die. However, so that people should not complain of this to Him, as many consider it disagreeable, God uses 'Azra'il as a veil in taking souls. Also, He puts illnesses or some calamities as veils between 'Azra'il and death so that people will not blame him for death.

Since 'Azra'il was created from "light," like all other angels, he can be anywhere and in any form simultaneously. He also can do many tasks at the same time. Like the sun giving heat and light to all things while being present through its images in innumerable transparent objects, 'Azra'il can take millions of souls at the same moment.

However, Archangels like Gabriel, Michael, Israfil, and 'Azra'il have subordinates that resemble them and are under their supervision. When righteous people die, angels come to them with smiles and radiant faces. After that 'Azra'il comes, either by himself or with his subordinates charged with taking such souls from the bodies. Sometimes just a subordinate comes. The verses: *By those who pluck out violently; by those who draw out gently* (79:1-2) indicate that these angels are different from those tasked with removing the souls of the wicked. Such souls are plucked out violently, and so have a sour, frightened face at death.

At the time of death, windows usually are opened for righteous believers from their places in Paradise, or they are shown the otherworldly forms of their good deeds and sayings. The Messenger stated that these souls are drawn out as gently as the flowing of water from a pitcher. Better than that, martyrs do not feel the agonies of death and do not know that they are dead; instead, they consider themselves to be transferred into a better world and enjoy happiness.[8]

Prophet Muhammad asked Jabir, whose father 'Abd Allah ibn Jahsh was martyred at Uhud:

> Do you know how God welcomed your father? He welcomed him in such an indescribable manner that neither eyes have seen it, nor ears have heard it, nor minds have conceived of it. Your father said: "O God, return me to the world so that I will explain to those left behind how pleasant martyrdom is." God replied: "There is no longer return. Life is lived only once. However, I'll inform them of the circumstances you are in," and He revealed: Never think of those slain in the way of God to be dead; rather they are alive and are provided in the Presence of their Master. (3:169) (Bayhaqi, *Dalail al-Nubuwwa*, 3:298.)

One dies how one lives. Those who live good, righteous lives have good deaths; those who live wicked lives do not. However, this does not mean that the righteous die easily or that those who seem to die easily were righteous, for God sometimes uses severe death agonies to cleanse people of sin. The Prophet says that whatever evil happens to a believer causes some of his or her sins to be erased. (Muslim, "Birr," Hadith No: 49.)

For righteous believers, death is not something to be feared. Although the body decomposes and seems to extinguish the light of life and destroy pleasures, in reality it is only a discharge from the heavy duties of worldly life, a changing of residence, a transferring of the body, an invitation to and the beginning of everlasting life. The world is continually enlivened through creation, and continually stripped of life through other cycles of creation, determination, and wisdom. Plants and trees appear to die. But their seeds, while underground and rotting, do not die; instead, they undergo chemical processes that cause them to re-form and reappear as new plants and trees. Given this, the apparent death of their seeds is really the beginning of a new plant or tree, a new, more perfect and elaborate life.

If this is true of such simple life forms, how can it not be true for human beings? Was not humanity created for greater purposes than plants and trees? Death discharges us from this narrow worldly life, which becomes more of a burden as we age and become ill, and causes us to enter the infinitely wide circle of the Eternal, Beloved One's Mercy. There, we enjoy the everlasting company of our loved ones and the consolation of a happy, eternal life. In effect, our grave is like our mother's womb: we leave both places for a more perfect life in another world.

The Spirit in the Intermediate World

Following death, the spirits of those people whose lives were characterized by faith, goodness, virtue, and refinement are wrapped in silk or silk-like substances and carried away by the angels charged with taking the spirit to God's Presence. While carrying the spirit of a good, righteous person through the heavens and all inner dimensions of existence, angels in every station it passes welcome it and ask: "Whose spirit is this? How beautiful it is!" Its bearers introduce it with its most beautiful titles by which it was called while in the world, and answer: "This is the spirit of that one who, for example, prayed, fasted, gave alms, helped others, and bore all kinds of hardship for God's sake." Finally, God welcomes it and tells the angels: "Return it to the grave where its body is buried, so that Munkar and Nakir, the interrogating angels, can investigate it."

The spirits of evil people are treated with disdain everywhere it passes and then thrown back into the grave, away from the Presence of God Almighty.

Whatever evil happens to us in this world is, with the exceptions of Prophets, because of our sins. If we are sincere believers who sometimes cannot avoid sinning, God, out of His Mercy, allows some misfortunes to befall us and thereby erases some of our sins. Or He may give us a hard death, so that still-unpardoned sins will be forgiven or so that we may attain higher (spiritual) ranks, but then take our spirits very gently. If we still have some unforgiven sins after this, we will undergo some sort of punishment in the grave and then be spared any punishment of Hell. Since the grave is the first station toward eternal life, almost everyone except the Prophets will be interrogated by the two above-mentioned angels and subjected to some suffering.

As recorded in reliable Tradition books, 'Abbas, the Prophet's uncle, desired very much to see 'Umar in a dream after the latter's death. When he finally saw him in a dream 6 months later, he asked him: "Where were you until now?" 'Umar answered: "Don't ask! I have just finished accounting (for my life)."[9]

In the grave or the intermediate realm, Munkar and Nakir ask each soul: "Who is your Master? Who is your Prophet? What is your religion, etc." Those who died as believers in God and the Prophet and Islam can answer these questions. Those who died as unbelievers cannot. Then the person's deeds are questioned.

Spirits interact with the body differently, for this relationship depends upon which world they inhabit. In this world, the spirit is confined within the "prison" of the body. If the evil-commanding self and bodily desires dominate it, the spirit inevitably deteriorates and the person is doomed. If a human being disciplines the evil-commanding self through belief, worship, and good conduct and frees himself or herself from servitude to bodily desires, his or her spirit becomes refined and acquires purity and laudable qualities. This will bring him or her happiness in both worlds.

After burial, the spirit is kept waiting in the intermediate world. Although the body decomposes and rots away into the ground, its essential particles (or atoms) do not. One *hadith* call this part the *ajb al-dhanab* (coccyx) (Muslim, "Fitan," HN: 141). Whatever it is, the spirit continues its relations with the body through it, as it is a foundation upon which God will resurrect each individual. God will make this part and its contents suitable for eternal life during the final destruction and rebuilding of the universe.

The intermediate world is the realm where spirits feel the "breath" of the bliss of Paradise or the punishment of Hell. If they led virtuous lives, their good deeds will appear to them as amiable fellows. Also, windows will be opened onto heavenly scenes and, as stated in a *hadith*, the grave will be like a garden of Paradise (Daylami, *al-Firdaws*, 3:231). However, those with unpardoned sins will have to undergo some sort of suffering in the intermediate world until their sins are purged and they are worthy of Paradise. Unbelievers and wicked people will meet their evil deeds in the form of bad fellows and vermin. They will see scenes of Hell, and the grave will be like one of Hell's pits.

While we live in the world, it is our spirit that suffers pain and feels joy and happiness. Although the spirit feels pain apparently through the nervous system and then uses it to communicate with all parts of the body, science still does not understand the spirit-body interaction, especially the role of the brain. Any failure in any part of the body can render the nervous system inoperative.

Science has established that certain brain cells continue to live for a while after death. Scientists have tried to receive signals through those cells. If they manage to receive and decipher those signals, the field of criminology will receive a great boost. The following verses give us an example of this. During the time of Moses, God revived a murdered person:

> When Moses said to his people: "God commands you to sacrifice a cow," ... they sacrificed her, a thing they had scarcely done. You had killed a living soul, and disputed thereon – God would disclose what you were hiding – so We said: "Smite him with part of it [the cow];" even so He brings to life the dead, and He shows you His signs, that haply you may have understanding. (2:67, 72-73)

Since the spirit and the body live the worldly life together and share all its joys and pains, God will resurrect people bodily and spiritually. The *Ahl al-Sunna wa al-Jama'a* (the great majority of Muslims who follow the way of the Prophet and his Companions) agree that the spirit and the body together will go to either Paradise or Hell. God will build bodies in forms specific to the Hereafter, where everything will be alive: *This life of the world is but a pastime and a game, but the home of the Hereafter, that is life if they but knew* (29:64).

Sending Gifts to the Spirit after Death

Spirits in the intermediate world will see and hear us, if God allows this. He may permit some saintly people to see, hear, and communicate with certain still-living people, or allow some of them to help us.

After we die, our record of deeds remains open if we have left behind good, virtuous children, books, or institutions that continue to benefit others. If we have raised or helped to raise people who benefit humanity, our reward increases; if we leave behind that which is evil, our sins increase for as long as they continue to harm people. So, if we want to help our loved ones in the intermediate world, we should be good heirs. By helping the poor, observing the rules of Islam, leading a good and virtuous life, and especially by spending to promote Islam, general Muslim well-being, and helping humanity, their reward will increase.

Answers to Questions about Paradise[10]

> Give glad tidings to those who believe and do good deeds. For them are Gardens underneath which rivers flow. Every time

they are provided with fruit thereof, they say: "This is what we were provided with before," and it is given to them in resemblance. There are pure spouses for them, and they shall abide there forever. (2:25)

The following are brief answers to questions about Paradise, which is everlasting. The Qur'anic descriptions, which are more beautiful than Paradise, leave nothing to be added. We shall point out some steps so that such brilliant, eternal, elevated, and beautiful verses can be understood easily. We also shall explain some fine points through five significant questions and answers.

QUESTION: What does the defective, changing, unstable, and pain-stricken body have to do with eternity and Paradise? The spirit's elevated pleasures must be enough. Why should a bodily resurrection take place for bodily pleasures?

ANSWER: Soil, despite its darkness and density when compared to water, air, and light, is the means and source of all works of Divine art. Therefore, it is somehow superior in meaning over other elements. Your selfhood, despite its density and due to its being comprehensive and provided it is purified, gains some kind of superiority over your other senses and faculties. Likewise, your body is a most comprehensive and rich mirror for the Divine Names' manifestations, and has been equipped with instruments to weigh and measure the contents of all Divine treasuries. For example, if the tongue's sense of taste were not the origin of as many measures as the varieties of food and drink, it could not experience, recognize, or measure them. Furthermore, your body also contains the instruments needed to experience and recognize most of the Divine Names' manifestations, as well as the faculties for experiencing the most various and infinitely different pleasures.

The universe's conduct and humanity's comprehensive nature show that the Maker of the universe wants to make known all of His Mercy's treasuries and all of His Names' manifestations, and to make us experience all of His bounties by means of the universe. Given this, as the world of eternal happiness is a mighty pool into which the flood of the universe flows, a vast exhibition of what the loom of the universe produces, and the everlasting store of crops produced in the field of this (material) world, it will resemble the universe to some degree. The All-Wise Maker, the All-Compassionate Just One, will give pleasures particular to each bodily organ as wages for their duty, service, and worship. To think otherwise would be contrary to His Wisdom, Justice, and Compassion.

QUESTION: As a living body is in a state of formation and deformation, it is subject to disintegration and thus noneternal. Eating and drinking perpetuate the individual; sexual relations perpetuate the species. These are fundamental to life in this world, but are irrelevant and unnecessary in the world of eternity. Given this, why have they been included among Paradise's greatest pleasures?

ANSWER: A living body declines and dies because the balance between what it needs to maintain itself and takes in is disturbed. From childhood until the age of physical maturity, it takes in more than it lets out and grows healthier. Afterwards, it usually cannot meet its needs in a balanced way. Either it takes in more and fattens or takes in less than it needs. This causes the balance to be destroyed and, in normal circumstances, finally leads to death. In the world of eternity, however, the body's particles remain constant and are immune to disintegration and re-formation. In other words, this balance remains constant.

Like moving in perpetual cycles, a living body gains eternity together with the constant operation of the factory of bodily life for pleasure. In this world, eating, drinking, and marital sexual relations arise from a need and perform a function. Thus, a great variety of excellent (and superior) pleasures are ingrained in them as immediate wages for the functions performed.

In this world of ailments, eating and marriage lead to many wonderful and various pleasures. Therefore Paradise, the realm of happiness and pleasure, must contain these pleasures in their most elevated form. Adding otherworldly wages (as pleasures) to them for the duties they performed in the world and the need felt for them here, in the form of a pleasant and otherworldly appetite, they will be transformed into an all-encompassing, living source of pleasure that is appropriate to Paradise and eternity.

According to: *The life of this world is but a pastime and a game, but the Abode of the Hereafter – it is all living indeed* (29:64), all lifeless and unconscious substances and objects here are living and conscious there. Like people and animals here, trees and stones there will understand and obey commands. If you tell a tree to bring you such-and-such a fruit, it will do so. If you tell a stone to come, it will come. Since stones and trees will assume such an elevated form, it will be necessary for eating, drinking, and marital relations to assume a form that is superior to their worldly forms to the same degree as Paradise is superior to this world. This includes preserving their bodily realities.

QUESTION: A *hadith* states that "a person is with the one he or she loves," (Bukhari, "Adab," 96) and so friends will be together in Paradise. Thus, a simple Bedouin who feels a deep love for God's Messenger in one minute of companionship with him should be together with him in Paradise. But how can a simple nomad's illumination and reward cause him to share the same place with God's Messenger, whose illumination and reward are limitless?

ANSWER: We can point to this elevated truth by a comparison. For example, a magnificent person prepared a vast banquet and a richly adorned event in an extremely beautiful and splendid garden. It included all delicious foods that taste can experience, all beautiful things that please sight, all wonders that amuse the imagination, and so on. Everything that would gratify and please the external and inner senses was present.

Two friends went to the banquet and sat at a table in the same pavilion. One had only limited taste and so received little pleasure. His weak sight and inability to smell prevented him from understanding the wonderful arts or comprehending the marvels. He could benefit only to the degree of his capacity, which was miniscule. But the other person had developed his external and internal senses, intellect, heart, and all faculties and feelings to the utmost degree. Therefore he could perceive, experience, and derive pleasure from all subtleties, beauties, marvels, and fine things in that exquisite garden.

This is how it is in our confused, painful, and narrow world. There is an infinite distance between the greatest and the least, who exist side by side in Paradise, the abode of happiness and eternity. While friends are together, it is more fitting that each receives his or her share from the table of the Most Merciful of the Merciful according to the degree of his or her ability. Even though they are in different Paradises or on different "floors" of Paradise, they will be able to meet, for Paradise's eight levels are one above the other and share the same roof – the Supreme Throne of God.

Suppose there are walled circles around a conical mountain, one within the other and one above the other, each one facing another, from its foot to the summit. This does not prevent each one from seeing the sun. (Indeed, various *hadith*s [Bukhari, "Tawhid," 22] indicate that the levels or floors of Paradise are somewhat like this.)

QUESTION: Some Prophetic Traditions say that some inhabitants of Paradise will be given a place as large as the world, and that hundreds of thousands of palaces will be granted to them. What is the reason for this, and why and how does one person need all these things?

ANSWER: If we human beings were only a solid object, a vegetable creature consisting of a stomach, or only had a limited, heavy, simple, and transient corporal or animal body, we would not own or deserve so many palaces or other blessings. But we are a comprehensive miracle of Divine Power. If we ruled this world and used all of its wealth and pleasure to satisfy our undeveloped senses' and faculties' needs, we still could not satisfy our greed during our brief life. However, if we have an infinite capacity in an eternal abode of happiness, and if we knock on the door of infinite Mercy in the tongue of infinite need, we will receive the Divine bounties described in such *hadith*s. We shall present a comparison to illustrate this elevated truth.

Like this valley garden, each vineyard and garden in this town has a different owner. Each bird, sparrow, or honey-bee, which has only a handful of grain, may say: "All of this town's vineyards and gardens are my places of recreation." Each may possess this town and include it in its property. The fact that others share it does not negate its rule. A truly human person may say: "My Creator made the world a home for me, with the sun as its chief lamp and the stars as its electric lights. Earth is my cradle spread with flowered carpets," and then thank God. This conclusion is not negated because other creatures live in this "house." On the contrary, the creatures adorn this home and are like its decorations.

If, on account of being human, we or even a bird were to claim the right of control over such a vast area in this narrow, brief world and to receive such a vast bounty, why should we consider it unlikely that we will own such property in a broad, eternal abode of happiness?

The inhabitants of Paradise (which is of light, unrestricted, broad, and eternal) will have bodies possessing the spirit's strength and lightness as well as the imagination's swiftness. They will be able to be in countless places simultaneously, and receive pleasure in an infinite number of ways. This is fitting for that eternal Paradise and infinite Mercy, and the Truthful Reporter told us that such is the reality and the truth. Nevertheless, these vast truths cannot be weighed on the scales of our tiny minds.

About Hell

Belief bears the seed of a sort of Paradise experienced by the spirit, while unbelief contains the seed of a sort of Hell experienced by the spirit. Just as unbelief is the seed of Hell, Hell is a fruit of unbelief. Unbelief is the cause of entering Hell as well as the cause of Hell's existence and creation. Denying Hell means that the unbeliever contradicts the infinitely Powerful One, Who has infinite dignity, glory, majesty, and greatness. Such a person accuses Him of impotence and lying, both of which are great affronts to His honor and dignity and offend His pride, glory, and majesty. If it did not exist already, Hell would have to be created to punish such unbelief and its possessor.

V. DIVINE BOOKS AND THE QUR'AN[11]

The Qur'an consists of the rhythmic verses, phrases, sentences, and chapters relayed by the Prophet as they were revealed to him by God, and which he proclaimed as the everlasting miracle testifying to his Prophethood. He challenged the Arabs of his time who doubted its Divine origin, as well as all unbelieving Arabs and non-Arabs who would come later.

Earlier Divine Revelations and the Qur'an

Another essential of Islamic faith is believing in all the Divine Books God sent to His different Messengers throughout history. God revealed His Books to His Prophets before Prophet Muhammad in exactly the same way. God informs us in the Qur'an of some of them: the Pages of Abraham, the Torah, the Zabur (the Psalms), and the Injil (the Gospel). We do not know the names of the books given to other Prophets, and therefore cannot say with certainty whether they were originally revealed books or not.

These earlier Divine Books were sent down in now-dead languages that only a few people today claim to understand. Given this, even if these books still existed in their original and unadulterated form, it would be virtually impossible to understand them correctly and to interpret and implement their injunctions. Furthermore, as the original texts of most of these earlier Divine Books have been lost with the passage of time, only their translations exist today. The Qur'an, on the other hand, exists in its original language, which is still spoken and understood by millions of people.

Defining the Qur'an

The general definition of the Qur'an is as follows: The Qur'an is the miraculous Word of God revealed to Prophet Muhammad, written down and transmitted to succeeding generations by many reliable channels, and whose recitation is an act of worship and obligatory in daily prayers.

The Qur'an describes some of its features as follows:

> The month of Ramadan in which the Qur'an was sent down as a guidance for humanity and clear proofs of the Guidance and the Criterion. (2:185)

> This Qur'an could not have been invented (by anyone) apart from God, but confirms what was (revealed) before it, a fuller

explanation of the Book – wherein there is no doubt – from the Lord of the Worlds. (10:37)

We have sent it as an Arabic Qur'an that you may understand and use your reason. (12:2)

This Qur'an guides to that which is most right, and gives good tidings to believers who do deeds of righteousness, that theirs will be a great reward. (17:9)

And in truth We have made the Qur'an easy to reflect and take lesson, but will any take heed? (54:17)

That this is a noble Qur'an, in a hidden, guarded Book. (56:77-78)

The Qur'an has other titles, each of which describes one of its aspects and thus can be regarded as one of its attributes, such as: the Book, the Criterion, the Remembrance, the Advice, the Light, the Guidance, the Healer, the Noble, the Book in Pairs, the Mother of the Book, the Truth, the Admonishment, the Good Tiding, the Book Gradually Revealed, the Knowledge, and the Clear.

Concerning the Qur'an, Prophet Muhammad says:

The Qur'an distinguishes between truth and falsehood. It is not for fun, for those who reject it will be punished. It contains the history of previous peoples and tidings of those who will come later, and rules on people's disagreements. Those who look elsewhere for guidance are led astray by God. It is God's strong rope, the wise instruction, and the Straight Path. It is a book that desires cannot deviate or tongues confuse, one that does not bore scholars or wear them out due to repetition, and one possessing uncountable admirable aspects. All who hear it say: "We heard a wonderful Qur'an guiding to righteousness, and so we believe in it." Those who base their words on it speak truly. Whoever judges by it judges justly, and whoever calls to it calls to truth. (Tirmidhi, HN: 3069)

We close this topic with Said Nursi's definition:

The Qur'an is an eternal translation of the great book of the universe and the everlasting translator of the various "languages" in which Divine laws of the creation and operation of the universe are "inscribed"; the interpreter of the books of the visible, material world and the world of the Unseen; the discoverer of the immaterial treasuries of the Divine Names hidden on Earth and in the heavens; the key to the truths that lie beneath the lines of events; the tongue of the Unseen world in the visible, material one; the treasury of the favors of the All-Merciful One and the eternal addresses of the All-Glorified One coming from the world of the Unseen beyond the veil of this visible world; the sun of the spiritual and intellectual world of Islam and its foundation and plan; the sacred map of the worlds of the Hereafter; the expounder, the lucid interpreter, articulate proof, and clear translator of the Divine "Essence," Attributes, Names and acts; the educator and trainer of the world of humanity and the water and light of Islam, which is the true and greatest humanity; the true wisdom of humanity and their true guide leading them to happiness. And for human beings it is a book of law, prayer, wisdom, worship and servanthood to God, commands and invitation, invocation, and a book of reflection. It is a holy book containing books for all the spiritual needs of humanity, and a heavenly book which, like a sacred library, contains numerous booklets from which all the saints and the eminently truthful, and all the purified and discerning scholars have derived their ways peculiar to each, and which illuminates each of these ways and answers the needs of all those with different tastes and temperaments who follow them.

Having come from the Supreme Throne of God, and originated in His Greatest Name, and issued forth from the most comprehensive rank of each Name, the Qur'an is both the word of God as regards His being the Lord of the worlds, and His decree in respect of His having the title of the Deity of all creatures; a discourse in the name of the Creator of all the heavens and Earth; a speech from the perspective of the absolute Divine Lordship; an eternal sermon on behalf of the universal Sovereignty of the All-Glorified One; a register of the favors of the All-Merciful One from the viewpoint of the all-embracing Mercy; a collection of messages, some of which begin with a cipher; and a holy book that, having descended from the surrounding circle of the Divine Greatest Name, looks over and surveys the circle surrounded by the "Supreme Throne of God."

It is because of all these that the title of "Word of God" has been, and will always be, given to the Qur'an most deservedly. After the Qur'an come the Scriptures and Pages which were sent to some other Prophets. As for the other countless Divine words, some of them are conversations in the form of inspirations coming as the particular manifestations of a particular aspect of Divine Mercy, Sovereignty, and Lordship under a particular title with particular regard. The inspirations coming to angels, human beings, and animals vary greatly with regard to their universality or particularity.

The Qur'an is a heavenly book that contains in brief the Scriptures revealed to the previous Prophets in different ages, the content of the treatises of all saints with different temperaments, and the works of all purified scholars each following a way particular to himself; the six sides of which are bright and absolutely free of the darkness of doubt and whimsical thought; whose point of support is with certainty Divine Revelation and the Divine eternal Word, whose aim is manifestly eternal happiness, and whose inside is manifestly pure guidance.

And it is surrounded and supported from above by the lights of faith, from below by proof and evidence, from the right by the submission of the heart and the conscience, and from the left by the admission of reason and other intellectual faculties. Its fruit is with absolute certainty the mercy of the Most Merciful One, and Paradise; and it has been accepted and promoted by angels and innumerable people and jinn through the centuries.[12]

Arguments for the Qur'an's Divine Authorship

- When we study the Qur'an's words, styles, and meanings even superficially, we notice immediately that it is unique. So, in rank and worth it is either below – even Satan cannot claim this, nor does he conceive of it – or above all other books. Since it is above, it must be the Word of God.

- The Qur'an declares: *You (O Muhammad) were not a reader of any Scripture before it, nor did you write (such a Scripture) with your right hand, for then those who follow falsehood might (have a right) to doubt it* (29:48). Moreover, it is undeniable that Prophet Muhammad was unlettered and that the Qur'an has presented an open-ended and eternal challenge to humanity: *If you are in doubt concerning that which We have sent down onto Our servant (Muhammad), produce a chapter of the like thereof, and call your witnesses, supporters, who are apart from God, if you are truthful* (2:23). No one has ever met this challenge successfully.

- The Revelation spanned 23 years. How is it that such a book, which deals with Divine truth, metaphysics, religious beliefs and worship, prayer, law and morality, the afterlife, psychology, sociology, epistemology, history, scientific facts, and the principles of a happy life, never contradicts itself? In fact, it openly declares that it contains no contradictions and is therefore a Divine Book: *Will they not then ponder on the Qur'an? If it had been from other than God they would have found therein much contradiction and incongruity* (4:82).

- The Qur'an is a literary masterpiece that cannot be duplicated. Its styles and eloquence, even its actual sentences, words, and letters, form a miraculous harmony. With respect to rhythm, music, and even geometric proportions, mathematical measures, and repetition, each is in its exact place and then perfectly interwoven and interrelated with others.

- Eloquence, poetry, and oratory enjoyed great prestige in pre-Islamic Arabia. Poetry competitions were held regularly, and winning poems were written in gold and hung on the Ka'ba's walls. The unlettered Prophet had never been heard to say even a couple lines of poetry. However, the Qur'an he brought eventually forced all known experts to surrender.

- Even the unbelievers were captivated by it. Nevertheless, to stop Islam from spreading, they said it was magical and should not be listened to. But when poets such as Khansa and Labid converted and then abandoned poetry out of respect for and awe of the Qur'an's styles and eloquence, the unbelievers had to confess: "If we call it a piece of poetry, it is not. If we designate it a piece of rhymed prose, it is not. If we describe it as the word of a soothsayer, it is not." At times, they could not help listening to the Prophet's recitation secretly at night, but they could not overcome their arrogance long enough to believe in its Divine origin.

- Despite the high level of poetry, Arabic's vocabulary was too primitive to express metaphysical ideas or scientific, religious, and philosophical concepts adequately. Islam, using the words and expressions of a simple desert people, made Arabic so rich and complex that it became the language of the most magnificent civilization, one that made many entirely original contributions in scientific, religious, metaphysical, literary, economic, juridical, social, and political areas. How could an unlettered person launch a philological revolution that has no parallel in human history?

- Despite its apparent simplicity, the Qur'an has many levels of meaning. It illuminates the way for poets, musicians, and orators, as well as for sociologists, psychologists, scientists, economists, and jurists. Founders of true spiritual orders and schools of law and conduct found in it all the principles needed to guide their adherents. The Qur'an shows everyone how to solve their problems and fulfill their spiritual quests. Can any other book do this?

- However beautiful and interesting a book is, we read it at most two or three times and then put it aside forever. Billions of Muslims, on the other hand, have recited portions of the Qur'an during their five daily prayers for the last 14 centuries. Many have recited it completely once a year, and sometimes even once or twice a month. The more we recite it, the more we benefit from it and the more desire we feel to recite it. People never tire of its wording, meaning, and content, and it never loses any of its originality and freshness. As time passes, it breathes new truths and meanings into minds and souls, thereby increasing their activity and liveliness.

- The Qur'an describes all our physical and spiritual aspects, and contains principles to solve all social, economic, juridical, political, and administrative problems regardless of time or place. Furthermore, it satisfies the mind and spirit simultaneously, and guarantees happiness in both worlds.

- No one, regardless of intelligence, can establish rules to solve all potential problems. Even the best system must be revised at least every 50 years. More importantly, no system can promise eternal happiness, for its principles are restricted to this transient human life that is infinitely short when compared to the afterlife.

• In contrast, no Qur'anic principle has become obsolete or needs revision. For example, it states that wealth should not circulate only among the rich (59:7); that government offices should be entrusted to competent, qualified persons, and that absolute justice should be the rule in public administration and all disputes (4:58); that people can have only that for which they strive (53:39); and that whoever kills a person unjustly is the same as one who would kill all humanity (5:32). These and many other principles (e.g., prohibiting usury, gambling, alcohol, and extramarital sexual relations; enjoining prayer, fasting, alms-giving, and good conduct), are strengthened through love and awareness of God, the promise of an eternal happy life, and the fear of punishment in Hell.

• The Qur'an also unveils the mystery of humanity, creation, and the universe. The Qur'an, humanity, and the universe are the three "books" that make the Creator known to us, and are three expressions of the same truth. Therefore, the One Who created humanity and the universe also revealed the Qur'an.

• You cannot find people who do exactly what they ask others to do, or whose deeds reflect them exactly. However, the Qur'an is identical with Prophet Muhammad, and is the embodiment of him in words, just as he is the embodiment of the Qur'an in belief and conduct. They are two expressions of the same truth. When asked about her husband's conduct, 'A'isha replied: "Don't you read the Qur'an? His conduct was the Qur'an." This clearly shows that the Qur'an and Muhammad are the works of God Almighty.

• Authors are usually so influenced by their surroundings that it is almost impossible for them to become detached. By contrast, even though revealed in parts on certain occasions, the Qur'an is as equally universal and objective when dealing with particular issues as it is exact and precise when dealing with universal matters. It uses precise expressions even while describing the beginning of creation and the end of time, and humanity's creation and life in the other world. Just as it sometimes draws universal conclusions from particular events, it sometimes goes from universal principles to particular events. This typical Qur'anic style cannot be found in any human work and is, therefore, another sign of its Divine origin.

- No author has ever written a book in his or her field that is as accurate as the Qur'an is in such varied fields as religion and law, sociology and psychology, eschatology and morality, history and literature, and so on. The Qur'an also contains at least the principles of all branches of knowledge, either in summary or in detail, and not even one piece of this knowledge has ever been contradicted. What more is needed to prove its Divine origin?

- Can any author claim that his or her work is absolutely correct and will remain so forever? Scientific conclusions change constantly. The Torah and Gospels undergo continuous alteration. Even a superficial study of Bibles published in different times and languages shows these alterations. Yet the Qur'an's truths retain their freshness or, in the words of Said Nursi, "as time grows older, the Qur'an grows ever younger." No mistake or contradiction has ever been found in it, and ever since the beginning of its revelation it has remained unchanged and displayed its uniqueness. It continues, even now, to conquer new hearts and reveal its hidden unlimited treasures, to bloom like a heavenly rose with countless petals.

- Based on your knowledge and reputation for honesty, can you speak on behalf of the president, the prime minister, and all other ministers; of associations for writers, lawyers, and workers; and of the board of university lecturers and scientists? If you can, can you claim to represent them as perfectly as each would want you to? If you can, can you legislate for all the affairs of the country? This is just what the Prophet, achieved through the Qur'an. How can you claim that an unlettered person, who was totally apolitical until he was 40, could achieve such results without Divine inspiration and support?

- The Prophet is admonished in the Qur'an. If he were its author, would he give such a noticeable place to the grave slander against his wife? Would he not hide the revelation ordering him to marry Zaynab, rather than publicize it, if it did not come from God? 'A'isha said later that if the Prophet could have concealed any part of the Qur'an, he would have concealed this. (Bukhari, "Tawhid," 22; Muslim, "Iman," 288.)

- His uncle Abu Talib, who had raised him since he was 8 and protected him for 10 years after his declaration of Prophethood, never embraced Islam. The Prophet loved his uncle deeply and desired his conversion, but was told that: *You guide not whom you love, but God guides whom He wills. He is best aware of those who are guided* (28:56). If he were the Qur'an's author, he could have claimed that Abu Talib had embraced Islam.

- Many verses begin with "They ask you" and continue with "Say (in answer)." These were revealed to answer questions asked by Muslims and non-Muslims, especially the Jews of Madina, about allowed or prohibited matters, the distribution of war spoils, (astrological) mansions of the moon, Judgment Day, Dhu'l-Qarnayn (an ancient believing king who made great conquests in Asia and Africa), the spirit, and so on. One without an all-encompassing knowledge cannot answer such questions. But his answers satisfied everybody. This shows that he was taught by God, the All-Knowing.

- The Prophet was very austere and shunned worldly gain, fame, rulership, wealth, and beautiful women. Also, he endured great hardship and persecution. To claim that he invented the Qur'an means that Muhammad the Trustworthy, as he was commonly known, was the greatest liar and cheat history has ever known. Why would he falsely claim Prophethood and expose himself and his family to severe deprivation and persecution? Such an accusation, as well as that of saying that he wrote the Qur'an, are totally groundless and lacking in evidence.

- The Jews and Christians were very strong opponents. Eventually, he had to fight the Jews of Madina several times and expel them. Despite this, the Qur'an mentions Prophet

Moses about 50 times and Jesus numerous times; it mentions Muhammad's name only four times. Why should a person who falsely claims Prophethood mention the Prophets of his opponents? Can there be any reasons other than jealousy, prejudice, selfishness, and other negative emotions for denying Muhammad's Prophethood?

• The Qur'an also refers to certain facts of creation only recently established by modern scientific methods. How, except for Divine authorship, could the Qur'an be literally true on matters of which the people listening to it being revealed had no idea? For example, if the Qur'an were a regular book, could it have contained: *Do not the unbelievers realize that the heavens and Earth were one unit of creation before we split them asunder?* (21:30).

Understanding the Qur'an

The Qur'an is the book that Prophet Muhammad conveyed to humanity as God's Word and that testifies to his Prophethood. Being his greatest miracle, it challenged the Arabs of that time and all people to come until the Last Day to produce even a single chapter like it. The Qur'an is unparalleled among Divine Scriptures as regards its preservation and transmittal to later generations without the slightest alteration. There is no difference among the copies of the Qur'an that have circulated throughout the world since its first revelation.

The first step to understanding the Qur'an is to understand Arabic, the language in which it was revealed, for language has the same meaning for a text as bodily features have for a person. The essential existence of a text lies in its meaning, just as a person's essential existence lies in his or her spirit. Bodily features are the externalized form assumed by the spirit, and therefore serve as a mirror in which to see into his or her character. In the same way, the Qur'an's language and styles are the form of its meaning and cannot be separated from it.

The second step is to penetrate its meaning, which requires living it. Although its language constitutes its outer form and structure, and therefore is very important in penetrating its meaning, restricting its understanding to linguistic understanding means restricting oneself to form or formalism. One can penetrate the Qur'an's meaning, in which its essential existence lies, through purifying the "heart" (the spirit's seat) by avoiding sin and evil, performing the necessary acts of worship, and living a pious life.

The Qur'an is "like a rose that continuously grows petals in the womb of time." As science develops and contributes to penetrating its depths of meaning, the Qur'an blooms to an even greater extent and grows younger and fresher. Thus, having sufficient knowledge of such topics as the abrogation of laws, laws and principles dependent upon certain conditions, and unconditioned, general, and particular rules and the occasions on which the verses were revealed is not enough; the general principles of natural science also must be known. Since Prophet Muhammad received the Qur'an and taught and practiced it in his daily life as an infallible authority, knowledge of his Sunna, his practice of the Qur'an, and his example of living Islam also are indispensable to understanding the Qur'an.

The Qur'an is not a book of science, history, or morality. Nor is it a book in the literal sense of the word. It is a book to be practiced, for it came to guide people to truth, to educate them intellectually and spiritually, and to govern their individual and social life. Therefore, it can be understood only through daily practice. Remember that the Qur'an was not revealed all at once, but over a 23-year period on many diverse occasions. Separating the Qur'an and practical life means reducing it to the status of an ordinary book to be read. It does not unfold itself to any significant degree to those who consider it to be no more than this.

Moreover, the Qur'an is a medium-sized book that, at first glance, contains repetition. However, it declares that *everything wet or dry is in a Manifest Book* (itself) (6:59). A Prophetic *hadith* states that it contains the history of previous peoples, tidings of those to come after its revelation, and solutions to disagreements among people (Tirmidhi, "Fadail al-Qur'an," 14). It addresses and satisfies all levels of understanding and knowledge, regardless of time and place.

Hundreds of interpreters have written commentaries on it during the 14 centuries of its existence, and none have claimed to understand all of its various aspects and meanings. Thousands of jurists have inferred laws from it and based their reasoning upon it, but none have asserted that they have inferred all of the laws contained therein or understood all of the reasons behind its injunctions and prohibitions. All pure and exacting scholars who "marry" mind and heart, all revivers (the greatest, saintly scholars who come when needed to revive and restore Islam) find their ways in it, all saints derive their sources of inspiration and ways of purification from it, and all authentic Sufi paths depend upon it. And yet, like a source of water that increases as it flows, it remains as if untouched.

The Qur'an's miraculous eloquence gives it this depth and richness of meaning. Its creative and artistically rich style is only one element upon which its eloquence is based. It frequently speaks in parables and adopts a figurative, symbolic rhetoric using metaphors and similes. This is natural, for the Qur'an contains knowledge of all things and addresses all levels of understanding and knowledge.

The Qur'an's Style

As the Qur'an deals with all issues of theological value and surpasses all scriptural records of pre- or post-Islamic ages in the abundant variety of its contents, its approach, presentation, and solution are unique. Rather than dealing with a topic in the usual systematic manner employed by theologians or apostolic writers, it expressly says that it has its own special manifold method: *tasrifi*. In other words, it shows variety, changes topics, shifts between subjects, reverts to the previous one, and deliberately and purposefully repeats the same subject in unique rhythmic and recitative forms to facilitate understanding, learning, and memorization: *See how We display the revelations and signs so that they may understand and discern* (6:65).

The Qur'an shows the universe's order. As almost all types or varieties of existing things present themselves to us side by side or mingled, the Qur'an displays varieties linked together with a spe-

cific rhythm to show the signs of God's Unity, even while acknowledging that such a style will cause some opponents to doubt its
Divine authorship (6:106). It also explains why it does this: to
encourage the human intellect to reflect upon unity in variety and
harmony in diversity. In fact, each chapter deals with numerous
topics in various ways, a characteristic that only adds to its unique
beauty and matchless eloquence. An attentive reciter or intelligent
audience can enjoy such rhythmical pitches to the extent that the
Qur'an itself declares:

> God has sent down the most beautiful message in the form of
> a book, consistent in itself, in pairs, whereat do shudder the
> skins of those who are in awe before their Lord, and then their
> skins and hearts become pliant to the remembrance of God.
> Such is God's guidance: He guides with it whomsoever He
> wills. And (as for) those whom God allows to go astray, there
> is no guide for them. (39:23)

In addition, the Qur'an's verses and chapters are not arranged
chronologically. Some verses revealed and placed together are preceded and followed by other verses. Some chapters and verses are
lengthy; others are short. This arrangement is an aspect of its
miraculousness and also one of the most important reasons why
many Orientalists and their Muslim imitators criticize it.

The Qur'an exhibits the universe's order. Just as there is both
a whole-part and holistic-partial (or universal-particular) relation
among its contents, the same relation is found in the Qur'an. In
other words, a body is a whole consisting of parts (e.g., the head,
arms, legs, and other organs). Any part cannot wholly represent
the body, although each part is a whole in itself, because the whole
body cannot be found in any of its parts. Humanity and all species
are holistic or universal, for each species is composed of the members, each of which contains all features of the species and therefore represents the species. Each person is an exact specimen of
humanity in structure.

In the same way, each Qur'anic verse is a whole in itself and
has an independent existence. It can be located anywhere in the
Qur'an without harming either the composition or the mean-

ing. In addition, there is an intrinsic relation among all verses or between one verse and all the others. Bediüzzaman Said Nursi writes that:

> The verses of the Qur'an are like stars in a sky among which there are visible and invisible ropes and relationships. It is as if each Qur'anic verse has an eye that sees most of the verses and a face that looks towards them, so that it extends to them the immaterial threads of relationship to weave a fabric of miraculousness. A single *sura* can contain the whole "ocean" of the Qur'an, in which the whole universe is contained. A single verse can comprehend the treasury of that *sura*. It is as if most verses are small *sura*s, and most *sura*s a little Qur'an. In fact, the whole Qur'an is contained in *Surat al-Fatiha*, which itself is contained in the *Basmala*.[13]

At first glance, this unique *tasrifi* style sometimes seems to produce contradictory verses. But this is not the case, for the Qur'an is like an organism having all of its parts interlinked. As a result of this whole-part arrangement and the holistic-partial relationship among verses, a correct understanding of a verse sometimes depends upon a complete understanding of the Qur'an. This is another unique characteristic, another aspect of its miraculousness, and another sign of its Divine authorship.

This characteristic is very important in Qur'anic interpretation, for the Qur'an is the written counterpart of the universe and humanity. In addition, the Qur'an, the universe, and humanity are three "copies" of the same book, the first being the "revealed and written universe and humanity," and the second and third each being a "created Qur'an." Given this, the Qur'an also teaches us how to view humanity and the universe. Therefore, any apparent contradiction among its verses is really due to the reader's misunderstanding. One whose being is unified with the Qur'an sees no contradiction, as he or she is free of all contradictions. If people view the Qur'an in light of their particular worlds, which are full of contradictions, of course they will see contradictions. This is why those who seek to approach the Qur'an first have to be free of all contradictions.

Arabic, the language of revelation, is the Qur'an's outer body. Religion does not consist only of philosophy or theology, but is a method of unifying all dimensions of our being. Therefore, Arabic is an essential, inseparable element of the Qur'an. It was chosen as the language of revelation not only so that the Arabs of that time would understand it, but because a universal religion requires a universal language.

The Qur'an views the world as the cradle of brotherhood and sisterhood. It seeks to unite all races, colors, and beliefs as brothers and sisters and servants of the One God. Its language is a basic factor that helps people ponder religious realities and unite all dimensions of their being according to Divine standards. Translations cannot be recited in prescribed prayers, for no translation is identical with the original Arabic. Without Arabic, one can be a good Muslim but can understand only a little of the Qur'an.

The Qur'an is the source of all knowledge in Islam, be it religious, spiritual, social, scientific, moral, legal, or philosophical. As the guide to all truth, it has four main purposes: to show God's Existence and Unity, establish Prophethood and the afterlife, promulgate the worship of God, and set forth the essentials of justice. Its verses mainly dwell upon these purposes, and thus contain creedal principles, rules governing human life, detailed information on the Resurrection and the afterlife, how to worship God, morality, direct or indirect information on some scientific facts, principles of civilizational formation and decay, historical outlines of previous civilizations, and so on.

The Qur'an is a source of healing, as applying it in daily life cures almost all psychological and social illnesses, as well as a cosmology, epistemology, ontology, sociology, psychology, and law revealed to regulate human life for all people, regardless of time or place. In fact, the Prophet declares: "The Qur'an is more lovable to God than the heavens and Earth and those in them." (Darimi, *Sunan*, 2:533.)

Recording and Preserving the Qur'an

God Almighty has sent more than 124,000 Prophets to humanity. Islam defines Prophets as those who came with important tidings ("the tidings of religion") concerning belief in God's Existence and Unity, angels, Prophethood's mission and Prophets, Revelation and Divine Scriptures, the Resurrection and afterlife, and Divine Destiny (including human free will). The tidings also include offering a life based upon this belief, promises related to accepting belief, and warnings related to rejecting it. The frequent corruption of religion by various communities has caused Prophets to be sent to revive and restore it, and also to amend some rules or bring new laws concerning daily life. Such Prophets usually were given a Book and are known as Messengers, the greatest of whom are Noah, Abraham, Moses, Jesus, and Muhammad (42:13).

The name of the religion that God Almighty revealed through all Messengers is Islam. Just as the laws ordering and operating the universe remain the same and constant, and just as all people have the same basic characteristics, essential needs, and final destination regardless of when and where they live, it is natural for religion to be based upon the same essentials of belief, worship, and morality.

Muhammad was sent as the last Messenger and with the perfected form of the Divine religion (Islam). God protects this final and perfected religion by promising to preserve the Qur'an: *Without doubt, We sent down the Message and We will preserve it* (15:9). People who followed the messages brought by Moses and by Jesus later on called them Judaism and Christianity, respectively, whereas Islam has retained its original and God-given name.

In this world, as God Almighty acts behind natural or material causes, He also uses causes or means to preserve the Qur'an. One of these is having the Qur'an written down during the Prophet's lifetime and under his direct supervision so that nothing could be deleted, added, or changed. All copies of the Qur'an in existence during the 14 centuries of Islam are exactly the same. Unlike other earlier Scriptures, the Qur'an has been preserved in its original form or text and in the language in which it was revealed.[14] Thus the following points are of considerable significance:

The Qur'an was revealed in parts. God Almighty undertook its preservation, due recitation, and its part's arrangement. He revealed to His Messenger where each revealed verse and chapter was to be placed:

> Do not move your tongue (with the revelation) so that you
> may hasten (committing) it (to memory). It is for Us to collect
> it and to promulgate it. But when We have promulgated it, fol-
> low its recital (as promulgated). Then it is also for us to explain
> it. (75:16-19)

> High above all (considerations) is God, the Sovereign, the Truth.
> Do not show haste to receive and recite the Qur'an before its rev-
> elation to you is completed; but rather say: "Lord, increase me
> in knowledge." (20:114)

The Almighty emphasizes that no falsehood can touch the
Qur'an or cast doubt upon its authenticity:

> These are the people who rejected the Message when it came to
> them. But the fact is that this is a noble, mighty Book. No false-
> hood can approach it from before or behind. It is a Revelation
> being sent down from One All-Wise, All-Praised. (41:41-42)

Once a year, the Messenger reviewed all that had been revealed
up to that point with Archangel Gabriel. In his last year, after the
Revelation was completed, Gabriel came twice for this purpose.
The Messenger concluded from this that he would die soon.[15]

From the very beginning, the Companions paid the utmost
attention to the Qur'an and tried their best to understand, memorize, and learn it. In fact, the Qur'an ordered them to do so:
*When the Qur'an is recited, give ear to it and pay heed, that you may
obtain mercy* (7:204).

Only a few people could read and write when the Revelation
began. After the Battle of Badr (624), the first military encounter
between the Muslims and the Makkan polytheists, Makkan prisoners of war were freed only after they taught 10 Madinan Muslims
how to read and write. The beneficiaries of this policy then tried
to memorize the Qur'an for several reasons: reciting some verses
is obligatory during the prescribed prayers; the Qur'an was very
original for them; it purified their minds of prejudice and wrong
assertions, their hearts of sins, and illuminated them; and it built a
society out of illuminated minds and purified hearts.

To understand the extent of their effort and the number of
those who did so, 70 Companions who had memorized it were

martyred at Bi'r al-Ma'una (625). During the Prophet's lifetime, another 70 or so were martyred. When the Prophet died, many Companions knew the Qur'an by heart, among them 'Ali ibn Abi Talib, 'Abdullah ibn Mas'ud, 'Abdullah ibn 'Abbas, 'Abdullah ibn 'Amr, Hudayfa ibn al-Yaman, Salim, Mu'adh ibn Jabal, Abu al-Darda, Ubayy ibn Ka'b, and 'A'isha and Umm Salama (two of the Prophet's wives). New converts or immigrants to Madina were sent to Companions to learn the Qur'an. As the subsequent reciting raised a humming noise, the Prophet asked them to lower their voices so that they would not confuse each other.[16]

The Qur'an was revealed piecemeal and mostly on certain occasions. Whenever a verse, chapter, or group of verses was revealed, it was memorized by many Companions and written down by scribes chosen by the Prophet specifically for that purpose. The Messenger also told them where to place it in the Qur'an. Known as the Scribes of the Revelation, these 40 or so Companions also copied the pieces for themselves and preserved them.[17]

At the time of the Prophet's death, 'Ali ibn Abi Talib, Mu'adh ibn Jabal, Abu al-Darda, Ubayy ibn al-Ka'b, and other Companions already had assembled these portions in book form. 'Ali arranged them chronologically.[18] After the Battle of Yamama (633), during which around 70 memorizers were martyred, 'Umar ibn al-Khattab asked Caliph Abu Bakr about compiling an "official" version. Zayd ibn Thabit, a leading scholar and memorizer, was chosen for the task. After a meticulous work, he prepared the official collection (*mushaf*).[19]

The Almighty declares: *It is for Us to collect it and to promulgate it* (75:17). The Qur'an's verses and chapters were arranged and collected according to the Prophet's instructions [while he was still alive], which were guided by the Revelation. The official version was formed after the Battle of Yamama. When a disagreement appeared over the pronunciation of certain words, the formal version was copied and sent to important centers during the reign of Caliph 'Uthman ibn 'Affan (644-56).[20]

One of the foremost reasons for the Qur'an's continued incorruptability is that it has been preserved in its original language. No one in the Muslim world has ever thought to supersede it with a translation, and so it was never exposed to imprecise or mistaken translations, or to additions or deletions.

In conclusion, the Qur'an that we hold in our hands today is the same Qur'an that the Prophet received from God. Its authenticity and genuineness cannot be contested. No Muslim scholar of any standard has ever doubted this, and none have questioned that the Prophet spoke every word that we find in the Qur'an today.

Matchless Eloquence and Profound Meaning

The Qur'an's verses, linked with rhythm and symmetry of form to show the signs of Divine Unity, stir our emotions and intellect to reflect upon unity in variety and harmony in diversity. Each chapter has a particular rhythm and presents several topics in various ways. Such a style discloses a unique beauty with matchless eloquence. Attentive reciters and intelligent listeners experience what the Qur'an describes:

> God has sent down the fairest discourse as a Book, some parts of which confirm and resemble others, whereat shiver the skins of those who fear their Lord; then their skins and their hearts soften to the remembrance of God. That is God's guidance. (39:23)

Although the Arabs of the Prophet's time were highly intelligent and well-versed in poetry and eloquence, they could not produce anything like the Qur'an. Likewise, none of the countless literary figures who have lived since then has duplicated it. In fact, the Prophet challenged his contemporaries and humanity at large, regardless of time or place, to create even one chapter like those of the Qur'an. That they have failed to do so is a proof of the Qur'an's Divine origin.

> If you doubt concerning what We have sent down to Our servant (Muhammad), bring a chapter like it, and call your witnesses, apart from God, if you are truthful. (2:23)

> This Qur'an cannot be forged by (any one) but (is a revelation from) God confirming (the Scriptures) that went before it and

(the clearest) explanation of the Book, wherein is no doubt, from the Lord of all being. Or do they say: "He (Muhammad) has forged it." Say: "Then bring a chapter like it and call on whomsoever you can (to help you), apart from God (for He has sent it down), if you are truthful." (10:37-38)

Say: "(Even) if humanity and jinn united to produce the like of this Qur'an, they will never be able to do so, even though some of them help the others." (17:88)

No one has produced a composition that can equal a chapter of the Qur'an, even the smallest one (*Surat al-Kawthar*), and no one will ever be able to do so. Those who oppose Islam always have taken up arms. But their attempts have come to naught, with the sole exception of Andalusia (Islamic Spain). As one Muslim scholar points out, if people could defeat the Qur'an or Islam through argument, science, or eloquence, they would not have to resort to arms. The Qur'an becomes younger and fresher as time passes, for this process allows its hidden unlimited treasures to be disclosed one by one. Today, Islam is the only way of life that offers us any hope.

As almost every verse has an independent existence, it also has intrinsic relations with every other verse and with the Qur'an as a whole. Given this, understanding and interpreting a verse requires a complete and holistic knowledge and understanding of the Qur'an. This is why Muslims say that the Qur'an's main interpreter is the Qur'an itself.

Said Nursi frequently draws our attention to the miraculous depths of meaning contained in the Qur'an's wording. For example, Arabic's definite particle al adds inclusiveness to the word, and so he interprets *al-hamdu* (the praise) at the beginning of *Surat al-Fatiha* as: "All praise and thanks that everyone has given and will give until the Last Day to others since the beginning of human life on Earth, for any reason and on any occasion, are for God."

Also, from the characteristics of the words used and their order in: *Out of what We have provided for them they give as livelihood* (2:3) he infers the following rules or conditions of giving alms:

- In order to make their alms-giving acceptable to God, believers must give out of their livelihood a certain amount that will not make it necessary for them to receive alms. *Out of* in *out of what* expresses this condition.

- Believers must not transfer another person's goods to the needy, but must give from their own belongings. The phrase *what We have provided for them* points to this condition. The meaning is: They give (to maintain life) out of what We have provided for you (to maintain your life).

- Believers must not remind those who receive their alms of the kindness they have received. *We* in *We have provided* indicates this condition, for it means: "I have provided for you the livelihood out of which you give to the poor. Therefore, you cannot put any of My servants under obligation, for you are giving out of My property."

- Believers must not fear that they may become poor through giving to others. *We* in *We have provided* points to this. Since God provides for us and commands us to give others, He will not cause us to become poor by giving to others.

- Believers must give to those who will spend it for their livelihood, and not to those who will waste it. *They give as livelihood* points to this condition.

- Believers must give for God's sake. *We have provided for them* states this condition. It means: "Essentially, you give out of My property and so you must give in My Name."

- *What* in *out of what* signifies that whatever God provides for a person is included in the meaning of provision. Therefore, believers must give out of their goods and also out of whatever they have, such as a good word, an act of help, a piece of advice, and teaching. All of these are included in the meaning of *rizq* (provision) and giving others as livelihood.

  Along with these conditions, the meaning of the original three-word expression becomes: "Out of whatever We have provided for them as goods, money, power, knowledge, and intelligence, etc., believing that it is We Who provide and therefore without feeling any fear that they may become poor because of giving and putting under obligation those to whom they give, they give to the needy who are sensible enough not to waste what is given to them, such amount that they themselves will not be reduced to needing to receive alms themselves."[21]

This is just one of the thousands of examples of the Qur'anic expressions' miraculous profundity and meaning.

VI. PROPHETHOOD AND PROPHET MUHAMMAD

The Meaning of the Prophets' Prophethood and Mission

God creates every community of beings with a purpose and a guide or a leader. It is inconceivable that God Almighty, Who gave bees a queen, ants a leader, and birds and fish each a guide, would leave us without Prophets to guide us to spiritual, intellectual, and material perfection.

Prophethood is the highest rank and honor that a man can receive from God. It proves the superiority of that man's inner being over all others. A Prophet is like a branch arching out from the Divine to the human realm. He is the very heart and tongue of creation, and possesses a supreme intellect that penetrates into the reality of things and events.

Moreover, he is the ideal being, for all of his faculties are harmoniously excellent and active. He strives and progresses steadily toward Heaven, waits upon Divine inspiration or Revelation for the solutions to the problems he faces, and is the connecting point between this world and the Beyond. His body is subject to and follows his heart, figuratively the seat of spiritual intellect, as does his heart. His perceptions and reflections are always directed to the Names and Attributes of God. He goes to what he perceives, and arrives at the desired destination.

A Prophet's perception, developed to the full – seeing, hearing, and thus knowing – surpasses that of all other people. His perception cannot be explained in terms of different light, sound, or some other wavelengths. Ordinary people cannot acquire a Prophet's knowledge.

Although we can find God by reflecting upon natural phenomena, we need a Prophet to learn why we were created, where we came from, where we are going, and how to worship our Creator properly. God sent Prophets to teach their people the meaning of creation and the truth of things, to unveil the mysteries behind historical and natural events, and to inform us of our relationship, and that of Divine Scriptures, with the universe.

Everything in the universe tries to exhibit the Names and Attributes of the All-Mighty, All-Encompassing Creator. In the same way, the Prophets note, affirm, and are faithful to the subtle, mysterious relation between God and His Names and Attributes. As their duty is to know and speak about God, they enter into the true meaning of things and events and then convey it directly and sincerely to humanity.

Without Prophets, we could not have made any scientific progress. While those who adopt evolutionary approaches to explain historical events tend to attribute everything to chance and deterministic evolution, Prophets guided humanity in intellectual – and thus scientific – illumination. Thus, farmers traditionally accept Prophet Adam as their first master, tailors accept Prophet Enoch, shipmakers and sailors accept Prophet Noah, and clock makers accept Prophet Joseph. Also, the Prophets' miracles marked the final points in scientific and technological advances, and urged people to them.

Prophets guided people, through personal conduct and the heavenly religions and Scriptures they conveyed, to develop their inborn capacities and directed them toward the purpose of their creation. Had it not been for them, humanity (the fruit of the tree of creation) would have been left to decay. As humanity needs social justice as much as it needs private inner peace, Prophets taught the laws of life and established the rules for a perfect social life based upon justice.

The Qur'an explicitly declares: *We sent among every people a Messenger (with the command): "Serve God and avoid evil"* (16:36). But many people gradually forgot these Divine teachings and fell into such errors as deifying the Prophets and others or engaging in idolatry. Even accepting that there must be a tremendous difference between the original and the current form of many religions, it is quite impossible to understand the conditions that caused Confucius to appear in China and Brahma and Buddha in India. It is equally difficult to guess what their original messages were and to what degree they have been corrupted.

If the Qur'an had not introduced Prophethood to us, we would not have an accurate idea of the character, lives, missions, and teachings of many Prophets. One accurate *hadith* says: "A Prophet's disciples will carry out his mission after his death, but some of his followers will later upset everything he established." This is a very important point. Many of the religions we now consider false turned to falsehood, superstition, and legend over time through the deliberate malice of their enemies (or the mistakes of their followers), despite their possible origin in the purest, Divine source.

To say that someone is a Prophet when he is not is unbelief, as is the case with refusing to believe in a true Prophet. We should consider what Buddhism or Brahmanism may have been in their true, original forms, as well as the doctrines attributed to Confucius or the practices and beliefs of Shamanism. Maybe they still have some remnants of what they originally were.

Many once-pure religions have been distorted and altered. Therefore, it is essential to accept the purity of their original foundation. The Qur'an says: *There never was a people without a warner having lived among them* (35:24), and: *We sent among every people a Messenger* (16:36).

These Revelations declare that God sent Messengers to each group of people. The Qur'an mentions the names of 28 Prophets, out of a total of 124,000. We do not know exactly when and where many of them lived. But we do not have to know such information, for: *We did in times past send Messengers before you; of them there are some whose stories We have related to you, and some whose stories We have not related to you* (40:78).

Recent studies in comparative religion, philosophy, and anthropology reveal that many widely separated communities share certain concepts and practices. Among these are moving from polytheism to monotheism, and praying to the One God in times of hardship by raising their hands and asking something from Him. Many such phenomena indicate a singular source and a single teaching. If primitive tribes cut off from civilization and the influence of known Prophets have a sure understanding of His Oneness, though they may have little understanding of how to live according to that belief, a Messenger must have been sent to them at some time in the past: *For every people there is a Messenger. When their Messenger comes, the matter is judged between them with justice, and they are not wronged* (10:47).

As pointed out above, whenever people fell into darkness after a Prophet, God sent another one to enlighten them again. This continued until the coming of the Last Prophet. The reason for sending Prophets Moses and Jesus required that Prophet Muhammad should be sent. As his message was for everyone, regardless of time or place, Prophethood ended with him.

Due to certain sociological and historical facts, which require a lengthy explanation, Prophet Muhammad was sent as "a mercy for all worlds (21:107)." For this reason, Muslims believe in all of the Prophets and make no distinction among them:

> The Messenger believes in what has been sent onto him by his Lord, and so do the believers. They all believe in God and his angels, His Scriptures and His Messengers: "We make no distinction between any of His Messengers" – and they say: "We hear and obey. Grant us Your forgiveness, our Lord; to You is the journeying." (2:285)

That is why Islam, revealed by God and conveyed to humanity by Prophet Muhammad, is universal and eternal.

Describing Prophethood and narrating the stories of all Prophets is beyond the scope of this book. By focusing on the Prophethood of the Seal of the Prophets, who told us about the other Prophets and Divine Scriptures and made our Lord known to us, we will make the other Prophets known and prove their Prophethood.

Belief in God, the source of happiness, and following the Last Prophet and Messenger of God are the keys to prosperity in both worlds. If we want to be saved from despair and all negative aspects of life and attain intellectual, spiritual, and material perfection, we must believe whole-heartedly that Muhammad is the Messenger of God and follow his guidance.

The Age of Ignorance

If we were to imagine ourselves in the world of the seventh century, we would find a completely different world. The opportunity to exchange ideas would be scanty, and the means of communication limited and undeveloped. Darkness would hold sway, and only a faint glimmer of learning, hardly enough to illumine the horizon of human knowledge, would be visible. The people of that time had a narrow outlook, and their ideas of humanity and things were confined to their limited surroundings. Steeped in ignorance and superstition, their unbelief was so strong and widespread that they refused to consider anything as lofty and sublime unless it appeared in the garb of the supernatural. They had developed such an inferiority complex that they could not imagine any person having a godly soul or a saintly disposition.

The Prophet's Homeland

In that benighted era, darkness lay heavier and thicker in one land than in any other. The neighboring countries of Persia, Byzantium, and Egypt possessed a glimmer of civilization and a faint light of learning, but the Arabian peninsula, isolated and cut off by vast oceans of sand, was culturally and intellectually one of the world's most backward areas. The Hijaz, birthplace of the Prophet, upon him be peace and blessings, had not passed through even the limited development of neighboring regions, and had not experienced any social evolution or attained any intellectual development of note. Although their highly developed language could express the finest shades of meaning, a study of their literature's remnants reveals the limited extent of their knowledge. All of this shows their low cultural and civilizational standards, their deeply superstitious nature, their barbarous and ferocious customs, and their uncouth and degraded moral standards and conceptions.

It was a land without a government, for every tribe claimed sovereignty and considered itself independent. The only law recognized was that of the jungle. Robbery, arson, and the murder of innocent and weak people was the norm. Life, property, and honor were constantly at risk, and tribes were always at daggers drawn with each other. A trivial incident could engulf them in ferocious warfare, which sometimes developed into a decades-long and country-wide conflagration. As one scholar writes:

> These struggles destroyed the sense of national unity and developed an incurable particularism; each tribe deeming itself self-sufficient and regarding the rest as its legitimate victims for murder, robbery and plunder.[22]

Barely able to discriminate between pure and impure, lawful and unlawful, their concepts of morals, culture, and civilization were primitive and uncouth. Their life was wild and their behavior was barbaric. They reveled in adultery, gambling, and drinking. They stood naked before each other without shame, and women circumambulated the Ka'ba in the nude.

Their prestige called for female infanticide rather than having someone "inferior" become their son-in-law and eventual heir. They married their widowed stepmothers and knew nothing of the manners associated with eating, dressing, and cleanliness. Worshippers of stones, trees, idols, stars, and spirits, they had forgotten the earlier Prophets' teachings. They had an idea that Abraham and Ishmael were their forefathers, but almost all of these forefathers' religious knowledge and understanding of God had been lost.

Prophet Muhammad, upon Him Be Peace and Blessings

This was Prophet Muhammad's homeland where he was born in 571. His father, 'Abdullah, died before he was born, and his mother, Amina, died when he was 6 years old. Consequently, he was deprived of whatever training and upbringing an Arab child of that time received. During his childhood, he tended flocks of sheep and goats with other Bedouin boys. As education never touched him, he remained completely unlettered and unschooled.

The Prophet left the Arabian peninsula only twice. As a youth, he accompanied his uncle Abu Talib on a trade mission to al-Sham (present-day Israel, Palestine, Lebanon, Syria, and Jordan). The other time was when he led another trade mission to the same region for the widow Khadija, a wealthy Makkan merchant 15 years his senior. They got married when he was 25, and lived happily together until she died more than 20 years later.

Being unlettered, he read no Jewish or Christian religious texts or had any appreciable relationship with them. Makka's ideas and customs were idolatrous and wholly untouched by Christian or Jewish religious thought. Even Makka's *hanifs*, those who followed some of Abraham's pure religion in an adulterated and unclear form and rejected idolatry, were not influenced by Judaism or Christianity. No Jewish or Christian thought is reflected in these people's surviving poetic heritage. Had the Prophet made any effort to become acquainted with their thought, it would have been noticed.

Moreover, Muhammad, upon him be peace and blessings, avoided the locally popular intellectual forms of poetry and rhetoric even before his Prophethood. History records no distinction that set him over others, except for his moral commitment, trustworthiness, honesty, truthfulness, and integrity. He did not lie, an assertion proven by the fact that not even his worst enemies ever called him a liar. He talked politely and never used obscene or abusive language. His charming personality and excellent manners captivated the hearts of those who met him. He always followed the principles of justice, altruism, and fair play with others, and never deceived anyone or broke his promise.

Muhammad, upon him be peace and blessings, was engaged in trade and commerce for years, but never entered into a dishonest transaction. Those who had business dealings with him had full confidence in his integrity. Everyone called him *al-Amin* (the Truthful and the Trustworthy). Even his enemies left their precious belongings with him for safe custody, and he scrupulously fulfilled their trust. He was the embodiment of modesty in society that was immodest to the core.

Born and raised among people who regarded drunkenness and gambling as virtues, he never drank alcohol or gambled. Surrounded by heartless people, his own heart overflowed with the milk of human kindness. He helped orphans, widows, and the poor, and was hospitable to travelers. Harming no one, he exposed himself to hardship for their sake. Avoiding tribal feuds, he was the foremost worker for reconciliation. He never bowed before any created thing or partook of offerings made to idols, even when he was a child, for he hated all worship devoted to that which was not God. In brief, his towering and radiant personality, when placed in the midst of such a benighted and dark environment, may be likened to a beacon of light illumining a pitch-dark night, to a diamond shining among a heap of stones.

What Was His Message?

Suddenly a remarkable change came over him. His heart, illuminated with Divine Light, now had the power for which he had yearned. He left the confinement of the cave to which he used to retire at regular intervals, went to his people, and addressed them in the following strain:

> The idols that you worship are mere shams, so stop worshipping them. No person, star, tree, stone, or spirit deserves your worship. Do not bow your heads before them in worship. The entire universe belongs to God Almighty. He alone is the Creator, Nourisher, Sustainer, and thus the real Sovereign before Whom all should bow down and Who is worthy of your prayers and obedience. So worship Him alone and obey His commands.

> The theft and plunder, murder and rapine, injustice and cruelty, and all the vices in which you indulge are sins in God's eyes. Leave your evil ways. Speak the truth. Be just. Do not kill anyone, for whoever kills a person unjustly is like one who has killed all humanity, and whoever saves a person's life is like one who has saved all humanity (5:32). Do not rob anyone, but take your lawful share and give that which is due to others in a just manner.

> Do not set up other deities with God, or you will be condemned and forsaken. If one or both of your parents reaches old age and lives with you, speak to them only with respect and, out of

mercy, be humble with them. Give your relatives their due. Give to the needy and the traveler, and do not be wasteful. Do not kill your children because you fear poverty or for other reasons. Avoid adultery, for it is indecent and evil. Leave the property of orphans and the weak intact.

Fulfill the covenant, because you will be questioned about it. Do not cheat when you measure and weigh items. Do not pursue that of which you have no knowledge, for your ears, eyes, and heart will be questioned about this. Do not walk around arrogantly, for you will never tear Earth open or attain the mountains in height. Speak kind words to each other, for Satan uses strong words to cause strife. Do not turn your cheek in scorn and anger toward others or walk with impudence in the land.

God does not love those who boast, so be modest in bearing and subdue your voice. Do not make fun of others, for they may be better than you. Do not find fault with each other or call each other by offensive nicknames. Avoid most suspicion, for some suspicion is a sin. Do not spy on or gossip about each other. Be staunch followers of justice and witnesses for God, even though it be against yourselves, or your parents and relatives, regardless if they are rich or poor. Do not deviate by following caprice. Be steadfast witnesses for God in equity, and do not let your hatred of others seduce you to be unjust toward them.

Restrain your rage and pardon the offences of others. Good and evil deeds are not alike, so repel the evil deed with a good one so that both of you can overcome your enmity and become loyal friends. The recompense for an intentional evil is a similar evil; but whoever pardons and amends the evildoer with kindness and love will be rewarded by God. Avoid alcohol and games of chance, for God has forbidden them.

You are human beings, and all human beings are equal in God's eyes. No one is born with the slur of shame on his or her face or the mantle of honor around his or her neck. The only high and honored people are the God-conscious and pious, true in words and deeds. Distinctions of birth and glory of race are no criteria of greatness and honor.

On a day after you die, you will appear before a Supreme Court and account for all your deeds, none of which can be hidden.

Your life's record shall be an open book to God. Your fate shall
be determined by your good or bad actions. In the court of the
True Judge – the Omniscient God – there can be no unfair recommendation and favoritism. You cannot bribe Him, and your
pedigree or parentage will be ignored. True faith and good
deeds alone will benefit you at that time. Those who have done
them fully shall reside in the Heaven of eternal happiness, while
those who did not shall reside in the fire of Hell.[23]

Muhammad as a Prophet and Messenger of God

For 40 years, Muhammad lived as an ordinary man among his
people. He was not known as a statesman, preacher, or orator. No
one had heard him impart wisdom and knowledge, or discuss
principles of metaphysics, ethics, law, politics, economy, or sociology. He had no reputation as a soldier, not to mention of being a
great general. He had said nothing about God, angels, revealed
Books, early Prophets, bygone nations, the Day of Judgment, life
after death, or Heaven and Hell. No doubt he had an excellent
character and charming manners and was well-behaved, yet nothing marked him out as one who would accomplish something
great and revolutionary. His acquaintances knew him as a sober,
calm, gentle, and trustworthy citizen of good nature. But when he
left Hira cave with a new message, he was completely transformed.

When he began preaching, his people stood in awe and wonder, bedazzled by his wonderful eloquence and oratory. It was so
impressive and captivating that even his worst enemies were
afraid to listen to it, lest it penetrate their hearts or very being and
make them abandon their traditional religion and culture. It was
so beyond compare that no Arab poet, preacher, or orator, no
matter how good, could equal its beautiful language and splendid
diction when he challenged them to do so. Although they put
their heads together, they could not produce even one line like the
ones he recited.

Facing immediate and severe opposition, he confronted his
opponents with a smile and remained undeterred by their criticism
and coercion. When the people realized that their threats did not
frighten this noble man and that the severest tribulations directed

toward him and his followers had no effect, they played another trick – but that too was destined to fail.

A deputation of the leading members of the Quraysh (his tribe) offered him a bribe to abandon his mission:

> If you want wealth, we will amass for you as much as you wish; if you want honor and power, we will swear allegiance to you as our overlord and king; if you want beauty, you shall have the hand of the most beautiful maiden of your choice.

The terms were extremely tempting for any ordinary person, but they had no significance in the Prophet's eyes. His reply fell like a bomb upon the deputation, who thought they had played their trump card:

> I want neither wealth nor power. God has commissioned me to warn humanity. I deliver His message to you. If you accept it, you shall have felicity and joy in this life and eternal bliss in the life hereafter. If you reject it, God will decide between you and me.

On another occasion he said to his uncle, who was being pressured by the tribal leaders to persuade him to abandon his mission:

> O uncle! Should they place the sun in my right hand and the moon in my left so as to make me renounce this mission, I shall not do so. I will never give it up. Either it will please God to make it triumph or I shall perish in the attempt.[24]

The faith, perseverance, and resolution with which he conducted his mission to ultimate success is an eloquent proof of the supreme truth of his cause. Had there been the slightest doubt or uncertainty in his heart, he would never have been able to brave the storm that continued in all its fury for 23 long years.

The unlettered Prophet spoke with a learning and wisdom that no one had displayed before and none could show after him. He expounded the intricate problems of metaphysics and theology; delivered speeches on why nations and empires rise and fall and supported his thesis with historical examples; taught ethical canons and principles of culture; and formulated such laws of social culture, economic organization, group conduct, and international relations that even eminent thinkers and scholars could grasp their true wisdom only after life-long research and vast experience. Their beauties, indeed, unfold themselves progressively as humanity advances in theoretical knowledge and practical experience.

This silent and peace-loving trader who had never handled a sword, who had no military training, and who had participated in only one battle (as a spectator!), suddenly turned into such a brave soldier that he never retreated in the fiercest battles, and became such a great general that he conquered Arabia in 9 years at a time of primitive weaponry and very poor means of communication. His military acumen and efficiency developed the military spirit to such a high pitch that he infused a motley crowd of Arabs with the training and discipline necessary to overthrow one of the two superpowers of his day – Sassanid Persia and the Eastern Roman Empire – and utterly defeat the other. These Arabs became the masters of the greater part of the then-known world within a few decades.

This reserved and quiet man who, for 40 years, had given no indication of political interest or activity, suddenly appeared on the world stage as such a great statesman that, without the aid of modern media or telecommunications, he united the scattered inhabitants of a 1.2 million square mile desert – a people who were warlike, ignorant, unruly, uncultured, and plunged in internecine tribal warfare – under one banner, law, religion, culture, civilization, and form of government. Sir William Muir, no friend of Islam, admits:

> The first peculiarity, then, which attracts our attention is the subdivision of the Arabs into innumerable bodies. . . each independent of the others: restless and often at war amongst themselves; and even when united by blood or by interest, ever ready on some significant cause to separate and give way to an implacable hostility. Thus at the era of Islam the retrospect of Arabian history exhibits, as in the kaleidoscope, an ever-varying state of combination and repulsion, such as had hitherto rendered abortive any attempt at a general union. . . The problem had yet to be solved, by what force these tribes could be subdued or drawn to one common center; and it was solved by Muhammad.[25]

He changed people's modes of thought, habits, and morals. He turned the uncouth into the cultured, the barbarous into the civilized, the evildoers and bad characters into pious, God-conscious, and righteous persons. Their unruly and stiff-necked natures were transformed into models of obedience and submission to law and order. A nation that had produced no great figure worth the name for centuries gave birth, under his influence and guidance, to thousands of noble souls who went to far-off lands to preach and teach the principles of religion, morals, and civilization.

In the cavalcade of world history, this sublime figure towers high above all the great people and heroes of all nations. None of them possessed the degree of genius that would allow them to make a deep impression on more than one or two aspects of human life. Some are exponents of theories and ideas but deficient in practical action, people of action who suffered from paucity of knowledge, or renowned only as statesmen; others were masters of strategy and maneuvering, totally focused on one aspect of social life so that others were overlooked, devoted their energies to ethical and spiritual verities but ignored economics and politics, or took to economics and politics but neglected morals and spirituality.

In short, one comes across heroes who are adepts and experts in one walk of life only. Prophet Muhammad is the only person in which all excellences are blended into one personality. He is a man of wisdom, a seer, and a living embodiment of his own teachings; a great statesman as well as a military genius; a legislator and a teacher of morals; and a spiritual luminary as well as a religious guide.

His vision penetrates every aspect of life, and he adorns whatever he touches. His orders and commandments cover a vast field, from regulating international relations to such daily habits as eating, drinking, and cleanliness. On the foundations of his teaching, he established a civilization and a culture and produced such a fine equilibrium among life's conflicting aspects that no flaw, deficiency, or incompleteness can be found therein. Can anyone point to another example of such a perfect personality?

He ruled his country, but was so selfless and modest that he remained very simple and sparing in his habits. He continued to live poorly in his humble thatch-and-mud cottage, sleeping on a mattress, wearing coarse clothes, eating the simplest food of the poor, and sometimes experiencing the pangs of hunger. He spent whole nights standing in prayer before his Lord, helped the destitute and penniless, and worked like a laborer when necessary, never considering it beneath his dignity.

Even when he lay dying, he showed not the slightest taint of royal pomp or hauteur so enjoyed by the rich. Like an ordinary man, he sat and walked with people and shared their joys and sorrows. He mixed and mingled with crowds so easily and naturally that a stranger or an outsider found it hard to recognize him as his nation's leader and ruler. Once a Bedouin came and asked for Muhammad while he was serving his Companions. His answer enshrines an eternal principle: "The master of the nation is the one who serves it." (Daylami, *al-Firdaws*, 2:324.)

This is the tribute of Lamartine, the French historian to the person of the Holy Prophet of Islam:

> Never a man set himself, voluntarily or involuntarily, a more sublime aim, since this aim was superhuman: to subvert superstitions which had been interposed between man and his Creator, to render God unto man and man unto God; to restore the rational and sacred idea of divinity amidst the chaos of the material and disfigured gods of idolatry then existing. Never has a man undertaken a work so far beyond human power with so feeble means, for he had in the conception as well as in the execution of such a great design no other instrument than himself, and no other aid, except a handful of men living in a corner of desert. Finally, never has a man accomplished such a huge and lasting revolution in the world, because in less than two centuries after its appearance, Islam, in faith and arms, reigned over the whole of Arabia, and conquered in God's name Persia, Khorasan, Western India, Syria, Abyssinia, all the known continent of Northern Africa, numerous islands of the Mediterranean, Spain, and a part of Gaul.

> If greatness of purpose, smallness of means, and astounding results are the three criteria of human genius, who could dare to

compare any great men to Muhammad? The most famous men created arms, laws, and empires only. They founded, if anything at all, no more than material powers which often crumbled away before their eyes. This man moved not only armies, legislation, empires, peoples, and dynasties, but millions of men [and women] in one-third of the then inhabited world; and more than that, he moved the altars, the gods, the religions, the ideas, the beliefs and the souls. On the basis of a Book, every letter of which has become law, he created a spiritual nationality which has blended together peoples of every tongue and of every race. He has left to us as the indelible characteristic of this Muslim nationality, the hatred of false gods and the passion for the One and immaterial God. This avenging patriotism against the profanation of Heaven formed the virtue of the followers of Muhammad: the conquest of one-third of the earth to his creed was his miracle. The idea of the unity of God proclaimed amidst the exhaustion of fabulous theogenies, was in itself such a miracle that upon its utterance from his lips it destroyed all the ancient temples of idols and set on fire one-third of the world. His life, his meditations, his heroic revilings against the superstitions of his country, and his boldness in defying the furies of idolatry; his firmness in enduring them for thirteen years at Makka, his acceptance of the role of public scorn and almost of being a victim of his fellow-countrymen: all these and, finally his incessant preaching, his wars against odds, his faith in his success and his superhuman security in misfortune, his forbearance in victory, his ambition which was entirely devoted to one idea and in no manner striving for an empire; his endless prayer, his mystic conversations with God, his death and his triumph after death; all these attest not to an imposture but to a firm conviction. It was his conviction which gave him the power to restore a creed. This creed was two-fold, the unity of God and the immateriality of God; the former telling what God is; the latter telling what God is not. Philosopher, orator, apostle, legislator, warrior, conqueror of ideas, restorer of rational dogmas, of a cult without images; the founder of twenty terrestrial states and of one spiritual state, that is Muhammad. As regards all standards by which human greatness may be measured, we may well ask: Is there any man greater than he?[26]

In spite of his greatness, the Prophet behaved as an ordinary man with all people. He sought no reward or profit to compensate him for his life-long struggles and endeavors, and left no property for his heirs, for he lived to serve his nation. He did not ask that anything be set aside for him or his descendants, and forbade his progeny from receiving *zakat* so that future Muslims would not give all of their *zakat* to them.

He was deeply loved by his Companions, as evidenced by this historical episode:

A group from the Adal and al-Qarah tribes, who were apparently from the same ancestral stock as the Quraysh and who lived near Makka, came to the Prophet during the third year of the Islamic era and said: "Some of us have chosen Islam, so send a group of Muslims to instruct us what Islam means, teach us the Qur'an, and inform us of Islam's principles and laws."

The Messenger selected six Companions to go with them. Upon reaching the Hudhayl tribe's land, the group halted and the Companions settled down to rest. Suddenly, a group of Hudhayli tribesmen fell upon them like a thunderbolt with their swords drawn. Clearly, the mission either had been a ruse from the beginning or its members had changed their minds en route. At any rate, they sided with the attackers and sought to seize the six Muslims. As soon as the Companions were aware of what was happening, they grabbed their arms and got ready to defend themselves. Three were martyred, and the rest were tied up and taken to Makka, where they were to be delivered to the Quraysh.

Near Makka, 'Abdullah ibn Tariq managed to free his hand and reach for his sword. However, his captors saw what he was doing and stoned him to death. Zayd ibn al-Dathina and Hubayb ibn Adiy were carried to Makka, where they were exchanged for two Hudayli captives. Safwan ibn Umayya al-Qurayshi bought Zayd from the person to whom he had been sold so that he could avenge the blood of his father, who had been killed during the Battle of Badr. He took him outside Makka to kill him, and the Quraysh assembled to see what would happen.

Zayd came forward with a courageous gait and did not even tremble. Abu Sufyan, a spectator who wanted to use this chance to extract a statement of contrition and remorse or an avowal of hatred of the Prophet, stepped forward and said: "I adjure you by God, Zayd, don't you wish that Muhammad was with us now in your place so that we might cut off his head, and that you were with your family?" "By God," said Zayd, "let alone wishing that, I do not wish that even a thorn should hurt his foot." Abu Sufyan, astonished, turned to those present and said: "By God, I swear I have never seen a man so loved by his followers as Muhammad."

After a while, Hubayb was taken outside Makka for execution. Requesting the assembled people to let him perform two *rak'at*s of prayer, to which they agreed, he did so in all humility, respect, and absorption. Then he spoke to them: "I swear by God that if I did not think that you might think that I was trying to delay my death out of fear, I would have prolonged my prayer."

After condemning Hubayb to crucifixion, his sweet voice was heard, with a perfect spirituality that held everyone in its spell, entreating God with these words: "O God! We have delivered the message of Your Messenger, so inform him of what has been done to us, and tell him my wish of peace and blessings upon him." Meanwhile, God's Messenger was returning his peace, saying: "Upon you be God's peace and blessings, O Hubayb!"[27]

The following account shows the indelible mark that God's Messenger has imprinted on people of every age:

One of Avicenna's (Ibn Sina) students told Avicenna that his extraordinary understanding and intelligence would cause people to gather around him if he claimed prophethood. Avicenna said nothing. When they were travelling together during winter, Avicenna woke up one morning at dawn, woke his student, and asked him to fetch some water because he was thirsty. The student procrastinated and made excuses. However much Avicenna persisted, the student would not leave his warm bed. At that moment, the cry of the muadhdhin (caller to prayer) called out from the minaret: "God is the greatest. I bear witness that Muhammad is the Messenger of God."

Avicenna considered this a good opportunity to answer his student, so he said:

> You, who averred that people would believe in me if I claimed
> to be a prophet, look now and see how the command I just

gave you, who have been my student for years and have benefited from my lessons, has not had the effect of making you
leave your warm bed to fetch me some water. But this muadhdhin strictly obeys the 400-year-old command of the Prophet.
He got up from his warm bed, as he does every morning
together with hundreds of thousands of others, climbed up to
this great height, and bore witness to God's Unity and His
Prophet. Look and see how great the difference is!"[28]

The Prophet's name has been pronounced five times a day
together with that of God for 1,400 years all over the world.
For further information on Prophet Muhammad with all the
aspects of his life, character, and mission, see, M. Fethullah Gülen,
*The Messenger of God: Muhammad - An Analysis of the Prophet's
Life*, and "Prophethood and Muhammad's Prophethood" in
Essentials of the Islamic Faith (The Fountain: 2000.)

A Short Biography of Prophet Muhammad

Prophet Muhammad (upon him be God's blessings and peace)
was born in 571 in Makka. His father, 'Abdullah, died several
weeks before his birth in Yathrib (Madina), where he had gone
to visit his father's maternal relatives. His mother died while on
the return journey from Madina at a place called Abwa when he
was 6 years old. He was raised by his paternal grandfather 'Abd
al-Muttalib (Shayba) until the age of 8, and after his grandfather's
death by Abu Talib, his paternal uncle. 'Abd al-Muttalib's mother,
Salma, was a native of Madina, and 'Abd al-Muttalib was born and
raised as a young boy in Madina before his uncle Muttalib brought
him to Makka to succeed him. Many years before Muhammad's
birth, 'Abd al-Muttalib had established himself as an influential
Qurayshi leader in Makka and took care of the Ka'ba. Makka was
a city-state well connected to the caravan routes to Syria and Egypt
in the north and northwest and to Yemen in the south. Muhammad
was a descendant of Prophet Ishmael.

Under Abu Talib's guardianship, Muhammad, upon him be
God's blessings and peace, began to earn a living as a business-
man and a trader. At the age of 12, he accompanied Abu Talib
with a merchant caravan as far as Bostra in Syria. Muhammad was

popularly known as al-Amin for his unimpeachable character by the Makkans and visitors alike. This title means "the Honest, the Reliable, and the Trustworthy," and signified the highest standard of moral and public life.

Upon hearing of Muhammad's impressive credentials, Khadija, a rich widowed merchant, asked him, upon him be God's blessings and peace, to take some merchandise for trade to Syria. Soon after this trip, when he was 25, Khadija proposed marriage to him through a relative. Muhammad accepted the proposal. At that time, Khadija was twice widowed and 40 years old. Khadija, may God be pleased with her, and Muhammad, upon him be God's blessings and peace, had 6 children – four daughters and two sons. His first son Qasim died at the age of two. (Muhammad was nicknamed Abu al-Qasim [the father of Qasim]). His second son, 'Abdulla, died in infancy. 'Abdulla was also called affectionately Tayyib and Tahir, because he was born after Muhammad's Prophethood. Their four daughters were Zaynab, Ruqayya, Umm Kulthum, and Fatima.

At this time, the Ka'ba was filled with 360 idols. Prophet Abraham's original pristine message had been lost and then mixed with superstitions and traditions brought by pilgrims and visitors from distant places who were used to idolatry and myths. In every generation, a small group of men and women detested the Ka'ba's pollution and kept pure their practice of the religion taught by Prophets Abraham and Ishmael. They used to spend some of their time away from this pollution in retreats to the nearby hills.

Muhammad, upon him be God's blessings and peace, was 40 when, during one of his many retreats to Mount Hira for reflection during Ramadan, he received the first Revelation from the Archangel Gabriel (Jibril). Gabriel, upon him be peace, said to Muhammad: "*Iqra'*," meaning "Read" or "Recite." Muhammad replied: "I cannot read," as he had received no formal education and was unlettered. Gabriel then embraced him until he reached the limit of his endurance and, after releasing him, said: "*Iqra'*." Muhammad's answer was the same as before. Gabriel repeated the embrace for the third time, asked him to repeat after him and said:

> Recite in the name of your Lord who created! He created
> humanity from an embryo suspended. Recite; and your Lord is
> the Most Munificent, He who has taught by the pen, taught
> humanity what it knew not.

These Revelations are the first five verses of *Surat al-'Alaq* (96:1-5). Thus, the Revelation began in the year 610.

Muhammad, upon him be God's blessings and peace, left the cave of Mt. Hira. When he reached his home, still under the influence of the Revelation, he asked his wife: "Cover me!" After his awe had somewhat abated, Khadija asked him about his great anxiety. She then assured him by saying: "God will not let you down because you are kind to relatives; you speak only the truth; you help the poor, the orphan, and the needy; and you are an honest man." (Bukhari, "Bad'ul-Wahy," 1:3.) She accepted the Revelation as truth, and was the first person to accept Islam. She supported her husband in every hardship, most notably during the 3-year boycott of the Prophet's clan by the pagan Quraysh. She died at the age of 65 during Ramadan, soon after the boycott was lifted in 620.

Gabriel, upon him be peace, visited the Prophet, as commanded by God, and revealed *ayat* (meaning signs, loosely referred to as verses) in Arabic over a 23-year period. The Revelations sometimes consisted of a few verses, part of a chapter, or an entire chapter. Some Revelations came down in response to an inquiry by the unbelievers. The revealed verses were recorded on a variety of available materials (e.g., leather, palm leaves, bark, shoulder bones of animals), memorized as soon as they were revealed, and were recited in daily prayers (80:13-16). Gabriel taught the order and arrangement of verses, and the Prophet instructed his scribes to record verses in that order (75:16-19; 41:41-42).

Once a year, the Prophet would recite all of the verses that had been revealed up to that time to Gabriel so that the latter could authenticate the recitation's accuracy and the verses' order (17:106). All of the revealed verses were compiled in the book known as Qur'an. The name Qur'an appears in the revealed verses. The Qur'an contains not even one word from the Prophet, and speaks in the first person (i.e., God's commands to His creation).

Gabriel also visited the Prophet throughout his mission to inform and teach him about events and strategy, as needed, to help complete the Prophetic mission. The Prophet's sayings, actions, and approvals are recorded separately in collections known as Hadith.

The Prophet's, upon him be God's blessings and peace, mission was to restore the worship of the One True God, the Creator and Sustainer of the universe, as taught by Prophet Abraham and all other Prophets of God; and to demonstrate and complete the laws of moral, ethical, legal, and social conduct, as well as all other matters of significance for humanity at large.

His first followers were his cousin 'Ali, his servant Zayd ibn Haritha, his friend Abu Bakr, and his wife and daughters. They accepted Islam by testifying that: There is no deity (worthy of worship) except The One True God and Muhammad is the Messenger of God.

Islam means peace by submission and obedience to the Will and Commandments of God and those who accept Islam are called Muslims, meaning those who have accepted the message of peace by submission to God.

In the first 3 years of his mission, 40 men and women accepted Islam. This small group was comprised of youth as well as older people from a wide range of economic and social backgrounds. The Prophet, directed by a Revelation, soon started reciting the Revelations public and inviting the people to Islam. The Quraysh, Makka's leaders, met this development with hostility. The most hostile people were his uncle Abu Lahab and his wife Umm Jamila. Initially, they and other Qurayshi leaders tried to bribe him with money, power, and kingship if he would abandon his message. When this failed, they tried to convince his uncle Abu Talib to accept the best young man of Makka in place of Muhammad, and then to allow them to kill Muhammad. His uncle tried to persuade him to stop preaching, but the Prophet said: "O uncle, if they were to put the sun in my right hand and the moon in my left hand to stop me from preaching Islam, I would never stop. I will keep preaching until God makes Islam prevail or I die." (I. Hisham, *Sira*, 1:282)

The Quraysh began to persecute Muslims by beating, tor-
turing, and boycotting their businesses. Those who were weak,
poor, or slaves were publicly tortured. The first martyr was
Umm 'Ammar (the mother of 'Ammar ibn Yasir). Muslims from
well-to-do families were physically restrained in their homes and
told that their freedom of movement would be restored when
they recanted. The Prophet was publicly ridiculed and humiliated by having filth thrown upon him in the street and while he
prayed in the Ka'ba. Despite great hardship and no apparent
support, the Muslims remained firm in their belief. As God told
the Prophet to be patient and to preach the message of the Qur'an,
the Prophet asked his followers to remain patient because he had
not received any Revelation that allowed retaliation.

When the persecution became unbearable for most Muslims
in 615, the Prophet advised them to emigrate to Abyssinia (modern Ethiopia) where Ashama (Negus, a monotheistic Christian
who later believed in Prophet Muhammad) ruled. Eighty people,
not counting the small children, emigrated in small groups to
avoid detection. No sooner had they left the Arabian coastline
than the Qurayshi leaders discovered their departure. Not willing
to let them escape, they immediately sent two envoys to Negus
requesting their return. However, Negus offered them his protection after he investigated their beliefs and heard the Revelations
about Jesus and Mary in *Sura Maryam*, peace be upon them both.
The emigrants were allowed freedom of worship in Abyssinia.

After this, the Quraysh made life even more difficult for the
Prophet by banning all contact with his family (Bani Hashim and
Muttalib). The ban was ended 3 years later, when the Qurayshi
leaders discovered that their secret document defining the ban's
terms, which they had stored in the Ka'ba, had been eaten by
worms – all except for the opening words: "In Your name, O
God." This ban left the Prophet with even more personal sorrow,
for shortly after its lifting his beloved wife Khadija and his uncle
Abu Talib passed away.

After his uncle's death, the Prophet went to Ta'if (about 50
miles east-southeast of Makka) to seek its people's protection.

They flatly refused, mocked him, and severely injured him by inciting their children to throw stones at him. Gabriel, upon him be peace, visited the Prophet and told him that the angels were ready to destroy the town if he would ask God to punish its people. But he answered that if even one of their descendants should accept Islam within 100 years, he could not desire their extermination. He prayed for future generations of Ta'if to accept Islam. On his return from this trip, he met in a vineyard a Christian slave named Addas, originally from Nineveh, who accepted Islam.

Soon after the terrible disappointment at Ta'if, the Prophet experienced the events of the Isra' and Mi'raj (621), during which Gabriel took him from the sacred mosque near the Ka'ba to al-Aqsa mosque in Jerusalem in a very short time during the latter part of the night. This was then followed by his journey through all the dimensions of existence so that he could be shown the greatest signs of God. During this event, the five daily prayers were prescribed. He was then taken back to the Ka'ba. Upon hearing of this, the Makkans mocked him. However, after he described Jerusalem, other things on the way, and the caravan that he had seen on this journey, including its expected arrival in Makka, turned out to be true, their ridicule stopped. These two events are mentioned in the Qur'an in 17:1 and in 53:1-18.

Occasional fairs were held in Makka and such nearby places as 'Arafat, Mina, Muzdalifa, and 'Aqaba. The Prophet would go to them every year, looking for receptive people. In the eleventh year of his mission, seven people from Madina believed in him in 'Aqaba. They returned the next year with 70 new converts and swore that they would protect him if he emigrated to Madina.

The Hijra and Madina

In 622, the Qurayshi leaders decided to kill the Prophet. They planned to choose one man from each Qurayshi tribe and attack him altogether. Gabriel informed him of this plan and told him to leave Makka immediately. The Prophet, after arranging to return that which several unbelievers had entrusted to him, left with Abu Bakr that very night. They went south of Makka to a mountain cave of Thawr [see Qur'an 9:40] and, after staying there for 3 nights, traveled about 250 miles north to Yathrib, which the Messenger changed into Madina.

When the Qurayshi leaders learned of his escape, they offered a reward of 100 camels for his capture, either dead or alive. But despite their best scouts and search parties, God protected the Prophet and he arrived safely in Quba, a suburb of Madina. This event is known as the Hijra (Emigration) and marks the beginning of the Islamic calendar. The people of Madina's Aws and Khazraj tribes greeted him with great enthusiasm in accordance with their pledge made at 'Aqaba. One by one, those Muslims (men and women) of Makka who were not physically restrained and who could make a secret exit, abandoned everything and left for Madina.

When the Prophet settled down in Madina, the Muslims built a mosque in which they could perform their daily prayers and use as their new city-state's headquarters.

The Prophet, upon him be God's blessings and peace, found complete anarchy in Madina, for the region had never had either a state or a ruler to unite its feuding tribes. In just a few weeks, he rallied the tribes together (and brought order), and established a city-state in which Muslims, Jews, pagan Arabs, and probably a small number of Christians as well, entered into a state organism by means of a social contract.

The constitutional law of this first Muslim state, which took the form of a confederacy due to its multiple population groups, has come down to us *in toto*. In it, we read "to Muslims their religion, and to Jews their religion," or "that there would be benevolence and justice," but even that "the Jews . . . are a community (in alliance) with the believers (i.e., Muslims)." All of these phrases appeared in clause 25.[29]

In other words, the autonomous Jewish villages voluntarily joined this confederate state and recognized Muhammad as its head. The document stated clearly that military defense was obligatory upon everyone, including the Jews. This implies their participation in discussing and then executing the policies adopted. In fact, section 37 laid down: "The Jews will bear their expenses and the Muslims theirs, and there will be mutual succor between them in case an aggressor attacks the parties to this document." Further, section 45 says that war and peace will be indivisible for the parties to the document.

Some months after establishing this city-state, the Prophet concluded treaties of defensive alliance and mutual aid with the pagan Arabs around Madina. Some of them embraced Islam about 10 years later. During this decade, mutual confidence was complete.

With the arrival of God's Messenger in Madina, the struggle between Islam and unbelief entered a new phase. In Makka, the Prophet had devoted himself almost exclusively to expounding Islam's basic principles and to his Companions' moral and spiritual training. After the Emigration (622), however, new Muslims belonging to different tribes and regions began to gather in Madina. Although the Muslims held only a tiny piece of land, the Quraysh allied itself with as many tribes as possible to exterminate them.

In these circumstances, the small Muslim community's success, not to mention its very survival, depended upon several factors. In order of importance, they were:

- Propagating Islam efficiently and effectively to convert others.
- Demonstrating the unbelievers' falsehoods so convincingly that nobody could doubt Islam's truth.
- Facing exile, pervasive hostility and opposition, economic hardship, hunger, insecurity, and danger with patience and fortitude.
- Regaining their wealth and goods usurped by the Makkans after they emigrated.
- Resisting, with courage and force of arms, any assault launched to frustrate their movement. While resisting, they should ignore the enemy's numerical or material superiority.

In addition to threats from Makka and its allies, the young community had, despite the signed pact, to contend with Madina's three Jewish tribes, which controlled its economic life. Although they had been waiting for a Prophet, the Jews opposed God's Messenger, because he was not Jewish, and continued to harbor considerable ill-will toward him and plot against him and Islam.

For example, the skilled Jewish poet Ka'b ibn Ashraf composed poems satirizing God's Messenger and instigating his enemies.

In Madina, another hostile element began to emerge: hypocrisy. The Hypocrites can be divided into four broad groups, as follows:

- Those who had no faith in Islam but entered the Muslim community to cause trouble within its ranks.
- Those who understood political realities and so sought some advantage by seeming to have converted. However, they maintained contacts with anti-Islamic forces in the hope that they could benefit from contacts with both sides and thus not be harmed.
- Those who had not made up their minds yet, but seemed to have converted because those around them were doing so.
- Those who accepted Islam as the true religion but found it difficult to abandon their inherited way of life, superstitions, and customs, as well as to exercise the self-discipline required by Islam.

Military Expeditions

In such severe circumstances, God's Messenger decided to dispatch military expeditions into the desert's heart. He had several goals in mind, some of which were as follows:

- Unbelievers tried to extinguish the Light of God with their mouth, but, although they were averse, God willed to perfect His Light (61:8). God's Messenger wanted to prove that the unbelievers could not exterminate Islam.
- Makka enjoyed a central position in the Arabian peninsula. As its most formidable power, all other tribes felt some sort of adherence to it. By sending military expeditions to neighboring areas, God's Messenger wanted to display Islam's power and break Qurayshi dominance. Throughout history, the concept of "might is right" has usually been a norm, for "right" is often too weak to rule. In Arabia, the Quraysh had might and wealth, so the neighboring tribes obeyed them. However, Islam came to make right prevail, and so God's Messenger had to break Makka's grip on the neighboring tribes.

- His mission was not restricted to a fixed period or nation, for he was sent as a mercy for all the worlds. Thus he was charged with conveying Islam as far as possible. To succeed, he had to know what was going on in the peninsula. These expeditions served as vanguards providing him with the information he needed to pave the way for the preaching of Islam.

- The Quraysh lived on trade with the international markets in the present-day regions of Syria and Yemen, and so had to secure their trade routes. But now that the Muslims were in Madina, these routes could be threatened. While strengthening his position, the Prophet also was dispatching military expeditions to paralyze the Quraysh's hopes and plans of defeating him.

- Islam's commands seek to guarantee security of life and property, of chastity and belief, as well as of physical, mental, and spiritual health. Given this, murder and theft, robbery and plundering, usurpation and interest (or usury), gambling, alcohol, illicit sexual relations, anarchy, and the propagation of atheism are all forbidden. The Arabic word for belief, *iman*, means giving peace and security. Thus a *mu'min* (believer) never cheats, and all are safe from a believer's tongue and hand. Believers do not lie, break their promise, or betray a trust. Also, they do not earn their livelihood through such un-Islamic ways as stealing, usurpation, and interest-based transactions. In addition, they seek to harm no one, for they are convinced that those who kill even one person are like those who kill humanity.

- When God's Messenger was raised as a Prophet, Arabia had no security of life or property, chastity or health, or belief. This was true on a global scale. One of his tasks, therefore, was to establish absolute security in every aspect of life. Once he said to Adiy ibn Khatam: "A day will come when a woman will travel, riding in a litter, from Hira to Ka'ba and fear nothing except God." (Bukhari, "Manaqib," 25.) By dispatching military expeditions, God's Messenger sought to establish security therein and show everyone that only Islam would bring them security.

Battles

The Messenger sent military dispatches into the desert until the Battle of Badr (624), which was the first major confrontation between the believers in Madina and the Makkan polytheists.

After his emigration to Madina, the enemies of Islam increased their assault from all sides. In the second year after the Hijra, the Makkans organized a trade caravan to the region of Syria under the leadership of Abu Sufyan. Their merchandise consisted of goods which the Muslims had left behind. When the caravan was en route back to Makka, Abu Sufyan feared a Muslim attempt to retrieve stolen property and so sent a messenger to Makka asking for help and reinforcements.

This caused an uproar throughout Makka. Leading Qurayshi chiefs decided to fight the Prophet. About 1,000 fighters left Makka, amidst much pomp and show, to crush the rising power of the Muslims. They also wanted, as always, to terrorize neighboring tribes to ensure the continued safety of their trade caravans. The Prophet faced them with 310 and so soldiers at Badr. This first confrontation ended in a decisive victory for the Muslims.

In order to take vengeance, the Quraysh prepared a new, powerful army composed of 3,000 soldiers and attacked Madina the following year. Informed of the Makkans' march upon Madina, God's Messenger, after consulting his Companions, met them with 1,000 soldiers in the skirts of the Mount Uhud, 5 kilometers north of Madina. In the first stage of the battle, the Muslims defeated the enemy easily. When the enemy began to flee, the Muslims gathered the spoils. Then, the archers that he had placed on the mountain pass left their positions.

Khalid ibn Walid, still an unbeliever and commander of the Qurayshi cavalry, seized this opportunity to lead his men around Mount Uhud and attacked the Muslims' flank through the pass. The fleeing enemy soldiers came back and joined the attack from the front. Now, the battle turned against the Muslims. Both of these sudden attacks by superior forces caused great confusion among them, and the Companions had to rally around the Prophet, who was wounded and had fainted. Many of them also were wounded.

They retreated to mountain's safety. When the Qurayshi army began to leave the battlefield, thinking they had revenged themselves for Badr and seeing that they could not crush the Muslims' resistance, they mounted their camels and, only leading their horses, headed for Makka.

In 627, a group of the expelled Banu Nadir Jews, including Sallam ibn Abi al-Huqayq, Huyayy ibn Akhtab, and some of the Banu Wa'il, went to Makka. They met with the Qurayshi leaders, urged them to continue the fight, and promised their help and support. These Jews then went to the Ghatafan and Qays Aylan tribes and, promising them help, encouraged them to fight against God's Messenger. These intrigues resulted in a great anti-Muslim confederacy of Makkan polytheists, the desert tribes of central Arabia, Jews already expelled from Madina, Madina's remaining Jews (the Banu Qurayza), and the Hypocrites (led by 'Abdullah ibn Ubayy ibn Salul). The last two constituted a fifth column within Madina.

When God's Messenger was informed of this anti-Muslim gathering of confederates (ahzab) through his intelligence service, he consulted his Companions. It was their unanimous view that they should remain in Madina and fight from there. Salman al-Farisi suggested that they dig a trench around the city. It took 6 days of feverish labor to dig this trench.

The allies advanced against Madina in the hope of destroying the Muslims on an open battlefield. However, when they faced this new strategy, they took the first blow. Numbering around 20,000, they camped near the trench. The Madinans had no more than 3,000 soldiers. Moreover, the Jewish Banu Qurayza and the Hypocrite fifth columns already had contacted the enemy. As stated in Qur'an 33:12-20, when the Hypocrites first saw the enemy, they were already in a defeatist mood.

The Messenger's sagacity and military genius showed themselves once again. He had kept the soldiers confined within the city and stationed them so that they could safeguard their homes against possible Banu Qurayza attacks. The most critical moment came when the Banu Qurayza sent a man into the city to learn the conditions of the Muslim women. However, when this man was killed by Safiyya, the Prophet's aunt, their hopes were frustrated.

The siege lasted for 27 days. The Muslims suffered greatly from hunger, cold, unending barrages of arrows and stones, attempts and concentrated assaults to cross the trench, and betrayals and intrigues within Madina. After almost 4 weeks, during which the enemy was disheartened by a lack of success and the believers proved their steadfastness and loyalty, there was a piercing blast of the cold wind from the east. The enemy's tents were torn up, their fires were extinguished, sand and rain beat their faces, and they were terrified by the portents against them. In the end, Abu Sufyan shouted: "Come on, we're going home!" The Muslims were victorious by God's help.

The Battle of the Trench was the last Qurayshi attempt to destroy Islam and the Muslims. Following their withdrawal in defeat and humiliation, God's Messenger declared: "From this moment we will march upon them; they will no longer be able to raid us."

Relations with the Jewish Tribes

Madina's Jewish tribes were not eager to honor their agreements with God's Messenger after his Emigration. During the Battle of Badr, they favored the Makkan polytheists; after Badr, they openly encouraged the Quraysh and other Arab tribes to unite against the Muslims. They also collaborated with the Hypocrites, who were apparently an integral part of the Muslim body-politic.

To sabotage the spread of Islam, they began to fan the flames of old animosities between the Aws and Khazraj, the two tribes of Madinan Muslims. Ka'b ibn Ashraf, chief of the Banu Nadir, went to Makka and recited stirring elegies for the Makkans killed at Badr in an attempt to provoke the Quraysh into renewed hostile action. He also slandered the Muslims and satirized God's Messenger in his poems.

The Jewish tribes' violation of their treaty obligations exceeded all reasonable limits. A few months after Badr, a Muslim woman was treated indecently by some Jews of the Banu Qaynuqa', the most anti-Muslim Jewish tribe. During the ensuing fight, a Muslim was martyred and a Jew was killed. When God's Messenger reproached them for this shameful conduct and reminded them of their treaty obligations, the Jews threatened him: "Don't be misled by your encounter with a people who have no knowledge of warfare. You were lucky. By God, if we fight you, you will know that we are men of war." But God's Messenger marched upon them and defeated them.

The Jewish Banu Nadir tribe was originally the sworn ally of the Muslims in Madina. However, its members secretly intrigued with the Makkan pagans and the Madinan Hypocrites. They even tried to kill the Prophet while he was visiting them, breaking the laws of hospitality and their treaty. God's Messenger asked them to leave their strategic position, about 3 miles south of Madina, and they agreed to do so. But when 'Abdullah ibn Ubayy, the Hypocrites' chief, promised them help in case of war, the Banu Nadir demurred.

The Muslim army then besieged them in their fortresses. The Banu Nadir, seeing that neither the Makkan polytheists nor the Madinan Hypocrites cared enough to help them, had to leave the city. They were dismayed, but their lives were spared. They were given 10 days to remove themselves, their families, and all they could carry. Many of them joined their brethren in the region of Syria and others in Khaybar.

When the Allies were routed during the Battle of the Trench (627) and returned to their homes in defeat, God's Messenger turned his attention to the Banu Qurayza. They had betrayed their agreement with God's Messenger, allied themselves with the Quraysh, and had given asylum to the Banu Nadir's leaders, like Huyay ibn Akhtab, who had been expelled from Madina and continued to conspire against the Muslims.

Immediately after the Battle of the Trench, God's Messenger ordered his Companions to march upon this Jewish tribe, and had his tent pitched opposite their fortresses. He would have forgiven them if they had asked, but they preferred to resist. The Messenger besieged them for 25 days. At last they asked for surrender terms, agreeing that they should submit to Sa'd ibn Mu'adh's judgment, who decreed their sentence according to the Torah. This was the end of the Banu Qurayza's conspiracies, as well as of the Jewish presence in Madina.

God's Messenger signed a treaty of 10 years of ceasefire with the Quraysh a year after the Battle of the Trench. This treaty was a clear victory that opened a door to new and greater victories for Islam. The Makkan threat ended, and God's Messenger sent envoys to neighboring countries to invite them to Islam. He also set out to solve the other problems he faced within Arabia.

Most of the Banu Nadir Jews had settled in Khaybar after their expulsion from Madina. Together with them, the Jews of Khaybar continued to work against Islam, sometimes with the Quraysh and sometimes with the Banu Ghatafan. The Banu Nadir had been instrumental in forming the 20,000-man anti-Muslim alliance that was defeated during the Battle of the Trench. Seeking to end this continually hostile Jewish presence so that Arabia could be made secure for the future and free preaching of Islam, the Muslims acted.

The Banu Qurayza's defeat roused the Jews of Khaybar to ally themselves with the Banu Ghatafan and attack Madina. They were making preparations for this when, after the treaty of Hudaybiya, God's Messenger marched upon Khaybar. After a fierce battle, the Muslims conquered Khaybar.

The Perfection of Divine Religion

As mentioned above, a year after the Battle of the Trench, the Prophet and 1,500 Companions left for Makka to perform the annual pilgrimage. They were barred from approaching the city at Hudaybiya, where, after some negotiations, a treaty was signed allowing them to come next year. This treaty facilitated the exchange of ideas among the people of the whole region without interference. Many delegations from all regions of Arabia came to the Prophet to investigate Islam, and a large number of people accepted it within a couple of years. The Prophet sent many of his Companions (who had memorized the Qur'an by heart) to new communities to instruct them about the practice of Islam. More than 50 of them were murdered by unbelievers.

A few weeks after Hudaybiya, the Prophet sent letters to several kings and rulers (including the two superpowers – Byzantium and Persia) inviting them to Islam. Negus, the king of Abyssinia, and the ruler of Bahrayn accepted Islam, and Emperor Heraclius acknowledged Muhammad's Prophethood. Some other rulers also entered the fold of Islam.

At the end of 629, the Quraysh violated the terms of the Treaty of Hudaybiya by helping the Banu Bakr in a surprise attack on the Banu Khuzaʿa, who were allied with the Prophet. Some Banu Khuzaʿa men escaped, took shelter in Makka, and sought redress. However, the Qurayshi leaders did nothing. They then sent a message to the Prophet for help.

The Prophet, after confirming all the reports of the attack and subsequent events, marched to Makka with an army of 3,000 Muslims from Madina. Muslims from other Arab communities joined him on the way, swelling the army's numbers. Before entering the city, he sent word to citizens of Makka that anyone who remained in his home, or in Abu Sufyan's home, or in the Kaʿba would be safe. The army entered Makka without fighting, and the Prophet went directly to the Kaʿba and extolled God for his triumphant entry. The Prophet pointed at each idol with a stick and said: *Truth has come and falsehood has perished. Surely falsehood is by nature bound to perish* (17:81). And one by one the idols fell down. The Kaʿba was then cleansed by having the 360 idols removed and restored to its pristine status for the worship of One True God (as built by Prophets Abraham and Ishmael).

The people of the city expected general slaughter in view of their persecution and torture of Muslims for the past 20 years. While standing by the Kaʿba, the Prophet, upon him be God's blessings and peace, promised clemency, stating: "O Quraysh, what do you think that I am about to do with you?" They replied, "Good. You are a noble brother, son of a noble brother." The Prophet forgave them all saying: "I will treat you as Prophet Yusuf (Joseph) treated his brothers. There is no reproach against you. Go to your homes. You are all free."

The Makkans then accepted Islam, including the Prophet's staunch enemies. A few of his staunchest enemies and military commanders had fled Makka, but, after receiving his assurance of no retaliation and no compulsion in religion, they came back and gradually embraced Islam. Within a year (i.e., by 630), almost all of Arabia accepted Islam. Among the Prophet's close companions were Muslims from such diverse regions as Persia, Abyssinia, Syria, and Rome. Several prominent Jewish rabbis, Christian bishops, and clergymen accepted Islam after discussions with the Prophet.

The great change in Arabia alarmed the two superpowers: Byzantium and Persia. Their governors, particularly the Byzantines, reacted with threats to attack Madina. Instead of waiting, the Prophet sent a small army to defend the northernmost border of Arabia. From this time onward, until his death, all of the major battles were fought on the northern front. As the Prophet did not have a standing army, whenever he received a threat he would discuss the situation with the Muslims and then call for volunteers to fight any aggression.

The Prophet performed his first and last pilgrimage in 632 in the company of tens of thousands of male and female Companions. He received the last Revelation during this time, and died 2 months later (upon him be God's blessings and peace), Monday, 12 Rabi al-Awwal, 11 AH [June 8, 632] in Madina after a short illness. He was buried in the place where he died.

Prophet Muhammad lived a most simple, austere and modest life. He and his family used to go without cooked meals several days at a time, relying only on dates, dried bread, and water. During the day he was the busiest man, as he performed his duties in many roles all at once as head of state, chief justice, commander-in-chief, arbitrator, instructor, and family man. He was the most devoted man at night, often spending one- to two-thirds of every night in prayer and reflection. He owned only mats, blankets, jugs, and other simple things even when he was the virtual ruler of Arabia. He left nothing to be inherited except a white mule (a gift from the ruler of Egypt), some ammunition, and a piece of land that he had made a gift during his lifetime. Among his last words were: "We, the community of Prophets, are not inherited. Whatever we leave is for charity." (Muslim, "Jihad," 52.)

At the end of his mission, the Prophet was blessed with around 100,000 men and women who had become his followers. Thousands prayed with him at the mosque and listened to his sermon. They would find every opportunity to be with him following the five daily prayers and at other times. They used to seek his advice for their everyday problems, and listened attentively to the interpretation and application of revealed verses to their situation. They followed the message of the Qur'an and the Messenger of God with utmost sincerity, and supported him with everything they had. The most excellent among them are Abu Bakr, 'Umar, 'Uthman, Ali, Talha, Zubayr, 'Abd al-Rahman ibn Awf, Sa'd ibn Abi Waqqas, Sa'id ibn Zayd, Abu 'Ubayda, Hasan, Hussayn, and several dozen others. They faithfully carried the message of Islam after the Prophet, and within 90 years the light of Islam reached Spain, North Africa, the Caucasus, northwest China, and India.

Jesus in the Qur'an

The Qur'an, the last of the Divine Books, which was revealed by the Creator to the Last of the Messengers and has come down to us uncorrupted, is a source of knowledge about Jesus that is generally unknown to most students of Christianity. The Qur'an not only leads us toward a better understanding of who he was, but also, through that understanding, increases our respect and love for him. The last Revelation, coming as it did some 600 years after Jesus' birth, tells us what is important for us to know about his life and teachings, and places his role as a Prophet in the vast perspective that the Unitarians (*Muwahhids*) realized lay behind prophecy itself. The Qur'an gives a perspective that no other source can provide:

> And truly We gave to Moses the Book and caused a train of Messengers to follow after him, and We gave to Jesus, son of Mary, clear proofs and supported him with the Pure Spirit. (2:87)

The following passage reminds us of the line of Messengers, of which Jesus was a part. After mentioning Abraham, it continues:

> And We bestowed on him (Abraham) Isaac and Jacob, each of whom We guided; We guided Noah in an earlier time; and of his progeny David, Solomon, Job, Joseph, Moses, and Aaron. Thus We reward the good. And Zechariah, John, Jesus, and Elijah, each of whom was of the righteous. And Ishmael, Elisha, Jonah, Lot, each of whom We preferred above the (other) creatures. (6:84-86)

> And the list of the Messengers is by no means complete, for there are Messengers We have mentioned to you before and Messengers We have not mentioned to you. (4:164)

In fact, Prophet Muhammad, peace of God be upon him, said that Jesus was one of the Prophets, about whom there is no cause for conflict or argument. God tells His Messenger:

> Say: "We believe in God and what is revealed to us; what was revealed to Abraham, Ishmael, Isaac, Jacob, and the Prophets among Jacob's descendants; and what was entrusted to Moses, Jesus, and the Prophets from their Lord. We make no distinction between any of them, and to Him we have surrendered." (3:84)

God sent all the Prophets with the same purpose, and Jesus was not different from them:

> We caused Jesus, son of Mary, to follow in their footsteps, confirming what was before him, and bestowed upon him the Gospel, wherein is guidance and light, confirming that which was before it in the Torah – a guidance and an admonition to those who are careful." (5:46)

> Jesus, son of Mary, said: "O Children of Israel! See! I am the messenger of God to you, confirming what was before me in the Torah, and bringing good news of a messenger who will come after me, whose name is Ahmad (the Praised One)." (61:6)

The Qur'an relates his birth and the nature of his mission:

> (Remember, O Muhammad) when the angels said: "O Mary, God gives you glad tidings of a word from Him, whose name is

the Messiah, Jesus, son of Mary, illustrious in the world and the Hereafter and one of those brought near (unto God). He will speak to humanity in his cradle and in his manhood, and he is one of the righteous." She said: "My Lord, how can I have a child when no man has touched me?" He said: "So (it will be). God creates what He wills. If He decrees a thing, He says to it only: 'Be!' and it is. He will teach him the Book and the wisdom, the Torah, and the Gospel, and will make him a Messenger to the Children of Israel, (saying): 'I come to you with a sign from your Lord. See! I fashion for you out of clay the likeness of a bird, and I breathe into it and it is a bird, by God's leave. I heal him who was born blind, and the leper, and I raise the dead, by God's leave. I announce to you what you eat and what you store up in your houses. Here truly is a portent for you, if you are to be sincere believers. (I come) confirming what was before me of the Torah, and to make lawful some of what was forbidden to you. I come to you with a sign from your Lord, so keep your duty to God and obey me. God is my Lord and your Lord, so worship Him. This is a straight path." But when Jesus became conscious of their disbelief, he called out: "Who will be my helpers in the cause of God?" The disciples said: "We will be helpers in God's (cause). We believe in God and bear witness that we have surrendered (to Him). Our Lord, we believe in what You have revealed and follow him whom You have sent. Enroll us among those who witness (to the Truth)." (3:45-53)

Such was Jesus, son of Mary. (This is) a statement of the Truth concerning that which they doubt. It does not befit (God's Majesty) that He should take to Himself a son. Glory be to Him! When He decrees a thing, He says to it only "Be!" and it is. And see! God is my Lord and your Lord. So serve Him. That is the right path. (19:34-36)

They say: "God has taken a son." Glorified be He! He has no needs! His is all that is in the heavens and all that is in the earth. You have no warrant for this. Do you tell concerning God that which you do not know? (10:68)

They indeed are unbelievers who say: "God is the Messiah, the son of Mary." Say: "Who then can do anything against God, if He had willed to destroy the Messiah, son of Mary, and his mother, and everyone on Earth?" God's is the Sovereignty of the heavens and Earth and all that is between them. He creates what He will. God is able to do all things. (5:17)

When God says: "O Jesus, son of Mary, did you say to humanity: 'Take me and my mother for two gods beside God?' he says: '(May You) be glorified! It was not mine to utter something that I had no right to utter. If I used to say it, then You know it. You know what is in my mind, and I know not what is in Your mind. You, only You, are the Knower of Things Hidden. I spoke to them only what You commanded me, (saying): "Worship God, my Lord and your Lord." I was a witness of them while I lived among them, and when You took me You were the Watcher over them. You are Witness over all things. If You punish them, they are Your slaves, and if You forgive them (they are Your slaves). You, only You, are the All-Honored with irresistible might, the All-Wise.'" (5:116-18)

Some Jews say: "Ezra is the son of God," and the Christians say: "The Messiah is the son of God." That is their saying with their mouths. They imitate the saying of those who disbelieved of old. God (Himself) fights against them. How perverse they are! They have taken as lords beside God their rabbis, their monks, and the Messiah, son of Mary, when they were ordered to worship only One God. There is no god except Him. (9:30-31)

O People of the Book! Do not exaggerate in your religion, nor utter anything concerning God except the Truth. The Messiah Jesus, son of Mary, was only a Messenger of God, and His word that He conveyed to Mary, and a spirit from Him. So believe in God and His Messengers, and do not say "Three" – Stop! (It is) better for you! – God is only One God. It is far removed from His transcendent majesty that He should have a son. His is all that is in the heavens and all that is in the earth. And God is enough as Defender. The Messiah will never scorn to be a slave to God, nor will the favored angels. Whoever scorns His service and is proud, all of them will He gather to Himself. As for those who believed and did good works, to them He will pay their wages in full, adding to them of His bounty. As for those who were scornful and proud, He will punish them with a painful doom, and they will not find any protecting friend or helper for themselves against God. (4:171-73)

Conclusion

Cardinal Articles of Belief

1. God is One, without any partners. The name "Allah," His special name, cannot be used for anybody or anything else.

2. He eternally exists without coming into existence. He is the Eternal without a beginning and endures without end.

3. There is nothing like Him. He is the Creator, neither created nor a part of His creation. He neither begets nor is begotten.

4. He cannot be conceived of in any human terms and qualities, and does not incarnate. He is different from any created being. He knows, but not as we know; He has power, but not as we have power; He sees, but not as we see; He hears, but not as we hear; and He speaks, but not as we speak. We speak via speech organs and sounds, whereas God Most High speaks without organs or sounds. He has neither body nor substance, neither accidental property nor limit, neither opposite nor like nor similitude.

5. There is no god other than Him. He is One, not in a numerical sense, but in the sense that He has no partner. He is the Eternal Refuge. He has absolute control over everything, and nothing has any control over Him. Nothing can be independent of Him, even for the blink of an eye.

6. Nothing can overwhelm Him. No limits or restrictions can be placed upon Him. He has no parts or limbs, and cannot be contained by the six directions, as all created things are.

7. No entity in the universe is worthy of worship besides Him.

8. Nothing happens except that He wills it to happen.

9. He is living and never dies, is eternally active and never sleeps.

10. He creates without being in need to do so, and provides for His creation without any effort.

11. He causes death without fear, restores to life without difficulty.

12. He has the power to do everything. Everything is dependent upon Him, and yet He needs nothing. There is nothing like Him.

13. He ordered His creatures to obey Him and forbade them to disobey Him.

14. He is Exalted beyond having opposites or equals.

15. No one can ward off His decree, delay His command, or overpower His affairs.

16. Muhammad, upon him be God's blessings and peace, is His chosen Servant, elect Prophet, His Messenger with whom He is well pleased, and the Seal of the Prophets.

17. Every claim to Prophethood after Him is falsehood and deceit.

18. He has been sent to the jinn and humanity with truth, guidance, light, and illumination.

19. The Qur'an is God's word, which He revealed to His Messenger. All Muslims accept it as absolute truth.

20. The Prophets, peace and blessings be upon them, are free of all major and minor sins, unbelief, and everything that is repugnant. Any insignificant lapses and errors that they might commit cause them to be corrected immediately by God.

21. God took Abraham as an intimate friend and spoke directly to Moses.

22. We believe in the angels, the Prophets, and the Books revealed to the Messengers, and we bear witness that they were all following the manifest Truth.

23. We call the people of our qibla Muslims and believers as long as they acknowledge what the Prophet brought and accept as true everything that he said and told us about. We do not consider any of them unbelievers because of any wrong action they have done, as long as they do not consider that action lawful.

24. A person enters unbelief only by disavowing what led him or her to it.

25. Whatever the Prophet, upon him be peace, said about the Shari'a and the explanation (of the Qur'an and of Islam) is true.

26. God loves all the believers, and the noblest of them in His sight are those who are the most obedient and who follow Islam most closely.

27. Belief consists of belief in God, His angels, His Books, His Messengers, the Last Day (along with the Resurrection and the Day of Judgment), and belief in Divine Destiny and Decree (including human free will).

28. We make no distinction between any of the Messengers, and accept as true what all of them brought.

29. God, the Guardian of those who recognize Him, will not treat them in the Hereafter in the same way as He treats those who deny Him, are bereft of His guidance, and have failed to obtain His protection. O God, You are the Protector of Islam and its people. Make us firm in Islam until the day we meet You.

30. We follow the Sunna of the Prophet and the Muslim community, and avoid deviation, differences, and divisions.

31. People's actions are created (given external existence in the material world) by God, but earned (done) by people themselves.

32. We do not accept as true anything said by soothsayers and fortune-tellers, nor do we accept the claims of those who affirm anything that goes against the Book, the Sunna, and the consensus of the Muslim community (*umma*).

33. We agree that holding together is the true and right path, and that separation is deviation and torment.

Importance and Virtues of Belief [30]

In the following four points, we will explain five out of the thousands of virtues of belief.

First Point

Through the light of belief, we reach the highest degree of perfection and become worthy of Paradise. The darkness of unbelief reduces us to the lowest level so that we deserve Hell. Belief connects us to our Majestic Maker, and our value derives from using our belief to demonstrate the Divine art and manifest the Divine Names. Unbelief breaks this relation, thereby veiling the Divine art and reducing our value to that of a mere physical entity with almost no value (a physical entity is perishable and is no more than a transient animal). We will explain this through a parable.

The value of the iron (or any other material) from which a work of art is made differs from the value of the art expressed in it. Sometimes they may be of the same value, or the art's worth may be far more than its material, or vice versa. An antique may fetch as much as a million dollars, while its material is not even worth a few cents. If taken to the antiques market, it may be sold for its true value because of its art and the brilliant artist's name. If taken to a blacksmith, it would be sold only for the value of its iron.

Similarly, each person is a unique, priceless work of God Almighty's art. We are His Power's most delicate and graceful miracles, beings created to manifest all His Names and inscriptions in the form of a miniature specimen of the universe. If we are illuminated with belief, these meaningful inscriptions become visible. Believers manifest these inscriptions through their connection with their Maker, for the Divine art contained in each person is revealed through such affirmations as: "I am the work of the Majestic Maker, the creature and object of His Mercy and Munificence." As a result, and because we gain value in proportion to how well we reflect this art, we move from insignificance (in material terms) to beings ranked above all creatures. We communicate with God, are His guests on Earth, and are qualified for Paradise.

But if unbelief is ingrained in us, all of the Divine Names' manifestations are veiled by darkness and thus nonexpressive. If the artist is unknown, how can the aspects expressing the worth of his art be identified? Thus most meaningful instances of that sublime art and elevated inscriptions are concealed. In material terms, unbelievers attribute such art and inscriptions to trivial causes, nature and chance, thereby reducing them to plain glass instead of sparkling diamonds. They are no more significant than any other material entity, self-condemned to a transient and suffocating life, and no better than a most impotent, needy, and afflicted animal that eventually will become dust. Unbelief thus spoils our nature by changing our diamond into coal.

Second Point

Just as belief illuminates human beings and reveals all the messages inscribed in their being by the Eternally-Besought-of-All, it also illuminates the universe and removes darkness from the past and future. We will explain this truth through what I experienced regarding the meaning of: *God is the Protecting Friend of those who believe. He brings them out of the layers of darkness into the light* (2:257).

I saw myself standing on an awe-inspiring bridge set over a deep valley between two mountains. The world was completely dark. Looking to my right, I imagined I saw a huge tomb. Looking to my left, I felt as if I were seeing violent storms and calamities being prepared amid tremendous waves of darkness. Looking down, I imagined I was seeing a very deep precipice.

In that darkness, my torch's dim light revealed a dreadful scene. All along the bridge's length were such horrible dragons, lions, and monsters that I wished I had no torch. Whichever way I directed it, I got the same fright. "This torch brings me only trouble," I exclaimed, angrily throwing it away and breaking it. Suddenly darkness was replaced by light, as if I had switched on a huge light by breaking my torch. I saw everything in its true nature.

I discovered that the bridge was a highway on a smooth plain. The huge tomb was a green, beautiful garden in which assemblies of worship, prayer, glorification, and discourse were being led by illustrious persons. The turbulent, stormy, frightening precipices now appeared as a banqueting hall, a shaded promenade, a very beautiful resting place behind lovely mountains. The horrible monsters and dragons were, in fact, camels, sheep, and goats. "Praise and thanks be to God for the light of belief," I said, and then awoke reciting: *God is the Protecting Friend of those who believe. He brings them out of the layers of darkness into the light.*

The two mountains are this life's beginning and end, and the life between death and Resurrection. The bridge is the lifespan, between the two phases of the past (on the right) and the future (on the left). The torch is our conceited ego that, relying on its own achievements, ignores Divine Revelation. The monsters were the worlds' events and creatures of all kinds.

Those who have fallen into the darkness of misguidance and heedlessness because of their confidence in their egos resemble me in the former state – in the dim light of a torch. With their inadequate and misguided knowledge, they see the past as a huge tomb in the darkness of extinction and the future as a stormy scene of terror controlled by coincidence or chance. The torch shows them events and creatures. In reality, these are subjugated to the All-Wise and All-Merciful, fulfill specific functions, and serve good purposes in submission to His Decree. However, they see such things as harmful monsters. These are the people referred to in: *As to those who do not believe, their protecting friends are false deities. They bring them out of light into layers of darkness* (2:257).

If, however, people are favored with Divine guidance so that belief enters their hearts and their Pharaoh-like egos are broken, thereby enabling them to listen to the Book of God, they will resemble me in my later state. Suddenly the universe will fill with Divine Light, demonstrating the meaning of: *God is the light of the heavens and Earth* (24:35).

Through the eye of their hearts, such people see that the past is not a huge tomb; rather, each past century is the realm of authority of a Prophet or a saint, where the purified souls, having completed the duties of their lives (worship) with "God is the Greatest," flew to higher abodes on the side of the future. Looking to their left and through the light of belief, they discern, behind the mountain-like revolutions of the intermediate world and the next life, a feasting place set up by the All-Compassionate One at palaces of bliss in gardens of Paradise. They understand that storms, earthquakes, epidemics, and similar events serve a specific function, just as the spring rain and winds, despite their apparent violence, serve many agreeable purposes. They even see death as the beginning of eternal life, and the grave as the gateway to eternal happiness.

Third Point

Belief is both light and power. Those who attain true belief can challenge the universe and, in proportion to their belief's strength, be relieved of the pressure of events. Relying upon God, they travel safely through the huge waves of events in the ship of life. They voyage through the world comfortably until their last day, since they entrusted their burdens to the Absolutely Powerful One's Power. The grave will be a resting place, after which they will fly to Paradise to attain eternal bliss. If they do not rely upon God, their worldly life will force them down to the lowest depths.

Belief, therefore, consists of affirming Divine Unity, which requires submitting to God, which requires relying upon God, which yields happiness in both worlds. Such reliance upon God should not be misunderstood as ignoring cause and effect. Rather, it means that one should think of causes as a veil covering Power's hand. One observes them by seeking to comply with the Divine Will, which is a sort of worship in action. However, such desire and seeking is not enough to secure a particular effect. We must understand that, in accordance with right belief, the result is to be expected only from God, the All-Mighty. As He is the sole producer of effects, we always should be grateful to Him.

To understand the truth and meaning of trust in God, consider this parable: Once two people boarded a ship with heavy burdens. One put his burden on the deck immediately after boarding and sat on it to keep it safe. The other one, even after being told to lay his burden down, refused to do so and said: "I won't put it down, for it might get lost. Besides, I'm strong enough to carry it." He was told:

> This reliable royal ship is stronger and can hold it better. You will most probably get tired, feel dizzy, and fall into the sea with your burden. Your strength will fail, and then how will you bear this burden that gets heavier every moment? If the captain sees you in this state, he might say you are insane and expel you from the ship. Or maybe he will think you do not trust our ship and make fun of us, for which he will imprison you. Also, you will be marked out and become the butt of jokes. Your vanity reveals

> your weakness, your arrogance reveals your impotence, and your
> pretension betrays your humiliation. And so you have become a
> laughing-stock – look how everybody is laughing at you.

These words convinced him to follow his companion's example. He told him: "May God be pleased with you. I have obtained relief and am no longer subject to imprisonment or becoming a laughing-stock." Trust in God and come to your senses, as the man in the parable did. Put your trust in God so that you may be delivered from begging from creation and trembling in fear at each happening. Doing so will deliver you from self-conceit, being ridiculous, the pressures of this life, and the torments of the Hereafter.

Fourth Point

Belief enables us to attain true humanity, to acquire a position above all other creatures. Thus, belief and worship are our most fundamental and important duties. Disbelief, by contrast, reduces us to the state of a brutal but very impotent beast.

A decisive proof for this truth is the difference between how human beings and animals come into existence. Almost from the very moment of birth, an animal seems to have been trained and perfected its faculties somewhere else. Within a few hours or days or months, it can lead its life according to its particular rules and conditions. A sparrow or a bee is inspired with the skill and ability to integrate into its environment within a matter of 20 days, while it would take a person 20 years to do so. This means that an animal's basic obligation and essential role does not include seeking perfection through learning, progress through scientific knowledge, or prayer and petitioning for help by displaying their impotence. Rather, their sole purpose is to act within the bounds of their innate faculties, which is the mode of worship specified for them.

People are born knowing nothing of life and their environment and so must learn everything. As we cannot do this even within 20 years, we must continue to learn until we die. We appear to have been sent here with so much weakness and inability that we might need 2 years to learn how to walk. Only after 15 years can we distinguish good and evil. Only by living in a society can we become smart enough to choose between what is good and what is bad.

Thus the essential and intrinsic duty of our existence is to seek perfection through learning and to proclaim our worship of and servanthood to God through prayer and supplication. We should look for answers to such questions as: "Through whose compassion is my life so wisely administered? Through whose generosity am I being so affectionately trained? Through whose favors and benevolence am I being so solicitously nourished?" Then we should pray and petition the Provider of Needs in humble awareness of our needs, none of which we can satisfy on our own. This understanding and confession of our impotence and poverty will become two wings on which to fly to the highest rank: being a slave of God.

And so our purpose here is to seek perfection through knowledge and prayer. Everything is, by its nature, essentially dependent on knowledge. And the basis, source, light, and spirit of all true knowledge is knowledge of God, of which belief is the very foundation. After belief, prayer is our essential duty and the basis of worship, for despite our infinite impotence, we are exposed to endless misfortune and innumerable enemies. And despite our infinite poverty, we suffer limitless need and demands.

Children express their need for something they cannot reach with words or tears. Both are a sort of plea or prayer, in word or deed, with the tongue of weakness. Eventually they get what they want. Similarly, we are quite like a beloved child, for at the Most Compassionate and Merciful Being's Court we either will weep (due to our weakness and impotence) or pray (due to our poverty and need) so that our need may be satisfied. In return, we should perform our duty of gratitude and thanksgiving for this provision. Otherwise, the ingratitude of those who claim to have so much intelligence and power over everything that they can meet their own needs finally will come to the point where they resemble mischievous children moaning about irritating flies. Such ingratitude is against our essential nature and makes us worthy of severe punishment.

CHAPTER THREE

The Pillars of Islam and
a Muslim's Daily Life

THE PILLARS OF ISLAM AND
A MUSLIM'S DAILY LIFE

I slam is based on five pillars: Bearing witness to God's Existence and Oneness and the Messengership of Muhammad, praying five times a day, fasting during the month of Ramadan, paying zakat (the prescribed purifying alms), and *hajj* or pilgrimage. The first pillar includes all essentials of belief, which were discussed in the previous chapter.

TAHARA (CLEANLINESS OR PURIFICATION)

Islam requires physical and spiritual cleanliness. On the physical side, Islam requires Muslims to clean their bodies, clothes, houses, and community, and they are rewarded by God for doing so. While people generally consider cleanliness desirable, Islam insists upon it and makes it an indispensable fundamental of religious life. In fact, books on Islamic jurisprudence often contain a whole chapter on this very requirement.

Prophet Muhammad, upon him be God's blessings and peace, advised Muslims to appear neat and tidy in private and in public. Once when returning home from battle he advised his army: "Soon you will meet your brothers, so tidy your saddles and clothes" (Abu Dawud, "Libas," 25). On another occasion he said: "If I had not been afraid of overburdening my community, I would have ordered them to use a *miswaq* (to brush and clean their teeth) for every prayer" (Bukhari, "Jumu'a" 8).

Moral hygiene also was emphasized, for the Prophet, upon him be God's blessings and peace, encouraged Muslims to make a special prayer upon seeing themselves in the mirror: "God, You have endowed me with a good form; likewise bless me with an immaculate character " (Ibn Hanbal, *Musnad*, 1:34, 6:155). He advised modest clothing, for men as well as for women, on the grounds that it helps one maintain purity of thought.

Being charitable is a way of purifying one's wealth. A Muslim who does not give charity (*sadaqa*) and pay the required annual *zakat* (the prescribed alms), contaminates his or her wealth by hoarding that which rightfully belongs to others: *Of their wealth take alms so that you may purify them* (9:103).

All the laws and injunctions given by God and His Prophet, upon him be God's blessings and peace, are pure. Any law established by Divine guidance is just and pure.

The Purity of Water

Pure water is used essentially in matters of purification or *wudu'* (minor ablution) and *ghusl* (major ablution). Hence the necessity to investigate water's purity. Water has four essential attributes: smell, color, taste, and fluidity. Any pure and purifying water is judged according to whether it retains these attributes or not. As a result, water is classified into two categories: *mutlaq* and *muqayyad* water.

Mutlaq water is "natural" water, such as that which comes from rain water, snow, hail, sea water, and water from the Zamzam well.

It is subdivided as follows:
- Water that is both pure and purifying (e.g., rain water, snow, hail, sea water, and water from the Zamzam well).
- Water that drips from a person after he or she has performed the minor or major ablution, and therefore is considered "used." It is considered pure, but cannot be used for another minor and major ablution.
- Water that is both pure and purifying, but whose usage is disliked (*makruh*) (e.g., water left in a container after a cat, bird, or another "allowed" animal has drunk from it).
- Water mixed with impure elements. Water whose taste, color, or smell has been altered by an impure substance cannot be used for purification. However, if the liquid is still considered water, meaning that the impure substance has not altered its taste, color, or smell, it can be used for purification.

- Water that is pure but may not be purifying. One example of this type of water is the water that remains in a pot after a donkey or a mule has drunk from it.

Muqayyad water includes naturally *muqayyad* water, such as fruit juices and water that has been mixed with various substances (e.g., soap, saffron, flowers) or objects that the Shari'a considers pure. Such water is considered pure until, due to being mixed with other substances, one can no longer call it water. In this case, the water is still considered pure, but it cannot be used for purification (minor and major ablution).

Types of Impurities

Najasa refers to impure substances that Muslims must avoid and wash off after coming into contact with them. God says: *Purify your raiment* (74:4) and: *God loves those who repent and who purify themselves* (2:222).

- Animals that died naturally (e.g., not killed in the Islamic manner) are impure, as is anything cut off a live animal. However, dead sea animals and those that have no flowing blood (e.g., bees and ants) are not impure. The bones, horns, claws, fur, feathers, and skin of dead animals, except for pigs, are pure.
- Any blood that flows from a person's or an animal's body (e.g., blood from a killed animal or menstrual blood) is impure. However, blood that remains in the veins is permissible. Also, any blood that remains in edible meat, livers, hearts, and spleens is not impure, provided that the animal was sacrificed in the Islamic way.
- A person's vomit, urine, excrement, *wadi* (a thick white secretion discharged after urination), *mazi* (a white sticky fluid that flows from the sexual organs when thinking about sexual intercourse, foreplay, and so on), prostatic fluid, and sperm is impure. However, according to some, sperm is not impure but should be washed off if it is still wet, and scratched off if it is dry. Any part of human flesh is impure.
- The urine, saliva, and blood of all animals whose meat is prohibited, and the excrement of all animals except birds whose meat is allowable, are impure.

- The excrement of poultry (i.e., geese, hens, ducks) is impure.
- Pig and alcohol are impure.
- Dogs are considered impure. Any container that a dog has licked must be completely washed and sterilized. If a dog licks a pot that has dry food in it, what it touched and what surrounds it must be thrown away. The remainder may be kept, as it is still pure. A dog's hair is considered pure.
- The impurities mentioned are considered "gross impurity" (*najasat al-ghaliza*). Any amount of them contaminates whatever it touches. However, if it is on person's body or clothes when he or she is praying, or on the ground or mat where he or she is praying, its amount is taken into consideration. Any solid filth weighing more than 3 grams, and any liquid more than the amount that spreads over a person's palm, invalidates the prayer.
- The urine of horses and domestic or wild animals whose meat is allowed to eat is weak impurity (*najasat al-khafifa*). When more than one-fourth of a limb or one-fourth of one's clothes are smeared with it, the prayer is invalidated.

The Ways of Purification

PURIFYING THE BODY AND CLOTHES. If these are contaminated, they must be washed with water until no impurity remains. This is especially so if the impurity is visible, such as blood. If some stains remain after washing, such as those that would be extremely difficult to remove, they can be overlooked. If the impurity is not visible, such as urine, wash and wring whatever it has contaminated three times.

PURIFYING THE GROUND. Purify the ground by pouring water over it. If the impurity is solid, the ground will become pure only by its removal or decay.

PURIFYING CONTAMINATED BUTTER AND SIMILAR SUBSTANCES. If a dead animal has fallen into a solid matter but has not swollen or disintegrated, whatever the corpse touches and what is around it must be thrown away, provided that one can make sure that it did not touch the rest of the matter. If it fell into a liquid substance, the majority say that the entire liquid becomes impure.

PURIFYING A DEAD ANIMAL'S SKIN. Tanning purifies a dead animal's skin and fur. The Prophet said: "If the animal's skin is tanned, it is purified" (Muslim, "Hayz," 105).

PURIFYING MIRRORS AND SIMILAR OBJECTS. Mirrors, knives, swords, nails, bones, glass, painted pots, and other smooth surfaces that have no pores are purified by removing the impurity.

Useful Points

- If an unknown liquid falls on a person, there is no need to ask about it or to wash one's clothes.

- If a person finds something moist on his or her body or clothes at night and does not know what it is, he or she does not need to smell it in order to identify it.

- Clothes that have street mud on them do not have to be washed.

- If a person finishes praying and sees some previously unseen impurity on his or her clothes or body, or was aware of but forgot about them, his or her prayer does not have to be repeated.

- If a person cannot determine what part of his or her clothes contains the impurity, the whole garment should be washed, for "if an obligation can be fulfilled only by performing another related act, that act also becomes obligatory."

- If a person mixes pure clothes with impure clothes (and cannot tell them apart), he or she should investigate the matter and pray once in one of the clothes.

- It is not proper to carry something that has God's Name upon it while going to the bathroom, unless he or she is afraid of losing it or having it stolen.

- One should not talk in the bathroom, respond to a greeting, or repeat what the muadhdhin is saying. One may speak if there is some necessity. In the event of sneezing, one should praise God silently by moving his or her lips.

- One should neither face nor turn his or her back on the *qibla* while answering a call of nature, especially if in an open area.

- One should seek a soft and low piece of ground to protect against any impurity. The Prophet said: "When one of you urinates, he should choose the proper place to do so."
- One should avoid shaded places and places where people walk and gather.
- One should not answer a call of nature in bathing places or in still or running water.
- One should not urinate while standing, though some allow it.
- One must remove any impurities from one's clothes and body after relieving oneself.
- One should not clean himself or herself with the right hand.
- One should remove any bad smell from one's hands after answering a call of nature.
- One should enter the bathroom with the left foot, saying: "I seek refuge in God from noxious male and female beings (devils)," and exit with one's right foot, saying: "O God, I seek your forgiveness."
- After a man has relieved himself, he should wait until the urine stops completely and make sure that none of it has fallen onto his clothes. This is called *istibra* (seeking full purification). Ibn 'Abbas related that the Messenger of God, upon him be God's blessings and peace, passed by two graves and said: "They are being punished, but not for a great matter (on their part). One of them did not clean himself from urine, and the other used to spread slander." (Tirmidhi, "Tahara," 53) To erase all doubt, the person should sprinkle his penis and underwear with water.

Acts That Correspond to Human Nature

God has chosen certain acts for all of His Prophets and their followers to perform. These acts, are known as *sunan al-fitra* (acts required by human nature), are as follows:

CIRCUMCISION. This prevents dirt from getting on one's penis and also makes it easy to keep clean. The Shafi'i scholars maintain that it should be done on the seventh day after birth, although it is permissible to do it later.

SHAVING PUBIC HAIRS AND PULLING OUT UNDERARM HAIRS. Doing so is *sunna*. However, it is enough to trim or pull it out. CLIPPING FINGERNAILS, TRIMMING AND SHAVING THE MOUSTACHE, AND KEEPING THE BEARD TIDY. Abu Hurayra reported that the Messenger of God, upon whom be God's blessings and peace, said, "Five things are part of one's *fitra*: Shaving the pubic hair, circumcision, trimming the moustache, removing any underarm hair, and trimming the nails." (Muslim, "Tahara," 49) A moustache should not be so long that food particles, drink, and dirt accumulate in it. If one grows a beard, it should not be untidy.

HONORING AND COMBING ONE'S HAIR. Abu Hurayra reported that the Prophet, upon whom be peace, said: "Whoever has hair should honor it" (Abu Dawud, "Tarajjul," 3:4163). Cutting one's hair off is permissible, and so is letting it grow if one honors it.

LEAVING GRAY HAIRS IN PLACE. This applies to both men and women. 'Amr ibn Shu'ayb related, on the authority of his father from his grandfather, that the Prophet said: "Do not pluck the gray hairs, as they are a Muslim's light. A Muslim never grows gray in Islam except that God writes for him, due to that, a good deed, raises him a degree, and erases for him, due to that, one of his sins" (Ibn Hanbal, 2:179; Tirmidhi, "Adab," 56).

DYEING ONE'S GRAY HAIR. According to the accepted opinion, dyeing one's gray hair by using henna, red dye, yellow dye, and so on is permissible, provided that the dyes are religiously allowable.

USING PERFUME. Using musk and other perfumes that are free of alcohol and similar forbidden things is highly advisable, for they are pleasing to the soul and beautify the atmosphere.

Menstruation and Post-childbirth Bleeding

Menstruation is a natural type of blood that flows at regular intervals from a woman's uterus after puberty. God has laid down certain rules in connection with this, as a concession to the woman, in consideration of her condition.

Menstruation usually lasts 3 to 10 days and nights, varying from woman to woman. Most women have a regular number of days for their monthly menstrual period. The number of days may fluctuate and the period might come a little early or a little late. So when a woman sees menstrual blood, she should consider herself to be menstruating. When it stops, she should consider herself clean. If more blood appears after her menstrual period has ended, but does not have the same color as menstrual blood, it should not be considered as menstruation.

Post-childbirth bleeding is the blood that comes during and after childbirth. It may begin to come 2 or 3 days before delivery and be accompanied by labor pains. There is no minimum limit as to how long a woman will bleed, but generally the upper limit is within 40 days.

Women are prohibited from performing certain acts while they are in this condition, such as follows:

- She cannot pray (*salat*) after she begins to bleed and does not have to make up any missed prayers.

- She cannot observe any obligatory (Ramadan) or supererogatory fasts. She must make up the obligatory fasting days after regaining her ritual cleanliness. If bleeding begins during a supererogatory fasting day upon which she had intended to fast, she must make it up.

- She can do all pilgrimage rites except circumambulating the Ka'ba (*tawaf*).

- She should avoid mosques or places of worship, and cannot touch the Qur'an, whether the original or in translation. She cannot recite it from memory, but can read the verses of prayer and supplication with the intention of praying. (She cannot perform *salat* but can supplicate and recite the prayers mentioned in the Qur'an with the intention of saying prayers or making supplications.)

- A man cannot have sexual intercourse with his wife while she has post-childbirth bleeding, for she is not allowed to make herself available to him. However, he can kiss, hug, or touch her anywhere besides the pubic region. It is better and highly advisable to avoid the area between the navel and the knees.

When a menstruating woman stops bleeding, she must perform a complete *ghusl* (major ablution). After this, she must resume praying and fasting, can enter the mosque, make *tawaf*, recite the Qur'an, and engage in allowable sexual intercourse. She must make up the fasting days that she missed during Ramadan, but not the prayers. The same rules apply to women in post-childbirth bleeding.

Istihadha (Non-menstrual Vaginal Bleeding)

In some women, bleeding never stops; in others, it continues for longer than normal. This blood is called *istihadha*. Likewise, any blood coming before puberty and after menopause is also considered *istihadha*.

A woman with this condition should calculate when her period would normally end, and then stop praying during the days of her calculated period and follow all of the other menstruation-related rules. For the rest of the days, her bleeding should be treated as *istihadha*. If she does not have a regular period or does not remember when it used to occur, but can distinguish between the two kinds of blood based on color, thickness, and smell (i.e., menstrual blood is dark, thick, and has a strong odor, while *istihadha* is bright red, thin, and less disagreeable in smell), she must act accordingly. If she does not have a regular period and cannot distinguish between the two types of blood, she must consider the blood coming for 3 to 10 days every month as menstruation and calculate it from the time she first noticed her vaginal bleeding.

There is no difference between a woman beset by *istihadha* and one who has a complete cessation of menstrual flow, except as follows:

- If the first woman wants to perform *wudu'* (ritual ablution), she should wash the blood from her vaginal area and then apply a menstrual pad or wrap the area with a clean rag on top of a wad of cotton to catch the blood. Any blood coming out after that is of no account.
- She must perform wudu' for every obligatory prayer.

Ghusl (Major Ablution)

Ghusl means major canonical ablution or a complete washing of the body. It becomes obligatory after sexual intercourse, even if only the head of the penis disappears into the vagina. Any discharge of semen, and the completion of menses and post-childbirth bleeding.

Taking *ghusl* every Friday before the congregational prayer is highly advisable, for the Prophet always did so. Before beginning *ghusl*, one should make the intention to perform it and, if one will pray after performing it, also the prayer.

Things Forbidden to a Ritually Impure Person

People who are in this state cannot pray, circumambulate the Ka'ba (*tawaf*), enter a mosque or place of worship unless necessary, or touch the Qur'an or any of its verses except with a clean cloth or something similar.

What Makes One's Ghusl Valid?

• Rinsing the mouth thoroughly so that all of its parts are cleaned properly.
• Rinsing the nose right up to the nasal bone.
• Washing all bodily parts thoroughly, including the hair.
  The best way to perform *ghusl* is as follows:
• Having the intention (*niyyat*) to cleanse the body from (ritual) impurity while washing oneself.
• Washing the hands up to the wrists three times.
• Washing the private parts thoroughly.
• Removing all filth from all bodily parts.
• Performing ablution.
• Washing all bodily parts three times, including the hair thoroughly. No part, even the size of a pinpoint, is allowed to remain dry. Rubbing and pressing the body is not obligatory.

Tayammum (Ablution with Clean Soil)

When a person is too sick to use water or none is around when it is time to pray, he or she can perform *tayammum* in place of *wudu'* and *ghusl*.

The requirements are as follows:

- Intending to perform *tayammum* to remove any impurity.
- Striking the pure soil lightly with the palms of both hands and passing the palms over the face one time.
- Striking the pure soil again with one's palms and rubbing the right and left arms alternately from the fingertips to the elbows.

Tayammum is nullified as soon as the cause for performing it is removed (i.e., the sick person recovers or pure water is found). If a person performs *tayammum* and then prays, he or she does not have to repeat the prayer if the conditions for it are removed before the time for that particular prayer ends.

Wudu' (Ablution)

Wudu' involves washing with water at least once the usually exposed bodily parts, namely, the face, hands and arms up to (and including) the elbows, and feet, and wiping one-quarter of the head. It is obligatory for any obligatory or supererogatory prayer, circumambulating the Ka'ba, and touching the Qur'an with bare hands.

Wudu' is performed in the following manner:

- Ensure that the water to be used is pure.
- Intend to perform *wudu'* to offer prayer, if you plan to pray after taking it.
- Recite: *"Bismillahir-Rahmanir-Rahim"* (i.e., in the Name of God, the All-Merciful, the All-Compassionate).
- Wash the hands up to the wrists three times, and do not miss the parts between the fingers.
- Clean your mouth with a brush or a finger, and gargle with water three times.
- Rinse the nostrils with water three times.
- Wash the face from the forehead to the chin and from ear to ear three times.
- Wash the right arm followed by the left up to the elbows three times.
- Wipe at least a quarter of the head with wet hands, pass the wet tips of the little fingers inside and the wet tips of the thumbs

outside the ears, and pass the palms over the nape and sides of the neck.

- Finally, wash the feet up to (and including) the ankles, the right foot first and then the left, taking care to wash in between the toes, each three times.

The obligatory acts are as follows:

- Washing the face.
- Washing both arms up to and including the elbows.
- Wiping a quarter of the head with wet hands.
- Washing both feet up to and including the ankles.

The following acts nullify *wudu'*

- Whatever comes out from the two private parts (front and back): waste matter, urine, wind, *wadi* (a thick white secretion discharged after urination), *mazi* (a white sticky fluid that flows from the sexual organs when thinking about sexual intercourse or Foreplay, and so on), and prostatic fluid. Semen, menstrual blood, and post-childbirth blood require *ghusl*.
- Emission of blood, pus, or yellow matter from a wound, boil, pimple, or something similar to such an extent that it flows beyond the wound's mouth.
- Vomiting a mouthful of matter.
- Physical contact for pleasure between men and women without any obstacle (e.g., clothes). If the head of one's penis disappears into a woman's vagina, *ghusl* is required.
- Loss of consciousness through sleep, drowsiness, and so on.
- Temporary insanity, fainting, hysteria, or intoxication.
- Audible laughter during prayer.

Wiping over Clean, Indoor Boots (Khuffayn)

While performing *wudu'*, one can wipe over (the top of) their clean, indoor boots once with wet hands instead of washing the feet.

- Boots should be waterproof and cover the whole foot up to (and including) the ankles. They must have no holes wider than three fingers in width. It does not matter if their mouths are so wide that the feet can be seen when looking down at them.

- They must be fit, strong, and tough enough so that the feet would not come out of them, and they should not fall down when walked in for 3 miles.
- They cannot be made out of wood, glass, or metal.
- One must put on the boots after washing one's feet while performing ablution. One can wear it for a whole day if one is resident. If traveling, one can wear it for 3 consecutive days.

SALAT (PRAYER)

Prayer is the most important type of worship, for it displays a person's sincerity and loyalty to God. In the words of God's Messenger, it is the pillar or main support of religious life (Daylami, *al-Firdaws*, 2:404).

There are several kinds of prayers, as follows:

- *Obligatory.* The five daily prescribed prayers and the *Jumu'a* (Friday) prayer. The latter is not obligatory for women, but they can pray it if they wish. The funeral prayer is obligatory, but not upon every individual. If some people perform it, others do not have to.
- *Necessary (wajib).* The 'Iyd (religious festive days) prayers and the *witr* prayer (performed after the late evening or night prayer until dawn).
- *Sunna (those performed or advised by the Prophet).* Those performed before or after the daily prescribed prayers, *tahajjud* (performed after the late evening prayer and before the *witr* prayer), *tarawih* (performed after the late evening prayer during Ramadan), *khusuf* and *kusuf* (performed during solar and lunar eclipses), and the prayer for rain (*salat al-istisqa*).
- *Supererogatory and rewarded. Salat al-ishraq* (performed some three quarters after sunrise), *salat al-duha* (forenoon or broad daylight prayer, performed until some three quarters before the noon prayer), and *salat al-awwabin* (performed between the evening and late evening prayers). There are some other supererogatory prayers, such as *salat al-tawba* (performed before asking God to forgive us), *salat al-istikhara* (performed to ask God to make something good for us), *salat al-tasbih* (the

prayer of glorifying God), the prayer performed when leaving on a journey, and the prayer performed when returning from a journey.

The Prayer's Meaning and Importance[1]

The prescribed prayers (*salat*) are Islam's pillars. To fully understand their importance, consider this parable: A ruler gives each of his two servants 24 gold coins and sends them to a beautiful farm that is 2 months' travel away. He tells them: "Use this money to buy your ticket, your supplies, and what you will need after you arrive. After traveling for a day, you will reach a transit station. Choose a method of transportation that you can afford."

The servants leave. One spends only a little money before reaching the station. He uses his money so wisely that his master increases it a thousandfold. The other servant gambles away 23 of the 24 coins before reaching the station. The first servant advises the second one: "Use this coin to buy your ticket, or else you'll have to walk and suffer hunger. Our master is generous. Maybe he'll forgive you. Maybe you can take a plane, so we can reach the farm in a day. If not, you'll have to go on foot and endure 2 months of hunger while crossing the desert." If he ignores his friend's advice, anyone can see what will happen.

Now listen to the explanation, those of you who do not pray, as well as you, my soul that is not inclined toward prayer. The ruler is our Creator. One servant represents religious people who pray with fervor; the other represents people who do not like to pray. The 24 coins are the 24 hours of a day. The farm is heaven, the transit station is the grave, and the journey is from the grave to eternal life. People cover that journey at different times according to their deeds and conduct. Some of the truly devout pass in a day 1,000 years like lightning, while others pass 50,000 years with the speed of imagination. The Qur'an alludes to this truth in 22:47 and 70:4.

The ticket is the prescribed prayers, all of which can be prayed in an hour. If you spend 23 hours a day in worldly affairs and do not reserve the remaining hour for the prescribed prayers, you are a foolish loser. You may be tempted to use half of your money for a lottery being played by 1,000 people. Your possibility of winning is 1:1,000, while those who pray have a 99 percent chance of winning. If you do not use at least one coin to gain an inexhaustible treasure, something is obviously wrong with you.

Prayer comforts the soul and the mind and is easy for the body. Furthermore, correct intention transforms our deeds and conduct into worship. Thus our short lifetime is spent for the sake of eternal life in the other world, and our transient life gains a kind of permanence.

The prescribed prayer is the pillar of religion and the best of good deeds. One who does not perform it cannot construct the building of religion on the foundation of faith. Any foundation on which a building was not built is liable to removal. The Messenger, upon him be peace and blessings, taught that it is like a river running by one's house. One who bathes in it five times a day is cleaned of all dirt (which may have smeared him or her during the periods between them). He also taught that the prescribed prayers can serve as an atonement for the minor sins committed between them (Muslim, "Tahara," 16).

The Qur'an declares that the prescribed prayer prevents one from committing indecencies and other kinds of evil deeds (29:45). Also, it serves as repentance and asking God for forgiveness. Similarly, any good deed done just after an evil one may cause it to be forgiven. So it is highly advisable that one should do good immediately after doing an evil deed. Like the prescribed prayer, this manner of action may also restrain one from doing further evil.

Prayer seems to be a strenuous demand, but in reality gives indescribable peace and comfort. Those who pray recite *ashhadu an la ilaha illa Allah* (I bear witness that there is no deity but God). Only He can give harm and benefit. He is the All-Wise, Who does nothing useless; the All-Compassionate, Whose mercy and bounty are abundant. Having faith, believers see in every event a door to the wealth of God's Mercy, and knock on it via supplication. Realizing that their Lord and Sustainer controls

everything, they take refuge in Him. Putting their trust in and fully submitting to God, they resist evil. Their faith gives them complete confidence.

As with every good action, courage arises from faith in and
loyal devotion to God. As with every bad action, cowardice arises from misguidance. If Earth were to explode, those servants of
God with truly illuminated hearts would not be frightened –
they might even consider it a marvel of the Eternally-Besought's
Power. A rationalist but nonbelieving philosopher might tremble at the sight of a comet, lest it should strike Earth.

Our ability to meet our endless demands is negligible. We are
threatened with afflictions that our own strength cannot withstand.
Our strength is limited to what we can reach, yet our wishes and
demands, suffering and sorrow, are as wide as our imagination.

Anyone not wholly blind to the truth understands that our
best option is to submit to God, to worship, believe, and have
confidence in Him. A safe road is preferable to a dangerous one,
even one with a very low probability of safe passage. The way
of belief leads one safely to endless bliss with near certainty; the
way of unbelief and transgression, meanwhile, is not profitable
and has a near certainty of endless loss. Even its travelers agree
on this truth, as do countless experts and people of insight and
observation.

In conclusion, just like the other world's bliss, happiness in
this world depends upon submitting to God and being His devoted servant. So always praise Him, saying: "Praise be to God for
obedience and success in His way," and thank Him that we are His
believing and worshipping servants.

Who Must Pray?

Prayer is obligatory upon every sane Muslim who has reached the
age of puberty. Only women having their menstrual period or
post-childbirth bleeding do not perform it. Prepubescent children
do not have to pray, but God's Messenger, upon him be peace and
blessings, advises us to tell them to pray when they reach the age
of 7 in order to prepare their hearts for it.

The Times of the Five Daily Prescribed Prayers

Every sane, adult Muslim must perform the five daily prescribed prayers each within its own time. The Qur'an mentions these times. For example:

> Establish the prayer at the beginning and the end of the day, and in the watches of night near to the day. Assuredly, good deeds wipe out evil deeds. This is advice and a reminder for the mindful who take heed. (11:114)

> Establish the prayer from the declining of the sun to the darkness of the night, and (be ever mindful of) the Qur'an's recitation at dawn. Assuredly, the Qur'an's recitation at dawn is witnessed (by angels and the whole creation awakening to a new day). (17:78)

> Bear patiently what they say, and glorify your Lord with His praise before the rising of the sun, and before its setting, and during some of the hours of the night glorify Him, and at the sides of the day, that you may become pleased with the reward which God shall give you. (20:130)

> Glory be to God whenever you reach evening and whenever you rise in the morning. All praise is for Him in the heavens and on Earth, in the late afternoon, and whenever you reach the noon. (30:17-18)

These verses circumscribe the five prescribed prayers. The prayers to be established at the sides of the day, at its beginning and end from the declining of the sun to the darkness of night, are the noon and afternoon prayers. The original word for "watches of night near to the day" is *zulef*, which is plural. In Arabic, plural includes at least three things, so it can be concluded that it refers to the three prayers to be established during night (e.g., the evening, late evening, and dawn [early morning] prayers). These five prayers were prescribed for the Muslims during the Messenger's Ascension in the ninth year of his Messengership, 4 years before the Hijra.

Verse 17:78 also alludes to the daily five prescribed prayers and each one's time. *Declining of the sun* means the sun's passing its zenith, and therefore hints at the noon prayer. After the noon prayer comes the afternoon prayer. Immediately after sunset and after night has fallen, the evening and late evening prayers are performed, respectively. The verse specifically mentions the dawn prayer because of its importance, and draws attention to reciting the Qur'an during it, for the Messenger, under Divine Revelation, used to lengthen his recitation during that prayer.

Some of the *hadiths* (i.e., Tirmidhi, "Salat," 1) narrate the Messenger's statements about the exact time of each prayer. According to these *hadiths*, as well as the practice of the Prophet and his Companions, the time of each prayer is as follows:

- The *fajr* (dawn or early morning) prayer is performed from the break of dawn until sunrise.
- The *zuhr* (noon) prayer is performed when the sun passes its zenith until a person's shadow is the same length as his or her height.
- The *'asr* (afternoon) prayer is performed when a person's shadow is the same length as his or her height and continues until the yellowing of the sun.
- The *maghrib* (evening) prayer is performed as long as twilight lasts until the sun's complete disappearance.
- The *'isha'* (night) prayer begins with the end of twilight and continues until a short while before the break of dawn.
- The *Jumu'a* prayer is performed during the time of the noon prayer on Friday. The time of the 'Iyd (religious festive days) prayers is some three quarters after sunrise on 'Iyd days. Their time continues until the sun reaches its zenith.

The Times When Prayers Cannot Be Performed

- During sunrise and sunset.
- From sunrise until the sun has completely risen to the length of a spear above the horizon (approximately three quarters after sunrise).
- When the sun is at its zenith until it moves slightly to the west.
- After the afternoon prayer till the sun sets.

Prayers must not be offered during the approximately three quarters in the last three times in which praying is forbidden.

However, if one has not been able to perform the afternoon prayer during its time, one can perform it until the sun begins to disappear in the west.

The Meaning of Different Prayer Times[2]

Each prayer time is the opening of a significant turning point, a mirror to the Divine disposal of power as well as the universal Divine bounties therein. We are told to pray at those specific times to give more adoration and glory to the All-Powerful One of Majesty, and to give more thanks for the bounties accumulated between any two periods. To comprehend this subtle and profound meaning a little better, consider these five points:

First Point

Each prayer stands for praising, glorifying, and feeling grateful to God. We glorify Him by saying *Subhana'llah* (Glory be to God) by word and action in awareness of His Majesty. We exalt and magnify Him by saying *Allahu akbar* (God is the Greatest) through word and action in awareness of His Perfection. We offer thanks to Him by saying *al-hamdu lillah* (All praise be to God) with our heart, tongue, and body, in awareness of His Grace. From this, we conclude that the heart of prayer consists of glorification, exaltation, praise, and thanksgiving. Thus, these three phrases are present in all words and actions of those who pray. Further, following each prayer, they are repeated 33 times each to confirm and complete the prayer's objectives. The meaning of prayer is pronounced consecutively with these concise utterances.

Second Point

We are God's servants. Aware of our defects, weakness, and poverty in the Divine presence, we prostrate in love and awe before His Lordship's perfection, His Divine Might on which every creature relies, and His Divine Compassion. Just as His Lordship's sovereignty demands devotion and obedience, His Holiness requires us to see our defects and seek His pardon, to proclaim that He has no defect, that the false judgments of the ignorant are meaningless, and that He is beyond all failings of His creatures.

His Might's Perfection requires that, realizing our weakness and the helplessness of all creatures, we proclaim: "God is the Greatest" in admiration and amazement before the majesty of the Eternally Besought One's works. Bowing humbly, we are to seek refuge in Him and place our trust in Him. His Compassion's boundless treasury demands that we declare our need and those of all creatures by praying and asking for His help, and that we proclaim His blessings through praise and gratitude by uttering *al-hamdu lillah*. In short, the prayer's words and actions comprise all these meanings, and so were ordered and arranged by God.

Third Point

Each person is a miniature of the universe. In the same way, the Qur'an's first *sura* (chapter), *Surat al-Fatiha*, is an illuminated miniature of the whole Book, and the prayer is a bright index involving all ways of worship, a sacred map hinting at the diverse kinds of worship practiced by all living entities.

Fourth Point

The consecutive divisions of day and night, as well as the years and phases of our life, function like a huge clock's wheels and levers. For example:

The time for *fajr* (before sunrise) may be likened to spring's birth, the moment when sperm takes refuge in the protective womb, or to the first of the 6 consecutive days during which Earth and the heavens were created. It recalls how God disposes His Power and acts in such times and events. The time for *zuhr* (just past midday) may be likened to the completion of adolescence, the middle of summer, or the period of humanity's creation in the world's lifetime. It also points to God's compassionate manifestations and abundant blessings in those events and times.

The time for *'asr* (afternoon) resembles autumn, old age, and the time of the Last Prophet (the Era of Happiness). It calls to mind the Divine acts and the All-Compassionate's favors in them. The time for *maghrib* (sunset or evening) reminds us of many creatures' decline at the end of autumn and also of our own death. It thus forewarns us of the world's destruction at the Resurrection's beginning, teaches us how to understand the manifestation of God's Majesty, and wakes us from a deep sleep of neglect.

The time for *'isha'* (nightfall or late evening) calls to mind the world of darkness, veiling all daytime objects with its black shroud, and winter covering the dead Earth's surface with its white shroud. It brings to mind the remaining works of the dead being forgotten, and points to this testing arena's inevitable, complete decline. Thus *'isha'* proclaims the awesome acts of the Overpowering One of Majesty. Night reminds us of winter, the grave, the Intermediate World, and how much our spirit needs the All-Merciful One's Mercy. The late-night *tahajjud* prayer reminds and warns us of how necessary this prayer's light will be in the grave's darkness. By recalling the True Bestower's infinite bounties granted during these extraordinary events, it proclaims how worthy He is of praise and thanks.

The next morning points to the morning following the Resurrection. Just as morning follows night and spring comes after winter, so the morning of the Resurrection or "spring" follows the intermediate life.

We understand that each appointed prayer time is the beginning of a vital turning point and a reminder of greater revolutions or turning points in the universe's life. Through the awesome daily disposals of the Eternally Besought One's Power, the prayer times remind us of the Divine Power's miracles and the Divine Mercy's gifts regardless of time and place. So the prescribed prayers, which are an innate duty, the basis of worship, and an unquestionable obligation, are most appropriate and fitted for these times.

Fifth Point

We are created weak, yet everything involves, affects, and saddens us. We have no power, yet are afflicted by calamities and enemies. We are extremely poor, yet have many needs. We are indolent and incapable, yet the burden of life is very heavy. Being human, we are connected with the rest of the world, yet what we love and are familiar with disappears, and the resulting grief causes us pain. Our mentality and senses inspire us toward glorious objectives and eternal gains, but we are unable, impatient, powerless, and have only a short lifetime.

Given all of this, several things become quite clear:

The *fajr* prayer is essential, for we must present a petition before the day's activities begin. Through prayer and supplication, we must beseech the Court of an All-Powerful One of Majesty, an All-Compassionate One of Grace, for success and help. Such support is necessary to bear and endure the troubles and burdens waiting for us.

The *zuhr* prayer is essential, for this is when the day starts to move forward to complete its course. People take a break from their activities. The spirit needs a pause from the heedlessness and insensibility caused by hard work, and Divine bounties are fully manifest. Praying at this time is good, necessary, agreeable, and proper. This prayer gives relief from the pressures of daily life and heedlessness. We stand humbly in the presence of the Real Bestower of blessings, express gratitude, and pray for His help. We bow to demonstrate helplessness before His Glory and Might, and prostrate to proclaim our wonder, love, and humility before His everlasting Perfection and matchless Grace.

The *'asr* prayer resembles and recalls the sad season of autumn, the mournful state of old age, and the distressing period at the end of time. The day's tasks are brought toward completion, and the Divine bounties received that day (e.g., health, safety, and good service in the way of God) have accumulated to form a great total. It is also the time when the sun fades away, proving that everything is impermanent. We, who long for eternity, are created for it and show reverence for favors received, also are saddened by separations. So we stand up, perform *wudu'* (ablution), and pray.

Thus praying *'asr* is an exalted duty, an appropriate service, a reasonable way of paying a debt of gratitude, and an agreeable pleasure. We acquire peace of mind and find true consolation and ease of spirit by supplicating at the Eternal Court of the Everlasting, the Eternally Self-Subsistent One, and by seeking refuge in His infinite Mercy, offering thanks and praise for His countless bounties, bowing humbly before His Lordship's Might and Glory, and prostrating humbly before His Eternal Divinity.

Evening reminds us of winter's beginning, the sad farewells of summer and autumn creatures, and our sorrowful separation from loved ones through death. The sun's lamp is extinguished, and Earth's inhabitants will emigrate to the other world following this one's destruction. It is also a severe warning for those who adore transient, ephemeral beloveds, each of whom will die.

By its nature, the human spirit longs for an Eternal Beauty. During this prayer, it turns toward the Eternal Being, Who creates and shapes everything, Who commands huge heavenly bodies. At this time, the human spirit refuses to rely on anything finite and cries *Allahu akbar* (God is the Greatest). Then, in His presence, we say *al-hamdu lillah* (all praise be to God) to praise Him in the awareness of His faultless Perfection, matchless Beauty and Grace, and infinite Mercy.

Afterwards, by declaring: *You alone do we worship, and from You alone do We seek help* (1:5), we offer our worship of, and seek help from, His unassisted Lordship, unpartnered Divinity, and unshared Sovereignty. Bowing before His infinite Greatness, limitless Power, and perfect Honor and Glory, we demonstrate, with the rest of creation, our weakness and helplessness, humility and poverty by saying: "Glory be to my Lord, the Mighty." Prostrating in awareness of the undying Beauty and Grace of His Essence, His unchanging sacred Attributes, and His constant everlasting Perfection, we proclaim, through detachment from all that is not Him, our love and servanthood in wonder and self-abasement. Finding an All-Beautiful Permanent, an All-Compassionate Eternal One to Whom we say: "Glory be to my Lord, the Most Exalted," we declare our Most Exalted Lord free of any decline or fault.

After that, we sit reverently and willingly offer all creatures' praises and glorifications to the Eternal, All-Powerful, and All-Majestic One. We also ask God to bestow peace and blessings on His holy Messenger in order to renew our allegiance to him, proclaim our obedience to His commands, and renew and strengthen our belief. By observing the universe's wise order, we testify to the Creator's Oneness and the Messengership of Muhammad, upon him be peace and blessings, herald of the sovereignty of God's Lordship, proclaimer of what pleases Him, and interpreter of the Book of the Universe's signs or verses.

Given this, how can we be truly human if we do not realize what the evening prayer represents: an agreeable duty, a valuable and pleasurable service, a fine and beautiful worship, a serious matter, a significant conversation with the Creator, and a source of permanent happiness in this transient guest-house?

The time of *'isha'* (nightfall), when night covers Earth, reminds us of the mighty disposals of God's Lordship as the Changer of Night and Day. It calls to our mind the Divine activities of the All-Wise One of Perfection as the Subduer of the sun and the moon, observed in His turning the white page of day into the black page of night, and in His changing summer's beautifully colored script into winter's frigid white page. It recalls His acts as the Creator of Life and Death in sending the dead entity's remaining works to another world. It reminds us of God's majestic control and graceful manifestations as the Creator of the Heavens and Earth, and that this narrow, mortal, and lowly world will be destroyed. The same is true for the unfolding of the broad, eternal, and majestic world of the Hereafter. It also warns that only the One Who so easily turns day into night, winter into summer, and this world into the other world can be the universe's Owner and True Master. Only He is worthy to be worshipped and truly loved.

At nightfall our spirits, which are helpless and weak, poor and needy, tossed to and fro by circumstances and whirling onward into an unknown future, perform the *'isha'* prayer. We say, like Abraham: *I do not love those that set* (6:76). We seek refuge at the Court of the Ever-Living, the Ever-Worshipped, the Eternal Beloved One. From our transient life in this dark, fleeting world and dark future, we beseech the Enduring, Everlasting One. For a moment of unending conversation, a few seconds of immortal life, we seek the All-Merciful and Compassionate's favors. We ask for the light of His guidance that will illuminate our world and our future, and bind up the pain from the decline of all creatures and friends.

We forget the world, which has left us for the night, and pour out our heart's grief at the Court of Mercy. Before death-like sleep comes, after which anything can happen, we perform our "last" duty of worship. To close our day's activities on a favorable note, we pray and enter the Eternal Beloved and Worshipped One's presence, rather than the mortal ones we loved all day; the All-Powerful and Generous One's presence, rather than the impotent creatures from which we begged all day; and the All-Compassionate Protector's presence in the hope of being saved from the evil of the harmful creatures before which we trembled all day.

We start the prayer with *Surat al-Fatiha*, which extols praising the Lord of the worlds, Perfect and Self-Sufficient, Compassionate and All-Generous. We move on to *You alone do We worship* (1:5). That is, despite our insignificance and being alone, our connection with the Owner of the Day of Judgment, the Eternal Sovereign, causes us to be treated like an indulged guest and important officer. Through *You alone do we worship and from You alone do we seek help* (1:5), we offer Him the worship of all creatures and seek His assistance for them. Saying *Guide us to the Straight Path* (1:6), we ask to be guided to eternal happiness and the radiant way.

Saying "God is the Greatest," we bow down and contemplate the Grandeur of the Majestic One, Who orders hidden suns and waking stars, that are like individual soldiers subject to His command just like the plants and animals that have now gone to sleep, and are His lamps and servants in this world.

We think of the universal prostration of all creatures. That is, like the creatures that have gone to sleep at night, when all creation living in a certain age or period is discharged from the duty of worship by the command of *"Be!" and it is* like a well-ordered army of obedient soldiers, and is sent to the World of the Unseen, it prostrates on the rug of death in perfect orderliness saying: "God is the Greatest." They are resurrected in the spring by an arousing, life-giving trumpet-blast from the command of *"Be!" and it is*, and rise up to serve their Lord. Insignificant humanity makes the same declaration in the presence of the All-Merciful One of Perfection, the All-Compassionate One of Grace, in won-

der-struck love, eternity-tinged humility, and dignified self-efface-
ment. We then prostrate and achieve a sort of Ascension.

Thus each prescribed prayer time points to a mighty revolution, is a sign to the Master's tremendous activity, and a token
of the universal Divine bounties. And so this matter is a result
of perfect wisdom.

Adhan (Call to prayer)

The *adhan* calls Muslims to prayer. Although it consists of few
words, it covers the essentials of faith, expresses Islamic practices, is a form of worship, and one of Islam's collective symbols
that shows that the place in which it is made is a Muslim land.
It is made at the beginning of each prescribed prayer's time, and
should be made by the man who can perform it in the best way
possible. Even if one is performing the prayer alone, he or she
is strongly advised to make it before beginning to pray.

The words of *adhan* are as follows:

Allahu akbar (God is the Greatest): 4 times.
Ashhadu an la ilaha illa'llah (I bear witness that there is no
deity but God): twice.
Ashhadu anna Muhammadan Rasululu'llah (I bear witness
that Muhammad is God's Messenger); twice.
Hayya 'ala's-salah (Come on, to prayer): twice.
Hayya 'ala'l-falah (Come on, to salvation): twice.
Allahu akbar (God is the Greatest): twice.
La ilaha illa'llah (I bear witness that there is no deity but
God): once.

The *adhan* for the dawn (early morning) prayer includes *as-
salatu khayrun mina'n-nawm* (Prayer is better than sleep [twice])
after *hayya 'ala'l-falah* (Come on, to salvation). God's Messenger
highly recommends that we pray after making the *adhan*.

The Obligatory Acts before the Prayer

For the prayer to be complete and acceptable by God, one must
perform the following acts:

- Purify oneself from all major and minor impurity by performing *ghusl* (the major ablution) and *wudu'* (the minor ablution), respectively. If one has not broken *wudu'* between two prayer times, it does not need to be renewed before the next prayer. The Prophet strongly recommended that one should clean his or her teeth with a *miswak*, or at least something clean, while making *wudu'*.

- Remove any impurity from one's clothes, body, and place of prayer. The impurities that invalidate prayer were mentioned in the section on *tahara*. They are divided into two categories: gross impurity (*najasat al-ghaliza*) or weak impurity (*najasat al-khafifa*). Vomit, urine, excrement, *wadi* (a thick white secretion discharged after urination), *mazi* (a white sticky fluid that flows from the sexual organs when thinking about sexual intercourse or foreplay, and so on), prostatic fluid, are included in gross impurity. Also included in this category are the urine, saliva, and blood of all animals whose meat is forbidden, the excrement of all animals (except birds) whose meat is allowable, the excrement of poultry (geese, hens, and ducks), any part of pigs, and alcohol. Any such solid filth that weighs more than 3 grams, and any liquid more than the amount that spreads over one's palm, invalidates the prayer.

- The urine of horses and domestic or wild animals whose meat is allowed is weak impurity. If such impurity is more than one-fourth of a limb or smears more than one-fourth of one's clothes, the prayer is invalidated.

- Covering the area of the body that cannot be shown in public. For the men, this is from the knee to the navel; for women, the whole body except the face, hands, and feet.

- Facing the *qibla* (the direction of the Sacred Mosque in Makka) during the prayer. If one does not know its location, one must search for it. If one prays in another direction after searching, the prayer is valid. If the chest is turned from the *qibla* during prayer, the prayer is invalid. If the head is turned even for a moment, the person must immediately turn it back toward the *qibla*.

- Performing the prayer in its time.

The Obligatory Acts during the Prayer

- Make the intention to perform a specific prayer. Bukhari, Muslim, and Abu Dawud relate from 'Umar that God's Messenger said: "Actions are judged according to intentions. One is rewarded for whatever one intends to do. Whoever emigrates for God and His Messenger has emigrated for God and His Messenger; whoever emigrates to acquire something worldly or to marry has emigrated for what is intended." (Bukhari, "Bed'ul-Wahy," 1; Muslim, "Iman," 155.) Thus the intention is the aim and purpose of something. It is a condition of the heart and does not have to be spoken out loud. This is why the Prophet and his Companions never spoke their intentions.

- Say the opening *takbir* and begin the prayer. When God's Messenger stood for prayer, he would stand straight, raise his hands as high as his ears, and, with his palms facing the *qibla*, say: *"Allahu akbar."*

- Stand while reciting *Surat al-Fatiha* (the Opening Chapter of the Qur'an) and a selection of verses. One must stand during the obligatory prayers, if at all possible. But if this is not possible, the prayer can be performed while sitting or, if even that is not possible, while lying on one's right side. The feet should be kept about a span or a little more apart while standing in prayer. The voluntary (supererogatory) prayers can be offered while sitting, although standing will bring a greater reward.

- Recite *Surat al-Fatiha* and another portion from the Qur'an. This is obligatory in the first two *rak'ats* (cycles) of the obligatory prayers and in every *rak'at* of necessary (*wajib*), recommended (*sunna*), and supererogatory (*nafila*) prayers. In the last cycle (i.e., the third *rak'at* of the evening prayer and the last two *rak'ats* of the obligatory noon, afternoon, and late evening prayers), reciting *al-Fatiha* is preferable, but one can glorify (*Subhana'llah*), praise (*al-hamdu li'llah*), exalt (*Allahu akbar*) God, and declare His Unity (*La ilaha illa'llah*). The portion to be recited after *Surat al-Fatiha* should be as long as the shortest *sura* (*Surat al-Kawthar*).

No translation of the Qur'an can be recited during the prayer, for the Qur'an is composed of both its meaning and wording and is from God with both its meaning and wording.

• Bow down and remain in that position (*ruku*) for some time (long enough to say "*Subhana'llah*" three times). The position of ruku' consists of bending down and grasping the knees with the palms, and leaving the fingers partly spread apart. This position is maintained until one attains "calmness." The back must be kept straight while bowing.

• Prostrate (*sujud*). God's Messenger explains: "Prostrate until you are calm in your prostration, then rise (and sit) until you are calm in your sitting, and then prostrate until you are calm in your prostration." The first prostration, sitting afterwards, the second prostration, and calmness during all of these acts are obligatory in every *rak'at* of every type of prayer offered.

  Bukhari relates ("Adhan," 133, 134, 137) from God's Messenger, concerning the parts of the body that must touch the ground during prostration, that he said: "I have been ordered to prostrate on seven bodily parts: the forehead (and he also pointed to his nose), the hands, the knees and the ends of the feet."

• The final sitting and recital of the *tashahhud*. In the prayer's last *rak'at*, one must sit long enough to recite the *tashahhud* before ending the prayer with giving greetings by turning one's head to the right and then to the left and saying: "*As-salamu 'alaykum wa rahmatu'llah*" (Upon you be peace and God's mercy). During this sitting, one says the tashahhud or tahiyyat. Reciting words of *salat wa salam* (God's peace and blessings) on Muhammad and his Family is necessary.

Necessary (But Not Obligatory) Things To Complete the Prayer

• To complete the prayer, one must recite correctly, understandably, and distinctly; carry out all of the obligatory acts correctly and in the proper order; attain calmness; straighten the body while standing, bowing down, and prostrating; bow, prostrate, and stand after bowing and before prostrating and sit between prostrations as long as it takes to say *Subhana'llah* at least.

- Unless there is an acceptable impediment, prayers should be performed in congregation.
- One who prays alone should recite *al-Fatiha* and a portion from the Qur'an inaudibly in both the prescribed or supererogatory prayers performed during the day. One can recite loudly or inaudibly during the night prayers. In congregation, the imam (the one leading the prayer) should recite audibly in all *rak'ats* of the morning, *jumu'a, tarawih,* and *witr* prayers, and the first two *rak'ats* of the evening and late evening prayers. He should recite inaudibly in all *rak'ats* of the noon and afternoon prayers, the last one *rak'at* of the evening prayer, and the last two *rak'ats* of the late evening prayer.
- Sitting between the second and third *rak'ats* of those prayers having three or four *rak'ats.*
- The obligatory acts during prayers should be done one after the other, without doing anything extra between them.
- Ending the prayer by giving greetings on both sides and saying *as-salamu 'alaykum wa-rahmatu'llah.*
- Having sincerity, humility, and concentration. Prayer is the most important kind of worship, so it must be performed in the best way possible. In addition to fulfilling its obligatory and necessary acts, praying in humility, with utmost sincerity and self-concentration on God are essential.

Sunna Acts

Each prayer contains certain acts that are *sunna,* meaning that the Messenger, upon him be peace and blessings, performed them and advised Muslims to do likewise. They are highly important for completing the prayer and receiving a greater reward.

- While beginning the prayer and saying the opening *takbir,* one should raise one's hands (according to the Hanafis) as high as the ears and the thumbs touch the earlobes.
- According to the Hanafis, the hands should be placed below the navel, (the Shafi'is say below the chest), and the right hand should grasp the wrist of the left arm.
- The prayer should begin with a supplication used by the Prophet, upon whom be peace, to begin his prayers. This is

said after the opening takbir and before reciting *al-Fatiha*. The Hanafis prefer: *Subhanaka'llahumma wa bi-hamdik. Wa tebaraka'smuk. Wa ta'ala jadduk. Wa la ilaha ghayruk.* (Glory be to You, O God, and to You is the praise. Blessed is Your Name and most high is Your honor. There is no deity besides You). The Shafi'is prefer: *Inni wajjahtu wajhiya li'llezi fatara's-samawati wa'l-ardi hanifan wa ma ana mine'l-mushrikin. Inna salati wa nusuki wa mahyaya wa mamati li'llahi Rabbi'l-alamin, la sharika lah; wa bi-dhalike umirtu; wa ana mina'l-muslimin* (I have turned my face to the One Who has originated the heavens and Earth as a sincere submissive one, and I am not one of the polytheists. My prayers, my sacrifice, my life and my death are all for God, the Lord of the Worlds. He has no partner. That is what I have been ordered and I am of those who submit.). Other supplications related from the Messenger also can be recited before *al-Fatiha*.

- Saying *Amin* after reciting *al-Fatiha*.
- Reciting considerably long passages from the Qur'an after *al-Fatiha* in the morning (about one page or more in each *rak'at*, being longer in the first one), noon, and afternoon prayers (about one page), either a somewhat long or shorter passages in the evening prayers, and short passages in the late evening prayer.
- Saying the *takbir* upon every bowing down, sitting down, moving to and rising from prostration, and standing up after sitting. Upon rising from the bowing, all Muslims should say: "*Sami'a'llahu li-man hamidah*" (God hears him who praises Him), and after it, "*Rabbana wa-laka'l-hamd*" (Our Lord, and to You is all praise).
- Saying "*Subhana Rabiyya'l-'Azim*" (Glory be to my Lord, the Mighty) three times while bowing, and "*Subhana Rabbiya'l-A'la*" (Glory be to my Lord, the Most High) while prostrating.
- Supplicating after the final *tashahhud* and before giving the final salutations (that end the prayer). These may consist of any supplication mentioned in the Qur'an or reported from the Messenger.

- Saying words of remembrance, asking forgiveness, and sup-
plicating after the prayer. The most famous and widespread
one reported from the Messenger is: *Astaghfiru'llaha'l-'Azim*
(I ask God the Mighty for forgiveness: three times), and
*Allahumma anta's-Salamu wa minka's-salam. Tabarakta ya
Dha'l-Jalali wa'l-Ikram* (O God, You are the Peace, and from
You is peace. All blessed and One bestowing blessings You
are, O One of Majesty and Munificence). Afterwards, reciting *Ayat al-Kursiy* (2:255) and saying words of glorification
(Subhana'llah), praise (*al-hamdu li'llah*), and exaltation (*Allahu
akbar*) each 33 times.

Disliked and Discouraged Things

- Beginning the prayer while feeling the need to answer a call
of nature.
- Omitting any *sunna* act.
- Thinking about worldly affairs while praying.
- Doing things that cannot be reconciled with being in God's
presence (e.g., cracking one's knuckles, playing with any part
of the body or clothes, smoothing the stones on the ground,
putting the hands on the hips while bending down or standing up, yawning, blowing something, coughing, or cleaning
the throat without a valid excuse).
- Leaning on a post, a wall, or something similar without a valid
excuse.
- Praying while having something to eat or chew in the mouth,
regardless of its size.
- Praying while angry or hungry, when food has been placed
nearby, or wearing something that may distract one's attention.
- Praying in the path of people who are passing in front of one.

Things That Invalidate the Prayer

- Omitting any of the prayer's obligatory acts, regardless if
doing so is intentional or out of ignorance or forgetfulness.
- Uttering a word, even if only 2 letters long, that is not included in the recitations of the prayer.

- Weeping, sighing and complaining about worldly things, and making any noise (except clearing the throat, coughing, or yawning) or speaking. Only weeping unintentionally out of fear or love of God and similar things does not invalidate the prayer.
- Answering any call or salutation.
- Reciting the Qur'an or supplications so incorrectly that it cannot be found in the Qur'an or among the reports from the Messenger and transforms the meaning so that it violates Islamic truths and principles.
- Saying prayers that are not found in the Qur'an or reported from the Messenger, and concerning worldly things, such as, "O Lord, enable me to pay my debts," or "Lord, let me marry such-and-such a woman (or man)."
- Moving aside or changing places when asked or ordered to do so by one who is not praying.
- Doing something that makes someone else think that one is not praying.
- Doing something that invalidates ritual purity.
- Turning one's chest from the *qibla*.
- Eating or swallowing anything bigger than a chickpea grain that has remained between the teeth.

How To Pray

The dawn (early morning [fajr]) prayer

Having done what is necessary to have the prayer accepted, one recites the *iqama* even if praying alone. Women are not required to recite the *iqama*. The iqama is as follows:

Allahu akbar (God is the Greatest): 4 times.

Ashhadu an la ilaha illa'llah (I bear witness that there is no deity but God): twice.

Ashhadu anna Muhammadan Rasululu'llah (I bear witness that Muhammad is God's Messenger); twice.

Hayya 'ala's-salah (Come on, to prayer): twice.

Hayya 'ala'l-falah (Come on, to salvation): twice.

Qad qamatu's-salah (Now the prayer is about to be performed): twice.

Allahu akbar (God is the Greatest): twice.

La ilaha illa'llah (I bear witness that there is no deity but God): once.

One should pause between each phrase of the *adhan*, but be quick when reciting the *iqama*.

After the *iqama*, one intends to perform the dawn prayer, and, while reciting the opening *takbir*, raises the hands with the palms facing the *qibla* to one's ears, with the thumbs touching the earlobes, and then puts them (according to the Hanafis) under the navel with the right hand grasping the left one at the wrist. Then, recite a supplication with which the Prophet, upon whom be peace, used to begin his prayers. The Hanafis prefer: *Subhanaka'llahumma wa bi-hamdik. Wa tabaraka'smuk. Wa ta'ala jadduk. Wa la ilaha ghayruk* (Glory be to You, O God, and to You is the praise. Blessed is Your Name and most high is Your honor. There is no deity besides You.).

Then recite *Surat al-Fatiha*, say Amin at its end, and recite a portion from the Qur'an. Then bow down and say: *Allahu akbar* and, attaining calmness with one's back straightened, say three times: *Subhana Rabiyya'l-'Azim* (Glory be to my Lord, the Mighty). Afterwards, rise up and say: *Sami'a'llahu li-man hamidah* (God hears him who praises Him), and then: *Rabbana wa-laka'l-hamd* (Our Lord, and to You is all praise). After a short pause, prostrate and say: *Allahu akbar* with one's palms, knees, toes, forehead, and nose touching the ground. While prostrating, recite three times: *Subhana Rabbiya'l-A'la* (Glory be to my Lord, the Most High). Then, sit up and say: *Allahu akbar*, and, after a short pause while sitting, prostrate again and say: *Allahu akbar*. Recite the same things that were recited during the first prostration. This is the first *rak'at* in all prayers except the 'Iyd (religious festive day) prayers and *salat al-tasbih* (prayer of glorification), which will be described below.

Rise from prostration saying: *Allahu akbar*, and then perform the second *rak'at* just as the first one was performed. After the second prostration, sit up and recite the *tashahhud* or *tahiyy-at*, which is as follows: *At-tahiyyatu li'llahi wa's-salawatu wa't-tayyibatu as-salamu 'alayka ayyuha'n-nabiyyu wa-rahmatu'llahi wa-barakatuh. As-salamu 'alayna wa 'ala 'ibadi'llahi's-salihin. Ashhadu an la ilaha illa'llah wa ashhadu anna Muhammadan 'abduhu wa-rasuluh* (Eternity and all dominion is God's, and from Him are all blessings and benedictions. Peace be upon you O the [greatest] Prophet, and God's mercy and gifts. Peace be also upon us and God's righteous servants. I bear witness that there is no deity but God, and I also bear witness that Muhammad is His servant and Messenger.).

Afterwards, one calls God's blessings and peace upon His Messenger: *Allahumma salli 'ala Muhammadin wa 'ala Al-i Muhammad, kama sallayta 'ala Ibrahima wa 'ala Al-i Ibrahim. Innaka Hamidun Majid. Allahumma barik 'ala Muhammadin wa 'ala Al-i Muhammad, kama barakta 'ala Ibrahima wa 'ala Al-i Ibrahim. Innaka Hamidun Majid* (O God, bestow Your blessings upon our master Muhammad and the Family of Muhammad, as You bestowed Your blessings upon Abraham and the Family of Abraham. Assuredly, You are All-Praised, All-Illustrious. O God, send Your abundant gifts and favors unto our master Muhammad and the Family of Muhammad, as You sent them unto Abraham and the Family of Abraham. Assuredly, You are All-Praised, All-Illustrious.).

Then, pray to God. Choose prayers from the Qur'an and the prayers of God's Messenger, upon him be peace and blessings. Then, give greetings, turning your head to your right and left, saying: *As-salamu 'alaykum wa rahmatu'llah* (Peace be upon you, and God's Mercy.). While giving greetings on your right, direct them to those sitting on the right (if praying in congregation) and the noble angel who records our good deeds, and while giving greetings on your left, direct them to those sitting on the left (if praying in congregation) and the noble angel who records our evil deeds. However, according to Bediüzzaman Said Nursi, one may also intend, while giving greetings on the right, God's Messenger, other Messengers, the believing members of their families, Companions, and all other saintly, pure, and scholarly people who have emigrated to the other world and, while giving greetings on the left, all believers to come until the Last Day.

The noon, afternoon, and night (zuhr, 'asr, and 'isha') prayers

Having done what is necessary to have the prayer accepted, recite *iqama* even if praying alone. Women are not required to recite *iqama*.

Then, perform the first two *rak'at*s just as in the dawn prayer, except that when sitting in the second *rak'at*, recite the *tashahhud*, stand up, and say: *Allahu akbar* (God is the Greatest). Perform another two *rak'at*s without reciting the opening *takbir*, and, while standing, recite only *al-Fatiha* preferably; although you can recite, instead of *al-Fatiha*, words of glorification (*Subhana'llah*), praise (*al-hamdu li'llah*), and exaltation (*Allahu akbar*); and declare God's Oneness (*La ilaha illa'llah*). While sitting in the last (fourth) *rak'at*, recite that which was recited in the dawn and all other prayers. End the prayer by giving salutations to the right and left.

The evening (maghrib) prayer

One begins the prayer and prays the first two *rak'at*s as outlined above. After reciting the *tashahhud* while sitting in the second *rak'at*, perform the third *rak'at* in the same way as the third *rak'at* of the noon, afternoon, and late evening prayers. However, after the second prostration, sit again, as in the second (or last sitting) of the other prayers or in the second *rak'at* of the dawn prayer. Do what is done in them.

Prostrations of Forgetfulness

If any of the necessary acts are omitted or delayed for some time due to forgetfulness (e.g., sitting between the second and third *rak'at*s of those prayers having three or four *rak'at*s, stopping between the obligatory acts more than a few seconds, or omitting the qunut in the *witr* prayer) after giving the first salutation to the right, make two prostrations just like the other prostrations and recite the *tashahhud (tahiyyat)* and calling of God's peace and blessings on God's Messenger. Then, give salutations and finish the prayer.

In the congregational prayer, the imam recites only the *tahiyyat* and the initial part of calling God's blessings and peace upon the Messenger and his Family (i.e., *Allahumma salli 'ala Muhammadin wa 'ala Al-i Muhammad*) before making the prostrations of forgetfulness.

Prostrating while Reciting

Whoever recites a verse of prostration or hears it, whether during a prayer or outside it, should pronounce the *takbir*, prostrate, recite *Subhana Rabbiya'l-A'la* three times, and rise from the prostration. There are 15 such verses in the Qur'an. If one of them is recited during a prayer, prostrate without interrupting the prayer and then continue it.

The *Sunna* Prayers

- Praying two *rak'at*s before the dawn prayer was highly recommended and stressed by God's Messenger. They are performed just as in the dawn prayer, except that one recites shorter Qur'anic passages after *al-Fatiha*.
- Praying four *rak'at*s before the noon prayer was highly advised and stressed by God's Messenger. They are performed just as in the noon prayer, except that one recites Qur'anic passages after *al-Fatiha* in all *rak'at*s. He also prayed another two or four *rak'at*s after the prescribed prayer, and Muslims are urged to follow his example.
- Praying four *rak'at*s before the afternoon prayer is also recommended. They are performed just as in the noon prayer, except that one recites the calls of God's blessings, peace, and gifts upon our master Muhammad and his Family after the *tashahhud* during the first sitting, and the supplication before *al-Fatiha* in the third *rak'at*, which one recites while beginning the prayer after the opening *takbir*.
- Praying two *rak'at*s after the evening and late evening prayer is highly recommended, while praying four *rak'at*s before the late evening prayer, just as in the afternoon prayer, is an unstressed *sunna* prayer.

Tahajjud and Witr

The *tahajjud* prayer has an extremely important place among the highly advisable, stressed *sunna* prayers. It was obligatory for the Messenger from the very beginning of his mission. Interrupting sleep for God's sake and turning to Him with devotion and pure feelings during the night is a great support and source of feeding for human spirit. While ordering the Messenger to pray it, the Almighty declared:

> O you, folded in garments! Rise to pray by night, but not all night – half of it, or a little less, or a little more, and recite the Qur'an in measured rhythmic tones and with great care and attention. We are about to cast upon you a weighty Word. Indeed, rising by night is most potent and good for governing the soul, and most suitable for reciting and understanding the Word. There is for you by day prolonged occupation with ordinary duties. So, keep in remembrance of God's Name and mention It, dedicating yourself devoutly to Him. He is the Lord of the east and the west. There is no deity save Him. Take Him for your Guardian and Disposer of Affairs (73:1-9).

Since every Muslim is a devoted servant of God and dedicated to His cause, the *tahajjud* prayer's importance is clear. According to most acceptable reports from the Messenger, together with the *Witr* prayer, it consists of eleven *rak'at*s and is performed in cycles of two, just like the morning prayer (Bukhari, "Tahajjud," 10). Although the *witr* prayer can be performed after the late evening prayer before going to bed, so that one will not miss it because of sleep, its preferable time is after *tahajjud*. It consists of three *rak'at*s and is performed like the evening prayer, but with the following exceptions:

In the third *rak'at*, a Qur'anic passage and the *qunut* prayers are recited after *al-Fatiha*. Before praying *qunut*, say *takbir* (*Allahu akbar*) by raising the hands as is done when beginning the prayer. The Messenger's reported qunut prayers are: *Allahumma inna nasta'inuka wa nastaghfiruka wa nastahdika wa nu'minu bika wa natubu ilayk; wa natawwakkalu 'alayka wa nuthni 'alayka'l-khayra kullahu nashkuruka wa la nakfuruk. Wa nakhla'u wa natruku man yafjuruk. Allahumma iyyaka na'budu wa laka nusalli wa nasjudu wa ilayka nas'a wa nahfidu; narju rahmataka wa nakhsa 'adhaba-ka inna 'adhabaka bi'l-kuffari mulhiq* (O God! We ask You for help, forgiveness, and guidance. We believe in You and turn to You in repentance for our sins, and place our trust in You. We praise You by attributing all good to You, and thank You, and never feel ingratitude to You. We reject and cut our relations with those who are in constant rebellion against You. O God, You alone do we worship, and we pray and prostrate for You alone. We endeavor in Your way to obtain Your good pleasure and approval. We hope and expect Your Mercy and fear Your chastisement, for Your chastisement is to surround the unbelievers.).

Tarawih

The specific prayers during Ramadan, which are known as *tarawih*, are *sunna* for both men and women and are to be performed after the prescribed late evening prayer and before *witr*. As generally accepted, it consists of 20 *rak'ats* and is performed preferably in cycles of two *rak'ats*.

Tarawih prayers can be performed in congregation or alone. The majority of scholars, however, prefer to pray them in congregation. The Messenger, upon him be peace and blessings, prayed it in congregation but then stopped doing so, fearing that it would be made obligatory. 'Umar established the practice of praying *tarawih* behind one imam.

The Prayer of the Sick (Salat al-Marid)

Whoever cannot stand due to illness or another valid reason can pray sitting. If this is not possible, one can pray while lying on one's right side by making gestures. In such a case, the gestures for *sajda* should be lower than those for *ruku'*.

The Prayer during Times of Fear or Danger (Salat al-Khawf)

All scholars agree about the legality of such prayers:

> (O Messenger!) When you are among the believers (who are on an expedition and fear that the unbelievers might harm them) and rise to lead the prayer for them, let a party of them stand in prayer

with you and retain their arms (while letting the other party take their positions against the enemy). When the first party has prostrated (and finished the rak'at), let them go behind you (to take their positions against the enemy), and let the other party, which has not prayed, come forward and pray with you, being fully prepared against danger and retaining their arms. Those who disbelieve wish that you should be heedless of your weapons and your equipment, so that they might swoop upon you in a surprise attack. But there shall be no blame on you if you lay aside your arms (during prayer) if you are troubled by rain (and the ground impedes your movement), or if you are ill. However, (always) be fully prepared against danger. Surely God has prepared for the unbelievers a shameful, humiliating chastisement. (4:102)

The Prayer of a Traveler (Salat al-Musafir)

If one begins a journey of at least 3 days, one shortens the prescribed prayers of four *rak'at*s (the noon, afternoon, and night prayers) and offers them as two *rak'at*s, just like the dawn prayer. Since at that time travel was generally by foot and a day's travel was counted as 6 hours, the distance of 3 days on foot was regarded as 90 kilometers (54 miles). However, many contemporary scholars maintain that since many people now travel by bus or train, the above-mentioned prayers can be shortened only if the distance is around 1,200 kilometers (720 miles).

Travelers are defined as people who have left their home and their town. So long as they are traveling, the above-mentioned prayers can be shortened. If they reach a place and intend to stay there for less than 15 days, they are considered as travelers and are therefore allowed to shorten their prayers as outlined above. If they are still there on the fifteenth day for reasons beyond their control, although they originally intended to stay for less than 15 days, they are still considered travelers and can shorten the appropriate prayers. Most scholars opine that travelers may offer the *sunna* and supererogatory prayers without shortening them.

The main reason for shortening the above-mentioned prayers is traveling, not the hardships of travel. Thus, these prayers are shortened even if no difficulty is encountered while traveling. The cause for establishing a rule differs from its expected wisdom and benefit. Wisdom or benefit is the reason for its preference, while the cause requires its existence. So, traveling Muslims shorten their prayers. The cause for this Divine dispensation is traveling, and the underlying wisdom is the hardship of traveling. Thus prayers are shortened even if no hardship is encountered, for the cause exists. Muslims who encounter hardships while at home cannot shorten their prayers, for the wisdom or benefit cannot be the cause for this dispensation.

Those who are traveling must pray whether they are on a ship or a train or a plane, if the prayer will be missed before reaching a place where one can offer it.

Specific *Sunna* Prayers

Asking for What Is Good (Salat al-Istikhara)

The Messenger advised all Muslims to follow his practice when confronted with having to make a choice between permissible alternatives: pray two non-obligatory *rak'at*s and then ask God to enable one to choose what is good or better.

The Prayer of Glorification (Salat al-Tasbih)

Ibn 'Abbas reports that God's Messenger said to 'Abbas ibn 'Abd al-Muttalib:

> O 'Abbas, O Uncle, shall I not give you, present to you, donate to you, tell you of ten things which, if you do them, God will forgive your first and last sins, past and present sins, intentional and unintentional sins, private and public sins? The ten actions are: pray four *rak'at*s, reciting in every *rak'at* al-Fatiha and a *sura*. When you finish the Qur'anic recitation of the first *rak'at*, say, while standing: *Subhana'llah, al-hamdu li'llah, wa la ilaha illa 'llahu wa'llahu akbar* (Glory be to God, all praise be to God, there is no deity save God, and God is the greatest) 15 times. Then make *ruku'*, and while in *ruku'*, say the same phrases 10 times. Then stand and say the same 10 times. Then go down and make *sajda*, and while you are in *sajda*, say the same phrases 10 times. Then sit after *sajda* and say the same phrases 10 times. Then make *sajda* and say the same phrases 10 times. Then sit after the second *sajda*, and say the same phrases another 10 times. That is 75 (repetitions of the phrases) in each *rak'at*. Do

that in each of the four *rak'at*s. If you can pray it once a day, do
so. If you cannot, then once every Friday. If you cannot do that,
then once a year. And if you cannot do that, then once during
your life. (Abu Dawud, "Salat," 303; Tirmidhi, "Salat," 350.)

After saying the phrases 10 times following the second *sajda* in
the second *rak'at*, recite the *tashahhud* and calls of God's blessings
and peace upon the Messenger and his Family, and then end the
first two *rak'at*s by giving salutation. Pray the second two *rak'at*s in
the same way.

The Prayer for Need (Salat al-Haja)

Make the proper ablution, pray two *rak'at*s, and say the prayer
reported from the Messenger concerning it (Tirmidhi, "Witr," 345).
If God's overall Wisdom requires it to be met, God will grant
whatever is asked, either sooner or later.

The Prayer of Repentance (Salat al-Tawba)

Make the appropriate minor or major ablution, offer a prayer of two
*rak'at*s, and ask for His forgiveness. Hopefully, God will grant it.

The Prayer during a Solar or Lunar Eclipse (Salat al-Kusuf and al-Khusuf)

Scholars agree that this is a *sunna mu'akkada*, a stressed or confirmed one, which is to be performed by both men and women.
It is best, but not absolutely necessary, to pray it in congregation.
Its time is from the eclipse's beginning until its end. It is preferred to say *takbir*, supplicate, give charity, and ask God for forgiveness during the eclipse. It should be noted that this has nothing to do with asking for the eclipse to end, for its beginning and
end are clear. An eclipse is only an occasion for such a prayer.

The Prayer for Rain (Salat al-Istisqa')

This prayer is performed to entreat to God for rain during a drought.

Supererogatory Prayers

Supererogatory prayers are important in that they make up for any
deficiencies in performing the prescribed prayers and to bring us
closer to God, Who declares:

My servant cannot get near to Me through anything else more lovable to Me than doing the obligatory religious duties. However, by doing supererogatory duties he gets nearer to Me, and when he becomes near to Me, I shall be his eyes to see with, his ears to hear with, his hands to grasp with, and his legs to walk on. (Bukhari, "Riqaq," 38)

Supererogatory prayers are offered in cycles of two *rak'at*s. Praying two *rak'at*s when around three quarters have passed after sunrise (*ishraq*), two to eight *rak'at*s in broad daylight until the sun reaches its zenith (*duha*), and four *rak'at*s between the evening and late evening prayers (*awwabin*).

Such supererogatory prayers are important, for as recorded by Ahmad ibn Hanbal, Muslim, and Abu Dawud, the Messenger said the following about the *duha* (broad daylight) prayer:

Charity is required from every part of your body daily. Every saying of "Glory be to God" is charity. Every saying of "All praise be to God" is charity. Every saying of "There is no deity but God" is charity. Every saying of "God is the Greatest" is charity. Ordering good is charity. Eradicating evil is charity. And what suffices for that (as a charity) are the two *rak'at*s of the *duha* (broad daylight prayer). (Muslim, "Musafirun," 84)

Offering Supererogatory Prayers at Home

Ahmad ibn Hanbal and Muslim relate from Jabir that the Messenger of God said: "If one of you offers his prayers in the mosque, then he should offer a portion of his prayers at home, as God has made saying prayers in one's home a means of betterment (for him)." Ahmad records from 'Umar that the Messenger of God said: "The supererogatory prayers prayed by a person at home are a light. Whoever wishes should light up his house."

Reciting Long Passages

It is preferred to prolong one's recitation during supererogatory prayers. God's Messenger would stand and pray until his feet or shanks swelled. When he was asked about it, he said: "Should I not be a thankful servant?" (Bukhari, "Tahajjud," 16)

The Friday Congregational Prayer

The Friday congregational prayer is obligatory and a significant Islamic symbol. God's Messenger declared that God seals the heart of one who misses it three consecutive times without a valid excuse (Abu Dawud, "Salat," 215; Tirmidhi, "Salat," 359). It also has aspects concerning the Muslim community's political freedom and condition, and cannot be offered alone.

When and Who

It is offered during the noon prayer's time, for the latter prayer is not performed on Friday. Every free, adult, sane, and resident Muslim who can attend must attend, unless he has a valid reason not to do so. It is not obligatory upon women, children, those with valid excuses (e.g., illness, lack of security, extreme cold), and travelers.

Preparations

Increase prayers, supplications, and calling God's blessings and peace upon the Messenger and his Family on Friday, especially before the Friday prayer. Perform the major ablution (*ghusl*) and wear the best clothes and the best allowable perfume. It is recommended to follow the Messenger's example of reciting 10 verses from the beginning and end of *Surat al-Kahf*. Also, go to the mosque early.

Conditions for Its Validity

The Friday congregational prayer has aspects concerning the Muslim community's political freedom, as follows:
* It is offered in a city (*misr*) that contains a government or a village having 30, 40, or more houses – which looks like a city in its outward form.
* It is preferably offered in a central, large mosque and led by the district or city governor or imam (prayer leader) who is able to lead it and has been appointed by the governor to do so. In the capital city, it is preferably offered by the president or a capable imam appointed by him.

- There must be at least three people to form a congregation after the imam.

The Adhan

The call to prayer (*adhan*) is made before the Friday sermon.

The Sermon

A sermon must be made before the Friday prayer. The imam gives it on a pulpit while standing. He begins it by praising God and calling God's blessings and peace upon His Messenger and his Family. Next, he gives a sermon in which he exhorts Muslims to good deeds, discourages them from evil, advises them, and seeks to enlighten them mentally and spiritually and to guide them. He should not lengthen the sermon. After this part of the sermon, he sits for a short while and then, standing up, praises God, calls God's blessings and peace upon God's Messenger and his Family, and prays for all Muslims. The congregation must listen carefully and silently.

Prayers before and after the Friday Prayer

The Friday prayer consists of two *rak'ats*. It is sunna to offer four *rak'ats* before it, just like the four *rak'ats* offered before the noon prayer. After the prayer, another supererogatory prayer of four *rak'ats* is recommended.

Scholars have had some doubts about the Friday prayer's validity for many centuries, due the Muslim community's condition. Therefore, to be sure about performance of the prescribed noon prayer, they have ruled that another prayer of four *rak'ats*, just like the noon prescribed prayer and with the intention of offering a later noon prayer, should be offered after the four-*rak'at* supererogatory prayer. They also advise to follow this with another supererogatory prayer of two *rak'ats* with the intention of offering the *sunna* prayer for that time.

'Iyd (Religious Festive Days) Prayers (Salat al-'Iydayn)

The two 'Iyd prayers are considered necessary (*wajib*) and are to be offered on the two annual religious festive days: 'Iyd al-Fitr

Büyükçelebi: Living in the Shade of Islam

(marking the end of Ramadan) and 'Iyd al-Adha (on Dhu al-Hijja 10, the Day of Sacrifice). The former continues for 3 days, and the latter for 4 days.

The Religious Festive Days

On these days, Muslims visit, congratulate and offer gifts to one another, and display greater generosity by honoring the elders and pleasing the needy and children especially. They amuse themselves within religious and moral bounds, occupy themselves with reciting the Qur'an, mentioning God's Names, and supplicating. It is advisable to perform *ghusl* (major ablution) and wear the best clothes and religiously allowed perfume. On the Day of Sacrifice, they offer cattle or sheep or goats to God as a sacrifice, as will be explained below.

The Prayer

The 'Iyd prayers can be offered from when the sun is three spears above the horizon (approximately three quarters after sunrise) until it reaches its zenith. All men, women (regardless of marital status, age, or if they are menstruating), and children go to the place of prayer. Menstruating women do not attend the prayer. There is no *adhan* or *iqama*, unlike the Friday prayer.

Offering the 'Iyd Prayer

The 'Iyd prayer consists of two *rak'ats* and is offered like the Friday prayer, except for extra *takbirs (Allahu akbar* [God is the Greatest]). Like other prayers, the imam and the congregation make the intention and the opening *takbir*, and then recite the supplication silently. After the supplication and before reciting *al-Fatiha*, the imam leads the congregation in three extra *takbirs* by raising his hands while saying the opening *takbir*. After the first two *takbirs*, they leave their arms down, and after the third, they hold their hands under the navel and begin to recite *al-Fatiha*. After completing the first *rak'at* and reciting *al-Fatiha* and another Qur'anic passage in the second *rak'at*, the imam leads the congregation in extra *takbirs* again. This time they say four *tak-*

birs and, leaving the arms down after the first three, bow after the fourth one. Then they complete the prayer.

Sermon

After the prayer, the imam gives a sermon just as he does during the Friday congregational prayer.

Takbirs during the 'Iyds

Muslims must exalt God on the Festive Days of Sacrifice by pronouncing: *Allahu akbar, Allahu akbar; la ilaha illa'llahu wa'llahu akbar; Allahu akbar wa li'llahi'l-hamd* (God is the Greatest, God is the Greatest. There is no deity but God, and God is the Greatest. God is the Greatest and for His is all praise.). It is pronounced after every prescribed prayer after the dawn prayer on the day before the Festive Day, and ends after the afternoon prayer on the fourth day of 'Iyd.

RELIGIOUS FESTIVALS

Almost every nation has religious festivals to commemorate important events in its history or to celebrate special occasions. There are two religious festivals in Islam: 'Iyd al-Fitr (marking the end of Ramadan's month-long dawn-to-sunset fast) and 'Iyd al-Adha (the festival of sacrifice), which falls on Dhu'l-Hijja 10, the last month of the Islamic year in which the pilgrimage is performed. Both festivals enjoy a special place in the life of Muslims, and leave indelible impressions upon their cultures.

Religious festivals are times of deepened Islamic thoughts and occasions of paradoxical feelings – pangs of separation and hopes of reunion, regrets and expectations, and joys and sorrows.

Muslims enjoy the pleasure of reunion and universal brotherhood and sisterhood on festive days. They smile at each other lovingly, greet each other respectfully, and visit each other. Members of families divided by modern, industrialized life and forced to live in different towns come together and enjoy the delight of eating and living together once again, if only for a few days.

Religious festivals are occasions for spiritual revival through seeking God's forgiveness and through praising and glorifying Him. Muslims are enraptured by special supplications, odes, and eulogies for the Prophet, upon him be peace and blessings. Especially in traditional circles where traces of the past are still alive, people experience the festival's meaning in a more vivid, colorful fashion, on cushions or sofas, or around furnaces in their humble houses, or under the trees among their garden's flowers, or in the spacious halls of their homes. They feel its meaning in each morsel they eat, in each sip they drink, and in each word they speak about their traditional and religious values.

Religious festivals have a much greater significance for children. They feel a different joy and pleasure in the warm, embracing climate of the festivals, which they have been preparing to welcome a few days before. Like nightingales singing on branches of trees, they cause us to experience the festivals more deeply through their play, songs, smiles, and cheerfulness.

Religious festivals provide the most practical means for improving human relationships. People experience a deep inward pleasure, and meet and exchange good wishes in a blessed atmosphere of spiritual harmony. When the festival permeates hearts with prayer and supplications performed consciously, souls are elevated to the realm of eternity. They then feel the urge to abandon the clutches of worldly attachments and live in the depths of their spiritual being. In the atmosphere overflowing with love and mercy, a new hope is injected with life.

Believing souls welcome the religious festivals with wonder and expectations of otherworldly pleasures. Indeed, it is difficult to understand fully what believing souls feel in their hearts during these religious festivals. To perceive the feelings thus aroused in pure souls who lead their life in ecstasies of otherworldly pleasures, we must experience such pleasures to the same degree. Having reached the day of the festival after fulfilling their prescribed duty of praying and responsibility, these souls display such a dignity and serenity, and such a grace and spiritual perfection, that those who see them think that they have all received a perfect religious and spiritual education. Some of them are so sincere and devoted to God that each seems to be the embodiment of centuries-old universal values. One may experience through

> their conduct and manners that taste of the fruits of Paradise,
> the peaceful atmosphere on its slopes, and the delight of being
> near to God.
>
> (M. Fethullah Gülen, *Towards The Lost Paradise* [trans.], Kaynak, Izmir, 1995.)

The Funeral Prayer

The Rights of a Dead Muslim upon Living Muslims

A dead Muslim has four rights over living Muslims: The right to
be washed, shrouded, prayed over, and buried. However, Muslims
are not obliged to do so for those who die as apostates or while
fighting against them.

Visiting a Sick Person

It is a highly recommended and meritorious act to visit a sick
person. Muslims suggest to the dying that they should declare
God's Oneness: *La ilaha illa'llah, Muhammadun Rasulu'llah* (There
is no deity but God, and Muhammad is His Messenger) or the
profession of faith: *Ashhadu an la ilaha illa'llah wa ashhadu anna
Muhammadan 'abduhu wa rasuluh* (I bear witness that there is no
deity but God, and that Muhammad is His servant and Messenger.).

Washing the Corpse

When a Muslim dies, the corpse should be washed by a knowledgeable Muslim three times. Before washing, he or she is giv-
en minor ablution. Women wash dead women, and men wash
dead men. However, a woman can wash her dead husband. The
deceased's relatives and others should not see the corpse being
washed, and the corpse should be scented with camphor, musk,
and similar scents.

Offering the Funeral Prayer

After washing, a dead Muslim is wrapped in a shroud and put
in a coffin. This holds true for everyone except martyrs, who are
buried in the clothes in which they were martyred. The corpse
is placed upon a raised platform or a smooth stone so that its
right side faces the *qibla*. The congregation then stands to pray

before the corpse. While this prayer is obligatory upon all Muslims and must be prayed in congregation, when only some of them offer it, the others do not have to. Women also can attend.

The imam makes the intention to pray for the deceased (the deceased's gender should be specified) for God's sake and good pleasure. The congregation makes the same intention and then adds the intention to pray behind the imam. Then, following the imam, they begin the prayer with the opening *takbir* (as in all other prayers), supplicate, say *takbir* while keeping the hands under the navel, call God's blessings and peace upon His Messenger and his Family (as in the final sittings of other prayers), repeat *takbir* while keeping the hands under the navel, pray for the deceased and all other Muslims (both alive or dead), say *takbir* for the third time, and give salutations to the right and left.

Burying the Deceased

Muslims place the deceased in the grave while saying: *"Bi'smi'llahi ala millet-i Rasuli'llah"* (In God's Name and according to the religion and way of God's Messenger.). The deceased is laid on the right side facing the *qibla*, and the shroud is then untied. A stone or something similar is placed in the grave diagonally and in a slanting position so that the corpse should not be covered with soil. Soil is placed on the stone and then is used to cover the grave. After reciting some Qur'anic passages and praying to God for the deceased one, the people leave.

Congregational Prayer

Performing the prayers in congregation is a *sunna mu'akkada* (a sunna emphasized by the Messenger). Many scholars consider it necessary (*wajib*).

Women

It is better for women to pray in their houses than to attend congregational prayers. However, they may go to the mosque and attend the congregational prayer if they do not wear any attractive clothing or use any tempting perfume.

Conditions To Be Met by the Muadhdhin (the Caller to Prayer)

The Messenger praised muadhdhin and gave them good tidings of great reward (Bukhari, "Adhan," 5). However, in order to deserve this praise and reward, they have to meet certain conditions, as follows:

- Make the call to prayer for God's sake, not for wages.
- Be clean from major or minor impurities.
- Stand and face the *qibla*.
- Turn his head, neck, and chest to the right upon saying: "*Hayya 'ala's-salah*" and to the left upon saying: "*Hayya 'ala'l-falah*."
- Insert his index fingers into his ears so that his voice may be higher.
- Raise his voice for the call, even if he is alone in the desert.
- Pause between each phrase of the *adhan*.
- Adorn the *adhan* with his beautiful voice and tune.

The *adhan* is one of the important, collective symbols of Islam, for it shows that the place in which it is called is a Muslim land. In addition, it is a declaration of Islam's basic principles.

Whoever Makes the Adhan Makes the Iqama

It is highly recommended and preferable that whoever makes the *adhan* makes the *iqama*. A man who prays alone is encouraged to make the adhan, if he did not listen to its public recitation, and should make the *iqama*.

The Adhan and Iqama for Women

Although some scholars state that there is no *adhan* or *iqama* for women, some maintain that women can form a congregation and pray, and that one of them can serve as the imam. However, she must stand in the middle of the first row.

The Imam

The imam must meet several conditions, as follows:

- If the congregation includes men and women, the imam must be a man.
- He must be well-versed in Qur'anic recitation and knowledgeable of the prayer's obligatory, necessary, and *sunna* acts.

- He should be of good character and reputation.
- He should be the most knowledgeable (of those present) of Islamic jurisprudence and Qur'anic recitation, have excellent qualities and character, a good voice, and a sound body.
- He should not have a health problem that causes him to continually lose his ablution, unless all others in the congregation have the same or a similar problem.
- According to scholars, anyone whose prayer is valid for himself is valid for others if he serves as the imam. However, Muslims do not like to pray behind an evildoer or an innovator.

Where the Imam and the Congregation Stand

The imam stands before the congregation. Preferably, one person stands to the imam's right. If there are two or more people, they stand behind the imam. The Messenger placed the men in front of the young boys and the women behind the young boys.

Correcting the Imam's Mistake

If the imam forgets a verse, recites incorrectly, or makes a mistake in praying, someone in the congregation should correct him, and anyone who is known to be able to correct him is preferred to stand just after the imam.

Straightening the Rows and Filling the Gaps

The imam should tell the members of the congregation, or the congregation should do so even if the imam does so, to straighten the rows and fill in any gaps before starting the prayer.

The Imam's and Congregation's Recitation

It is enough for the imam to recite *al-Fatiha* and another Qur'anic passage, and for the congregation to keep silent. The congregation makes all other recitations, including *takbirs*, the supplication before *al-Fatiha*, the words of glorification in *ruku'* and *sujud*, and *tashahhud* and calls of God's blessings and peace upon God's Messenger and his Family.

Following the Imam

Every member of the congregation must follow the imam without delay, and must not to precede him in any action during the prayer.

Putting a Partition in front of Oneself While Praying

Anything that one sets in front of himself or herself while praying qualifies as a partition, even if it is only the bed's end. The Messenger said: "When one of you prays, he should make a partition for his prayer, even if it is an arrow." (Ibrahim Canan, *Hadis Ansiklopedisi* [An Encyclopedia of Hadiths], Ist., 8:179) This is done so that others cannot pass in front of one who is praying. It is forbidden to pass in front of one who is praying (i.e., between the person and his or her partition). If there is no such probability, making a partition is not necessary. The partition should be close enough that there is only room enough to prostrate.

One can make a gesture to stop someone from passing in front of him or her; however, this must not of the kind that will invalidate one's prayer, like speaking. The prayer is not invalidated if a person or an animal passes in front of the one who is praying.

Joining the Congregation

Whoever joins a congregation must say the opening *takbir* while standing and then move directly to the act that the congregation is performing. For instance, if the congregation is prostrating one should perform the opening *takbir* and then prostrate. If one joins the congregation during the *ruku'* following any standing position (*qiyam*), one is considered to have performed that *rak'at*. If it belongs to the first *rak'at*, one who joins the congregation during it and completes the prayer after the imam is considered to have performed the whole prayer.

If one joins after the *ruku'*, one is considered to have missed the *rak'at* or *rak'ats* preceding it. If one joins during the second *rak'at*, no matter in which prayer it occurs, after the imam gives the first salutation (to his right), one stands up and performs the first missed *rak'at*, reciting *al-Fatiha* and a Qur'anic passage, performs the *ruku'*, *sujud*, and the final sitting, and ends the prayer with salutations.

If one joins after the *ruku'* of the second *rak'at* in the dawn prayer, one stands up after the imam gives the first salutation and performs the prayer completely, without, however, saying the opening *takbir*. If one joins the evening prayer, one follows the imam until he gives the first salutation, and then stands up, recites *al-Fatiha* and a Qur'anic passage, performs the *ruku'* and *sujud*, and sits. This is one's second *rak'at*. After reciting the *tashahhud*, one stands up and recites *al-Fatiha* and a Qur'anic passage, does the *ruku'* and *sujud*, performs the final sitting, and ends the prayer with salutations. If one joins the noon, afternoon, or late evening prayers, one follows the imam until he gives the first salutation and then stands up. One completes the prayer by performing the two first *rak'at*s missed as if performing a prayer of two *rak'at*s.

If one joins the congregation in the fourth *rak'at* or after the *ruku'* following the third *rak'at*, one follows the imam until he gives the first salutation and then stands up. One performs the first *rak'at* missed by reciting *al-Fatiha* and a Qur'anic passage, doing the *ruku'* and *sujud* and sits. After reciting the *tashahhud*, one stands up, recites *al-Fatiha* and a Qur'anic passage, does the *ruku'* and *sujud*, and stands up. Then one recites only *al-Fatiha*, does the *ruku'* and *sujud*, and sits to recite *tashahhud*, calls of God's blessings and peace upon the Messenger and his Family, and end the prayer by giving salutations.

If one joins the congregation after the *ruku'* of the last *rak'at* of any prayer, one has missed that prayer and, standing when the imam gives the salutation to the right, offers the prayer completely without, however, saying the opening *takbir*.

If one is offering the dawn or evening prayer alone and people form a congregation behind an imam in the place where one is praying, and if one has not yet prostrated after the second *rak'at*, one must join the congregation. If one is offering a prayer of 4 *rak'at*s and is offering the first *rak'at*, one also joins the congregation. If one is offering the second *rak'at*, one completes the first two *rak'ats*, as if performing a prayer of 2 *rak'ats*, and joins the congregation. If one is offering the third *rak'at*, one joins the congregation. If one is offering the fourth *rak'at*, one completes the prayer without joining the congregation.

Earth as a Mosque

A Muslim can pray anywhere, provided that the place does not have enough dirt to invalidate the prayer, has not been usurped, or belongs to one who will not allow prayer therein. This is a special blessing of God for the Muslim community. Given this, the whole Earth can serve as a mosque.

Three Most Excellent Mosques

One can pray in any mosque. However, three mosques have a particular sacredness and provide those praying within far more merit than praying in others. In order of merit and sacredness, they are the Sacred Mosque in Makka, the Prophet's Mosque in Madina, and the Masjid al-Aqsa in Quds (Jerusalem).

Making Up Missed Prayers

Prayer is the most important kind of worship. It is the support of religion, and therefore can never be omitted. However, scholars agree that all prayers that have been missed for whatever reason (e.g., forgetfulness, sleep, having an operation or a serious illness) must be made up. One can perform the missed prayer at any time, except when praying is prohibited.

Missed prayers should be performed in the proper order. For example, if one has missed less than six prayers, he or she should first perform that missed prayer before performing a new prayer whose time it is in. Doing so shows that one is a person of order, and making up missed prayers reinforces this. However, if one has missed more than six prayers, one can make up them in all times when praying is permissible.

SAWM AL-RAMADAN (FASTING THE MONTH OF RAMADAN)

The fourth pillar of Islam is the Ramadan fast, during which Muslims abstain from eating, drinking, and sexual relations or satisfaction from dawn until sunset. Concerning the order to fast, the Qur'an declares:

> The month of Ramadan, in which the Qur'an (began to be) sent down as a pure source of guidance for people, and, (when practiced,) as clear signs of guidance and the Criterion (between truth and falsehood). Therefore, whoever of you is present at this month must fast it, and he who is so ill that he cannot fast or is on a journey must fast the same number of other days. God desires ease for you, and desires not hardship for you, so that you can complete the number of the days required, exalt God for that He has guided you, and it is hoped that you may give thanks (due to Him). (2:185)

Types of Fasting

There are two types of fasting: obligatory and voluntary. Obligatory fasts can be further subdivided into the fast of Ramadan, the fast of expiation, and the fast of fulfilling a vow. Here we shall discuss the Ramadan and voluntary fasts.

When Does Ramadan Begin and End?

Ramadan is the ninth month of the Islamic lunar calendar. A lunar month is approximately 29.5 days, which is the time it takes for the moon to orbit Earth. Since a lunar month is, on average, one day shorter than a solar month, a lunar year is 10 to 12 days shorter than a solar year. Therefore, Ramadan comes 10 to 12 days earlier each year and so moves through the seasons, providing equal conditions for people living in different lands.

A new lunar month begins when, during the moon's orbit around Earth, the moon is in conjunction with the sun and the sun's light hits the side of the moon that is turned away from Earth. In this position, the moon is said to be a "new moon," with its dark side turned toward Earth. By definition, a new moon is not visible from Earth, as the sun's light shines only on the side facing Earth.

As the moon continues to orbit around Earth, it starts to form a crescent. This will be minutes after the new moon forms, even though the crescent will not be visible for several hours. In some traditional Islamic countries, Muslims do not start fasting until they see the actual crescent. This event is confirmed by sighting the new moon, even if it is seen by only one person, or by the passage of 30 days in the immediately preceding month of Sha'ban. However, according to some modern scholars, God has given us scientific knowledge to determine exactly when a lunar month will begin and end. Therefore, any observatory or other astronomy-related center should have this information for the area in which we live.

Fasting starts on the first dawn of the new month. During the few hours between the new moon and the following dawn, Muslims can eat and drink, and then start fasting when the first thread of light is observed in the sky.

Different Locations

Most scholars say that it does not matter if the new moon has been seen elsewhere. In other words, after the new moon is seen anywhere in the world, all Muslims must begin fasting.

The End of Ramadan

The Ramadan fast ends when the new moon (Shawwal) is seen. Most jurists state that the new moon must have been reported by at least two just witnesses.

The Hours Decreed for Fasting

According to the Qur'an, the fasting hours are as follows: *You can eat and drink until you can discern the white streak (of dawn) against the black streak (of night); then complete the Fast until night sets in* (2:187). Thus, the fast should start at the first thread of light at dawn (between 1.5 and 2 hours before sunrise, depending on the time of year), and maintained until sunset (the beginning of night).

Who Must Fast

All scholars agree that fasting is obligatory upon every sane, adult, healthy Muslim male who is not traveling or fighting on a battlefield at that time. As for women, those who are menstruating or having post-childbirth bleeding cannot fast. In addition, the following groups of people do not have to fast: those who are insane, minors, or travelers; pregnant women who fear that their unborn child might be harmed; the old and sick who think that fasting might harm them; and those who work in harsh circumstances or suffer such hunger or thirst that they fear fasting might result in death.

Making up the Missed Days

People who are (not chronically) ill and travelers can break their fast during Ramadan, but must make up the missed days. If travelers make the intention to fast during the night, they can still break their fast during the day. If they have already made the intention to fast while resident but then decided to travel during the day, most scholars maintain that they must fast.

Those who have broken their fast because of harsh circumstances also must make up the missed days. The scholars agree that menstruating women, women with post-childbirth bleeding, and pregnant and breast-feeding women who fear that fasting might harm them or the baby, must make up the missed days.

Paying a Recompense

Those who are too old to fast, as well as the chronically ill, are permitted to break their fast, for fasting would place too much hardship on them. However, they must feed one poor person for each day that they did not fast. If those who were traveling or had another excuse die before making up the missed days, no recompense has to be paid. If they requested their heirs to pay such a recompense, however, the money should be taken out of the deceased's estate. If those who died without making up the missed days, even though they had enough time to do so, must request their heirs to pay the necessary recompense.

Days When Fasting Is Forbidden

All scholars agree that fasting on the two 'Iyds ('Iyd al-Fitr and 'Iyd al-Adha) is forbidden. It does not matter if the fast is obligatory or voluntary. Fasting voluntarily on Friday exclusively is disliked. If one fasts on the day before or after it, if it is a day on which one customarily fasts (e.g., the 13th, 14th, or 15th of the month), or if it is the day of 'Ashura (Muharram 10), then it is not disliked to fast on such a Friday. The same rule applies to Saturday. Fasting on the "day of doubt," when one is not sure if it is the last day of Sha'ban or the first day of Ramadan, is also disliked, as is fasting on consecutive days without eating at all (*al-wisal*).

Voluntary Fasts

The Messenger exhorted Muslims to fast on the following days: six days of Shawwal; Muharram 10 ('Ashura) and the days immediately preceding and following it; most of Sha'ban (the month preceding Ramadan); every Thursday, Friday, and Saturday during the sacred months (Dhu'l-Qa'da, Dhu'l-Hijja, Muharram, Rajab); every Monday and Thursday; and the thirteenth, fourteenth, and fifteenth days of each month. He also permitted those who can fast every other day, which is called *sawm Dawud* (the fast of Prophet David), to do so.

The Predawn Meal and Breaking the Fast

Having a predawn meal between the middle of the night and dawn is *sunna* (recommended). It is considered best to delay it so that it will be eaten as close to dawn as possible. Those who are fasting should hasten to break the fast when the sun has set and, just before eating, make the following supplication (highly recommended): "O God, I have fasted for You, believed in You, placed my trust in You, and break my fast with Your provisions."

The Essential Elements of Fasting

Making the proper intention to fast the month of Ramadan is required. Preferably, this intention should be made before dawn and during every night of Ramadan. However, it is valid if made during any part of the night and can even be made as late as noon if one forgot to make it before dawn. It does not have to be spoken out loud, for it is, in reality, an act of the heart that does not involve the tongue. In addition, it is fulfilled by one's intention to fast out of obedience to God and to seek His pleasure. According to many jurists, the intention for a voluntary fast can be made until noon.

During the fasting hours, one cannot eat, drink, or engage in marital sexual relations. Before the Qur'an's revelation, married couples could not engage in sexual intercourse during the fasting period. This rule was alleviated by 2:187, which allows sexual intercourse between married couples during the nights of Ramadan:

> It is made lawful for you to go in to your wives on the night of the Fast; (there is such an inalienable intimacy between you that) they are a garment for you (enfolding you to protect you against illicit relations and beautifying you,) and you are a garment (of the same sort) for them. (2:187)

However, it is still forbidden during the fasting hours.

Avoiding Unbefitting Actions

Fasting, a type of worship for drawing closer to God, was ordered to purify the soul and train it in good deeds. Those who are fasting must guard against any act that might cancel the benefits of their fast. Thus, their fast will increase their personal God-consciousness and piety. Fasting is more than not eating and drinking; it also means to avoid everything else that God has forbidden. The Messenger said: "Fasting is not (abstaining) from eating and drinking only, but also from vain speech and foul language. If one of you is being cursed or annoyed, he should say: 'I am fasting, I am fasting.'"

Being Generous and Doing Other Meritorious Acts

Being generous, studying the Qur'an, and supplicating to God are recommended at all times, but are especially stressed during Ramadan. During the last 10 days of Ramadan, God's Messenger would wake his wives during the night and then, remaining apart from them, engage in acts of worship. He would exert himself in worshipping his Lord during this time more than he would at any other time. (Bukhari, "Sawm," 2:9; Muslim, "Siyam," 164)

Permitted Acts

- Pouring water over oneself and submerging oneself in water.
- Applying kohl, eye-drops, or anything else to the eyes.
- Kissing, provided that one has self-control.
- Rinsing the mouth and nose, without swallowing any water.
- Tasting a liquid, food, or something else that one wants to buy. However, anything edible must not be swallowed.
- Chewing gum (unlike something that has no sweetness or fragrance) is disliked but does not invalidate the fast.
- Eating, drinking, or having sexual intercourse during the night until dawn.
- If one eats due to forgetfulness, the day does not have to be made up later or expiated.
- Performing *ghusl* before dawn is not required, but it is advisable to be pure before fasting.
- If a woman's menstrual or post-childbirth bleeding stops during the night, she can delay *ghusl* until the morning and still fasts. However, she must perform *ghusl* before the dawn prayer.
- Those who are fasting can use a tooth stick or a brush to clean their teeth. It does not matter if this is done at the beginning or at the end of the day.
- Smelling perfumes.
- Swallowing anything wet with saliva remaining in the mouth after rising.
- Swallowing only a few drops of tears and sweat, the taste of which one does not feel.
- Eating anything edible remaining between teeth and which is smaller than a chickpea.
- Anything that is inedible and enters the mouth without intention (e.g., smoke, dust, and the taste of medicine put on teeth) does not invalidate the fast.
- Kissing, touching, and stroking the opposite sex, provided that no ejaculation occurs, as well as any sexual activity that does not result in ejaculation. Any ejaculation that is the result of looking and thinking does not invalidate the fast.

- Having a wet dream during the day or any ejaculation of seminal fluid.

Forbidden Acts Requiring a Make-up Day

- Eating due to a mistake (other than forgetfulness) or coercion.
- Swallowing the blood more than the saliva with which it is mixed and the taste of which one feels.
- Swallowing more than a few drops of tears and sweat the taste of which one feels.
- Removing from the mouth anything edible that remains between the teeth and which is greater than a chickpea, and then eating it.
- Vomiting a mouthful. Anything less and which goes back into the stomach does not invalidate the fast. However, if one intentionally takes it back, the fast is broken.
- Ejaculation that occurs with pleasure by kissing, touching, and masturbation.
- Menses and post-childbirth bleeding, even if either begins just before sunset.
- If one eats, drinks, or has intercourse, thinking that the sun has set or that *fajr* has not occurred.
- Any injections, whether for feeding or for medicinal purposes. It does not matter if the injection was intravenous or underneath the skin, or whether what was injected reaches the stomach.
- Any drink or medicine that passes through throat or nose. However, water that passes through the ears is allowed.
- Any fluid going into body through the rectum.

Acts that Invalidate the Fast and Require a Make-up Day and Expiation

Intentional eating, drinking, and having sexual intercourse during the day require making up the day and an expiation. Expiation is defined as freeing a slave if one can do so; if the person has no slaves or cannot free one for a valid reason, he or she must fast for 60 consecutive days; if one cannot do so, he or she must feed a poor person for 60 days or 60 poor people for one day with meals that are similar to what one would eat at home.

Most scholars say that both men and women have to perform acts of expiation if they intentionally have sexual intercourse during the day even if they had intended to fast on that day. If they engaged in it out of forgetfulness, coercion, or having no intention to fast, they do not have to perform any act of expiation. If the woman was raped or coerced by the man, only the man has to make an act of expiation.

All scholars agree that people who intentionally broke the fast and made expiation, and then broke it again in a way that requires another expiation, they must perform another act of expiation. Similarly, they all agree that if people break the fast twice during a day, before performing the expiation for the first act, they need to perform only one act of expiation. If people break their fast and then repeat it during the same Ramadan without expiation, they only have to make expiation one time. The reason for this is because there is a punishment for acts that are repeated, and if the expiation or punishment is not carried out, all of these acts are combined into one.

Places with Very Long Days and Very Short Nights

Muslims who are in such areas (e.g., close to the polar regions) should follow the norms of the areas in which the Islamic legislation took place (e.g., Makka or Madina) or follow the schedule of the closest area that has "normal" days and nights.

The Virtue of the Night of Power (*Laylat al-Qadr*)

This night is the year's most virtuous night. God says: *We revealed it (the Qur'an) on the Night of Power [Laylat al-Qadr]. What will tell you what the Night of Power is? It is better than a thousand months.* For example, any action therein (e.g., reciting the Qur'an, remembering God) brings as much reward as would doing the same action for 1,000 months that do not contain this night.

It is preferred to seek this night during the last 10 nights of Ramadan, as the Prophet, upon whom be peace, strove his best to seek it during that time. For example, he would stay up during the last 10 nights, wake his wives, and then stay apart from them in order to worship. However, according to Abu Hanifa, any night during the year may be the Night of Power (Canan, *ibid.*, 1:260), and so Muslims should keep vigils for some time every night in order to catch it. Such night vigils have a special importance.

Al-Bukhari records from Abu Hurayra that the Messenger, upon whom be peace, said: "Whoever prays during the Night of Power with faith and hoping for its reward will have all of his or her previous sins forgiven." (Bukhari, "Fadl Laylat al-Qadr")

The Meaning and Principles of I'tikaf

I'tikaf literally means to stick to something, whether good or bad, and to block out everything else. As a term, it denotes devoting oneself, especially during the last 10 days of Ramadan, to praying in a mosque. God's Messenger, upon him be peace and blessings, performed *i'tikaf* for 10 days every Ramadan. In the year that he died, he performed it for 20 days.

I'tikaf is not acceptable from an unbeliever, a non-discerning child, a person requiring major purification because of (sexual) defilement, and a menstruating woman and a woman with post-childbirth bleeding.

I'tikaf will be fulfilled if a person stays in the mosque with the intention of becoming closer to God. If these conditions are not met, it is not *i'tikaf*. If an individual intends to perform a voluntary *i'tikaf* but ends it before the 10-day period has ended, he or she must make up the remaining days later.

The Holy Month of Ramadan[3]

The month of Ramadan, in which the Qur'an (began to be) sent down as a pure source of guidance for people, and, (when practiced,) as clear signs of guidance and the Criterion (between truth and falsehood). (2:185)

First Point

Fasting Ramadan is one of Islam's foremost pillars and greatest symbols. Many of its purposes relate to God's Lordship and giving thanks for His bounties, as well as to humanity's individual and collective life, self-training, and self-discipline.

One purpose connected with His Lordship is that God displays His Lordship's perfection and His being the All-Merciful and All-Compassionate upon Earth's surface, which He designed as a table to hold His bounties in a way beyond human imagination. Nevertheless, people cannot perfectly discern this situation's reality due to heedlessness and causality's blinding veil. But during Ramadan, like an army waiting for its marching orders, believers display an attitude of worship toward the end of the day as if they expect to be told to help themselves to the banquet prepared by the Eternal Monarch. Thus they respond to that magnificent and universal manifestation of Divine Mercifulness with a comprehensive and harmonious act of collective worship. I wonder if those who do not worship or share in the honor of being so favored deserve to be called human.

Second Point

From the viewpoint of its being related to gratitude to God, one of the instances of wisdom in fasting during Ramadan is this: As stated in "The First Word," there is a price for the food brought by a servant from the king's kitchen. Obviously, it would be an incredible folly to tip the servant and not recognize the king, [for this would show] a clear disrespect for that gift. In the same way, God Almighty spreads His countless bounties on Earth and bestows them for a price: thanksgiving.

The apparent causes of those bounties or those who bring them to us are like the servant in the above example. We pay servants, feel indebted to and thank them, even though they are only causes or means. We sometimes show them a degree of respect they do not merit. The true Giver of Bounties is infinitely more deserving of thanks for these bounties. Such thanksgiving assumes the form of acknowledging one's need for the bounties, appreciating them fully, and ascribing them directly to Him.

Fasting Ramadan is the key to a true, sincere, comprehensive, and universal thanksgiving. Many people cannot appreciate most of the bounties they enjoy, for they do not experience hunger. For example, a piece of dry bread means nothing to those who are full, especially if they are rich. However, the believers' sense of taste testifies at the time of breaking the fast that it is indeed a very valuable bounty of God. During Ramadan, everyone is favored with a heartfelt thanksgiving by understanding the value of Divine bounties.

While fasting, believers think: "These bounties do not originally belong to me, and so I cannot regard them as mere food or drink. Since the One owns and grants them to me, I should wait for His permission to eat them." By thus acknowledging food and drink as Divine gifts, believers tacitly thank God. This is why fasting is a key to thanksgiving, which is a fundamental human duty.

Third Point

Fasting is related to humanity's collective life, for God's decision not to give each person livelihood means that the rich are to help the poor. Without fasting, many rich and self-indulgent people cannot perceive the pain of hunger and poverty or to what extent the poor need care. Care for one's fellow beings is a foundation of true thanksgiving. There is always someone poorer, so everyone must help such people. If people do not experience hunger, it is nearly impossible for them to do good or to help others. Even if they do, they can do so only imperfectly because they do not feel the hungry one's condition to the same extent.

Fourth Point

Fasting Ramadan contains many Divine purposes related to self-training and self-discipline, such as: The carnal self desires – and considers itself – to be free and unrestricted. It even wishes, by its very nature, for an imagined lordship and free, arbitrary action. Not liking to think that it is being trained and tested through God's countless bounties, it swallows up such bounties like an animal and in the manner of a thief or robber, especially if its wealth and power are accompanied by heedlessness.

During Ramadan, everyone's selfhood understands that it is owned by One Other, not by itself; that it is a servant, not a free agent. Unless ordered or permitted, it cannot do even the most common things, like eating and drinking. This inability shatters its illusory lordship and enables it to admit its servanthood and perform its real duty of thanksgiving.

Fifth Point

Fasting Ramadan prevents the carnal self from rebelling and adorns it with good morals. A person's carnal self forgets itself through heedlessness. It neither sees nor wants to see its inherent infinite impotence, poverty, and defect. It does not reflect upon how it is exposed to misfortune and subject to decay, and that it consists of flesh and bones that disintegrate and decompose rapidly. It rushes upon the world with a violent greed and attachment, as if it had a steel body and would live forever, and clings to whatever is profitable and pleasurable. In this state it forgets its Creator, Who trains it with perfect care. Being immersed in the swamp of immorality, it does not think about the consequences of its life here or its afterlife.

But fasting the month of Ramadan causes even the most heedless and stubborn to feel their weakness and innate poverty. Hunger becomes an important consideration and reminds them of how fragile their bodies really are. They perceive their need for compassion and care and, giving up haughtiness, want to take refuge in the Divine Court in perfect helplessness and destitution, rising to knock at the door of Mercy with the hand of tacit thanksgiving – provided, of course, that heedlessness has not yet corrupted them completely.

Sixth Point

God began revealing the Qur'an during Ramadan. This has many implications, such as: In order to welcome the month when the Qur'an, that Divine address, was revealed, believers should try to be like angels by abandoning eating and drinking. They also should seek to divest themselves of the carnal self's vain preoccupations and gross needs. During Ramadan, they should recite or listen to the Qur'an as if it were being revealed for the first time. If possible, they should listen to it as if they were hearing Prophet

Muhammad recite it, or Archangel Gabriel reciting it to Muhammad, or God revealing it to Muhammad through Gabriel. They should respect the Qur'an in their daily actions and, by conveying its message to others, demonstrate the Divine purpose for its revelation.

Ramadan transforms the Muslim world into a huge mosque in which millions recite the Qur'an to Earth's inhabitants. Displaying the reality of: *The month of Ramadan, in which the Qur'an (began to be) sent down* (2:185), Ramadan proves itself to be the month of the Qur'an. While some in the vast congregation in the great mosque of the Muslim world listen to its recitation with solemn reverence, others recite it. It is most disagreeable to forsake that heavenly spiritual state by obeying the carnal self, and thus eating and drinking in the sacred "mosque," for this provokes the whole congregation's hatred. It is also most disagreeable, and must provoke the Muslim world's dislike and contempt, to counter and defy those Muslims who fast Ramadan.

Seventh Point

Fasting Ramadan has many purposes related to a person's spiritual rewards, as everyone is sent here to sow this world with the seeds of the next life. The following paragraphs explain one such purpose, as follows:

The rewards for good deeds done during Ramadan are multiplied by a thousand. One Tradition states that 10 rewards are given for each letter of the Qur'an. Reciting one letter means 10 good deeds and brings forth 10 fruits of Paradise. But during Ramadan, this reward is multiplied by 1,000 and even more for such verses as the "Verse of the Throne":

> Allah! There is no god but He, the Ever-Living, Self-Subsisting, Supporter of all. Slumber and sleep do not seize Him. Everything in the heavens and on Earth belongs to Him. Who can intercede in His presence unless He permits it? He knows what (appears) before and after and behind His creatures, and they can only acquire as much of His knowledge as he permits. His Throne extends over the heavens and Earth. He feels no fatigue while guarding and preserving them, for He is the Most High, the Supreme. (2:255)

The reward is even greater on Ramadan's Friday nights. Furthermore, each letter is multiplied 30,000 times if recited during the Night of Power.

During Ramadan the Qur'an, each letter of which yields 30,000 permanent fruits of Paradise, becomes like a huge blessed tree producing millions of permanent fruits of Paradise. Consider how holy and profitable this trade is, and how great a loss for those who do not appreciate the Qur'an's letters.

So Ramadan is the most proper time for such a profitable trade in the afterlife's name. It is like a most fertile field to cultivate for the afterlife's harvest. Its multiplication of rewards for good deeds make it like April in spring. It is a sacred and illustrious festival for the parade of those who worship His Lordship's Sovereignty.

This is why fasting Ramadan is obligatory, why believers are not allowed to gratify the carnal self's animal appetites and indulge in its useless fancies. Since they become like angels while fasting or engaging in such a trade, each believer is a mirror reflecting God's Self-Sufficiency. They move toward becoming a pure spirit manifested in corporeal dress by abandoning the world for a fixed period. In fact, Ramadan contains and causes believers to gain, through fasting, a permanent life after a short period in this world.

One Ramadan may enable believers to gain 80 years' worth of reward, for the Qur'an declares the Night of Power to be more profitable than 80 years having no such night (97:3). A king may announce a few holidays to mark a special occasion, like his enthronement, and then honor his faithful subjects on those days with special favors. Likewise, the Eternal and Majestic King of the 18,000 worlds revealed the Qur'an, His exalted decree, to each world during Ramadan. Thus wisdom requires that Ramadan be a special Divine festival during which God's Lordship pours out bounties and spirit beings come together. Given that Ramadan is a Divinely ordained festival, fasting is commanded so that people withdraw from their bodily preoccupations to some extent.

Fasting also enables people to abandon sins committed by their bodily senses or members and use them in the acts of worship particular to each. For example, those who fast should stop their tongue from lying, backbiting, and swearing by busying it with reciting the Qur'an, glorifying God, seeking His forgiveness, and calling His blessing upon Prophet Muhammad. They should prevent their eyes from looking at, and their ears from listening to, forbidden things; rather, they should look at things that give a spiritual lesson or moral warning and listen to the Qur'an and truths. When the factory-like stomach is stopped from working, other members (small workshops) can be made to follow it easily.

Eighth Point

One purpose of fasting is to put people on a physical and spiritual diet. If the carnal self acts, eats, and drinks as it wishes, people's physical health is harmed. But, and more importantly, their spiritual life is harmed because they do not discriminate between the allowed and the forbidden. Such a carnal self finds it very difficult to obey the heart and spirit. Recognizing no principles, it takes the person's reins and drives him or her as it pleases.

However, fasting Ramadan accustoms it to dieting, and self-discipline trains it to obey. The stomach is not harmed from overeating before the previous meal has been digested properly and, learning to forsake what is allowed, can follow the decree of reason and religion to refrain from what is forbidden. Thus the carnal self tries not to corrupt its owner's spiritual life.

Also, most people suffer hunger to various degrees. To endure a long-lasting hunger patiently, people should train themselves in self-discipline and austerity. Fasting Ramadan provides this patience-based training by causing people to feel hungry for 15 hours, or even for 24 hours if the predawn meal is missed. Thus fasting cures impatience and the lack of endurance, which double humanity's misfortune.

Many bodily members somehow serve the stomach. If that "factory" does not stop its daytime routines during a certain month, it keeps those members busy with itself and forgetful of their own worship and sublime duties. This is why saints always prefer austerity as a way to spiritual and human perfection. Fasting Ramadan reminds us that our bodily members were created for more than just serving the stomach. During Ramadan, many bodily members take and experience angelic and spiritual – as opposed to material – pleasures. As a result, fasting believers receive degrees of spiritual pleasure and enlightenment according to their level of spiritual perfection. Fasting Ramadan refines a person's heart, spirit, reason, and innermost senses. Even if the stomach complains, these senses rejoice.

Ninth Point

Observing the fast of Ramadan breaks the carnal self's illusory lordship and, reminding it that it is innately helpless, convinces it that it is a servant. As the carnal self does not like to recognize its Lord, it obstinately claims lordship even while suffering. Only hunger alters such a temperament.

God's Messenger relates that God Almighty asked the carnal self: "Who am I, and who are you?" It replied: "You are Yourself, and I am myself." However much God punished it and repeated His question, He received the same answer. But when He subjected it to hunger, it replied: "You are my All-Compassionate Lord; I am Your helpless servant."

O God, grant peace and blessings to our master Muhammad in a way to please You and to give him his due, to the number of the rewards for reciting the Qur'an's letters during Ramadan, and to his Family and Companions. Glorified be your Lord, the Lord of Honor and Power; exalted above what they falsely ascribe to Him. Peace be upon the Messengers, and all praise be to God, Lord of the Worlds. Amen.

OATHS

Making an oath means to swear by God that one will not do something. In Islam, one can swear only by God. People who make such an oath must do their best to fulfill it, and so should not make one carelessly.

People who make false statements by mistake or unknowingly, and then swear to them by God, are not held responsible for them and do not have make any expiation. However, consciously lying and then swearing by God or declaring God as a witness to the lie is an extremely grave sin that many times has resulted in misfortune descending upon the liar. Such people must perform an act of expiation, earnestly seek God's forgiveness, and repair any damage caused by the lie.

If people swear by God not to do something in the future and then do that very act, they must seek God's forgiveness and make an expiation. In this case, this involves emancipating a slave. If this is not possible, the oath-breaker must feed a poor person for 10 days with meals that are similar to what his family eats. If this is not possible, he or she must fast for 3 consecutive days.

VOWS

A vow is a solemn promise to do, in God's name, something that resembles an act of worship and make obligatory upon oneself that which is not obligatory. A vow is considered "Islamic" only if it is made in God's name and involves an obligatory or necessary act of worship (e.g., to fast or help the poor). Therefore, one can vow to perform two *rak'at*s of prayer or fast, but not to make a prostration of recitation or perform ablution, for these latter two acts are not obligatory acts of worship in themselves but rather are the means to such acts. Also, vows can be made concerning only that which can be fulfilled.

There are two kinds of vows: appointed and unappointed. An appointed vow can be, for example, vowing to fast on a certain day if one's desire for something religiously lawful is met. If the desired thing happens, the vow must be fulfilled. An unappointed vow can be, for example, a vow to fast for one day or to give charity to the poor if one's desire for something religiously lawful is met. If the desired thing happens, the vow must be fulfilled.

If one vows to do something resembling an act of worship if something does not occur, he or she must either fulfill the vow or make an expiation. For example, if one addicted to lying vows to fast for a week if he or she does not lie again, but then does so, he or she either has to fulfill the vow or make an expiation like that made for broken oaths.

ZAKAT (THE PRESCRIBED PURIFYING ALMS)

The second important duty of servanthood is *zakat*. God's Messenger, who depicts prayer as Islam's pillar or support, describes *zakat* as its bridge (Canan, *ibid.*, 6:346), for *zakat* not only brings the social strata closer to each other and fills in the gaps between them and their members, but also stops such gaps from forming.

Zakat means purity and growing. Since it purifies wealth and people's attachment to it, and causes both it and Muslims to grow in purity and sincerity, the Qur'an calls it *zakat* (or the prescribed alms):

> (O Messenger,) take alms (prescribed or voluntary) out of their wealth so that you may cleanse them thereby and cause them to grow in purity and sincerity, and pray for them. Indeed your prayer is a source of comfort for them. God is All-Hearing, All-Knowing. (9:103)

Taking into account its very nature, *zakat* constitutes one of Islam's five pillars. It is associated with prayer (*salat*) in 82 Qur'anic verses. God, the Exalted One, prescribed it in His Book (the Qur'an), His Messenger corroborated it by his *sunna*, and the Muslim community by consensus upheld it. Ibn 'Abbas reported that when the Prophet sent Mu'adh ibn Jabal to Yemen (as its governor), he said to him:

> You are going to a people who are People of the Book. Invite them to accept the *shahada*: that there is no deity but God and I am His Messenger. If they accept and affirm this, tell them that God, the Glorious One, has enjoined five prayers upon them during the day and night. If they accept that, tell them also that He has enjoined *sadaqa* (meaning *zakat*) upon their assets, which will be taken from the rich of the (Muslim) community and distributed to the poor. If they accept that, refrain from laying hands upon the best of their goods and fear the cry of the oppressed, for there is no barrier between God and it. (Bukhari, "Zakat," 1:41; Muslim, "Iman," 31.)

Many verses exhort Muslims to pay *zakat* and forbid hoarding wealth. For example:

The believers, both men and women, they are guardians, confidants and helpers of one another. They enjoin and promote what is right and good and forbid and try to prevent the evil. They establish the prayer in conformity with its conditions, and pay the *zakat* (prescribed purifying alms) fully. They always obey God and His Messenger. Those are the distinguished ones whom God shall treat with mercy. Assuredly, God is the All-Honored with irresistible might, All-Wise. (9:71)

and:

Those who hoard gold and silver and do not spend it in God's way (to exalt His cause and help the poor and needy: O Messenger,) give them the glad tidings of a painful chastisement. (9:34)

Who Must Pay

Zakat must be paid by every free Muslim, man or woman, who has a *nisab* (the required amount of wealth). As for the insane and children who have a *nisab*, if their wealth is under disposal or in circulation, their guardians pay it on their behalf. If a person dies before paying it, it must be taken from the estate before paying off any debts, if there are any, and the heirs share the inheritance.

Conditions for Nisab

Nisab is conditioned by the following:

- *Nisab* is the amount of wealth remaining after meeting all expenses for such vital necessities as food, clothes, housing, and a mount. Thus, one does not have to pay *zakat* on what he or she needs to make a living, such as tools or machines related to carpentry, farming, tailoring, or working as a doctor. All debts are subtracted from one's wealth. If one has enough secured credit to pay off the debt, it is added to one's wealth, and if the resultant wealth reaches the *nisab*, one must pay *zakat*.

- For many items subject to *zakat* (e.g., money, gold, silver, and cattle), a full year of the Islamic calendar should pass, starting from the day of the *nisab's* possession. If the wealth possessed decreases during the year but is still possessed one year later, *zakat* must be paid. What matters is the availability of *nisab* at the beginning and end of the year. However, this condition does not apply to plantations and fruits, for their *zakat* should be paid, or at least calculated, on the harvest day and include what has been consumed before the harvest.

- In short, there are two types of *zakat*: one grows by itself (e.g., crops and fruits), and the other is used for growing and production (e.g., money, merchandise, and cattle). In the former case, *zakat* should be paid at harvest time; in the later, at the end of the year.

- The wealth subject to *zakat* should be actively or potentially increasing, growing, or productive. This condition will be explained below.

- One must have private, doubtless ownership or possession and the right of disposal of the wealth liable to *zakat*.

Intention

Since paying *zakat* is an act of worship, its validity depends upon one's sincere intention to pay it for God's sake. If one pays it without making the intention, one can still intend while the wealth expended as *zakat* has not yet been consumed.

Paying Zakat at Its Due Time

Zakat must be paid immediately at its due time. Deferring it is prohibited, unless there is a valid reason not to do so.

Holdings Subject to Zakat and Their Nisab

Islam enjoined *zakat* on currencies and similar things, such as shares, bonds and checks, gold and silver, crops, fruit, livestock, merchandise, minerals, and treasure.

The Standard of Richness

Islam does not criticize earning; rather, it encourages working and earning one's livelihood. But it does not approve of earning for luxury and a luxurious life, and urges Muslims to work, earn, and live for the other life as their goal. It encourages mutual helping in society and spending in God's way and for the needy, and has not established a fixed standard of living. It regards having a house, a mount, two suits and other articles of clothing, and one month worth of livelihood (some say that one can keep a year of livelihood at the most) as the necessary commodities or wealth upon which one does not have to pay *zakat*. Bediüzzaman Said Nursi expresses a standard that can be valid for all times, as follows: While most Muslims are below the average standards of living, a Muslim cannot live a luxurious, comfortable life.

The Sunna has established approximately 90 grams of gold or about 600 grams of silver or 40 sheep or 30 heads of cattle or 5 camels as the standard. If, according to the place or the general standard of living of the people in a particular place, one has banknotes, merchandise, or other kinds of increasing income or capital whose value is equal to any of the standard values given, he or she must pay *zakat*. However, in establishing the *nisab*, the minimum amount or value, which favors the poor, is considered.

The Nisab and Zakat for Gold, Silver, and Other Jewelry

The nisab for gold is 20 dinars (approximately 90 grams) and for silver is 200 dirhams (approximately 600 grams), both being owned for one year. The due on them is one-fortieth of their value. Any additional amount is to be calculated in this manner. Gold and silver are combined. Thus, if one has gold and silver whose value is equal to 200 dirhams of silver, *zakat* must be paid. Likewise, gold, silver, banknotes and the like, and commercial merchandise are also combined. Things made of gold and silver are treated like gold and silver. In other words, if the weight of gold and silver they contain amounts to the *nisab*, their *zakat* is paid.

Although most of the scholars opine that no *zakat* has to be paid on diamonds, pearls, sapphires, rubies, corals, or other precious stones that women wear as ornaments and unless they are used for trade, it is piety and a measure to be saved from the obligation of *zakat*, which is both God's and people's right on rich people, to make some payment due to them. One should not buy such precious stones in order to avoid paying *zakat*.

Banknotes, Checks, and Bonds

As these are documents with guaranteed credits, banknotes, checks, and bonds are subject to *zakat*, at the rate of one-fortieth of their value, when they are owned for one year and attain the minimum of *nisab* (being equal in value to 200 silver dirhams). A person may change them into currency immediately. They are combined with currencies, gold and silver, and commercial merchandise.

Commercial Merchandise

Any commercial merchandise that is religiously lawful to use, consume, buy, and sell (e.g., clothes, grain, iron, copper, cattle, sheep, houses, shops, and cars) is subject to *zakat*. Their due is one-fortieth. Due to gold's stable value, jurists maintain that it should be the basis upon which the *nisab* of commercial merchandise is determined.

Buildings and Vehicles of Transportation That Are Sources of Income

One who rents out a house, a shop, tools, vehicles, or land, or who has vehicles working in transportation, must pay *zakat* on the rent and income received. If their annual revenue is equal to *nisab*, after the money spent on them is deducted, the owner pays their *zakat* every month. Since they are compared with land and land products, their *zakat* rate is one-tenth.

Industrial Investments and Means of Production

These items are currently among the greatest sources of income. Although people's private houses, tools, and machines by which they earn their living are not subject to *zakat*, industrial investments and means of production (e.g., factories) are, for they are growing and sources of revenue. Some jurists compare them to land and land products, and say that their *zakat* rate is one-tenth. Others compare them to commercial activities and merchandise, and say that their *zakat* rate is one-fortieth of the value remaining after debts, expenses on necessary material, workmanship, production, marketing, and financing have been subtracted.

Wages, Salaries, and Independent Businesses

Since wages, salaries, and earnings from independent businesses are steady and continuous and potentially growing, they are subject to *zakat* if the amount remaining after the yearly average expenditure on livelihood reaches *nisab*. The rate is one-fortieth. Although there are diverse standards of living, Muslims do not think of living a comfortable life when the majority of Muslims and humanity are living a below-average life. Some jurists say that this type of *zakat* should be paid after one year; others say that it should be paid monthly.

Cattle, Sheep, and Goats

Cattle, camels, sheep, and goats are subject to *zakat*. They must be commercial or grazing, and have been in one's possession for a year. The *nisab* of each is as follows:

- When one has 5 grazing camels for one year, their due is 1 sheep, which is also the due for 5 to 9 camels. The due for 10 to 14 camels is 2 sheep, for 15 to 19 camels is 3 sheep, and for 20 to 24 camels is 4 sheep. The due for 25 to 35 camels is a 2-year-old she-camel, for 36 to 45 is a 3 year-old she-camel, for 46 to 60 is a 4-year-old she-camel, for 61 to 75 is 5-year-old she-camel, for 76 to 90 is 2 3-year-old she-camels, and for 91 to 120 is 2 5-years-old she-camels.

- The *nisab* for cattle is 30. For 30 to 40 heads of cattle, a 2.5-year-old male or female weaned calf; for 40 to 60, a 3-year-old weaned calf; for 60, 2 1-year-old calves. When there are more than 60 heads of cattle, the rate is 1 calf for each 30 heads and 1 weaned calf for each 40 heads.

- When one has 40 sheep or goats, their due is 1 sheep or goat. For 40 to 120 it is the same, for 120 to 200 it is 2 sheep, for 200 to 399 it is 3 sheep, and for 400 to 500 it is 4 sheep.

Farm Products

The *zakat* on farm products is paid when they are harvested. One must calculate them in advance if he or she wants to use or benefit from them. Most scholars maintain than their *nisab* is about 50 quarters, that is, if one has that amount of farm products, one must pay their *zakat*. The due for farm products naturally irrigated (with rain) is one-tenth; if they are irrigated by their owner, who must pay the related expenses, the due is one-twentieth.

Minerals, Mines, Buried Treasure, and Sea Products

The *zakat* on such items is one-fifth. If a buried treasure is found in a land whose owner is unknown or belongs to the state, one-fifth of it is given as *zakat* and the rest belongs to the finder. If it is found in a land whose owner is known, one-fifth is given to the owner. Scholars have ruled that there is no *nisab* for such items. However, some maintain that when these items are worth about 600 dirhams of silver or 90 grams of gold, *zakat* must be paid.

Recipients

Scholars have divided property into two categories: hidden (kept at home, such as money, gold, and silver) and property kept in the open (e.g., animals and farm products). During the Prophet's lifetime and that of the caliphs, *zakat* was collected by officials appointed for that purpose. There was even a special *zakat* fund in the state budget. In later times, the state began to collect *zakat* on the property in the open and let the owners of hidden properties take care of it by themselves.

Muslims or Muslim communities must find a good, preferable way to collect *zakat* in the absence of an Islamic authority and distribute it properly, as mentioned in 9:60. They are:

- Poor people who do not earn enough to keep themselves and their families alive.
- The destitute who cannot meet their basic needs.
- *Zakat* collectors.
- Those whose hearts, due to their weak Islam, need to be reconciled or strengthened for Islam; whose hearts can be swayed toward Islam; or those whose evil against Islam and the Muslims could be avoided.
- To free Muslim prisoners-of-war and emancipate slaves.

- To help those who are overburdened with debt.
- To support those who exalt God's word, strive for God's cause (*mujahidun*), and provide for students and pilgrims.
- Travelers, either at home or abroad.

The recipients of *zakat* are mentioned in the following verse:

> The prescribed alms are meant only for the poor and those in destitution (although, out of self-respect, they do not give the impression that they deserve help); those in charge of collecting and administering them; those whose hearts or friendship and support are to be won over for God's cause, (including those whose hostilities might be prevented thereby); to free those in the bondage of slavery and captivity; to help those overburdened with debt; and in God's way (to exalt God's word, to provide for students and help pilgrims); and for the wayfarer (in need of help). This is an ordinance from God. God has full knowledge of everything, All-Wise. (9:60)

Zakat is distributed among the recipients according to their need and priority, assigned to those in greater need, or according to circumstances. But *zakat* is not voluntary charity given to please the poor; rather, it is spent to eradicate poverty, provide capital for the needy in order to save them from their need, to fill the gaps between classes, or to prevent such gaps from appearing in society.

Sadaqa al-Fitr (The Charity of Fast-Breaking)

Sadaqa al-fitr must be paid by every free Muslim whose wealth meets one's basic needs and has extra wealth equal to 600 grams of silver. A Muslim must pay it for himself, his wife, children, and servants at the end of Ramadan to purify those who fast, to protect them from indecent act or speech, and to help the poor and needy. It is given before the 'Iyd prayer on the 'Iyd (Religious Festive) Day. One who forgets to pay it, or cannot pay it at this time due to some valid excuse, must pay it when one remembers it or has no more excuse.

Traditionally, sadaqat al-fitr has been calculated on the basis of, and paid as, wheat, barley, dates, and dried grapes. However, the amount to be paid must be sufficient to meet an average person's daily food intake. It can be paid either in the kind, as mentioned above, or in its monetary equivalence.

Infaq (Spending in God's Way)

Islam views wealth realistically – as an essential aspect of life and the main means of individual and group subsistence. God Almighty says: *Do not give to those devoid of good judgment and sanity your property, which God has put in your charge as means of support for you (and the needy)* (4:5). This amounts to saying that wealth is to be distributed to meet basic needs (e.g., food, clothing, lodging, and other indispensables), and that no one is to be lost, forgotten, or left without support. The best way to distribute wealth so that everyone's basic needs are met is through *zakat*, for it places no burden upon the wealthy, meets the basic needs of the poor, and relieves them of life's hardships and deprivation's pain.

Zakat is not a favor of the wealthy to the poor; rather, it is a due that God entrusted to the rich so that they might deliver it to the poor and distribute it among the deserving. This establishes the following truth: Wealth is not exclusively for the rich, but for the rich and the poor. This is what is meant by God's saying: *so that this (wealth) may not circulate solely among the rich from among you* (59:7). *Zakat* must be paid by those who can pay it, and must be given to the poor and the needy so that they can meet their basic needs, not go hungry, and acquire a sense of security and general well-being. If there is not enough *zakat* to meet such needs, the rich can be subjected to further taxation. How much should be taken is not specified, for that depends upon the needs of the poor.

The Qur'an urges the wealthy to spend in God's way and for His cause. For example, in praising the believers, it declares:

> They spend in God's way (of whatever God has bestowed upon them) both in ease and hardship, restrain their rage (even though they are able to retaliate and avenge), and pardon people their offenses. God loves (such) people devoted to doing good (ever conscious that God always sees them). (3:134)

> They establish the (prescribed) prayer (in awe and veneration of God and in conformity with its conditions), and spend as subsistence out of whatever We provide for them (of wealth, knowledge, power, and so on to those really in need purely for His good pleasure and without placing others under obligation). (8:3)

The Qur'an tells us to give from what we love and not to place people under obligation because of what we spend in God's way or give to them:

> Those who spend their wealth in God's way and then do not follow up what they have spent with placing under obligation and taunting, their reward is with their Lord. There shall be no fear on them (both in this world and the next, for they shall always find My help and support with them), nor shall they grieve. A kind word and forgiving (people's faults) are better than almsgiving followed by taunting. God is All-Wealthy and Self-Sufficient, (absolutely independent of people's charity), All-Clement (Who shows no haste in chastising). (2:262-63)

> You will never be able to attain godliness until you spend of what you love (in God's way or as sustenance to the needy). Whatever you spend, God has full knowledge of it. (3:92)

> Spend (of whatever you have) in God's way, and do not cast yourselves into destruction with your own hands (by refraining from doing so). Whatever you do, do it, conscious that God sees it, and in the best way possible. God loves those who are devoted to doing good, conscious that God always sees them. (2:195)

God promises great reward to those who spend their wealth in His way, and warns against being miserly and spending only to attract people's attention:

> The example of those who spend their wealth in God's way is like that of a grain that sprouts seven ears, and in every ear there are a hundred grains. Thus God multiplies for whomever He wills. God is One Who embraces all (with His mercy), All-Knowing. (2:261)

> Those who act miserly (in spending of what God has granted them) and urge others to be miserly, and conceal the things God

has granted them out of His bounty (such as wealth and certain truths in their Book), We have prepared for (such) disbelievers a shameful, humiliating chastisement. And (also) those who spend their wealth (in charity or for another good cause) to make a show of it to people and be praised by them, when they believe neither in God nor in the Last Day. Whoever has Satan for a comrade, how evil a comrade he is!! (4:37-38)

Another point to stress here is that generalizing certain matters sometimes has caused great misunderstanding and wrong applications, as in the cases of condemning the world and asceticism. Humanity is God's vicegerent on Earth, meaning that people have the right to interfere with things (i.e., the ecological equilibrium and 'nature's" universal laws) within the bounds established by God, improve Earth, and rule it in God's name and according to His laws. This duty falls first of all upon believers, because denying God in any way severs the link between God and humanity, causes bloodshed and unrest upon Earth.

Since maintaining human existence depends upon belief and the existence of a formidable group of believers with the potential to bear the Divine Trust, Earth's Divine bounties belong, first of all, to believers. In return, they are obliged to administer them and distribute them justly among people. Thus, they are to use Earth's bounties in accordance with God's Will, and to thank Him in return. However, they are forbidden to go beyond the lawful limits in benefiting from them and make eating and drinking the goal of their lives.

In addition to engendering competitive clashes over such items, overconsumption also leads to accumulated energy that, if not controlled, causes such destructive sins as adultery and prostitution. So, to avoid such destruction, individuals can adapt, and are even advised to embrace, asceticism. But the Muslim community cannot leave earthly bounties, as well as their administration and distribution, to others in the name of asceticism. As Bediüzzaman Said Nursi puts it, believers must not set their hearts on the world but must work and earn to maintain themselves, uphold God's Word, and spend in His way.

SOME GLIMPSES OF ISLAM'S ECONOMIC SYSTEM[4]

Islam guides its followers in all phases and activities of life, material as well as spiritual. Its basic teaching on economics is mentioned in several Qur'anic passages. We find it stated clearly in several verses, as in some of those mentioned above, that God created everything on Earth, in the seas, and the heavens for humanity's benefit, meaning that everything submits to Him and can be used by humanity, who is tasked with knowing and profiting from the creation in a rational way and by paying due regard to the future.

Islam's economic policy is explained in unequivocal terms: *so that this (wealth) may not circulate solely among the rich from among you* (59:7). Equality of all people in wealth and comfort – even if it is ideal – does not promise to be an unmixed blessing. For example, since people do not have equal natural talents, even if complete equality were achieved, spendthrifts would soon fall into difficulties and begin envying and coveting other people's good fortune. Furthermore, on philosophic and psychological grounds, it seems to be in humanity's interest that there be differences in wealth.

Human livelihood is in constant progress, for humanity continues to dominate and exploit one thing after the other in God's creation, whereas animals have changed nothing in their livelihood since God created their species. One cause of this difference, as discovered by biologists, is the simultaneous existence of a society – a cooperation and a liberty of competition among the people who live in that society. Perhaps the most developed social cooperation is found among bees, ants, and termites, all of which live collectively and with complete equality in livelihood. But there is no competition among its members, and so any bee which is more intelligent or industrious cannot live more comfortably than others. Thus none of these species evolves, changes, or makes any progress in the human sense of those terms.

Human history shows that every advance and discovery of how to become more comfortable came into existence through competition and the desire for improvement, as well as through the existence of grades of wealth or poverty. Yet absolute liberty would lead devilish people to exploit the needy and gradually draw them out. So each progressive civilization and healthy culture had to impose certain duties (e.g., paying taxes, forbidding oppression and cheating), and to recommend certain supererogatory acts (e.g., charity and spending for God's sake), while nevertheless allowing a great deal of liberty of thought and action to its members, so that each person benefits his or her self, family, friends, and society at large. This is the exigency of Islam.

Islam has based its economic system on this fundamental principle. If it tolerates richness, it imposes heavier obligations on the rich. For example, they have to pay taxes to help the poor, and cannot engage in immoral economic practices (e.g., exploitation, hoarding, and wealth accumulation). To achieve this goal, it makes various laws, as well as some recommendations (e.g., charity and sacrifice), with the promise of a spiritual (otherworldly) reward. Furthermore, it distinguishes between the necessary minimum and the desirable plenitude, and between those laws that are accompanied by material sanctions and those that are not by persuading and educating.

We shall describe this moral aspect first through several illustrations. Islam has used very emphatic terms to show that begging charity from others is abominable and a source of shame. Yet at the same time, it highly praises those who help others, calling the "best of people" those who sacrifice and prefer others to themselves. Similarly, avarice and waste are prohibited.

One day the Prophet needed considerable funds for a public cause. One of his friends offered a certain amount and, when asked by the Prophet, replied: "I have left nothing at home but the love of God and of His Messenger." This person received the warmest praise from the Prophet. But on another occasion, another Companion who was seriously ill told him, when he came to inquire about his health: "O Messenger of God, I am a rich man and want to bequest all that I possess for the welfare of the poor." The Prophet replied, "No, it is better to leave your relatives with an independent means of livelihood so that they will not be depend-

ent upon others and have to beg." When the man decreased it
to two-thirds and then one-half, the Prophet still refused, saying
that it was too much. When the man finally proposed one-third
of his property in charity, the Prophet said: "Well, even one-third
is a large amount." (cf. Abu Dawud, "Zakat," 45).

One day the Prophet saw a Companion in miserable attire.
When asked why, he replied: "O Messenger of God, I am not at
all poor, but I prefer to spend my wealth on the poor rather than
on myself." The Prophet remarked: "No. God likes to see on His
servant traces of the bounty that He has accorded him." (cf. Abu
Tirmidhi, "Birr," 63).

There is no contradiction in these accounts, for each has its
own context and relates to distinct individual cases. Muslims are
allowed to determine how much charity they will give after their
wealth has exceeded the obligatory minimum.

Inheritance

Both the individual right of controlling one's wealth and the
right of the collectivity vis-à-vis each person's wealth, inasmuch
as one is a member of society, have to be satisfied simultaneously. Individual temperaments differ enormously, and sickness or
other accidents may affect a person all out of proportion to the
norm. Therefore, a certain discipline should be imposed upon
the individual in the interest of the collectivity.

Thus Islam has taken two steps: distributing a deceased person's goods among his or her close relatives according to a method
that cannot be challenged, and restricting the freedom of bequest
through wills and testaments. The legal heirs require no testamen-
tary disposition and inherit the property in the proportions determined by law. A testament is required only for those who have no
right to inherit.

Parents and grandparents inherit, and one cannot award to
one son (elder or younger) more than to the other, regardless of
age. Before the property is distributed, however, the burial expenses have to be paid first, and then the creditors, as paying debts has
priority over the inheritors' rights. After this, the will is executed

in such a way that it does not exceed one-third of the remaining property. Only after satisfying these obligations are the heirs considered. The surviving spouse, parents, and descendants (sons and daughters) are the first-class heirs and inherit in all cases. Brothers, sisters, and more remote relatives (e.g., uncles, aunts, cousins, nephews, and others) only inherit if there are no nearer relatives.

Wills

Wills are operative only for one-third of property and favor persons other than creditors and heirs. The goal of this rule seems to be twofold: To permit a person to adjust things, in extraordinary cases, when the normal rule causes hardship (one-third of the property is enough for fulfilling such moral duties) and to prevent the accumulation of wealth among a few people. This could happen if one willed all of his or her property to only one person. Islam desires that wealth circulate as widely as possible, taking into account the family's interest.

Public Goods

One also has obligations as a member of a larger family (i.e., society and the state of residence). In the economic sphere, one pays taxes that the government then redistributes in the collectivity's interest. Tax rates differ according to the sources of income. Interestingly, the Qur'an, which gives precise directions about budgetary expenditure, contains no rules or rates of the income for the state. While scrupulously respecting the practice of the Prophet and his immediate successors, this silence may be interpreted as allowing the government to change the rules for income according to circumstances and in the people's interest.

Social Insurance

This consists of risks involving heavy charges from objects of insurance, and differs according to the times and social conditions. Among the Arabs of the Prophet's time, daily ailments were unknown and the cost of medical care was practically nothing. The average man built his house and paid for almost none of the material. Thus it is easy to understand why one did not need fire, health, and other types of insurance. However, insurance against captivity and assassination was a real need. The Prophet's contemporaries were aware of this and so desired certain flexible dispositions that could be modified and adapted to different circumstances when necessary.

For example, in the Constitution of Madina, which was formulated during the first year of the Islamic era, this insurance is called *ma'aqil* and worked as follows. If someone became a prisoner of war, paying a ransom could procure his freedom. Similarly, all bodily torts or culpable homicides required the payment of damages or blood money. The person concerned often could not afford the sum demanded. Thus, the Prophet organized an insurance system on the basis of mutuality. A tribe's members could count on the tribe's central treasury, to which everybody contributed according to his means. If the treasury proved inadequate, other related or neighboring tribes had to help. Thus a hierarchy was established for organizing the units into a complete whole. At Madina, the Ansar tribes were well known. The Prophet ordered the Makkan refugees in Madina to form their own "tribe," even though they belonged to different Makkan or regional tribes, or were Abyssinians, in order to provide social insurance.

Under Caliph 'Umar, the branches of insurance were organized according to which professional, civil, or military administration one belonged (or even of regions). Whenever needed, the central or provincial government helped those branches, as we described above when speaking of state expenditure.

Insurance signifies the spreading of one individual's burden among as many people as possible in order to lighten each person's burden. Unlike modern capitalistic insurance companies, Islam organized insurance on the basis of mutuality and cooperation, aided by a pyramidal gradation of the branches that culminated in the central government.

Such a branch could engage in commerce with the help of the unutilized funds at its disposal, so that the capital would be augmented. A time might come when a branch's members could be exempted from paying further contributions or might even receive some of the profits of commerce. Such elements of mutual aid could insure against risk (e.g., traffic accidents, fire, and loss in transit). Also, the insurance industry can be nationalized in order to deal with certain risks (e.g., such temporary motives as dispatching parcels).

Without entering into technical details, Islam does not tolerate the capitalist version of insurance, for the insured person does not participate in the company's benefits in proportion to his or her contributions, which makes it resemble a game of chance.

Games of Chance

Qur'an 5:90 prohibits all games of chance and characterizes them as the "work of Satan" for cogent reasons. First, most social evils emanate from an inequitable distribution of the national wealth, which allows some to become too rich and others to become too poor. As a result, the rich can exploit the poor. In games of chance and lotteries, there is great temptation for quick and easy gain, although such easy gain is often bad for society. If people spent 3 million dollars every week on horse races, public or private lotteries, and other games of chance, as is the case in certain countries, over the course of only 10 years, 1.56 billion dollars would be collected from a large number of people and distributed among a ridiculously small number of people. Less than one percent of the people thrive at the expense of the remaining 99 percent. In other words, 99 percent of the people are impoverished in order to enrich 1 percent.

Whether games of chance and lotteries are private or nationalized, the evil of a few people accumulating wealth at the expense of the vast majority works with full force. This is why Islam prohibits such activities. As is the case with capitalistic insurance, games of chance bear one-sided risks.

Interest on Money-Lending

Probably every religion has prohibited usury. However, only Islam provides remedies to undermine the causes leading to this evil institution: Nobody willingly pays interest on borrowed money.

He or she pays interest because the money is needed and there is no other choice.

Islam has made a very clear distinction between commercial gain and interest on money-lending: *God permits trading and forbids interest* (2:275) and

> If you do not give up (interest), be warned of war against God and His Messenger. If you repent, you shall have your principal, (without interest); neither you wrong nor be wronged. (2:279)

The basis of this prohibition is also unilateral risk, for one who borrows money on interest earns money for the rich. In games of chance and lotteries, where there is a great temptation for quick and easy gain, circumstances may not have been propitious enough for the borrower to earn enough money to pay back the promised interest, and the lender assumes none of the risk involved.

People do not deprive themselves of their money in order to make interest-free loans to others. Since Islam tells the state to help those who are in financial difficulty, the public treasury organized interest-free loans in addition to, and to supplement, the loans offered by charitable people or organizations to help the poor and the needy. The principle here is mutual aid and cooperation.

In the case of commercial loans, there is the system of *mudaraba*, in which one lends money and participates equally in any potential gain or risk. For example, if two people form a company, each one furnishing half of the capital and labor, the resulting profit distribution is quite easy. However, if the capital comes from one party and the labor from the other, if both furnish the capital though only one of them works, or their shares are not proportionally equal, in such cases a reasonable remuneration for labor, based upon previously agreed conditions, is taken into consideration before distributing any gains and profit. Although all precautions are taken to prevent risk, Islam demands that both contracting parties to any contractual negotiation must share the profit as well as the loss.

To sum up, the principle of mutual participation in profits and risks must be observed in all commercial contracts.

Statistics

When planning, one needs to have an idea about the available resources. The Messenger organized a census of the Muslim population, as al-Bukhari informs us. During 'Umar's caliphate, a census of animals, fruit trees, and other goods was organized, and cultivable lands were measured in the newly acquired provinces. With a large spirit and full of concern for the public's well-being 'Umar would invite representatives of the people of different provinces, after taxes were collected, to find out if they had any complaints about the collector's behavior during the year.

Daily Life

We end this brief sketch by mentioning two important prohibitions that are characteristic of a Muslim's daily life: games of chance and alcoholic drinks. Having already discussed the first one, which causes the vast majority of its participants to spend money for years without gaining anything in return, we now turn to a discussion of alcohol. Alcohol has a very interesting quality: drinking only a little of it makes one happy and weakens any resolution to stop drinking. While drunk, people lose control over their actions. For example, they may squander money without being aware of what they are doing. In addition, various unhygienic effects of alcohol are transmitted to their children and future generations. Qur'an 2:219 speaks about such matters in the following terms: *They question you about wine and games of chance. Say: "In both is great sin and some profits for people, but the sin of them is greater than their usefulness."*

The Qur'an does not deny that alcohol has some benefits, but still declares it a sin against society, the individual, and the Legislator. In 5:90, alcohol is relegated to the same level as idolatry and declared to be the handiwork of Satan. It adds that if one wants to be happy in both worlds, one should avoid games of chance and alcohol.

Fulfilling Agreements

All financial and other dealings are based on some expressed or implicit agreements. Honoring these agreements is the key to happy and smooth relationships among members of a community or a society. Therefore, the Qur'an stresses this principle and, in several places, actually lists it as being among a believer's most important characteristics.

> (Believers are those) who are faithful to their trusts and to their commitments. (23:8)

> Those who fulfill their covenant when they have engaged in a covenant. (2:177)

> O you who believe, fulfill the bonds (you have entered into with God and people). (5:1)

> Fulfill the covenant. One is responsible for one's covenant and will be called to account for it (on the Day of Judgment). (17:34)

The failure to honor agreements is a primary cause of difficulty in dealings among people, especially financial dealings. If we analyze broken business partnerships or other difficulties in financial dealings, we will always find their root in the failure of one or more parties to fulfill one or more of the implicit agreements related to those dealings.

Writing and Witnessing the Deal

To avoid such problems due to forgetfulness or other reasons, and to reduce any chance of misunderstanding and bad faith, the Qur'an orders that all financial deals be committed to paper and witnessed, as we read in the following passage:

> O you who believe, when you contract a debt between you for a fixed term, record it in writing. Let a scribe write it down between you justly, and let no scribe refuse to write it down as God has taught him (via the Qur'an and His Messenger). So let him write. Let the debtor dictate, and let him avoid disobeying God, his Lord, (Who has created him and brought him up with mercy and grace,) and curtail no part of it. If the debtor be weak of mind or body, or incapable of dictating, let his guardian dictate justly. And call upon two (Muslim) men among you as witnesses. If two men cannot be found, let one man and two women from among those of whom you approve as witnesses,

so that if either woman errs (through forgetfulness), the other may remind her. Let the witnesses not refuse when they are summoned (to give evidence). (And you, O scribes,) be not loath to write down (the contract), whether it be small or great, with the date of its payment. Your doing so, (O you who believe,) is more equitable in God's sight, more upright for testimony, and more likely that you will not be in doubt. If it be a matter of buying and selling concluded on the spot, there shall be blame upon you if you do not write it down. But take witnesses when you settle commercial transactions with one another, and let no harm be done to either scribe or witness, (nor let either of them act in a way to injure the sides). If you act (in a way to harm either side or the scribe and witnesses,) indeed it will be transgression in you. (Always) act in reverence for God and try to attain piety. God teaches you (whatever you need in life and the way you must follow in every matter); God has full knowledge of everything. If you are (in circumstances like being) on a journey and cannot find a scribe, a pledge in hand shall suffice. But if you trust one another, let him (the debtor) who is trusted fulfill his trust, and let him act in piety and keep from disobedience to God, his Lord (by not fulfilling the contract's conditions). Do not conceal the testimony, (for) he who conceals it, surely his heart (which is the center of faith) is wholly contaminated with sin. God has full knowledge of what you do. (2:282-83)

In these verses, the Qur'an distinguishes between financial transactions that involve credit for a definite period and those that are carried out on the spot. Examples of the first type include loans for a definite period and the purchase or sale of goods with either the payment or delivery promised for some fixed future date. An example of the second type include buying something in a shop on a cash-and-carry basis.

Some people might be surprised that the Qur'an recommends that even on-the-spot transactions (e.g., sale of goods on cash-and-carry basis) should have some proof in writing or through witnesses. Perhaps because at first sight it looks unnecessary, this recommendation has been almost completely ignored in the Muslim world. However, as business became more organized, the wisdom behind this recommendation has been independently discovered in modern times. These days, whenever we make any purchase, no matter how small, we receive a receipt. This receipt serves many purposes, such as enabling the customer to return defective items with little or no argument, prosecuting merchants who overcharge or cheat the customer in some way, catching and prosecuting shoplifters, and making it easier for buyers and sellers to keep accounts.

After briefly discussing the usefulness and relevance of the Qur'anic orders to write and/or witness financial deals, we now consider just how obligatory they are.

Avoiding Bad Faith

Writing a clear, detailed agreement and having it duly signed and/or witnessed can prevent two problems: forgetfulness and misunderstanding. In addition, it can reduce the chance of any involved party being tempted to take advantage of the other parties by lying, cheating, or other crooked ways resulting from bad faith. But to avoid bad faith, more than just recording the deal in writing is needed. What is needed here is piety, on which Islam lays such emphasis, defined as the respect for moral values that comes through fear and consciousness of God and belief in the Hereafter.

Enforcing Agreements

However, there will always be people who do not give too much importance to piety and thus will break an agreement whenever it suits them. To counter such people, there must be a legal apparatus to enforce any deals that they may willingly sign.

Justice as the Basis of Economic Life

Justice ('adl) means to divide two things equally or keep the balance. The Qur'an uses it for justice in all matters, and Islam teaches the believers to be fair in their dealings, as we read in:

> God commands you to deliver trusts (all public affairs, duties and posts and positions) to those entitled to them. And, when you judge between people, judge with justice. How excellent is what God exhorts you to do. Assuredly, God is All-Hearing, All-Seeing. (4:58)

Islam commands the believers to be just among themselves and exhorts them to be fully just even to their enemies:

> O you who believe, be upholders and standard-bearers of right for God's sake, being witnesses for establishing absolute justice, and never let your hatred for a people move you to deviate from justice. Be just, (for) this is nearer and more suited to piety. Try to attain piety and always act in reverence for God. Assuredly, God is fully aware of whatever you do. (5:8)

Justice and righteousness are the cornerstone of the Islamic way of life. God's Messenger was known for this justice even before he declared his Prophethood. Throughout his life, he exhorted his followers to be truthful and just. Moreover, he set a perfect example of justice even to the followers of other religions and his enemies.

In accordance with the Divine law, the concept of social justice lays down certain conditions to treat people as individuals having liberty and equality as their birthright. This concept provides them with equal opportunities for personal development so that they are better able to fill the position to which they are entitled, to give each person his or her due, and to regulate his or her relations with society in terms of value and welfare.

Duties to Society

This concept of social justice is achieved by giving people a better understanding of their individual duties in society and the reward thereof, as provided by Islam. The Messenger made education, being the measure and touchstone in this context, obligatory upon every Muslim, both men and women. More specifically, he said and knew that knowledge enabled one to distinguish right from wrong.

A society's progress depends upon the interaction between the individual and society, for this establishes and maintains a balance in human affairs. Humanity should always keep in mind that God created the universe for a particular purpose and that humanity has been asked to strive for its fulfillment.

Equality and Freedom

Broadly speaking, human rights center on equality and freedom. Caliph 'Umar reprimanded the governor of Egypt, whose son had struck a Copt (an Egyptian Christian), with the following instructive words: "Since when have you enslaved men whom their mothers delivered free?" Again, his instructions to establish equality among people demonstrate the best egalitarian features: highly placed people cannot take advantage of their position, and the weak are not made to despair of their condition.

All people are God's servants. The only permissible characteristic by which one can claim superiority, distinction, and preeminence over others is the virtue of piety. All people are equal in social status. This is fully manifested in the congregational prayers, where there is no room for rank and special privilege. All are equal in God's sight, whether one happens to be a caliph or a slave. The Messenger declared that all people were equal, like the teeth of a comb.

The Qur'an says:

> O humanity, We created you from a single (pair) of a male and female, and made you into nations and tribes that you may know each other. Verily, the most honored of you in God's sight is (the one who is) the most righteous of you. (49:13)

Balance in Society

Islam avoids extremes in order to maintain social balance and order. Therefore, monopoly and cut-throat competition are disapproved. Islam's essence is justice for all, which enables people to lead a good and happy life while, at the same time, strengthens the bonds of human brotherhood and the social fabric.

The social framework prevalent today in most Muslim countries is not Islamic. Many places are characterized by monstrous and oppressive conditions for the poor, rampant corruption, poverty, and need. A few people have acquired substantial wealth and thus enjoy the numerous amenities and luxuries of life, whereas the majority do not even receive two square meals a day. An Islamic social order stresses simple and austere efforts that are free from ostentation. The Messenger strove to bridge the gap between the rich and the poor, the high and the low. He advocated a society in which one sector would not exploit another, for Islam seeks a balanced life that represents the equilibrium of social forces.

The fullest development of humanity's potential can be achieved through the implementation of Islamic principles. The optimum level of civilization, which embodies the maximum well-being, can never be possible without spiritual and moral development. All Islamic principles, which descend from Divinity, are perfect and absolute. The Islamic approach is therefore just, natural, humane, and perfectly balanced and rational.

Abu'l-Fazl Ezzati outlines the Islamic economic system as follows:

- Islam represents a complete way of life. There is no compartmentalization of human activity is Islam. Its economic policy is, therefore, an integral part of the religion of Islam.
- Islamic economic system is based on equality, justice, moderation, and collective self-sufficiency.
- Man's spiritual development is fundamental but his physical welfare is instrumental.
- Islam is based on faith in God, Who has given man the capability to choose between good and evil, and assume full responsibility for his conduct. "Man has only that for which he makes effort, and and this effort will be seen." (53:39-40)
- Islam is a universal system embodying eternal values which safeguard man's rights while constantly reminding him of his obligation to himself and society.
- Islam forbids exploitation and monopoly in all forms and strictly prohibits unearned interest such as usury, gambling, betting, etc.
- Islam honors labor and contracts, enjoins work and toil, encourages man to earn his own living by honest means and to spread his earnings.
- Islam encourages mutual helping and never likes "wealth to circulate among the rich only" (59:7). Every member of the

Muslim community feels obliged to help his poor brother
while he is equally entitled to live a private life and to own
property.[5]

HAJJ (PILGRIMAGE)

Hajj is a rehearsal of life in both this world and the next, a theater of all Islamic life based upon deep devotion to God and perception of one's servanthood and God's Divinity and Lordship.
It consists of love, action, humility, God-consciousness, sacrifice,
and dominion over the carnal self.

It has two pillars: staying at 'Arafat for a certain length of time
on Dhu'l-Hijja 9 (the last day of the Islamic lunar calendar) and circumambulating the Ka'ba any day after staying at the 'Arafat. *Ihram*
is also essential to both the major (*Hajj*) and minor (*'Umra*) pilgrimage. *Ihram* is the intention to perform either *Hajj* or *'Umra*, or
both, and marks the beginning of *Hajj* or *'Umra*, or both if they are
performed together. It also signifies making some things forbidden.
Men wear special attire while in *ihram*, and this is why some people call this attire *ihram*.

The Virtue of *Hajj*

Hajj mabrur (a faultless *Hajj* that is free of sin and graced with
Divine acceptance and pleasure) is one of the best, most virtuous
deeds in Islam."

Bukhari and Muslim record from God's Messenger: "He who
performs *Hajj* for God's good pleasure and avoids all lewdness and
sin will return after *Hajj* as free from all sins as he was the day his
mother gave birth to him" (Zayn al-Din al-Zabidi, *Tajrid al-Sarih*,
"Hajj," 756) and: "Pilgrims and those performing *'Umra* are God's
guests. Their prayers are answered and their supplications for forgiveness are granted. The reward of *Hajj* mabrur is Paradise." (Canan,
ibid., 17:383)

Concerning the importance of *Hajj*, the Qur'an says:

> Behold, the first House (of prayer) established for humanity is
> the one at Bakka (Makka), as a blessed place and a center of guid-
> ance for the whole world. Therein are clear signs (showing that

it is a blessed sanctuary chosen by God as the center of guidance), and the Station of Abraham. Whoever enters it is secure (against attack and fear). Pilgrimage to the House is a duty owed to God by all who can afford a way to it. Whoever rejects (this obligation) or is ungrateful to God (by not fulfilling this command), God is All-independent of all creatures. (3:96-97)

Some Facts

Hajj is Obligatory Only Once

All Muslim scholars agree that *Hajj* is obligatory only once during a Muslim's lifetime, unless someone vows to perform an extra *Hajj*, in which case the vow must be fulfilled. Whatever is done over and above is supererogatory or optional.

When Hajj Must Be Performed

Although some scholars opine that *Hajj* may be performed at any time during one's life, and that one who must perform *Hajj* can postpone it, it is preferred that *Hajj* be performed as soon as one is physically and financially able to do so. This is because if the person dies before performing the obligatory *Hajj* or a vowed one, one's heirs must carry out this duty. Even if the deceased did not specify this in his or her will, if one-third of the estate is enough for an heir to make *Hajj*, an heir had better perform it for the deceased. All ensuing *Hajj* expenses, as well as any debts, must be paid from the deceased's property. However, the heir who wants to do this must obtain all of the other heirs' agreement, or at least resignation, before departing. If such an agreement is not reached, the heir must pay all expenses out of his or her own property.

Prerequisites

All jurists agree upon the following:
* Being an adult, free Muslim. Children can make *Hajj* along with their parents, but they have to perform it again after reaching the age of responsibility (puberty).
* Being of sound mind.
* Being physically fit and healthy enough to perform it.

- Finding a safe way to reach Makka, so that the pilgrim's life and possessions are not in danger.
- Having the necessary provisions, meaning that they must be able to take care of themselves while performing *Hajj*, meet their family's needs back home, and be able to make the trip in in a way acceptable in Islam. All of the money spent to perform *Hajj* must have been earned in lawful means according to Islam.
- A woman who performs *Hajj* from such a distance that she will be considered a traveler must be accompanied by her husband, or a man who cannot legally marry her, or one or more reliable women.

Hajj on Behalf of Others

If people can perform *Hajj* but do not do so, and then are over-taken by sickness, old age, or death, they must arrange for someone else to perform it on their behalf, for they might never have another chance to do it. If sick people recover after having sent someone in their place, some scholars say that their duty to make *Hajj* has been fulfilled and that they do not have to "repeat" it. However, most scholars opine that the recovered people still must perform *Hajj*, for a "substitutory" *Hajj* is not enough.

Doing Business

Pilgrims can pursue trade and business during *Hajj* or *'Umra*, provided that they are making *Hajj* solely to fulfill their responsibility for God's sake. The Qur'an declares:

> There is no blame on you if you should seek something of the bounty of your Lord (by trading during the Pilgrimage. But beware that you should not be over-occupied with trading to neglect any of its rituals). When you press on in multitude from 'Arafat (after you have stayed there for some time,) mention God at Mash'ar al-Haram (i.e., Muzdalifa). Mention Him, conscious of how He has guided you, for formerly you were surely of those astray. (2:198)

Ihram

Ihram is the intention to perform *Hajj* or *'Umra*, either singly or together, and marks the beginning of either one, or both, if they are performed together. It also signifies making some things forbidden. Men wear a special attire of two white, unstitched, cloth sheets. One of these is wrapped around the body's upper part (except the head), and the other (*izar*) is wrapped around the body's lower part. There is no special *Hajj* attire for women.

Fixed Time

This refers to the specific time during which the rites have to be performed in order to be valid. The Qur'an states: *They ask you, (O Messenger,) about the new moons. Answer them: "They are signs for the people to determine time and the period of the Pilgrimage"* (2:189) and: *The Pilgrimage is in the months well-known to people* (2:197). Muslim scholars agree that the known months are Shawwal, Dhu'l-Qa'da and the first ten days of Dhu'l-Hijja. Therefore, putting on the attire for *Hajj* is not valid outside these months, except for *'Umra*, which can be performed at any time of the year.

Fixed Places (Mawaqit) for Ihram and Donning the Special Hajj Attire

Mawaqit (plural of miqat) are the specific places where pilgrims or people intending to perform *Hajj* or *'Umra* must declare their intention to do so and enter the state of *ihram*. Men put on their special *Hajj* attires in these places. Anyone intending to perform *Hajj* or *'Umra* must not pass beyond these places without *ihram*.

God's Messenger, upon him be peace and blessings, specified these places (Canan, *ibid.*, 17:385):

- For the people of Madina and those coming through Madina, the *miqat* is Dhu'l-Hulayfa, 450 kilometers north of Makka.
- For those coming from Syria, Jordan, Palestine, and Lebanon, the *miqat* is al-Juhfa, 187 kilometers northwest of Makka, and close to Rabigh, 204 kilometers from Makka. Rabigh became the *miqat* for people coming from Syria and Egypt after the settlement of al-Juhfa disappeared completely.
- The *miqat* for the people of Najd is Qarn al Manazil, a mountain 94 kilometers east of Makka, overlooking 'Arafat.
- Yalamlam, a mountain 54 kilometers south of Makka, is the *miqat* for those coming from Yemen.

- For the people of Iraq, the *miqat* is Dhat 'Irq, 94 kilometers northeast of Makka.

- For those living in Makka who intend to perform *Hajj*, the *miqat* is the place where they are staying in Makka. However, if they intend to perform *Umra*, they should go to al-Khol or at-Tan'im, for that is the proper *miqat* for *Umra*.

- Those who live between a *miqat* and Makka can make their *ihram* from their house.

- Those whose way does not pass through any of these places must enter the state of *ihram* in that place which shares the same line (latitude) as they do.

Etiquette of Ihram

This involves clipping the fingernails, trimming the moustache, shaving the hair under the armpits, shaving the pubic hair, making wudu' or (preferably) performing ghusl, and combing their beard and hair (men only). Men can put perfume on their body and *Hajj* attire, even if it continues to smell afterwards. After cleansing oneself in accord with these rules, one should pray two *rak'ats*, intend to assume the state of *ihram*, and perform either *Hajj* or *Umra*, or both, if one intends to perform them together.

Kinds of Ihram or Hajj

These are divided into three categories, each of which all scholars say are legitimate: *Qiran* (combining *Umra* and *Hajj* in one state of *ihram*), *Tamattu'* (combining *Hajj* and *Umra* with a break in between), and *Ifrad* (*Hajj* only).

Qiran

Here, pilgrims declare their intention to perform both *Hajj* and *Umra* together, and say when doing *talbiya*: "O God, I answer your call to perform *Hajj* and *Umra*." [*Talbiya is: Labbayk, Allahumma labbayk; labbayk la sharika laka; inna'l-hamda wa'l-minnata laka wa'l-mulk, la sharika lak.* (Here I am, my God, here I am at Your service. Here I am at Your service. You have no partner. Assuredly, all praise and gratitude are for You, and all dominion. You have no partner.)]. Such pilgrims must remain in the state of *ihram* until they have performed all the rites of *Umra* and *Hajj*.

Tamattu'

In this case, pilgrims perform *Umra* during the *Hajj* season and then perform *Hajj*. It is called *tamattu'* (enjoyment) because these pilgrims have the added advantage of performing *Hajj* and *Umra* together without having to go back home, and also because after performing *Umra* they can wear their usual clothes, apply perfume, and do other things until they have to put on their attire for *Hajj*.

Anyone intending to do *tamattu'* should, on approaching the *miqat*, make the intention for *Umra*. While uttering *talbiya*, they should say: *Labbayk bil Umra* (O God, I answer Your call to perform *Umra*). They should wear their *Hajj* attire (women have no special *Hajj* attire) until they circumambulate the Ka'ba, walk between Safa and Marwa to perform *sa'y*, and then cut off a little of their hair or shave it off altogether (men only). After that, they may wear their usual clothes and do all that is permissible but that is prohibited while in the state of *ihram*. On Dhu'l-Hijja 8, they must declare their intention to perform *Hajj*, re-enter the state of *ihram*, and put on their special attire from Makka.

Ifrad

Ifrad means that pilgrims intending to perform *Hajj* only should only make the intention for *Hajj* while at the *miqat*. While saying *talbiya*, they should say: *Labbayk bi-hajj* (O God, I answer your call to perform *Hajj*) and wear their *Hajj* attire until all the rites of *Hajj* are completed. After that, they can make *Umra* if they so desire.

Restrictions during Ihram

These are as follows:
- Sexual intercourse and all matters leading to it (e.g., kissing, touching, or talking to one's wife about intercourse or related matters).

- Committing sins that cause deviation from the path of obeying God.
- Disputing, arguing, or fighting with companions, servants, and other people. God declares:

> The Pilgrimage is in the months well-known to people. Whoever undertakes the duty of Pilgrimage in them, there is no sensual indulgence, wicked conduct, or disputing during the Pilgrimage. (In addition to obeying this command,) whatever good you do (and help others), God knows it. Take your provisions for the Pilgrimage (and do not be a burden upon others). In truth, the best provision is piety, so be provided with piety to guard against My chastisement, O people of discernment. (2:197)

- Wearing any sewn clothes (e.g., a shirt, hooded robes, cloak, underpants), wrapping anything around the head (e.g., a cap or a fez), wearing clothes dyed with a nice fragrant dye, or wearing shoes or sewn slippers.
- Killing any animal or game or showing it to someone else so that he or she may kill it, or cutting any green grass or trees (whether within or outside the sacred precincts of Makka).

Penalty for Violating the Sanctity of *Ihram*

- Wearing perfume or similar things on any part of the body or henna on the head; wearing a stitched garment or covering one's head (for men) for a day; shaving at least one-fourth of one's head; clipping one's fingernails; omitting one of the necessary things of *Hajj*; performing the arrival or farewell circumambulation while menstruating; or being in a state of major impurity or doing the obligatory circumambulation of visiting without having wudu'. If one does any of these things in the state of *ihram*, one must sacrifice a sheep or a goat.

    If one does any of these things while in the *ihram* for *qiran*, two sheep or goats must be sacrificed. If one does such things because of coercion or absolute necessity, one either sacrifices within Makka's sacred precincts or fasts for 3 days wherever he or she pleases, or gives charity in an amount equivalent to the *fitra* (that which provides a person with two average-sized meals) to a poor person.

- Having sexual intercourse while in the state of *ihram* before or while at 'Arafat nullifies *Hajj*. If one has sexual intercourse before shaving oneself or cutting some hair after staying in 'Arafat, or performs the obligatory circumambulation of visiting in the state of major ritual impurity or menstruation or post-childbirth bleeding, one must sacrifice a cow, an ox, or a camel. If, however, one repeats the circumambulation after being purified, this sacrifice is cancelled. If one has sexual intercourse after shaving oneself or cutting some hair, but before the circumambulation, one must sacrifice a sheep or a goat.

- If one wears perfume or something similar on some part of the body, wears a stitched garment or covers one's head for some part of the day, shaves less than one-fourth of one's head, clips only a fingernail or another person's fingernails, shaves someone else, or performs the arrival and farewell circumambulation without having performed *wudu'*, one must give a *fitra* amount of charity. Plucking a broken fingernail entails no penalty.

- If one kills a grasshopper, a louse, or a flea on one's own body or on that of somebody else, he or she must pay charity less than a *fitra*. If one kills more than three of these vermin, one must pay a *fitra* amount of charity.

- If one in the state of *ihram* kills an animal whose meat is not edible or a game animal, an assessment should be made and then one should make compensation. For an animal whose meat is not edible, this cannot be more than a sheep or a goat. If one has an animal of equivalent value for the animal or game animal killed, one must sacrifice it and give its meat in charity. If one does not have such an animal, its value should be assessed by two just persons, and the person must give that amount of food to the poor. If one does not have enough money for this, he or she must fast according to how many poor

people could be fed with that money. For example, if it is
estimated that that money could feed 10 needy people, the
person has to fast for 10 days. The food given to the needy
must be enough to satisfy their hunger.

•   If one in the state of *ihram* cuts off or plucks green grass or
    trees within Makka's sacred precincts, and these are not pri-
    vately owned, their value is given away as charity. If they are
    privately owned, the compensation doubles, for the owner
    is indemnified and its value is given to the poor as charity.

The Sacred Precincts of Makka (*Haram Makka*)

The Sacred Precincts of Makka include the area around Makka,
which are marked by stones a meter high, on all roads leading to
or from the city. In this area, killing game animals and cutting
green trees are prohibited. On the northern side, Haram Makka
extends to Tan'im, 6 kilometers from the Sacred Mosque; on the
southern side to Adah, 12 kilometers from Makka; on the eastern side to al-Ji'rana, 16 kilometers away; on its northeastern side
to the valley of Nakhla (14 kilometers away); and on the western side 15 kilometers away (al-Hudaybiya).

Sacred Precincts of Madina (*Haram Madina*)

In the Sacred Precincts of Madina, killing game animals and cutting trees also are prohibited, with the exception that Madina's
residents can use trees and grass for their animals. The sacred
precincts of Madina extend from Eer to Thawr. Eer is a mountain at the *miqat* for Madina, and Thawr is a mountain to the
north near Uhud.

The Necessary Acts (*Wajib*) of Hajj

The obligatory acts consist of staying for some time in
'Arafat after noon on the eve of 'Iyd al-Adha (Dhu'l-Hijja 9), and
performing the obligatory circumambulation (*tawaf*) of visiting.
Ihram is also essential for *Hajj*.

The necessary acts for *Hajj* are as follows:

•   Getting into the state of *ihram* in any of the *miqat* places.

- Doing nothing forbidden while in *ihram*.
- Staying in 'Arafat until sunset on Dhu'l-Hijja 9, the eve of 'Iyd al-Adha.
- Staying in Muzdalifa between dawn and sunrise on the 'Iyd al-Adha for at least one hour. Muzdalifa is located about 20 kilometers from Makka and 10 kilometers from 'Arafat.
- Performing the last three turns of the obligatory circumambulation (*tawaf al-ifada* or *ziyara*) around the Ka'ba. (The first four turns are obligatory.)
- Doing the obligatory circumambulation of visiting during the first 3 days of 'Iyd al-Adha, during which sacrifice is offered.
- Performing the farewell circumambulation. (This is necessary for pilgrims coming from outside of Makka.)
- Performing the circumambulation in the state of ritual purity and covering all parts of the body that must be covered.
- Beginning the circumambulation from a point on line with the Black Stone and with the Ka'ba on one's left.
- Offering two *rak'ats* of prayer after every circumambulation.
- While performing the circumambulation, turning outside and around Hijr Isma'il, a place to the north of Ka'ba and surrounded by a semicircular wall.
- Performing *sa'y* (slightly running seven times between the hills of Safa and Marwa, going from Safa to Marwa four times, and the other way three times).
- Throwing seven pebbles at each of three stone columns (*jamarat*) standing in Mina with some distance between them. These are called Jamrat al-'Ula, Jamrat al-Wusta, and Jamrat al-'Aqaba. On the first day of 'Iyd al-Adha, one throws pebbles at Jamrat al-'Aqaba, and at all of them on the following two days.
- Those coming from outside of Makka and performing *Hajj* al-Tamattu' or *Hajj* al-Qiran should sacrifice a sheep or a goat any time within 3 days after throwing pebbles on the first day of 'Iyd al-Adha, and shave or cut some of their hair within Makka's sacred precincts. Women only clip a little of their hair.

If one of these necessary acts is omitted, a sacrifice must be offered.

Sunna Acts

- Performing *wudu'* or *ghusl* before putting on the *Hajj* attire to enter the state of *ihram*.
- Before wearing the *Hajj* attire, wearing permitted perfume.
- Offering two *rak'ats* of prayer as a *sunna* act of *ihram*, and reciting *Surat al-Kafirun* and *Surat al-Ikhlas* in each *rak'at* after *Surat al-Fatiha*.
- Uttering *talbiya* loudly as soon as one enters the state of *ihram*, and doing so whenever one climbs a hill, descends into a valley, meets one or more people, early in the morning, and after every prescribed prayer until throwing stones at Jamrat al-'Aqaba on the first day of 'Iyd al-Adha. (Women do not raise their voices while uttering *talbiya*.)
- Calling God's blessings and peace upon our Prophet Muhammad, upon him be peace and blessings, and upon his Family many times after each *talbiya*.
- Praying after calling God's blessings and peace upon the Messenger and his Family.
- Performing *ghusl* before entering Makka, praying upon seeing the Ka'ba, and exalting and glorifying God and declaring His Oneness in front of the Sacred Mosque.
- Those coming from outside of Makka perform the arrival circumambulation.
- Making voluntary circumambulations while staying in Makka.
- Walking fast, moving the shoulders vigorously, and taking small steps in order to give a sense of strength and energy during the first three turns of the obligatory *tawaf* of visiting.
- Being quicker between the green markers while doing *sa'y* (between Safa and Marwa).
- Leaving for Mina on Dhu'l-Hijja 8 after sunrise, and spending that day and night there.
- Leaving for 'Arafat on Dhu'l-Hijja 9 after sunrise.

- Leaving for Muzdalifa after sunset and spending that night there, and proceeding to al-Mash'ar al-Haram (near the hill of Quzah in Muzdalifa) at dawn.
- Praying sincerely and in utmost humility, especially after the daily prayers performed in 'Arafat and Muzdalifa.
- Leaving for Mina before sunrise on the first day of 'Iyd al-Adha, and staying in Mina for its last 3 days.
- While throwing pebbles at the Jamarat, standing so that Mina will be on one's right and Makka on one's left, and throwing in turn beginning with Jamrat al-Ula and proceeding to Jamrat al-Wusta and Jamrat al-'Aqaba.
- If possible, throwing the pebbles between sunrise and noon on the first day of throwing, and between noon and sunset on the other days.
- Going quickly from Mina to Makka. If leaving Mina on Dhu'l-Hijja 12 or the third day of 'Iyd al-Adha, leave before sunset.
- While going to Makka, staying in Muhatab and Abtah for a short time.
- Drinking Zamzam water to one's full satiation after making the farewell circumambulation and offering two *rak'ats* of prayer.
- Rubbing one's face and chest against Multazam, a part of the Ka'ba between the Black Stone and its gate.
- Holding onto the curtain covering the Ka'ba and praying without bothering and troubling anyone.
- Visiting the tomb of God's Messenger in Madina.

Performing these *sunna* acts increases the reward for *Hajj*, and omitting any of them incurs no penalty.

Performing *Tawaf*

One must begin *tawaf* (circumambulation) with one's right shoulder uncovered, the Ka'ba on the left, and, while facing the Black Stone, kissing it (if possible), or touching it with one's hand, or pointing in its direction. Jogging lightly through the first three circumambulations is encouraged. One should walk fast, keep as close to the Ka'ba as possible, and take short steps. In the next four rounds, one should walk at a normal pace. Touching the Yemeni corner (*ar-Ruknu'l-Yemeni*) is encouraged, and so is kissing or touching the Black Stone in each of the seven rounds of *tawaf*, if possible. Remembering God and supplicating as much as possible is also encouraged.

There are several kinds of *tawaf*, as follows:

* *Tawaf al-Qudum* (Arrival Circumambulation). This is *sunna* for those coming from outside of Makka.

* *Tawaf al-Ifada or Ziyara* (Obligatory Circumambulation of Visiting). This is one of the two basic pillars of *Hajj*, and should be done during the first 3 days of the 'Iyd al-Adha. If this is not possible, one can do it at any time during one's life, but must offer a sacrifice as penalty.

* *Tawaf al-Wada'* (Farewell Circumambulation). This is necessary for all pilgrims coming from outside of Makka.

* *Tawaf al-Tatawwu'* (Supererogatory Circumambulation). Pilgrims can perform this as often as they want to during their stay in Makka.

Making Sa'y between Safa and Marwa

Pilgrims, whether they are performing *Hajj* or *'Umra* perform *sa'y* after *tawaf*. *Sa'y* means running from Safa to Marwa four times and the other way three times. The Qur'an stresses that each person meets that for whatever one strives or endeavors (53:39). Sa'y means endeavoring or making effort. For *Hajj*, this is held to commemorate Hagar's running between Safa and Marwa seven times in order to find water for her son, Ishmael, whom she was still breast-feeding. God told Abraham to leave Hagar and Ishmael, upon him be peace, in Makka, which was then an uninhabited barren valley. Both Abraham and Hagar submitted to God's order wholeheartedly. However, their submission did not prevent Hagar from trying to find water for her son, for both of them needed it and she also needed it to produce breast-milk.

Islam is the harmonious combination of submission and endeavor. Hagar did not wait for a miracle, but tried to find water in a desolate desert without losing hope. The water came miraculously from an unexpected place: under Ishmael's feet. That water, known as Zamzam, continues to meet the needs of millions of pilgrims every year, even after so many centuries. This miracle was the result of sincere belief, confidence in and submission to God, endeavor (humanity's duty), and never being desperate. People act, and God creates the result. This is why it has unanimously been said: "God is not found by looking for Him, but those who have found Him are those who have looked for Him."

Pilgrims begin *sa'y* from Safa and end in Marwa. They walk from Safa to Marwa four times, and the other way three times. They jog between the two green markers along the way. They supplicate and recite the Qur'an while walking and upon reaching either hill, and face the Ka'ba while supplicating.

'Umra

The word *'umra* is derived from *al-i'timar*, which means "to visit." In this context, it means visiting the Ka'ba, performing *tawaf*, walking between Safa and Marwa seven times, and then shaving one's head or cutting one's hair short. It is a *sunna* act of worship.

The Time

Most scholars have ruled that 'Umra may be performed any time during the year. Abu Hanifa, however, opines that it is disliked to perform 'Umra on five days: the Day of 'Arafat (eve), the Day of Nahr (Dhu'l-Hijja 10, the first day of 'Iyd al-Adha), and the 3 days of Tashriq (Dhu'l-Hijja 11, 12, and 13).

The Miqat

If people who are intending to perform 'Umra are outside the *miqat* fixed for *Hajj*, they must not cross these *miqat*s (places fixed for *ihram*) without declaring *ihram*. Those people who are already well within the *miqat* area, even within Makka's Sacred Precincts, must go out to the *miqat* and declare *ihram* there.

Hajj and 'Umra from Beginning to End

- People who intend to perform *Hajj* must ensure that all of the money to be spent during *Hajj* was earned in Islamically lawful ways. Debts must be paid off, and everyone who has rights upon the intending pilgrim must be asked to suspend those rights. In addition, the intending pilgrims must seek forgiveness from those whom they have wronged and forgive any wrongs done to them. They seek God's forgiveness, and offer two *rak'ats* of prayer without leaving home.

• While journeying, they must occupy themselves with reflecting upon God's works, reciting the Qur'an, supplicating, and avoiding sin, speaking in vain, and harming any living creature.

• On arriving at the *miqat* (the place fixed for entering the state of *ihram*), pilgrims should shave themselves, clip their fingernails, perform *ghusl* or *wudu'*, and wear some perfume. Men don their special *Hajj* attire, which is also called *ihram*, as it is the beginning and symbol of entering the state of *ihram*. There is no special attire for women. Pilgrim candidates should offer a two-*rak'at* prayer and declare their intention (to perform *Hajj*, *Hajj* and *'Umra* together, or *'Umra*). It is recommendable to perform *Hajj Tamattu'* (*Hajj* and Umra together, with a break in between,) for pilgrims who come from far away. If one performs *Hajj Tamattu'*, one makes the intention for *'Umra* at the *miqat*. Wearing *ihram* and declaring the intention for *Hajj* or *'Umra* is an essential part of both, and neither will be correct without *ihram* and intention.

As soon as they enter the state of *ihram*, they must utter the *talbiya* loudly (women do not raise their voices) and continue saying it whenever climbing a hill, descending into a valley, meeting one or more people, early in the morning, and after every prescribed prayer until one throws pebbles at the Jamrat al-'Aqaba on the first day of 'Iyd al-Adha.

While in the state of *ihram*, pilgrims must avoid sexual intercourse and whatever leads to it, wrangling and useless bickering, marriage or joining others in marriage, wearing any sewn clothes or shoes that cover the feet above the ankles, covering their heads (men) or faces (women), wearing perfume, cutting their hair or nails, engaging in hunting game animals, or cutting trees or grass within Makka's Sacred Precincts.

- When entering Makka, pilgrims perform *ghusl*; hasten to the
  Sacred Mosque, and, upon reaching it, say the *talbiya*; ask God
  for forgiveness and pray to Him; call His blessings and peace
  on our master Muhammad, upon him be peace and blessings,
  and his Family and Companions; and recite words of God's
  Oneness, glorification, praise, and exaltation. As soon as they
  see the Ka'ba, they should pray for themselves, their parents,
  relatives, and all Muslims. In addition, they must always be
  humble. After this, they should proceed directly to the Black
  Stone and kiss it quietly or touch it with their hand. If this
  is not possible or doing so will harm others, one may just
  point toward it.

- After this, one should begin circumambulating the Ka'ba and
  repeating the Prophet's supplications, upon him be peace and
  blessings. In the first three turns, men should uncover their
  right shoulder and jog slowly. In the remaining rounds, they
  may walk at a normal pace. It is *sunna* to touch the Yemeni
  Corner and to kiss the Black Stone in every round. After
  completing this rite's seven rounds, the pilgrims should go to
  the Station of Abraham, for God said:

> Remember, again, that We made the House (the Ka'ba in
> Makka) a sign showing people to the truth, a resort and place
> of rewarding visit for them, and a center and means of safety.
> (As in older times,) you too (O believers), stand in prayer in
> the Station of Abraham. We imposed a duty on Abraham and
> Ishmael: Purify My House for those who go around It as an
> act of devotion, for those who abide in devotion, and for
> those who bow and prostrate (in prayer). (2.125)

There, they should pray two *rak'ats* of *tawaf*, if possible. If
not, they can pray anywhere in the Mosque.

- Then they should approach Safa to begin *sa'y* in compliance
  with God's words:

> (The hills of) Safa and Marwa are among the emblems that
> God has appointed (to represent some aspects of Islam and the
> Muslim community). Hence, whoever performs *Hajj* to the
> House (of God – the Ka'ba) or does *'Umra*, there is no blame

on him to run between them (and let them run after they go round the Ka'ba as an obligatory Pilgrimage rite). (2:158)

They should climb Safa, look toward the Ka'ba, and supplicate using one of the Messenger's supplications. After this, they should climb down and start walking toward Marwa as the first of seven rounds between the two hills, while remembering God and supplicating.

On approaching one of the two green markers, pilgrims should jog to the second green marker and, after passing it, resume one's normal walking speed toward Marwa. Upon reaching Marwa, one should climb it, turn toward the Ka'ba, and supplicate and glorify God. This marks one complete round. They should perform the remaining six rounds in the same manner, thereby completing all seven rounds.

- If pilgrims are performing *Hajj Tamattu'*, they should shave their head or cut their hair short, for this ends all *ihram*-related restrictions. After this, all things that were forbidden are allowed, including sexual intercourse with one's spouse. Those who intend to perform *Hajj Ifrad* (*Hajj* only) or *Hajj Qiran* (*Hajj* and *'Umra* together without a break) must continue in the state of *ihram*.

- On Dhu'l-Hijja 8, those intending to perform *Hajj Tamattu'* must resume *ihram*, make the intention to perform *Hajj* from their residences, proceed to Mina with those who have remained in *ihram*, and spend the night there.

- At sunrise on Dhu'l-Hijja 9, the pilgrims leave for 'Arafat. Staying at 'Arafat begins only after the sun has passed its zenith. During this time, they should stand by its rocks (*Jabal al-Rahma*) or as close as possible, because this is where the Prophet used to stand. Staying at 'Arafat is the *Hajj*'s principal rite. During it, they should face the *qibla*, glorify and remember God, and supplicate as much as possible until nightfall.

- After nightfall, the pilgrims must leave for Muzdalifa. Upon arriving there, they must offer the *maghrib* and *'isha'* prayers, combining them after an imam, and spend the night there.

- At dawn, the pilgrims stand by al-Mash'ar al-Haram, and perform *waqfa* there. That is, they must stay there for some time and remember and glorify God until it is almost sunrise, as God declares:

> When you press on in multitude from 'Arafat (after you have stayed there for some time,) mention God at Mash'ar al-Haram (in Muzdalifa). Mention Him, conscious of how He has guided you, for formerly you were surely of those astray. (In vainglory, do not choose to remain in Muzdalifa without climbing 'Arafat and staying there for some time. Instead,) press on in multitude from where all the (other) people press on, and implore God for forgiveness (for your opposition until now and the errors you have done during the Pilgrimage). God is All-Forgiving, All-Compassionate (especially toward His believing servants). (2:198-99)

- Before sunrise, they should return to Mina after collecting pebbles at Muzdalifa. After sunrise, the pilgrims must throw seven pebbles at Jamrat al-'Aqaba. Then they offer their sacrifice, have their hair cut, remove their *ihram*, and lead their normal life – with the exception of having sexual intercourse with their spouse.

- Then they go to Makka to perform the obligatory *tawaf* of visiting, an essential part of *Hajj*. Performing this *tawaf* on the first day of 'Iyd al-Adha is recommended, but one can perform it during the following two days. After this *tawaf*, sexual intercourse with one's spouse becomes permissible. If the pilgrims are performing *Hajj Tamattu'*, they must perform a *sa'y* after this *tawaf*. Those who are performing *Hajj Qiran* or *Ifrad* do not have to make this second *sa'y* if they had performed the Arrival *Tawaf* and *sa'y* upon their arrival in Makka.

- The pilgrims must now return to Mina and spend the 3 days of 'Iyd al-Adha there. After midday on the second and third day (Dhu'l-Hijja 11 and 12), they throw seven pebbles at each of three Jamras, beginning with Jamrat al-'Ula and then Jamrat al-Wusta and Jamrat al-'Aqaba. They exalt God at each throwing and, after finishing their throwing at the first two Jamras, pray for themselves, their parents and relatives, and for all Muslims. If they want to stay in Mina on the fourth day of 'Iyd al-Adha, they throw pebbles at the Jamras before noon.

- After returning to Makka, those pilgrims who will be returning to their native lands must perform the Farewell *Tawaf*. Afterwards, they should go to the Zamzam well and drink as much of its water as possible. Then they go to al-Multazim, rub their face and chest against it, hold the curtain covering the Ka'ba, pray, and supplicate.

Those Prevented from Completing *Hajj* or *'Umra*

- If the pilgrims intended to perform either *Hajj* or *'Umra* but were prevented from approaching the House of God, they must sacrifice whatever animal they can afford (e.g., a sheep or a larger animal) within Makka's sacred precincts. After this, they can leave the state of *ihram* and remove their special *Hajj* attire.
- If the reason why they cannot complete this duty is removed before staying in 'Arafat, they must complete their *Hajj*. If they are prevented (from doing so) after staying in 'Arafat, they are not regarded as being prevented from completing their *Hajj*, for they can perform the obligatory *tawaf* anytime during their life, provided that they offer a sacrifice.
- If they are prevented from staying in 'Arafat but can perform the obligatory *tawaf*, they do not have to sacrifice, but must make up their *Hajj* later.
- If they intended to perform the obligatory *Hajj* and were prevented from doing so, they must make it up later.

OFFERING A SACRIFICE

Offering a sacrifice (a sheep, a goat, and for seven people a camel, a cow, or an ox) is incumbent (*wajib*) upon every adult Muslim who has the *nisab* amount of wealth. The difference between having to pay *zakat* and sacrificing is that *zakat* must be paid on it if the person has had it for one year, while a sacrifice must be offered if the person has had it for only one day. The sacrifice must be made on any of the first 3 days of 'Iyd al-Adha.

Sacrifice during Hajj

Pilgrims performing *Hajj Qiran* and *Hajj Tamattu'*, who miss any necessary act (e.g., throwing pebbles, putting on *ihram* from a *miqat*, or performing *sa'y*), or violate any *ihram* restriction or the sanctity of Haram Makka, must sacrifice.

Sacrificial Animals

The most common sacrificial animal is a sheep or a goat. Cattle and camels also can be offered as sacrifice. Pilgrims must sacrifice a camel if they perform *tawaf* in a state of major ritual impurity (*junub*), are still menstruating or having post-childbirth bleeding, have sexual intercourse with their spouse after spending Dhu'l-Hijja 9 (eve) in 'Arafat but before shaving or clipping the hair, or have vowed to sacrifice a camel.

Conditions for Sacrifice

A sacrificial animal should satisfy the following conditions:
- If it is a sheep, it must be at least 1 year old, or as fat and healthy as a 1-year-old sheep if it is more than 6 months old. A camel must be at least 5 years old, a cow 2 years old, and a goat 1 year old.
- The animal should be healthy and without defect (i.e., it must not be one-eyed, have a limp, have a broken horn, be mangy, very thin, or weak).

Time of Offering

The sacrifice must be made at a specific time, as follows:
- Whether one is performing *Hajj* or not, a sacrifice must be offered on any of the first 3 days of 'Iyd al-Adha.
- A sacrifice made to fulfill a vow, atone for sins, or perform a supererogatory act of worship may be offered any time during the year.

Place of Offering

A sacrifice that will be offered during *Hajj*, whether it is necessary (*wajib*) or voluntary, must be offered within Makka's Sacred Precincts.

Who Must Sacrifice the Animal

The one who slaughters the animal must be a Muslim or belong to the People of the Book (a Christian or a Jew). He must say *Bismillah* before sacrificing, for the meat of an animal slaughtered by an atheist, an agnostic, an apostate, or one who intentionally does not say *Bismillah* cannot be eaten.

Eating the Meat of the Sacrificial Animal

God commands Muslims to eat the meat of sacrificed animals: *eat thereof and feed the poor such as (beg not but) live in contentment and such as beg with due humility* (22:36). It is advisable to eat one-third, give one-third to the poor, and one-third to one's friends and relatives. Apparently, this command applies to both the obligatory and supererogatory sacrifice. However, one cannot eat the meat of any animal sacrificed in fulfillment of a vow, for all of the meat must be distributed among the poor and needy.

The sacrificed animal's skin can be used as a rug or in another way, after it is tanned, or given away as charity. One cannot sell it.

Visiting the Prophet's Mosque and Tomb

Going to Madina and visiting the Prophet's Mosque and tomb is sunna and brings great reward. God's Messenger gave the glad tiding that visiting him after his death is like visiting him while he was alive. This visit may be made before or after *Hajj*. He also said: "The space between my house (where he died and was buried) and my pulpit is one of the gardens of Paradise (Rawda), and my pulpit is at my Fountain in Paradise." (Bukhari, "Fazl al-Salawat," 5)

It is recommended that one calls God's blessings and peace upon the Messenger as many times as possible and approaches his mosque calmly and with composure. One should wear perfume, nice clean clothes, and enter the mosque with the right foot. It is recommended that pilgrims first go to the Rawda and offer two *rak'ats*, with calmness and humility, to "greet" the mosque.

After this one should move toward the Prophet's grave, face it, give greetings of peace to him, and call God's blessings and peace upon him. Then, moving about a yard to the right, one should offer one's greetings to Abu Bakr and, moving another yard in the same direction, offer greetings to 'Umar ibn al-Khattab. Then, facing the *qibla*, they should supplicate for themselves, their family, friends, relatives, and all Muslims, and then leave.

One should also visit the Jannat al-Baqi cemetery, where many Companions and members of the Prophet's Family are buried. During the visit, people should talk only loudly enough to hear themselves, and behave with utmost humility and sincerity.

Offering Prayers in the Quba Mosque

God's Messenger, upon him be peace and blessings, used to go to Quba, riding or on foot, every Saturday and offer a two-*rak'at* prayer. He advised others to do the same: "Whoever makes ablutions at home and then goes and prays in the Quba Mosque will have a reward like that of an *Umra*." (Nasai, "Masajid" 9:2, 37) Thus, pilgrims who visit Madina should also visit the Quba Mosque and pray there.

WORSHIP

Worship means one's sincere acknowledgement of himself or herself as a servant and God as the sole and true Object of Worship. It consists in a servant designing his or her life in accordance with the relations between a true servant and the True Object of Worship, in the light of the fact that one is the created and the other the Creator.

ﻩﻭ ﻩﻭ

Worship means one's thankfulness for the bounties with which he or she is endowed, such as life, consciousness, power of perception and faith, while neglecting the duty of worship is crude ingratitude. Worship is a road to travel, opened by the Being Who commands us to belief, and is a set of good manners that He ordered us to observe so that we could finally reach Him and obtain happiness in both this life and the next.

ﻩﻭ ﻩﻭ

Worship is the safest way to reach the most unshakable certainty in one's conscience about the greatest truth known only theoretically at the outset.

Worship is a blessed, growing resource feeding a person's thoughts and deliberations of being good, righteous, and virtuous, and a mysterious elixir that reforms the selfhood's innate tendencies toward evil.

ॐ ॐ

Worship is developing a person's potential to be like angels in order to be fitted for Paradise, and bringing under control the bestial inclinations and potentialities. So far in human history, by means of their worship many have surpassed angels, while many others, refusing to worship, have fallen to the lowest of the low.

ॐ ॐ

The most meritorious of the acts or services of worship is knowing and loving God Almighty and being beneficial to humanity. If there is something more meritorious and commendable than this, it is seeking God's approval and good pleasure in whatever one does and, moved by the command, "Be straightforward as you are commanded," always being in pursuit of what is the truest and highest ideal in life.

(M. Fethullah Gülen, *Pearls of Wisdom*, The Light, Inc., 2005.)

MARRIAGE AND FAMILY LIFE[6]

God has created humanity as His vicegerent on Earth in order that human beings might populate and rule it. Obviously this purpose cannot be realized unless humanity perpetuates itself, living, thriving, cultivating, manufacturing, building, and worshipping its Creator. Accordingly, the Creator has placed certain appetites and impulses in humanity so that its members are impelled toward activities that guarantee humanity's survival. The Qur'an declares:

> Men innately feel a passionate attraction toward women, children, treasures of gold and silver (money hoarded), branded horses, cattle, and plantations. Such are the enjoyments of the life of this world; yet with God is the best of the goals to pursue. (3:14)

God has inculcated such impulses in human nature so that humanity could survive on Earth and evolve spiritually and mentally by disciplining them to transform each one into a virtue in order to develop into being a true, perfect human from being only potentially human. Humanity is not like other species, for it has been created with a different disposition, multiple potentialities, and various mental and spiritual faculties. So, there must be a significant purpose behind its creation. To realize this purpose and being perfected require self-discipline. Islam is the name of the set of principles for that self-discipline.

According to Imam al-Ghazzali, Islam's legal principles seek to protect and secure five basic values in human life, namely, religion, life, intellect, personal property, and reproduction, and forbid acts that will nullify them. When we consider the Divinely established prohibitions (e.g., unbelief, hypocrisy, associating partners with God, apostasy, killing a person, taking intoxicants and drugs, usurpation, theft, adultery, fornication, and homosexuality), we can deduce that they have been given to protect and secure those values. In order to secure these values for a virtuous life based upon justice, the observation of mutual rights, mutual helping, and righteousness, we also see that Islam has taken some measures and precautions. As regards marriage and family life, we can point to the following:

Prohibition of Approaching Adultery and Fornication

Islam prohibits illegal sexual relationships, for they lead to a confusion of lineage, child abuse, family break-ups, bitterness in relationships, the spread of venereal diseases, and a general laxity in morals. Moreover, it opens the door to a flood of lust and self-gratification. God's command: *And do not approach adultery and fornication; indeed, it is an abomination and an evil way* (17:32) is absolutely just and true.

Prohibition of Privacy between a Man and a Woman Who Are not Married to Each Other

Islam prohibits a man and woman who are not married to each other from being alone together in a private place where there is no fear of being interrupted by someone else. This is done to prevent such illicit sexual activities as touching, kissing, embracing, or having sexual intercourse.

Looking with Desire at the Opposite Sex

Islam prohibits people from looking lustfully at people of the opposite sex, for the eye is the key to the feelings, and the look triggers desire. The Qur'an declares:

> Tell the believing men that they should lower their gazes and guard their chastity; that is purer for them. God is well-acquainted with what they do. And tell the believing women that they should lower their gazes, guard their chastity, and not display their adornment, except that which is apparent of it, and that they should draw their head-coverings over their bosoms. (24:30-31)

Looking at the Private Parts of Others

Islam defines "the private parts" as those parts of the body that must be covered in front of others. For men, this is the area between the navel and the knees, which other men and women are not allowed to see. For women, this area is her whole body, except her face, hands and, according to some scholars, her feet. This prohibition applies to all men who are allowed to marry the woman in question.

Muslim, Abu Dawud, and al-Tirmidhi report from God's Messenger: "A man should not look at the *'awra* (private parts) of another man, nor a woman of a woman, nor should a man go under one cloth with another man, nor a woman with another woman."

Islam equipped and adorned Muslim men and women with chastity, dignity, self-respect, and modesty, while most of the men and women of the "ages of ignorance" were and have been vain, showy, and anxious to display their attractions.

Sexual Perversion

Islam, while regulating one's sexual drive, has prohibited illicit sexual relations and all ways that lead to them, as well as homosexuality. Homosexuality is considered a reversal of the natural order, a corruption of male sexuality, and a violation of the rights of women. The spread of this unnatural practice disrupts a society's natural life. It also makes those who practice it slaves to their lusts, thereby depriving them of decent taste, decent morals, and a decent manner of living. The Qur'anic account of Prophet Lut's (Lot) people should be sufficient for us.

No Monasticism

Although Islam is against sexual license, and thus prohibits fornication and adultery and blocks all ways leading to them, it does not seek to suppress the sexual urge. Therefore, it encourages people to get married and prohibits renunciation and castration.

Muhammad Abu Zahra, a modern scholar, defines marriage as follows: "Marriage is a contract that results in the man and woman living with each other and supporting each other within the limits of what has been laid down for them in terms of rights and obligations." Ibn Uthaymin adds: "It is a mutual contract between a man and a woman, whose goal is for each to enjoy the other, become a pious family and a sound society."

The Purpose and Goals of Marriage

Like anything a Muslim does, marriage should be undertaken only after gaining an understanding of what God has prescribed in terms of rights and obligations, as well as gaining an understanding of the wisdom behind this institution. Nearly all peoples and societies practice marriage in some form, just as they practice business. 'Umar ibn al-Khattab used to expel people from Madina's marketplace if they did not know the Islamic rules of buying and selling. Likewise, Muslims should not engage in something as important as marriage without understanding its purpose or having a comprehensive understanding of the ensuing rights and obligations.

One of marriage's most important purposes is to continue and increase the Muslim community's population. Clearly, this goal could be achieved without marriage, but when actions are undertaken in disobedience to God, they do not receive His blessing and corrupt society. The goal is not just to produce children for the next generation, but to produce righteous children who will obey God, serve people, and be a source of reward for their deceased parents.

Islam takes humanity's natural instincts and needs into consideration. It is not like the human-made (or modified) religions or systems that place unnatural constraints on people or set them free without any restrictions. Men are inclined toward women, and women are inclined toward men. Marriage fulfills this desire and channels it in ways pleasing to God and befitting humanity's honor and mission in life.

The desire of men and women for each other needs to be fulfilled. If left unfulfilled, it will be a source of discord and disruption in society. For this reason, God's Messenger, upon him be peace and blessings, ordered all men who can meet the responsibilities of marriage to get married: "Whichever of you is capable should marry, for it will aid him in lowering his gaze and guarding his body (from sin). As for one who is not capable, fasting is his protection."

MARRIAGE AND THE HOME

The purpose of marriage is not pleasure; rather, it is to establish a family, ensure the nation's permanency and continuation, save the individual from dispersed feelings and thoughts, and to control physical pleasures. Just as with many other matters related to the basic nature that God has given to each being, pleasure is a payment made in advance to invite and encourage marriage.

෧ ෯

One should not marry for reasons of dress, wealth, or physical beauty; rather, marry for spiritual beauty, honor and morality, and virtue and character. Every union made in the name of marriage, but without careful thought, has left behind crying wives, orphans, and those who wound the family's heart. Some marriages based on logic and judgment were initiated by taking refuge in God. They are so sacred that, throughout a lifetime, they function just like a school, and their "students" guarantee the nation's permanency and continuation.

If a couple wishes to divorce, the most intelligent criteria are of no use to those who did not (or could not) get married for the correct reasons. The important thing is not to escape from the fire in the home with the least harm, but to prevent it from ever starting.

ༀ ༀ

The soundest foundation for a nation is a family in which material and spiritual happiness flows, for such a family serves as a sacred school that raises virtuous individuals. If a nation can make its homes as enlightened and prosperous as its schools, and its schools as warm as its homes, it has made the greatest reform and has guaranteed the contentment and happiness of future generations.

ༀ ༀ

The word home is used according to the people in it. They are considered happy to the degree that they share human values. Yes, we can say that people live humanly with those in their home; a home becomes a home because of its inhabitants.

ༀ ༀ

A home is a small nation, and a nation is a large home. One who successfully manages a home and who has raised its members to a level of humanity can manage a large organization with a little effort

(M. Fethullah Gülen, *Pearls of Wisdom*, The Light, Inc., 2005.)

Men and Women To Be Preferred in Marriage

Making sure that Muslims are well-matched to their spouses is a most important matter. Those who want to get married must have their priorities straight and be clear on what characteristics are most important in ensuring a marriage's success. Many characteristics are important in a husband or a wife, but some are far more important than others. God's Messenger said: "A woman is married for the excellence of her religious belief and life, her wealth or her beauty. You must prefer the one with an excellent religious belief and life." (Canan, *a.g.e.*, 17:190) Thus, the first thing to be sought for in a potential spouse is excellence of religious belief and life.

Character is of extreme importance, and goes hand in hand with belief and piety. The Messenger described it as the purpose of his mission: "I have only been sent to perfect good character or morality" (Tabarani, *Mu'jam al-Awsat*, 7:74) and "That which will weigh the heaviest in the Balance in the Hereafter is good character" (Tirmidhi, 61, HN:2070). Believers with the most perfect belief are those with the best character.

God's Messenger advised marrying child-bearing women and preferring virginity, and said that a virgin woman is more likely to be pleased by a man and less likely to be devious and deceiving. Scholars stress that this good attribute applies to both the husband and the wife. Especially if it is each person's first marriage, both the man and the woman should be virgins.

Beauty has a certain undeniable role to play, since one of marriage's purposes is to keep both spouses from sin. The best way to do this is to have a strong attraction between the spouses. However, this is something that surely grows over time, and in some cases first impressions can become an obstacle to a successful marriage.

Recommended Steps

The following are important steps for those who want to get married and for those seeking to facilitate a marriage.

- The entire process, in order to be successful with God's blessing, should be proper and consistent with the teachings of the Qur'an and the Sunna.
- Both spouses should seek to get married purely for God's good pleasure, fulfill the purpose of marriage, and put their full trust in God.
- If they do everything properly and in accordance with the rules of Islam, God will grant them a successful marriage.
- Both the man and the woman are allowed to see their perspective spouse before taking further steps.

Prohibited Proposals and 'Idda for Women

A divorced or widowed woman cannot remarry during her *'idda* (the waiting period during which she is not allowed to remarry) and a man cannot propose marriage to such a woman, for this waiting period is part of the previous marriage and must not be violated.

A pregnant woman's *'idda* ends when she delivers the baby. If she is widowed but not pregnant, her *'idda* is 4 months and 10 days. If she is divorced and it is not known if she is pregnant, her *'idda* is three menstrual cycles. This *'idda* relates to women who have menstrual periods; for women who do not menstruate, the *'idda* is 3 months.

The Girl's Consent

A girl has the right to decide about her marriage, and her father or guardian cannot override her objections or ignore her wishes.

Women to Whom Marriage Is Prohibited

Muslim men cannot marry women who belong to one of the following categories: The father's wife, whether divorced or widowed (this prevents any sexual attraction between the son and his stepmother, who should develop a relationship of respect and honor between themselves), the mother (including grandmothers on both sides), the daughter (including granddaughters from the son or the daughter), the sister (including half- and stepsisters), the paternal aunt (whether she is the father's real, half-, or stepsister), the maternal aunt (whether she is the father's real, half-, or stepsister), the brother's daughter (his niece), and the sister's daughter (his niece).

Marriages Prohibited by Reason of Fosterage

These are as follows:

- **THE FOSTER MOTHER:** Muslim men cannot marry women who suckled them during their infancy, even if it was only for one time. Although some jurists opine that in order for such a woman to be forbidden she must have suckled him five or even seven times, in order to avoid committing a sin they must not be allowed to marry each other.
- **FOSTER SISTERS:** Just as a woman becomes a mother to a child by virtue of suckling, so do her daughters become his

sisters, her sisters his aunts, and so on. Tirmidhi (rada', 1) reports from the Messenger, upon him be peace and blessings, that: "What is forbidden by reason of genealogy is forbidden by reason of fosterage." Thus, marriage to foster-sisters, foster-aunts, and foster-nieces is forbidden.

In-Law Relationships

These are as follows:

*   THE MOTHER-IN-LAW: Marriage to the wife's mother is prohibited from the time a man marries a woman, whether he and his wife have engaged in sexual intercourse or not. The act of marriage itself gives the mother-in-law the same status as the mother.
*   THE STEPDAUGHTER: A man cannot marry his stepdaughter if he has had legal sexual intercourse with her mother (his wife). However, if a man divorces his wife before consummating the marriage, he may marry his stepdaughter.
*   THE DAUGHTER-IN-LAW: This woman is the wife of the real son, not of the adopted son. In fact, Islam abolished legal formalized adoption, because it is contrary to fact and reality, and results in prohibiting what is essentially lawful and permitting what is essentially forbidden.

Sisters and Aunts as Co-Wives

As opposed to the pre-Islamic practice, Islam forbade taking two sisters as co-wives and being married at the same time to a woman and her maternal and paternal aunt.

Married Women

A woman can only be married to one man at a time. She may marry another man only if her husband has died or she has been divorced, or if she has completed her *'Idda* (the period of waiting before remarrying).

Female Idolaters

Muslim men cannot marry women who practice idolatry (associating partners with God in His Divinity or Lordship).

Marrying Women of the People of the Book

Islam allows Muslim men to marry Jewish or Christian women, for they are considered People of the Book (Jews and Christians), or people whose tradition is based upon a Divinely revealed Scripture.

Prohibiting Muslim Women from Marrying Non-Muslim Men

Muslim women cannot marry non-Muslim man, regardless of whether they belong to the People of the Book or not.

Women Who Engage in Fornication

Islam forbids marrying women who are engaged in prostitution, adultery, and fornication. If one has engaged habitually in such activities or is a prostitute, other people are forbidden to marry them. But if one has committed it only once or twice and is not a prostitute, it still is highly advisable not to marry them. However, it is not forbidden to do so. God permits Muslims to marry chaste believing Muslim, Jewish, or Christian women. Similarly, He has made marriage lawful to men on the condition that they seek it in honest wedlock, not in lust (4:24).

Temporary Marriage (Mut'a)

Islam considers marriage a strong bond and a binding contract based upon both partners' intention to live together permanently in order to attain, as individuals, the benefit of the repose, affection, and mercy mentioned in the Qur'an. In addition, its purpose is to attain the social goal of reproduction and perpetuation of the human species:

> God has made for you spouses of your own kind, and has made for you from your spouses children and grandchildren, and has provided you with pure, wholesome things. Do they, then, believe in falsehood and associate partners with God in denial of His blessings? (16:72)

Temporary marriage (*mut'a*), which is contracted by two people to marry for a specified period of time in exchange for a specified sum of money, does not realize the above-mentioned purposes of marriage. Thus, there is no room for it in Islam.

CHILDREN

Adam, the first man, and Eve, the first woman, were created together at the very beginning of human existence. This indicates that marriage is natural. Reproduction is the most important purpose of this natural state. A marriage made for reasons other than bringing up new generations is no more than a temporary entertainment and adventure.

☙ ❧

Human generations come and go. Those who have attained high levels of spiritual and moral attainment are worthy of being considered human. Those who do not develop their spiritual faculties, due to their low level of education, scarcely merit being called human. They are nothing more than strange creatures, even though they are descended from Adam. And their parents, to whom they are a burden, are unfortunate to have nurtured them.

☙ ❧

Those of you who bring children into this world are responsible for raising them to the realms beyond the heavens. Just as you take care of their bodily health, so take care of their spiritual life. For God's sake, have pity and save the helpless innocents. Do not let their lives go to waste.

☙ ❧

If parents encourage their children to develop their abilities and be useful to themselves and the community, they have given humanity a strong new pillar. If, on the contrary, they do not cultivate their children's human feelings, they will have released scorpions into the community.

☙ ❧

Parents have the right to claim their children as long as they educate and equip them with virtue. They cannot make such a claim, however, if they neglect them. But what shall we call parents who introduce their children to wickedness and indecency, and cause them to break with humanity?

THE RIGHTS OF CHILDREN

A child has the same meaning for humanity's continuation as a seed for a forest's continued growth and multiplication. People who neglect their children decay gradually.

Children form the most active and productive part of a community after every 30 or 40 years. Those who ignore their young children should consider how important an element of their own community's life they are disregarding, and then shudder.

⌘ ⌘

The vices observed in today's generation, the incompetence of some administrators, and other social problems are the direct result of the conditions prevailing 30 years ago, and of that time's ruling elite. Likewise, those entrusted with educating today's young people are responsible for the vices and virtues that will appear 30 years from now.

⌘ ⌘

Those who want to secure their future should apply as much energy to raising their children as they devote to other problems. While the energy devoted to many other things may go in vain, whatever is spent for raising a young generation elevates them to the rank of humanity. Such people will be like an inexhaustible source of income.

⌘ ⌘

Those people in our community who are miserable and lost, such as drug addicts, alcoholics, and other dissolute people, were once children. We failed to educate them properly. I wonder whether we are sufficiently aware of the kind of people we are preparing to walk our streets tomorrow.

⌘ ⌘

Communities that pay close attention to the family institution and their young people's education, as opposed to those who are more advanced in sciences and technology, will have the upper hand in the future.

(M. Fethullah Gülen, *Pearls of Wisdom*, The Light, Inc., 2005.)

The Marriage Contract (*Nikah*)

Islam views marriage as a contract. Thus, as with any contract, several elements are considered essential to its existence. Each of these should be understood properly to ensure that the marriage is performed properly and that each spouse receives his or her full rights.

All the scholars agree that one essential act is the "offer and acceptance," for no marriage contract is valid without it. Either party can initiate this process. The presence of two witnesses and the dowry paid by the husband are necessary elements as well.

Conditions for a Sound Marriage Contract

These conditions are as follows:

- The woman cannot be one of those forbidden to the man by relation, nursing, or any of the other preventing factors mentioned above.
- The offer and acceptance is permanent and certain. If anything in the contract indicates something of a temporary and uncertain nature, the marriage is invalid. This is why the words of acceptance must be in the past tense, which expresses certainty.
- Two credible witnesses should be present, and the marriage should be announced and publicized.
- Both parties should willingly accept the marriage.
- The bride and groom should be identified and known.
- Neither of the contracting parties must be in the state of *ihram*.
- The parties and witnesses are not bound to keep it quiet.
- The presence of the woman's guardian or representative (*waliy*). The *waliy* is a Muslim man charged with marrying a woman entrusted to his care to a man who will be good for her.
- The man and woman must be legally competent (i.e., adult and sane). If they are not, the marriage is invalid. The woman cannot be from any category of women that her intended spouse cannot marry. For example, suppose the couple get married and he then learns that they had been breast-fed by the same woman. In this case, the marriage becomes null and void, because their breast-milk relationship disqualifies them from marrying each other.
- The offer and acceptance of the contract must be done in one sitting. In general, this means that the response must be immediate. The acceptance must correspond to what is being offered, and the marriage must be effective immediately.
- The bride must receive a dowry (bridal-due [*mahr*]).

Mahr (Dowry or Bridal-Due)

The groom gives the *mahr* only to the bride to honor her, show his respect for her, his serious desire to marry her, and his sense of responsibility, obligation, or effort to her. The Qur'anic injunction: *Give to the women (whom you marry) their bridal-due all willingly and without expecting a return* (4:4) is addressed to either the husband (because it is his duty to give it) or to the guardian (because before Islam came they used to keep a woman's dowry for themselves). This verse shows that this particular pre-Islamic custom was no longer permitted. The exact amount of the dowry has not been determined, for the groom should pay it according to his capacity or wealth. The region's customs also are considered in determining its amount.

Fulfilling Agreements

Generally speaking, Muslims must comply with any agreements that they make. God says about the believers: *They fulfill their covenant when they have engaged in a covenant* (2:177) and orders them: *O you who believe, fulfill the bonds (you have entered in with God and people)* (5:1). God's Messenger mentioned breaking one's promise and covenant as among the signs of hypocrisy.

Wedding Ceremony and Feast

It is permissible, even advisable, to arrange a wedding ceremony within an Islamic framework. The husband is required to sponsor the wedding feast, which can last for 3 days, after the marriage contract.

Mutual Love, Mercy, Respect, Understanding, and Thankfulness

The Qur'an declares:

> O humanity, avoid disobedience to your Lord, Who has created you from a single original human self, and from it created its mate, and from the pair of them scattered abroad a multitude of men and women. (4:1)

The original expression translated as "a single original human self" is *nafs wahida* (literally, a single self or soul). *Nafs* has two cardinal meanings: a being's self, and the animating energy or faculty that is the source of each person's and jinn's worldly life.

Considering both meanings together, *nafs wahida* is understood to mean a single original human self.

This point is very important to understanding the nature of the male-female relationship. The Qur'an points out this very point: *And of His signs is that He has created for you, from your selves, mates, that you might repose in them, and He has engendered love and mercy between you* (30:21); *God has given you, from your selves, mates, and He has given you, from your mates, children and grandchildren* (16:72); *The Originator of the heavens and Earth; He has given you, from your selves, mates, and from the cattle mates* (42:11). What these refer to by *your selves* is the human kind, self, or nature. In addition, they indicate that everything in the universe was created in pairs: *And everything We have created in pairs* (51:49).

However, these verses do not mean that by being the two halves of a perfect unit, men and women are identical or the same. While a woman's rights and responsibilities are equal to a man's, they are not necessarily identical with them. Equality and sameness are two quite different things. This difference is understandable, because men and women are not identical but are created as equals. Bearing this in mind, there is no problem. In fact, it is almost impossible to find even two identical men or women.

This distinction between equality and sameness is vital. Equality is desirable, just, and fair; but sameness is not. People are created as equals, and not as identical to each other, and so there is no basis to consider a woman to be inferior to a man. There is no reason to assume that she is less important than he just because her rights are not identical to his. Had her status been identical with his, she would have been no more than a duplicate of him, which she is not. The fact that Islam gives her equal – but not identical – rights shows that it takes her into due consideration, acknowledges her, and recognizes her independent personality.

In: *And of His signs is that He has created for you, from your selves, mates, that you might repose in them, and He has engendered love and mercy between you* (30:21), the Qur'an stresses that male-female relations are – and must be – based upon mutual love and mercy. What satisfies the needs of a human being the most is having an intimate life companion with whom one can share love, joy, and grief. However, we should acknowledge that a woman's heart is the most compassionate, loving and generous of all hearts. This is why the Qur'an stresses men's inclination toward and attachment to women, rather than the other way. In fact, it states that the most beautiful blessing in Paradise for a man will be a pure woman.

On the other hand, the Qur'an also says: *Men (who are able to perform their responsibilities) are the protectors and maintainers of women, for God has endowed some of the people with greater capacity than others (in some respects) and that they (men) spend of their wealth (for the family's maintenance)* (4:34). This verse is highly significant with respect to male-female relations and family law, and draws attention to the following cardinal points:

God has not created all people exactly the same in all respects; rather, He has given each superiority in some respect to others, as required by social life, the division of labor, and the choice of occupation. Although it is not true to the same degree for all men and women, as He has created men superior to women in some respects, He also has given women superiority over men in others. For example, God has given men greater physical strength, endowed them with a greater capacity for management, and has charged them with the family's financial upkeep. This is why He has made men the head of the family. However, this does not mean that men have absolute authority over the family, for this authority must be exercised according to the Prophetic principle: The master of a people is he who serves them. In addition, responsibility is proportionate to authority and authority is proportionate to responsibility.

In short, Islam proposes a male-female relation based upon mutual love, mercy, understanding, and respect. It also exhorts the couples to be thankful to each other for their kindness and efforts to please each other. Such things should be fundamental in any marriage. Each spouse should acknowledge the other's efforts, show them gratitude, and repay them with kindness.

Islam is primarily concerned with enabling people to attain the status of true humanity or perfection. Its legislation is based upon this cardinal point, and it considers legal rules or laws only as a means of reinforcement.

The Wife's Rights

These are as follows: receipt of a dowry, support or maintenance, kind and proper treatment and due respect, marital relations, privacy, justice between multiple wives, to be taught Islam, defense of her honor, and not revealing their secrets to others.

The Husband's Rights

These are as follows: enjoying due respect for being responsible for bringing up and maintaining the family, and marital relations. In addition, she must not allow in the house anyone of whom he disapproves, leave the house and go to places of which he disapproves without his permission, or undertake a voluntary fast without his permission. She also must defend his honor and not disclose their secrets to others.

Housework

The above-mentioned rights are noncontroversial and agreed upon by scholars. The wife's duties in the house (e.g., cooking, cleaning and generally serving her husband in the house), however, have been the subject of debate. While this has been the traditional Muslim custom, given that the man is obliged to look after the entire family, it is considered as ihsan (good treatment and excellence) for the wife to do the housework and meets her husband's needs (e.g., sewing, ironing, cooking, and taking care of the babies).

Sex

The Qur'an does not neglect humanity's sensual aspect and the married couple's sex life, for it guides humanity to the best path and enables them to fulfill their sexual urges while avoiding harmful or deviant practices.

It is reported that the Jews and Zoroastrians wo.
extremes in order to avoid any physical contact with me..
ing women. For example, Jewish laws and regulations are ext.
ly restrictive in this regard. The Old Testament considers a mun-
struating woman unclean and impure. Moreover, her impurity
"infects" other people, for whoever or whatever she touches becomes
unclean for a day (Leviticus 15:19, 23). Thus a menstruating woman
was sometimes banished to the "house of impurity" so that no
contact with her would be possible during this time. The Talmud
considers a menstruating woman "fatal," even without any physical contact, whereas Christians will have sex with such women.
The pre-Islamic Arabs would not eat, drink, or sit with menstruating women and would send them to separate dwellings, just
as the Jews and Zoroastrians did.

When some Muslims asked the Messenger, upon him be peace
and blessings, about menstruating women, God revealed:

> (O Messenger,) they also ask you about (the commands concern-
> ing) the monthly course (of their wives). Answer (them):
> "Menstruation is a state that causes suffering and ritual impurity, so
> avoid women during menstruation and do not approach them until
> they are cleansed. After they are cleansed, (you can) come to them
> as required by the inherent urge that God has implanted in your
> nature and within the rules that He has established. God loves those
> who turn to Him in sincere repentance of their errors and improve
> themselves, and try their best to cleanse themselves." (2:222)

What is meant by *avoid women* is sexual intercourse or benefiting from their genitals. Thus a man can fondle and enjoy his menstruating wife, avoiding only the place of hurt. Islam's position, as in
all other matters, is a middle one between the two extremes of ban-
ishing a menstruating woman from the house and of having sexual
intercourse with her. Islam has established no rules concerning the
way or position of intercourse. However, it has forbidden anal sex.

Contraception

Marriage's primary objective is to preserve humanity through continued reproduction. Accordingly, Islam encourages large families

and blesses both boys and girls. However, family planning is allowed for only valid reasons and recognized necessities. At the time of the Prophet, the common method of contraception was *coitus interruptus* (withdrawing the penis from the vagina just before ejaculation, thereby preventing the influx of semen). The primary valid reason for contraception is that the pregnancy or delivery might endanger the mother's life or health. Past experience or a reliable physician's opinion should guide the couple in such matters.

Abortion

While Islam permits preventing pregnancy for valid reasons, it does not allow terminating the pregnancy once it occurs. Muslim jurists agree unanimously that abortion is forbidden after the fetus is completely formed and has been given a soul, which is, according to the hadiths, about 6 weeks after the beginning of pregnancy (Muslim, "Qadar," 3). This is considered a crime under Islamic law, for it is an offense against a complete, live human being. Jurists insist that blood money (*diyat*) must be paid if the baby was aborted alive and then died, and that a lesser amount must be paid if it was aborted dead.

There is only one exception, according to the jurists: If, after the baby is completely formed, it becomes clear that continuing the pregnancy will cause the mother's death, the couple has recourse to the general Islamic legal principle that the lesser of the two evils should be chosen. In such a case, the fetus must be aborted.

Artificial Insemination

Islam safeguards lineage by prohibiting adultery and fornication (*zina*) and legal adoption, thus keeping the family line clear and "uncontaminated" by any foreign element. Thus, artificial insemination is forbidden unless the donor is the husband.

Polygamy

Islam is a way of life consonant with human nature, provides human solutions to complex situations, and avoids extremes. This characteristic can be observed most clearly in the issue of polygamy, which Islam allows only to resolve pressing individual and social problems. Many peoples and religions prior to Islam permitted marriage to as many women as one desired. Islam, on the other hand, laid down definite restrictions and conditions.

Some people criticize Islam wrongly as being polygamous. However, such criticisms are not justifiable for several reasons, as follows:

- Polygamy is an ancient practice found in many societies. The Bible does not condemn it, and the Old Testament and rabbinic writings frequently attest to its legality. King Solomon and King David had many wives and concubines (2 Samuel 5:13). According to Father Eugene Hillman in his insightful book, *Polygamy Reconsidered:* "Nowhere in the New Testament is there any explicit commandment that marriage should be monogamous or any explicit commandment forbidding polygamy." Moreover, Jesus did not speak against it, even though it was practiced by the Jews of his society. Father Hillman stresses that the Church in Rome banned polygamy in order to conform to the Greco-Roman culture (which prescribed only one legal wife while tolerating concubinage and prostitution). The Qur'an, contrary to the Bible, limited the maximum number of wives to four and mandated equal and just treatment for each wife. The Qur'an does not encourage polygamy or consider it an ideal. Rather, it tolerates or allows it and no more, for the following reason: There are places and times in which there are compelling social and moral reasons for polygamy. Islam, as a universal religion suitable for all places and all times, could not ignore such compelling obligations.
- In most societies, women outnumber men. For example, America currently has at least 8 million more women than men. What should be done about such unbalanced sex ratios? There are various solutions, such as lawful polygamy or celibacy, female infanticide (which still happens), or sexual permissiveness (e.g., prostitution, extramarital sex, and homosexuality).

- This problem becomes truly problematic at times of war. Native American Indian tribes used to suffer highly unbalanced sex ratios after wartime losses. Their women, who enjoyed a fairly high status, accepted polygamy as the best protection against indulgence in indecent activities. After WWII, there were 7.3 million more women than men in Germany (3.3 million of them were widows). Many needed a man for companionship as well as to provide for the household in a time of unprecedented misery and hardship. What is more dignifying for a woman: to be an accepted and respected second wife or a virtual prostitute? In 1987, a poll conducted by the student newspaper at the University of California at Berkeley asked students whether polygamy should be permitted as a way to deal with a perceived shortage of marriageable men in California. Almost all of the students polled approved of this idea.

- Polygamy continues to be a viable solution to some of the social ills of modern societies. In his provocative *Plural Marriage for Our Time*, Philip Kilbride, an American anthropologist of Roman Catholic heritage, proposes polygamy as a solution to some of America's social ills. He argues that plural marriage may be a potential alternative for divorce, in many cases, in order to obviate divorce's damaging impact upon children.

- Polygamy is quite rare in many contemporary Muslim societies, for there is no large gender imbalance. In fact, one can say that the rate of polygamous marriages in the Muslim world is far less than the rate of extramarital affairs in the West. In other words, Muslim men are far more monogamous than their Western counterparts.

- Billy Graham, the eminent Christian evangelist, has recognized this fact:

  > Christianity cannot compromise on the question of polygamy. If present-day Christianity cannot do so, it is to its own detriment. Islam has permitted polygamy as a solution to social ills and has allowed a certain degree of latitude to human nature but only within the strictly defined framework of the law.

Christian countries make a great show of monogamy, but actually they practice polygamy. No one is unaware of the part mistresses play in Western society. In this respect Islam is a fundamentally honest religion, and permits a Muslim to marry a second wife if he must, but strictly forbids all clandestine amatory associations in order to safeguard the moral probity of the community. (Abd al-Rahman Doi, *Woman in Shari'a*, London 1994, 76.)

- There are even psychological factors calling for polygamy. For example, many young African brides, whether Christian, Muslim, or otherwise, prefer to marry a married man who has already proved himself to be a responsible husband. Many African wives urge their husbands to get a second wife so that they do not feel lonely. A survey of over 6,000 women, ranging in age from 15 to 59, conducted in Nigeria's second largest city showed that 60 percent of them would be pleased if their husbands took another wife. In a survey undertaken in rural Kenya, 25 out of 27 women considered polygamy better than monogamy and felt that it could be a happy and beneficial experience if the co-wives cooperated.

- Modern civilization rejects polygamy as unwise and harmful to social life. As observed even in animals and plants, the cardinal purpose for and wisdom in sexual relations is reproduction. The resulting pleasure is a small payment determined by Divine Mercy to realize this duty. Marriage is for reproduction and perpetuation of the species. Being able to give birth at most once a year, to become pregnant during half of a month, and entering menopause around 50, one woman is usually insufficient for a man, who can sometimes impregnate until the age of 70 or more. That is why, in most cases, modern civilization is obliged to admit prostitution. Even if the purpose of marriage were sexual gratification, polygamy would be a lawful way to realize it.

The condition that Islam lays down for permitting polygamy is that the husband be able to treat each wife equitably as regards food, drink, housing, clothing, expenses, and spending time with them. Any man who feels that he cannot fulfill such obligations justly cannot have more than one wife: *But if you fear that you will not be able to do justice (among them), (marry) only one* (4:3).

The Status of Woman in Islam[7]

The status of woman in Islam is not a problem. The attitude of the Qur'an and the early Muslims bear witness to the fact that woman is, at least, as vital to life as man himself, and that she is neither inferior to him nor of a lower species. Had it not been for the impact of foreign cultures and alien influences, this question would have never arisen among the Muslims. The status of woman was taken for granted to be equal to that of man. It was a matter of course and a fact, and so no one considered it a problem.

Equity, Equality, or Sameness?

In order to understand what Islam has established for woman, there is no need to deplore her plight in the pre-Islamic era or in the modern would. Islam has given woman rights and privileges that she has never enjoyed under other religious or constitutional systems. This can be understood when the matter is studied as a whole and in a comparative, rather than in a partial, manner. The rights and responsibilities of a woman are equal to those of a man, but are not necessarily identical with them, for equality and sameness are two quite different things. This difference is understandable, because man and woman are not identical, but are created as equals. With this distinction in mind, there is no problem. It is almost impossible to find even two identical men or women.

This distinction between equality and sameness is of paramount importance. Equality is desirable, just, fair; but sameness is not. People are not created identical, but they are created equal. With this distinction in mind, there is no room to imagine that woman is inferior to man. There is no ground to assume that she is less important than him just because her rights are not identical to his. Had her status been identical with his, she would have been simply a duplicate of him, which she is not. The fact that Islam gives her equal – but not identical – rights shows that it takes her into due consideration, acknowledges her, and recognizes her independent personality.

Islam's View of Woman and Original Sin

Islam does not consider woman to be the product of the devil, the seed of evil, or man to be her dominating lord to whom she must surrender without any choice. In addition, Islam never asked whether a woman had a soul or not. Never in the history of Islam has any Muslim doubted the human status of woman and her possession of a soul and other fine spiritual qualities.

Unlike other popular beliefs, Islam does not blame Eve alone for the first sin. The Qur'an states that both Adam and Eve were tempted, that both sinned and were pardoned by God after repenting, and that God addressed them jointly (2:35-36; 7:19, 27; 20:117-23). In fact, the Qur'an gives the impression that Adam was more to blame for the first sin, from which all prejudice against and suspicion toward women have emerged. Islam does not justify such prejudice or suspicion, because Adam and Eve were equally in error. Thus if we blame Eve, we should blame Adam to the same degree – or even more.

The Status of Modern Woman

The status of woman in Islam is something unique, something novel, something that has no similarity in any other system. If we look even to the democratic nations, we find that woman is not really in a happy position. Her status is not enviable. She has to work so hard to live, and sometimes she may be doing the same job that a man does but is paid less. She enjoys a kind of liberty that, in some cases, amounts to libertinism. To get to where she is nowadays, woman struggled hard for decades and centuries. To gain the right of learning and the freedom of work and earning, she had to offer painful sacrifices and give up many of her natural rights. To establish her status as a human being possessing a soul, she paid heavily. Yet in spite of all these costly sacrifices and painful struggles, she has not acquired what Islam has established by a Divine decree for the Muslim woman.

The rights of woman in modern times were not granted voluntarily or out of kindness to women. Rather, she reached her present position by force, and not through natural processes, mutual consent, or Divine teachings. She had to force her way, and various circumstances came to her aid. A manpower shortage during wars, economic pressures, and the requirements of industrialization forced her out of her home – to work, to learn, to struggle for her livelihood, to appear as an equal to man, to run her race in the course of life side by side with him. She was forced by circumstances and, in turn, she forced herself through and acquired her new status. Whether all women were pleased with these circumstances being on their side, and whether they are happy and satisfied with the results of this course, is a different matter. But the fact remains that whatever rights modern woman enjoys fall short of those given to her Muslim counterpart.

What Islam has established for woman is that which suits her nature, gives her full security, and protects her against disgraceful circumstances and uncertain channels of life. We do not need here to elaborate on the status of modern woman and the risks she runs to make her living or establish herself. We do not even need to explore the miseries and setbacks that encircle her as a result of the so-called "rights of woman." Nor do we intend to manipulate the situation of many unhappy homes which break up because of the very "freedom" and "rights" of which modern woman is proud.

Most women today exercise the right of freedom to go out independently, to work and earn, to pretend to be equal to man. But sadly enough, this is at the expense of their families. This is all known and obvious. What is not known is the status of woman in Islam. An attempt will be made in the following passages to sum up the attitude of Islam with regard to woman.

Understanding the Modern View of Woman

The Qur'an draws the attention to an important point by declaring that those communities distant from Divine guidance usually call upon female deities. That is, those that reject belief in One

God adopt male and female deities. While they have usually chosen their supreme deity to be male, their other deities have been female. This is because they adore their own selves and consider, first of all, the satisfaction of their interests and animal desires. Since men's primary appetite is for women, and since they tend to exploit their deities to satisfy their needs, they choose many of their deities from among women. They desire to see a physically comely woman wherever they look, and tend to eternalize them by making statutes and pictures of them. This is the most abominable way of degrading the meaning of women, and means viewing them as no more than physical objects. Women are no more than simple objects to gratify men's desires and interests. They no longer receive any respect and affection when they need them most.

People also have many fears. They feel awe before that which they fear, and so conceive of their supreme deity (of whom they are afraid) as a man. By considering him above all other deities, they fawn on him. Even if such people may be Pharaoh-like tyrants, people degrade themselves in order to kiss the feet of any power above themselves and in whose hand they see the satisfaction of their needs and desires.

The Status of Woman in Islam

Islam recognizes woman as a full and equal partner in the process of procreation. He is the father, she is the mother, and both are essential for life. Her role is no less vital than his. This partnership gives her an equal share in every aspect. She is entitled to equal rights, undertakes equal responsibilities, and has as many qualities and as much humanity as her partner. Concerning this equal partnership in human reproduction, God says: *O humanity, We have created your from a single (pair) of a male and a female, and made you into nations and tribes that you may know each other* (49:13; cf. 4:1).

Woman is equal to man in bearing personal and common responsibilities and in receiving rewards for her deeds. She is acknowledged as an independent personality with human qualities and worthy of spiritual aspirations. Her human nature is neither inferior to nor deviant from that of a man. Both are members of one another. As we read in the Qur'an:

> And their Lord has accepted (their prayers) and answered them (saying): "Never will I cause to be lost the work of any of you, be he male or female. You are members, one of another. (3:195; cf 9:71, 33:35-36, 66:19-21).

She is equal to man in the pursuit of education and knowledge. When Islam enjoins the seeking of knowledge upon Muslims, it makes no distinction between man and woman. Almost 14 centuries ago, Prophet Muhammad, upon him be peace and blessings, declared that pursuing knowledge is incumbent upon every Muslim. This declaration was very clear and has been implemented by Muslims throughout history.

She is entitled to freedom of expression as much as a man is. Her sound opinions are taken into consideration and cannot be disregarded just because of her gender. The Qur'an and history both record that women not only expressed their opinions freely but also argued and participated in serious discussions with the Prophet and other Muslim leaders (58:1-4; 60:10-12). In addition, there were occasions when Muslim women expressed their views on legislative matters of public interest and opposed the caliphs, who then accepted their sound arguments. A specific example took place during 'Umar's caliphate.

Historical records show that women participated in the early Muslim community's public life, especially during emergencies. Women accompanied Muslim armies to nurse the wounded, prepare supplies, serve the warriors, and so on. They were not shut behind iron bars, considered worthless and deprived of souls.

Islam grants woman equal rights to contract, enterprise, earn, and possess independently. Her life, property, and honor are as sacred as those of a man. If she commits any offense, her penalty is no more or less than that of a man's in a similar case. If she is wronged or harmed, she receives due compensation equal to what a man in her position would receive (2:178; 4:45, 92-93).

Islam does not state these rights in a statistical form and then relax. Rather, it has taken all measures to safeguard and implement them as integral articles of faith. It does not tolerate those who are inclined to prejudice against woman or gender-based discrimination. Time and again, the Qur'an reproaches those who used to believe that woman was inferior to man (16:57-59, 62; 42:47-59; 43:15-19; 53:21-23).

Apart from recognizing woman as an independent human being and as equally essential for humanity's survival, Islam has given her a share of inheritance. Before Islam, she could inherit nothing as was even considered property to be inherited by man. Islam made this "transferable property" an heir, thereby acknowledging woman's inherent human qualifies.

Whether she is a wife or a mother, a sister or a daughter, she receives a certain share of the deceased kin's property. This share depends upon her degree of relationship to the deceased and the number of heirs. This share is hers, and no one can take it from her or disinherit her. If the deceased wishes to deprive her by willing his estate to other relatives or a cause, the law will not respect his desire. Any person can use a will to dispose of only one-third of his or her property, so that no male or female heir will be treated unjustly. This matter will be discussed below within the framework of the Islamic law of inheritance.

Bearing Witness

Women were not allowed to bear witness in early Jewish society. The rabbis counted a woman's not being allowed to bear witness among the nine curses inflicted upon all women because of the Fall.

In Israel today, women are not allowed to give evidence in rabbinical courts. The rabbis justify this prohibition by citing Genesis 18:9-16, where it is stated that Sara, Abraham's wife, had lied. The rabbis use this incident as evidence that women are unqualified to bear witness. The Qur'an also mentions this incident more than once, in 11:69-74, 51:24-30, without any hint that Sara had lied. In the Christian West, both ecclesiastical and civil law debarred women from giving testimony until the late eighteenth century.

If a man accused his wife of unchastity, the Bible says that her testimony is not admissible. Furthermore, she had to undergo a trial by ordeal, a complex and humiliating ritual that supposedly proved her guilt or innocence (Numbers 5:11-31). If she was found guilty after this ordeal, she would be sentenced to death. If she was found innocent, her husband was considered innocent of any wrongdoing.

If a man married a woman and then accused her of not being a virgin, her own testimony would not count. Her parents had to prove her virginity before the town elders. If they could not prove her innocence, she would be stoned to death on her father's doorstep. If the parents were able to prove her innocence, the husband would only be fined 100 silver shekels and could not divorce his wife as long as he lived.

By giving women the right to testify, the Qur'an made a revolution. In some instances of bearing witness to certain civil contracts, two men are required or one man and two women. This does not, however, indicate that a woman is inferior to a man. Rather, it is a means to secure the rights of the contracting parties, because a woman generally is not so experienced in practical life as a man. As this lack of experience may cause a loss to any of the contracting parties, the law requires that at least two women should bear witness with one man. If a woman witness forgets something, the other one would remind her; if she makes a mistake due to a lack of experience, the other would help correct her.

The reason why the Qur'an demands two women in place of one man in commercial transactions is quite clear. The Qur'an does not regard a woman as half of a man; rather, what is important here is not the status of women or men, but accuracy, justice, and equity in business.

Generally, men are supposed to be more engaged in business than women, which is actually the case, and are responsible for supporting the family. Furthermore, women are more emotional than men and more susceptible to forgetting. However, there are always women who have a better memory than men, and men who are more emotional then women. But rather than the exceptions, the law considers the majority of people in all matters relating to the community. Women also are expected to be more susceptible to mistakes and forgetfulness over a matter in which they are not so engaged as men. This precautionary measure guarantees honest transactions and proper dealings between people. In fact, it gives woman a role to play in civil life and helps to establish justice. Such a lack of experience does not denote inferiority, for every person lacks one thing or another. Yet no one questions their human status.

Islam does not demand two women in place of one man in all cases. For example, whichever spouse accuses the other of adultery must swear by God four times. In this instance, a woman's testimony can even invalidate a man's. For example, if a man accuses his wife of unchastity, he must swear five times by the Qur'an as evidence of the wife's guilt. If she denies the charge and swears similarly five times, she is considered innocent. In either case, the marriage is dissolved (24:6-11). Likewise, both men and women can scan the sky for the crescent moon to determine whether a lunar month has begun or ended. In addition, the testimony of two women can be sought exclusively in matters in which women have greater knowledge or specialty than men.

Privileges

A woman enjoys certain privileges that a man does not. For example, she is exempt from some religious duties (i.e., prayers and fasting while menstruating or experiencing post-childbirth bleeding) and all financial liabilities. As a mother, she enjoys more recognition and higher honor in God's sight (31:14-15; 46:15). The Prophet acknowledged this honor when he declared that Paradise is under the feet of mothers.

A mother is entitled to three-fourths of the son's love and kindness, with one-fourth left for the father. As a wife, she can demand a suitable dowry, which belongs to her alone, from her prospective husband. She is entitled to complete provision and maintenance by the husband, does not have to work or share any of the family expenses, and can retain whatever she possessed before her marriage. Her husband has no right to any of her belongings. As a daughter or sister, she is entitled to security and provision by her father and brother(s), respectively. If she wishes to work, be self-supporting, and participate in handling the family responsibilities, she is quite free to do so, provided that her integrity and honor are safeguarded.

The fact that women stand behind men during the prayers does not indicate inferiority. Women, as already mentioned, are exempt from attending the congregational prayers, which are necessary for men. If they do attend, they stand in separate lines made up of women exclusively. This is a regulation of discipline in prayers, not a classification of importance. In men's rows, the head of the state stands shoulder to shoulder to the pauper. Men of the highest social ranks stand in prayer side by side with men of the lowest ranks.

The order of the prayer lines are intended to help every person concentrate while praying. Such discipline is very important, because the prayers are not simply chanting or singsongs, but involve specific actions and motions (e.g., standing, bowing, prostrating). If men and women pray in the same line, they might be distracted by something and loose their concentration. Thus the prayer's purpose will not be fulfilled.

Moreover, no a man cannot touch a woman's body while praying, and vice versa. If they stand side by side while praying, they cannot avoid touching each other. Furthermore, if a woman prays in front of a man or beside him, part of her body most likely may be revealed when she is bowing or prostrating. He might look at that uncovered part, which will embarrass her and distract him and expose him to evil thoughts. In order to concentrate on praying, prevent any unforeseen accidents, maintain harmony and order among worshippers, to fulfill the prayer's true purposes of prayers, Islam ordains praying in rows: the men in the front, then the children, and then the women. Anyone who

understands what praying means to a Muslim can easily understand the wisdom of organizing the lines of worshippers in this
manner.

The Veil

The Muslim woman is always associated with an old tradition
known as the "veil." She is to beautify herself with the veil of
honor, dignity, chastity, purity, and integrity; and refrain from all
deeds and gestures that might stir the passions of people other
than her husband or cause people to suspect her morality. She is
warned not to display her charms or expose her physical attractions before strangers. The veil is one way to save her soul from
weakness, her mind from indulgence, her eyes from lustful looks,
and her personality from demoralization. Islam is most concerned
with a woman's integrity, safeguarding of her morals and morale,
and protecting her character and personality (cf. Qur'an, 24:30-31).

Conclusion

By now it is clear that the status of woman in Islam is unprece-
dentedly high and realistically suitable to her nature. Her rights
and duties are equal to those of a man, but not necessarily or
absolutely identical with them. If she is deprived of one thing in
some aspect, she is fully compensated for it with more things in
many other aspects. The fact that she is a woman has no bearing
on her human status or independent personality, and is no basis
for justifying any prejudice or injustice toward her. Islam gives her
as much as is required of her. Her rights match beautifully with her
duties. This balance between rights and duties is maintained, and
no side outweighs the other. As we read in the Qur'an:

> In a fair manner women have the same rights against men as
> men have against them, but men (due to the heaviness of their
> duty and responsibility,) have a degree above them (which they
> should not misuse. (2:228)

This degree is not a title of supremacy or an authorization to
dominate women, but rather corresponds with a man's extra

responsibilities and compensates him for his unlimited liabilities. The above-mentioned verse is always interpreted in the light of:

> "Men (who are able to perform their responsibilites) are the protectors and maintainers of women, for that God has endowed some people with greater capacity than others (in some respects) and that they (men) spend of their wealth (for the family's maintenance). (4:34)

These extra responsibilities give men a degree over women in some economic aspects, not in humanity or character. Nor is it a dominance of one over the other, or a suppression of one by the other. Rather, it is a distribution of God's abundance according to the needs of each gender's nature, of which God is the Maker. As He alone knows what is best for men and women, the following words are absolutely true:

> O humanity, avoid disobedience to your Lord Who has created you from a single original human self, and from it created its mate, and from the pair of them scattered abroad a multitude of men and women. (4:1)

Inheritance and Women

Since Biblical days, Judaism has given no female members of the household, including the wife and daughters, the right to inherit any part of the family estate. In the more primitive inheritance process, the women of the family were considered part of the estate and as remote from any legal personality of an heir as was a slave. Under rabbinic law, daughters could inherit if there were no male heirs. However, even in such conditions the wife could not inherit anything. Why were the women of the family considered part of the estate? Because of the attitude: "They are owned – before marriage by the father, and after marriage by the husband."

Christianity followed suit for a long time. Both the ecclesiastical and civil laws of Christendom barred daughters from sharing with their brothers in their father's patrimony. Wives also had no inheritance rights. These laws survived until late in the twentieth century.

Among the pre-Islamic Arabs, inheritance rights were confined exclusively to the male relatives. Islam also made a great revolution in this respect, for the Qur'an declared:

> For the male heirs is a share of what parents and near kindred (who die) leave behind, and for the female heirs is a share of what parents and near kindred (who die) leave behind, whether it (the heritage) be little or much – a share ordained by God. (4:7)

This short verse contains the basic principles of the Islamic law of inheritance and a significant warning[8]:

- Both women and men have a share in the inheritance.
- A deceased person's property is inherited, whether it be little or much.
- It makes no difference whether the inherited property is movable or immovable.
- The survivors (e.g., parents, grandparents, and nearest relatives) can inherit. If there are any "nearest kindred," "collateral relations" cannot inherit.
- Heirs cannot be deprived of their share of the inheritance.

The significant warning is: Women in pre-Islamic, idolatrous, Christian, and Jewish societies could not inherit. By mentioning female heirs separately, but in the same words as it mentions male heirs, at the risk of repetition and emphasizing that the estate's size does not matter, the verse warns that women cannot be deprived of their share of the inheritance on such pretexts as "the estate is too small."

Then, the Qur'an details the laws for inheritance (4:11-12). Its basic principles and standards were laid down, and its precise details were established on these standards, the Prophet's practice, and that of his Companions.

With the exception of the parents, and the siblings in some cases, a son receives twice as much as a daughter, a brother twice as much as a sister, and a husband twice as much as a wife. This has been the target of unjust objections. However:

- First, it should be noted that Islam is not a religion that answers objections, for whatever it decrees is right and just. Therefore, all other religions, systems, and ideologies must design themselves according to the Islamic precepts. So while explaining Islam's position in matters to which objections have been raised, we intend to illuminate sincere minds.

- Second, the verses present Islam's law of inheritance as God's absolute command, and in their conclusive pronouncements declare that they are based on God's Knowledge and Wisdom. So we should try to find the instances of Divine wisdom in them. Breaching them means disobeying God and His Messenger, while rejecting them amounts to unbelief.

- Third, Islam is universal and thus considers and addresses the conditions of all ages and communities. Its worldview is holistic and deals with particular matters in its universal frame. So while viewing its law of inheritance, we should consider such psychological and sociological factors as the psychology of women and men; their positions and financial, familial, and social responsibilities; and their contributions to the economy. As the matter is never a matter of equality between men and women, we should evaluate every matter with respect to its own nature and context.

In order to understand the rationale behind Islam's giving a woman half of a man's share, one must remember that the man's financial obligations far exceed those of a woman. A groom must provide his bride with a marriage gift, which then becomes her exclusive property and remains so even if she is divorced. The bride is under no obligation to present any gifts to the groom.

Moreover, the husband must maintain his wife and children. The wife, on the other hand, is not obliged to help him do so. Her property and earnings are for her use alone, except for what she may offer to her husband voluntarily. Besides, one has to realize that Islam strongly advocates family life, encourages young people to get married, and discourages divorce. Therefore, in a truly Islamic society, family life is the norm and single life is the rare exception, for almost all marriage-aged women and men get married. In light of these facts, one would appreciate that men generally have greater financial burdens than women, and that the inheritance rules are meant to offset this imbalance.

When a woman receives less than a man, she is not deprived of anything for which she has worked. The property she inherits is not the result of her earning or endeavor, but something coming from a neutral source, something additional or extra. Thus it is a type of aid, and any aid has to be distributed according to the needs and responsibilities, especially when the distribution is regulated by God's law.

The Qur'anic injunction of inheritance is a perfect mercy for women, in addition to its being perfectly just, for a girl is delicate, vulnerable, and thus held in great affection by her father. Her father, in turn and thanks to the Qur'an, does not see her as a child who will cause him any loss by carrying away some of his wealth to others. In addition, her brothers feel compassion for her and protect her without feeling envious, as they do not consider her as a rival in the division of the family's possessions. Thus, the affection and compassion which the girl enjoys through her family compensate her for the apparent loss in the inheritance.

Some still object on the grounds that a woman's share of the inheritance should be equal to that of a man so that there would be no need to compensate her through a dower and maintenance by her husband.

Those who make this objection think that the dower and maintenance are the effects of women's peculiar position with regard to inheritance, whereas the real position is just the reverse. Further, they seem to be under the impression that the financial aspect is the only consideration. If this were so, there would have been no need for dower and maintenance or for any disparity between the shares of men and women. As in every other case, however, Islam has considered all aspects connected to the individual's nature and psychology. It has considered women's unique needs arising out of their procreative function. Moreover, a woman's earning capacity is less than a man's, and her consumption of wealth is usually more. In most cases, in her parents' house her contribution to the family income is far less than her brother(s). In addition, there are several other finer aspects of their respective mental make-up. For example, a man always wants to spend on the woman of his choice. Other psychological and social aspects that help consolidate domestic relations also have been considered. Taking all of these points into consideration, Islam has made dower and maintenance obligatory.

Thus it is a severe injustice, not a kindness, to give a girl or woman more than her due out of unrealistic feelings of compassion – unrealistic because no one can be more compassionate than God. Rather, if the Qur'anic bounds are exceeded, women may become vulnerable to exploitation and tyranny in the family. As for the Qur'anic injunctions, all of them, like those pertaining to inheritance, prove the truth expressed in: *We have not sent you (O Muhammad), save as a mercy unto all beings.*

Modern civilization wrongs mothers more than girls by depriving them of their rights. Being the purest and finest reflection of Divine compassion, a mother's affection is the most revered reality in creation. A mother is so compassionate, self-sacrificing, and intimate a friend that she sacrifices all she has, including her life, for her children. For example, a timid hen, whose motherliness represents the lowest degree, has been observed to attack a dog to protect her chicks.

Islam does not approve of wealth circulating only among a few people; rather, it wants wealth to be distributed among as many people as possible. In inheritance, considering that God's grace and bountifulness have a share in it, it strongly advises and even orders that distant relatives, orphans, and the poor should also benefit from it.

WOMEN

Women train and educate children, and establish order, peace, and harmony at home. They are the first teachers in the school of humanity. A house that contains an honorable, well-mannered woman loyal to her home is a corner from Heaven. The sounds and breaths heard there are no different from the musical voices of the young people of Paradise and the burbling of the Kawthar stream in Heaven.

ॐ ॐ

A woman's inner depth, chastity, and dignity elevate her higher than angels and cause her to resemble an unmatched diamond.

A woman awake to virtue in her inner world resembles a crystal chandelier that, with every movement, sends light throughout the house.

၆ ၆

Women often have been used as objects of pleasure, means of entertainment, and material for advertising. Most champions of woman's rights and freedom only excite women with physical pleasures and then stab her spirit.

၆ ၆

In the past, a son was called *makhdum* and a daughter *karima*. Meaning "pupil (of the eye)," this word expresses a member that is very valuable, as necessary as it is valuable, and as delicate as it is necessary.

၆ ၆

A good woman speaks wisdom and has a delicate, refined spirit. Her behavior inspires admiration and respect. Familiar looks sense this sacred side of her, and turn instinctive feelings to contemplation.

၆ ၆

Like a flower worn on the breast, a physically beautiful woman may receive admiration and respect for some short period. But, if she has not been able to get the seeds of her heart and spirit to blossom, she will eventually fade and, like falling leaves, be trampled underfoot. What a sad ending for those who have not found the road of immortality!

၆ ၆

Thanks to the good successors she raised and left behind, the home of a spiritually mature woman constantly exudes a scent of joy like an incense burner. The "heavenly" home where this aroma "blows" is a garden of Paradise beyond description.

၆ ၆

A woman whose heart is illuminated with the light of faith and whose mind is enlightened with knowledge and social breeding builds her home anew each day by adding new dimensions of beauty to it.

(M. Fethullah Gülen, *Pearls of Wisdom*, The Light, Inc., 2005.)

Divorce

Christianity abhors divorce, and the New Testament unequivocally advocates the indissolubility of marriage. Judaism, on the other hand, allows divorce without cause. The Old Testament gives the husband the right to divorce his wife if he just dislikes her (Deuteronomy 24:1-4).

Islam, which rejects and is free from all extremities, occupies the middle ground between Christianity and Judaism with respect to divorce. It considers marriage a sanctified bond that should not be broken except for compelling reasons. Couples are instructed to pursue all possible remedies whenever their marriages are in danger. Divorce is not to be resorted to except when there is no other solution. In a nutshell, Islam recognizes divorce and yet it discourages it by all means. For example, the Qur'an warns: *And consort with them in kindness, for if you dislike them, it may be that you dislike something in which God has placed much good* (4:19).

God's Messenger emphasizes: "Let a believing man not dislike a believing woman. If something in her is displeasing to him, another trait may be pleasing"; "Among all of the permitted acts, divorce is the most hateful to God" (Abu Dawud, "Talaq," 3); and: "The most perfect believers are the best in character, and the best of you are the kindest to their families" (Canan, *ibid.*, 17:212).

However, Islam recognizes that there can be circumstances in which a marriage will be on the verge of collapse. In such cases, a mere advice of kindness or self-restraint is not a viable solution. So, what should be done to save the marriage in such cases? The Qur'an offers some practical advice for the spouses, takes some measures, and gives the spouses the possibility to reconsider their decision.

No Divorce during Menstruation

A man cannot divorce his wife at any time; rather, he must wait for a suitable time. According to the law, the suitable time is when the wife had cleansed herself after her menstrual or post-childbirth bleeding periods and before they resume sexual relations, or when she is not pregnant.

The reason for prohibiting divorce during menstruation or post-childbirth bleeding is that since sexual intercourse is forbidden during such periods, a husband is given the time and opportunity to withdraw his decision by waiting until his wife is clean and there can be a new atmosphere of love, understanding, and reconciliation between them. Divorce is also forbidden between menstrual periods (i.e., "the period of purity") if the husband has had sexual intercourse with his wife after the end of her previous period.

Repeated Divorce

A man is given three chances on three different occasions to divorce his wife, provided that each divorce is pronounced during the time when his wife is in "the period of purity" and he has not had intercourse with her.

He may divorce her once and let the *'Idda* pass. During that time, the divorced wife must stay in her home (i.e., her husband's house). She cannot move somewhere else, and her husband cannot evict her without a just cause. During *'Idda*, he must provide for her. This requirement leaves the way open for reconciliation. They have the option of reconciliation without having to remarry. If, however, this waiting period expires without reconciliation, they are considered divorced and therefore each former spouse can marry someone else or remarry each other. If they decide to remarry, a new marriage contract is required.

If they remarry, the husband has one more chance to divorce his wife, as in the first instance. But if he divorces his wife for a third time, they can no longer turn to each other unless the woman marries another man and divorces or is divorced by him in normal conditions.

Appointing Arbitrators

The Qur'an advises that two arbitrators be appointed if dissension occurs between the two spouses and its source cannot be determined. One arbitrator should be from the husband's family and the other from the wife's family. If that is not possible, other people may be appointed, depending on what is in the best interest of those concerned. They also agree that when a possible resolution has been devised to reconcile the spouses, it should be implemented. However, if they disagree, their opinions are not to be implemented.

Imam al-Shafi'i records in his book *al-Umm* from Ubayda al-Salmani, who said:

> A man and a woman came to 'Ali ibn Abi Talib, each of them accompanied by a group of people. 'Ali told them to appoint a male arbitrator from his family and one from her family. Then he said to the arbitrators: "Do you know what your responsibilities are? If you find that you can bring them back together, do so. If you find that they should be separated, do so."

Reconciling Honorably or Separating with Kindness

If any reconciliation does not occur and the period of *'idda* ends, they have two alternatives if only one or two instances of divorce have occurred: either to reconcile honorably (i.e., to remarry with the intention of living in peace and harmony), or to free the woman and part with her in kindness, without argument and harsh words, and without setting aside any of their mutual rights.

The Divorced Woman's Freedom to Remarry

After a divorced woman's *'idda* ends, her ex-husband, guardian, or anyone else cannot prevent her from marrying anyone she chooses. As long as she and the man who proposes to her follow the procedure required by the law, no one has the right to interfere.

The Woman's Right to Demand Divorce

If the wife chooses to end the marriage, she may return the marriage gifts to her husband. This is a fair compensation for the husband who is keen to keep his wife, while she chooses to leave him. The Qur'an instructs the man not to take back any of the gifts he has given to his wife, unless she chooses to end the marriage (2:229).

Once, a woman came to the Prophet, upon him be peace and blessings, seeking to dissolve her marriage. She said that she had no complaint against her husband's character or manners, but that she honestly disliked him so much that she could no longer live with him. The Prophet asked her: "Would you give him his garden (his marriage gift to her) back?" she said: "Yes," she replied. The Prophet then instructed the man to take back his garden and accept the dissolution of the marriage (Tajrid al-Sarih, HN: 1836).

In some cases, a wife might want to keep her marriage but find herself forced to seek divorce for a compelling reason (e.g., cruelty, desertion without a reason, non-fulfillment of his conjugal responsibilities). In such cases, the Muslim court dissolves the marriage.

As another case, a husband can confer the power of divorce on the wife. This delegation of power can be general or limited to certain specified circumstances. To make it irrevocable, it is included in the marriage contract as a binding clause that empowers the wife to dissolve the marriage based upon the agreed-upon specified circumstances.

Adoption

Islam has abolished the type of adoption that makes an adopted child a member of the family, which would give him or her full rights of inheritance and to mix freely with other members of the household, and prohibit him or her to marry certain women or men, and so on.

But the word *adoption* is also used in another sense, one that is not prohibited by Islam. In this context, adoption means bringing home an orphan or an abandoned child to rear, educate, and treat as his own child as regards protection, feeding, clothing, teaching, and loving. However, he does not consider the child to be his own and does not give the child any of the rights that Islamic law reserves for natural children.

The Prophet, His Wives, and Children[9]

Prophet Muhammad personifies the roles of a perfect father and husband. He was so kind and tolerant with his wives that they could not envisage their lives without him, nor did they want to live away from him.

He married Sawda, his second wife, while in Makka. After a while, he wanted to divorce her for certain reasons. She was extremely upset at this news, and implored him: "O Messenger of God, I wish no worldly thing of you. Please don't deprive me of being your wife. I want to go to the Hereafter as your wife. I care for nothing else" (Muslim, "rada'," 47). The Messenger did not divorce her.

Once he noticed that Hafsa was uncomfortable over their financial situation. "If she wishes, I may set her free," he said, or something to that effect. This suggestion alarmed her so much that she requested mediators to persuade him not to do so. He kept his faithful friend's daughter as his trusted wife.

His wives viewed separation from the Messenger of God as a calamity, so firmly had he established himself in their hearts. They were completely at one with him. They shared in his blessed, mild, and natural life. If he had left them, they would have died of despair. If he had divorced one of them, she would have waited at his doorstep until the Last Day.

After his death, there was much yearning and a great deal of grief. Abu Bakr and 'Umar found the Messenger's wives weeping whenever they visited them. Their weeping seemed to continue for the rest of their lives. Muhammad left a lasting impression on everyone. He dealt equally with his wives and without any serious problems. He was a kind and gentle husband, and never behaved harshly or rudely. In short, he was the perfect husband.

Each wife, because of his generosity and kindness, thought she was his most beloved. The idea that any man could show complete equality and fairness in his relationships with more than one women seems impossible. For this reason, the Messenger of God asked God's pardon for any unintentional leanings. He would pray: "I may have unintentionally shown more love to one of them than the others, and this would be injustice. So, O Lord, I take refuge in Your grace for those things beyond my power" (Tirmidhi, "Nikah," 41:4; Bukhari, "Adab," 68).

His gentleness penetrated his wives' souls so deeply that his departure led to what they must have felt to be an unbridgeable separation. They did not commit suicide, as Islam forbids it, but their lives now became full of endless sorrow and ceaseless tears.

The Messenger was kind and gentle to all women, and advised all other men to follow him in this regard. Sa'd ibn Abi Waqqas described his kindness as follows:

'Umar said: One day I went to the Prophet and saw him smiling. "May God make you smile forever, O Messenger of God," I said, and asked why he was smiling. "I smile at those women. They were chatting in front of me before you came. When they heard your voice, they all vanished," he answered still smiling. On hearing this answer, I raised my voice and told them: "O enemies of your own selves, you are scared of me, but you are not scared of the Messenger of God, and you don't show respect to him." "You are hard-hearted and strict," they replied (Bukhari, "Adab," 68).

'Umar also was gentle to women. However, the most handsome man looks ugly when compared to Joseph's beauty. Likewise, 'Umar's gentleness and sensitivity seem like violence and severity when compared to those of the Prophet.

The Prophet's Consultation with His Wives

The Messenger discussed matters with his wives as friends. Certainly he did not need their advice, since he was directed by Revelation. However, he wanted to teach his nation that Muslim men were to give women every consideration. This was quite a radical idea in his time, as it is today in many parts of the world. He began teaching his people through his own relationship with his wives.

For example, the conditions laid down in the Treaty of Hudaybiya disappointed and enraged many Muslims, for one condition stipulated that they could not make the pilgrimage that year. They wanted to reject the treaty, continue on to Makka, and face the possible consequences. But the Messenger ordered them to kill their sacrificial animals and take off their pilgrim attire. Some Companions hesitated, hoping that he would change his mind. He repeated his order, but they continued to hesitate. They did not oppose him; rather, they still hoped he might change his mind, for they had set out with the intention of pilgrimage and did not want to stop half way.

Noticing this reluctance, the Prophet returned to his tent and asked Umm Salama, his wife accompanying him at that time, what she thought of the situation. So she told him, fully aware that he did not need her advice. In doing this, he taught Muslim men an important social lesson: There is nothing wrong with exchanging ideas with women on important matters or on any matters at all.

She said: "O Messenger of God, don't repeat your order. They may resist and thereby perish. Offer your sacrificial animal and change out of your pilgrim attire. They will obey, willingly or not, when they see that your order is final" (Bukhari, "Shurut," 15). He did what his wife suggested, and the Companions began to do the same, for now it was clear that his order would not be changed.

Women are secondary beings in the minds of many, including those self-appointed defenders of women's rights as well as many self-proclaimed Muslim men. For us, a woman is part of a whole, a part that renders the other half useful. We believe that when the two halves come together, the true unity of a human being appears. When this unity does not exist, humanity does not exist – nor can Prophethood, sainthood, or even Islam.

Our master encouraged us through his enlightening words to behave kindly to women. He declared: "The most perfect believers are the best in character, and the best of you are the kindest to their families" (Abu Dawud, "Sunna," 15; Tirmidhi, "rada'," 11). It is clear that women have received the true honor and respect they deserve, not just in theory but in actual practice, only once in history – during the period of Prophet Muhammad.

A Perfect Head of the Family

Some of his wives had enjoyed an extravagant lifestyle before their marriage to him. One of these was Safiya, who had lost her father and husband, and had been taken prisoner, during the Battle of Khaybar. She must have been very angry with the Messenger, but when she saw him, her feelings changed completely. She endured the same destiny as the other wives. They endured it because love of the Messenger had penetrated their hearts.

Safiya was a Jewess. Once, she was dismayed when this fact was mentioned to her sarcastically. She informed the Messenger, expressing her sadness. He comforted her saying: "If they repeat it, tell them: 'My father is Prophet Aaron, my uncle is Prophet Moses, and my husband is, as you see, Prophet Muhammad, the Chosen One. What do you have more than me to be proud of?'" (Tirmidhi, "Manaqib," 64).

The Qur'an declares that his wives are the mothers of the believers (33:6). Although 14 centuries have passed, we still feel delight in saying "my mother" when referring to Khadija, 'A'isha, Umm Salama, Hafsa, and his other wives. We feel this because of him. Some feel more love for these women than they do for their real mothers. Certainly, this feeling must have been deeper, warmer, and stronger in the Prophet's own time.

The Messenger was the perfect head of a family. Managing many women with ease, being a lover of their hearts, an instructor of their minds, an educator of their souls, he never neglected the affairs of the nation or compromised his duties.

The Messenger excelled in every area of life. People should not compare him to themselves or to the so-called great personalities of their age. Researchers should look at him, the one to whom angels are grateful, always remembering that he excelled in every way. If they want to look for Muhammad they must search for him in his own dimensions. Our imaginations cannot reach him, for we do not even know how to imagine properly. God bestowed upon him, as His special favor, superiority in every field.

God's Messenger and Children

The Messenger, upon him be peace and blessings, was an extraordinary husband, a perfect father, and a unique grandfather. He was unique in every way. He treated his children and grandchildren with great compassion, and never neglected to direct them to the Hereafter and good deeds. He smiled at them, caressed and loved them, but did not allow them to neglect matters related to the afterlife.

In worldly matters he was extremely open. But when it came to maintaining their relationship with God, he was very serious and dignified. He showed them how to lead a humane life, and never allowed them to neglect their religious duties and become spoiled. His ultimate goal was to prepare them for the Hereafter. His perfect balance in such matters is another dimension of his Divinely inspired intellect.

In a hadith narrated by Muslim, Anas ibn Malik, honored as the Messenger's servant for 10 continuous years, says: "I've never seen a man who was more compassionate to his family members than Muhammad" (Muslim, "Fada'il," 63). If this admission were made just by us, it could be dismissed as unimportant. However, millions of people, so benign and compassionate that they would not even offend an ant, declare that he embraced everything with compassion. He was a human like us, but God inspired in him such an intimate affection for every living thing that he could establish a connection with all of them. As a result, he was full of extraordinary affection toward his family members and others.

All of the Prophet's sons had died. Ibrahim, his last son born to his Coptic wife Mary, also died in infancy. The Messenger often visited his son before the latter's death, although he was very busy. Ibrahim was looked after by a nurse. The Prophet would embrace, kiss, and caress him before returning home. When Ibrahim died, the Prophet took him on his lap again, embraced him, and described his sorrow while on the brink of tears. Some were surprised. He gave them this answer: "Eyes may water and hearts may be broken, but we do not say anything except what God will be pleased with." He pointed to his tongue and said: "God will ask us about this" (Bukhari, "Jana'iz," 44; Muslim, "Fada'il," 62).

He carried his grandsons Hasan and Husayn on his back. Despite his unique status, he did this without hesitation to herald the honor that they would attain later. One time when they were on his back, 'Umar came into the Prophet's house and, seeing them, exclaimed: "What a beautiful mount you have!" The Messenger added immediately: "What beautiful riders they are!" (Muttaqi al-Hindi, Kanz al-'Ummal, 13:650).

The Messenger was completely balanced in the way he brought up his children. He loved his children and grandchildren very much, and instilled love in them. However, he never let his love for them be abused. None of them deliberately dared to do anything wrong. If they made an unintentional mistake, the Messenger's protection prevented them from going even slightly astray. He did this by wrapping them in love and an aura of dignity. For example, once Hasan or Husayn wanted to eat a date that had been given to distribute among the poor as alms. The Messenger immediately took it from his hand and said: "Anything given as alms is forbidden to us" (Muslim, "Zakat," 161). In teaching them while they were young to be sensitive to forbidden acts, he established an important principle of education.

Whenever he returned to Madina, he would carry children on his mount. On such occasions, the Messenger embraced not only his grandchildren but also those in his house and those nearby. He conquered their hearts through his compassion. He loved all children.

He loved his granddaughter Umama as much as he loved Hasan and Husayn. He often went out with her on his shoulders, and even placed her on his back while praying. When he prostrated, he put her down; when he had finished, he placed her on his back again (Bukhari, "Adab," 18). He showed this degree of love to Umama to teach his male followers how to treat girls. This was a vital necessity, for only a decade earlier it had been the social norm to bury infant or young girls alive. Such public paternal affection for a granddaughter had never been seen before in Arabia.

The Messenger proclaimed that Islam allows no discrimination between son and daughter. How could there be? One is Muhammad, the other is Khadija; one is Adam, the other is Eve; one is 'Ali, the other is Fatima. For every great man there is a great woman.

He loved them and directed them toward the Hereafter, to the otherworldly and eternal beauty, and to God. For example, he once saw Fatima wearing a necklace (a bracelet, according to another version), and asked her: "Do you want the inhabitants of Earth and the Heavens to say that my daughter is holding (or wearing) a chain from Hell?" These few words, coming from a man

whose throne was established in her heart and who had conquered all her faculties, caused her to report, in her own words:
"I immediately sold the necklace, bought and freed a slave, and
then went to the Messenger. When I told him what I had done,
he rejoiced. He opened his hands and thanked God: 'All thanks
to God, Who protected Fatima from Hell'" (Nasa'i, "Zinat," 39).

Fatima did not commit any sin by wearing this necklace.
However, the Messenger wanted to keep her in the circle of the
muqarrabin (those made near to God). His warning to her was
based on *taqwa* (righteousness and devotion to God) and *qurb*
(nearness to God). This was, in a sense, a neglect of worldly things.
It is also an example of the sensitivity befitting the mother of the
Prophet's household, which represents the Muslim community
until the Last Day. To be a mother of such godly men like Hasan,
Husayn, and Zayn al-'Abidin was certainly no ordinary task. The
Messenger was preparing her to be the mother first of his own
household (Ahl al-Bayt), and then of those who would descend
from them.

Bukhari and Muslim gave another example of how he educated them. 'Ali narrates that:

> We had no servant in our house, and so Fatima did all the house-
> work by herself. We lived in a house with just a small room.
> There, she would light a fire and try to cook. She often singed
> her clothes while trying to increase the fire by blowing. She also
> baked our bread and carried water. Her hands became covered
> with calluses from turning the millstone, as did her back from
> carrying water.

> Meanwhile some prisoners of war were brought to Madina.
> The Messenger gave them to those who applied. I suggested to
> Fatima that she ask for a servant from her father. And she did.

Fatima continues:

> I went to my father, but he was not at home. 'A'isha said she
> would tell him when he came, so I returned home. As soon as
> we went to bed, the Messenger came in. We wanted to get up,
> but he did not let us and instead sat between us. I could feel the

cold of his foot on my body. He asked what we wanted, and I explained the situation. The Messenger, in an awesome manner, replied: "Fatima, fear God and be faultless in all your duties to Him. I will tell you something. When you want to go to bed, say *subhana'llah* (All glory be to God), *al-hamdu li'llah* (All praise be to God), and *Allahu akbar* (God is the Greatest) 33 times each. This is better for you than having a maid" (Bukhari, "Fada'il al-Ashab," 9; Muslim, "Dhikr," 80, 81).

Affection toward and Respect for Parents[10]

O you who are unaware of filial responsibility toward parents, whose house contains an elderly parent, a helpless and invalid relative, or a coreligionist unable to earn a living. Heed these verses and see how they insist in five ways that you show filial affection.

As paternal affection for children is a sublime reality of worldly life, filial gratitude is a most urgent and heavy duty. Parents lovingly sacrifice their lives for their children. Given this, children who try to please them and gain their approval without showing them sincere respect or serving them willingly have no humanity and are monsters of ingratitude. Uncles and aunts are considered parents.

Know, you who neglect such duties, how terribly disgraceful and unscrupulous it is to be bored with their continued existence and so hope for their deaths. Know this and come to your senses! Understand what an injustice it is to desire the deaths of those who sacrificed their lives for you.

O you immersed in earning your livelihood, know that your disabled relative, whom you consider a burden, is a means of blessing and abundance. Never complain about the difficulty of making a living, for were it not for the blessing and abundance bestowed upon you, you would face even more hardship. If I did not want to keep this letter brief, I would prove this to you.

I swear by God that this is a reality that even my devil and evil-commanding self accept. All existence can see that the infinitely merciful and compassionate, gracious and munificent Generous, Majestic Creator sends children here along with their sustenance: their mother's breast milk. He sends sustenance for the elderly, who are like children and even more worthy and needy of compassion, in the form of blessing and unseen, immaterial abundance. He does not load their sustenance onto mean, greedy people.

The truth expressed in: *God is the All-Provider, the Possessor of Strength and the Steadfast* (51:58) and: *How many an animate creature bears not its own provision, but God provides for it and you* (29:60) is proclaimed by all living creatures through the tongue of their disposition. So not only is the sustenance of elderly relatives sent in the form of blessings, but also that of pets, created as friends to people who feed and take care of them. I have personally observed this: Years ago, my daily ration was half a loaf of bread. I barely managed with this until four cats became my daily guests. As soon as they began sharing my bread, the same ration was always enough for all of us. I saw this so often that I became convinced that I benefited from the blessing coming through the cats. I declare that they were not a burden upon me; rather, I was indebted to them.

O people, you are the most esteemed, noble, and worthy-of-respect of all creatures. Among people, believers are the most perfect. Among believers, the helpless and the elderly are the most worthy and needy of respect and compassion. Among the helpless and elderly, relatives deserve more affection, love, and service than others. Among relatives, parents are the most truthful confidants and most intimate companions. If an animal is a means of blessing and abundance when it stays as a guest in your house, consider how invaluable a means of blessing and mercy your elderly parents are if they stay with you. The following Tradition shows what an important means for removing calamities they are: "But for the old bent double, calamities would pour down upon you."

So come to your senses. If you have been assigned a long life, you also will grow old. If you do not respect parents, then, according to the rule that one is rewarded or punished in accordance with one's action, your children will not respect you. Further, serious reflection on your afterlife shows that gaining your parents' approval and pleasing them through service is a precious provision for your afterlife. If you love this worldly life, please them so that you may lead a pleasant life. If you consider them a burden, break their easily offended hearts, and desire their deaths, you will be the object of the Qur'anic threat: *He [She] loses both the world and the world to come* (22:11). So, those who wish for the All-Merciful's mercy must show mercy to those entrusted to them by God.

HALAL (LAWFUL) AND HARAM (FORBIDDEN)[11]

Halal is a Qur'anic term that means permitted, allowed, lawful, or legal. Its opposite is *haram* (forbidden, unlawful or illegal). Determining what is *halal* and *haram* is one matter that, prior to the advent of Islam, over which the peoples of the world were very far astray and utterly confused. Thus, they permitted many impure and harmful things and forbade many things that were good and pure.

They erred grievously, either going far to the right or the left. On the extreme right was India's ascetic Brahmanism and Christianity's self-denying monasticism. In addition, other religions were based on mortifying the flesh, abstaining from good food, and avoiding other enjoyments of life that God has provided for humanity. On the extreme left was Persia's Mazdak philosophy, which advocated absolute freedom and allowed people to take whatever they wanted and to do whatever they pleased. It even exhorted them to violate what is naturally held inviolable.

When Islam came, the errors, confusion, and deviations with respect to *halal* and *haram* were widespread. One of Islam's initial accomplishments was, therefore, to establish certain legal principles and measures for rectifying this situation. These principles were made the determining criteria on which defining *halal* and *haram* were based. Thus this vital aspect was determined according to the correct perspective, and the related rules were established on the basis of such principles as justice, morality, righteousness, and perfect goodness. As a result, the Muslim community occupied a position between the extreme deviations mentioned above and was described by God as a *middle community, the best community that has ever been brought forth for humanity* (3:110).

Basic Principles

• The first principle is that all that God has created and the benefits derived from them are for humanity's use are permissible. Nothing is *haram* except what is forbidden by a sound and explicit nass (i.e., either a Qur'anic verse or a clear, authentic, and explicit *sunna* [practice or saying] of the Prophet, upon him be peace and blessings. These are the two main sources of Islamic law.).

• In Islam, the sphere of forbidden things is very small, while that of permissible things is vast. In relation to acts of worship, the principle is limitation: Nothing can be legislated in this regard except what God Himself has legislated. But as far as living habits are concerned, the principle is freedom, because nothing can be restricted in this regard except what God Himself and the Messenger, as based upon His Revelation, have forbidden. No rabbi, priest, king, or sultan has the right to forbid something permanently to God's servants. The Qur'an took to task the People of the Book (the Christians and Jews) for giving their priests and rabbis the power to make things and actions lawful or forbidden.

'Adiy ibn Hatim, who was a Christian before accepting Islam, once came to God's Messenger, upon him be peace and blessings. When he heard him reciting:

> The Jews take their scholars (teachers of law), and the Christians take their monks, as well as the Messiah, son of Mary, for Lords beside God, whereas they were commanded to worship none but the One God. There is no deity but He. Glory be to Him, that He is infinitely exalted above that they associate partners with Him (9:31),

he said, "O Messenger of God, but they do not worship them." The Messenger replied, "Yes, but they forbid to the people what is *halal* and permit them what is *haram*, and

the people obey them. This is indeed their worship of them."
(Tirmidhi, "Tafsir," HN: 3292)

- One of Islam's beauties is that it forbids only that which is unnecessary, harmful, and discardable (useless and unwanted), while providing alternatives that are better and give greater ease and comfort. For example: God forbids seeking omens by drawing lots, but provides the alternative of *istikhara*. Islam teaches that Muslims facing a problem should consult other Muslims and seek God's guidance. *Istikhara* means to ask for God's guidance in choosing between two conflicting decisions. For this there is a *salat* and a *du'a* (a supplication for guidance). He forbids usury but encourages profitable trade; forbids (to men) the wearing of silk, but gives them the choice of wool, linen, cotton, and so on; forbids adultery, fornication, and homosexuality, but encourages lawful marriage; forbids intoxicating drinks but provides other delicious drinks that are wholesome for the body and mind; and forbids unclean food but provides alternative wholesome food.

   Thus, when we survey all of Islam's injunctions, we find that if God limits His servants' choice in some matters, He provides them with a still wider range of more wholesome alternatives. Assuredly, God has no will to make peoples' lives difficult, narrow, and circumscribed; on the contrary, He wills ease, goodness, guidance, and mercy for them.

- Another Islamic principle is that whatever leads to something that is forbidden is also forbidden. In this way, Islam intends to block all avenues leading to what is *haram*. For example, Islam forbids extramarital sex as well as anything that leads to it or makes it attractive (e.g., seductive clothing, private meetings and casual mixing between men and women, depicting nudity, pornography, obscene songs, and so on).

- Just as Islam forbids whatever leads toward the *haram*, it forbids resorting to technical legalities in order to do what is *haram* by devious means and excuses. For example, God forbade the Jews to hunt on the Sabbath (Saturday). To get around this, they would dig ditches on Friday so that the fish would fall into them on Saturday and be caught on Sunday. Those who resort to rationalizations and excuses to justify their actions consider such practices permissible. However, Muslim jurists consider them *haram*, since God's purpose was to prevent them from hunting on the Sabbath, whether by direct or indirect means.

- Renaming a *haram* thing or changing its form while retaining its essence is a devious tactic, since both actions are of no consequence as long as the thing and its essence remain unchanged. Thus, when some people invent new terms in order to deal in usury or to consume alcohol, the sin of dealing in usury and drinking remains. As we read in the Traditions: "A group of people will make peoples' intoxication *halal* by giving it other names" and: "A time will come when people will devour usury, calling it 'trade.'"

- In all of its legislation and moral injunctions, Islam emphasizes the nobility of feelings, loftiness of aims, and purity of intentions. Indeed, in Islam, having a good intention transforms life's routine matters and mundane affairs into acts of worship and devotion to God. Accordingly, if one eats food with the intention of sustaining life and strengthening one's body so that he or she can fulfill his or her obligations to the Creator and other people, eating and drinking are considered worship and devotion to the Almighty. If one enjoys sexual intimacy with his or her spouse, desiring a child and seeking to keep both spouses chaste, it is considered an act of worship that deserves a reward in the Hereafter.

When Muslims perform a permissible action along with a good intention, the action becomes an act of worship. But the case of the *haram* is entirely different: It remains *haram* no matter how good the intention, how honorable the purpose, or how lofty the aim may be. Islam can never consent to employing a *haram* means to achieve a praiseworthy end. Indeed, it insists that both the aim and the means chosen to attain it must be honorable and pure. "The end justifies the means" has no place in Islam.

- It is God's mercy to people that He did not leave them in ignorance concerning what is lawful and forbidden. Indeed, He has made these matters very clear. Accordingly, one may do what is lawful and must avoid what is forbidden insofar as one has the choice to do so. However, there is a gray area of doubt between the clearly *halal* and the clearly *haram*. Some people may not be able to decide whether a particular matter is permissible or forbidden, either because of doubtful evidence or of doubt concerning the text's applicability to the circumstance or matter in question. In such cases, Islam considers it an act of piety to avoid doing what is doubtful in order to stay clear of doing something *haram*.

- In Islam, the *haram* has universal applicability, for that which is forbidden to a non-Arab cannot be permitted to an Arab, or that is restricted for a black person cannot be allowed to a white person. Islam contains no privileged classes or individuals who, in the name of religion, can do whatever they please according to their whims. No Muslim can forbid something to others but allow it for himself or herself, for God is the Lord of all and Islam is the guide for all. Whatever God has legislated through the religion He has sent for humanity is lawful for all people, and whatever He has forbidden is forbidden to all people until the Day of Resurrection.

Eating and Drinking

The following products are definitely lawful: Milk (from cows, sheep, and goats), honey, fish, plants that do not intoxicate, fresh or naturally frozen vegetables, fresh or dried fruits; legumes and nuts (e.g., peanuts, cashew nuts, hazel nuts, walnuts), and grains (e.g., wheat, rice, rye, barley, oats). Such animals as cows, sheep, goats, deer, geese, chickens, ducks, and game birds are lawful, but they must be sacrificed according to Islamic rites before being eaten.

Sacrificing animals in the Islamic manner (*zabiha*) and following Islam's dietary rules are excellent ways to avoid certain diseases. Sacrificing is done to ensure the meat's quality and to avoid any microbial contamination. Lawful animals must be offered in such a way that all of the blood is drained from the animal's body.

The Islamic method of sacrificing an animal is to cut its throat, so that the blood runs out and does not congeal in the veins. Thus, animals that have been strangled, beaten to death, or died in a fight or accident cannot be eaten. One who sacrifices the animal must be a mature sane Muslim, who sacrifices it while reciting *Bismi'llah* (In God's Name) with a sharp device and without severing it. The animal must be completely dead before it is skinned.

A product is considered *haram* if it has any contact with, or contains anything from:

- Pigs, dogs, donkeys, and carnivorous animals (e.g., bears and lions).
- Reptiles and insects that are considered ugly or filthy (e.g., worms, lice, flies, and cockroaches).
- Animals killed by strangulation, a blow to the head (clubbing), a headlong fall, natural causes (carrion), or being gored or attacked by another animal. Fish are exempted from this class. When the Messenger was asked about the sea, he replied: "Its water is pure and its dead are halal."
- All animals, except fish, that are not sacrificed according to Islamic rules.
- Alcohol, harmful substances, and poisonous and intoxicating plants or drinks (e.g., hashish, opium, and contemporary drugs, whether natural or chemical).
- Animals with protruding canine teeth (e.g., monkeys, and cats, lions).
- Amphibians (e.g., frogs, crocodiles, and turtles).
- Animals slaughtered for worship of, or in the name of, that which is not God.
- Scorpions, centipedes, rats, and similar animals.
- Animals that are forbidden to be killed (e.g., bees).
- Birds with talons (e.g., owls and eagles).
- Any meat that has been cut off of a live animal.
- Blood.
- Animals won in a bet or a game of chance.

- Food additives whose raw materials are forbidden and pro-duced through a process incompatible with Islam.
- Such impurities as dogs and pigs, alcohol, dead bodies not killed according to Islamic principles (except fish), blood, human and animal urine and waste matter, parts obtained from still-living animals (except for wool, hair, horns, and so on), and the milk of animals that cannot be eaten (e.g., donkeys, cats, and pigs).

Medical Necessity

Jurists differ over whether some of the forbidden food substances can be used as medicine. Some do not classify medicine as a "com-pelling necessity" like food based upon the following *hadith*: "Assuredly God did not provide a cure for you in what He has forbidden to you." Others consider the need for medicine equal to that of food, for both are necessary for preserving life. However, they maintain that any medicine containing a *haram* substance is permissible only under the following conditions: If the patient's life is endangered if the medicine is not taken; if there is no entire-ly *halal* alternative or substitute medication available; and if the medication is prescribed by a Muslim physician who is both knowl-edgeable and God-conscious.

Hunting and Game Animals

- For game animals to be lawful, the hunter must be a Muslim or a member of the People of the Book. A Muslim cannot hunt while in the state of *ihram*.
- The hunter should not hunt merely for sport, meaning that he or she kills animals but has no intention to eat them or to otherwise benefit from them.
- The weapon should pierce the animal's body, making a wound, for death by impact (e.g., hitting a deer with a car) does not make it halal.
- The hunter must say *Bismi'llah* when hurling or striking with the weapon, or dispatching the hunting animal.
- If a dog, a falcon, or a similar animal is used, it should be a trained animal and catch the game animal only for its owner.

Intoxicants

Khamr, translated as intoxicants, signifies any alcoholic drink that causes intoxication. Humanity has been afflicted with no greater calamity than alcohol. If statistics were collected worldwide of all the patients in hospitals who, due to alcohol, suffer from mental disorders, delirium tremens, nervous breakdowns, and digestive ailments and added to those collected worldwide regarding the suicides, homicides, bankruptcies, sales of properties, and broken homes related to alcohol consumption, the number of such cases would be so staggering that, in comparison, all exhortation and preaching against it would seem too little.

Whatever Intoxicates Is Haram

The first declaration made by the Messenger concerning this matter was that wine is forbidden and that khamr means any substance which intoxicates, in whatever form or under whatever name it may appear. Thus, beer and similar drinks are *haram*. When the Messenger was asked about certain drinks made from honey, corn, or barley by the process of fermentation until they became alcoholic, he replied succinctly: "Every intoxicant is *khamr*, and every *khamr* is *haram*."

Whatever Intoxicates in Large Amounts Is Haram in Any Amount

Islam takes an uncompromising stand in prohibiting intoxicants, regardless of whether the amount is little or much. If an individual is permitted to take just one step down this road, other steps follow. The person starts walking and then running, and does not stop at any stage. This is why the Messenger said: "Of that which intoxicates in a large amount, a small amount is *haram*."

Trading in Alcohol

The Messenger forbade any trading in alcohol, even with non-Muslims.

Drugs or "Khamr Is What Befogs the Mind."

'Umar ibn al-Khattab declared from the Messenger's pulpit, that "*khamr* is what befogs the mind," thus providing us with a decisive criterion for classifying items as *khamr*. There is no room for any uncertainty, for any substance that befogs or clouds the mind, as well as impairs its faculties of thought, perception, and discernment, is forbidden by God and His Messenger until the Day of Resurrection. This definitely includes such drugs as marijuana, cocaine, and opium.

The Consumption of Tobacco and Other Harmful Things

A general Islamic rule is that it is *haram* to eat or drink anything that may cause death, either quickly or gradually, such as poison or substances that injure one's health or harm one's body. Thus, if tobacco or another substance is proven to harm one's health, it is *haram*, especially if a physician has told the patient to quit smoking. Even if it were not injurious to one's health, it is still a waste of money and brings no religious or secular benefit, and the Messenger forbade wasting one's property. This becomes more serious when the money spent on such items is needed to support oneself and one's family.

Clothing and Adornment

From the Islamic point of view, clothing has two purposes: to cover the body and to beautify the appearance. God Almighty counts His bestowal of clothing and adornment upon human beings as one of His favors to humanity: *O children of Adam! Verily, We have bestowed upon you clothing to cover your shame as well as to be an adornment to you* (7:26).

Before dealing with questions of adornment and good appearance, Islam addressed itself in considerable depth to the question of cleanliness, for cleanliness is the essence of good appearance and the beauty of every adornment.

Gold Ornaments and Pure Silk Clothing

Islam forbids gold ornaments and clothing of pure silk to men, but permits them to women.

Women's Clothing

Islam makes it *haram* for women to wear clothes that do not cover the body, that are transparent, and that are so tight fitting that they delineate the parts of the body, especially those that are sexually attractive.

Dressing for Ostentation and Pride

The general rule for enjoying life's good things (e.g., food, drink, and clothing) is that they should be enjoyed without extravagance or pride. Extravagance consists of exceeding the limits of what is beneficial in the use of the *halal*, while pride is something related to the intention and the heart rather than to what is apparent. Pride is defined as the intention to look superior and above others, and God does not love any proud boaster (57:23). In order to avoid even the suspicion of pride, the Messenger forbade garments of "fame" (i.e., clothes worn to impress others and that generate competition in vain and idle pursuits).

Going to Extremes in Beautification

Islam denounces such excesses in beautifying oneself that require altering one's physical features as God has created them. The Qur'an considers such alterations as inspired by Satan, who will command them (his devotees) to change what Allah has created (4:119).

Items Related to Luxurious Living and Paganism

Muslims may adorn their houses with flowers, decorated fabrics, and other permitted ornamental objects. They are free to desire beauty in their homes and elegance in clothing. However, Islam disapproves of excess, and the Messenger did not like Muslims to fill their houses with luxurious and extravagant items or items related to paganism, for Islam has condemned luxury, extravagance, and paganism.

Useful Information

Gold and Silver Utensils

In accordance with what has been stated above, Islam has forbidden the use of gold and silver utensils and pure silk spreads.

Commemorating Great People

Islam abhors any excessive glorification of people, no matter how "great" they may be or whether they are living or dead. The Messenger, upon him be peace and blessings, also gave similar warnings. For example, he said: "Do not glorify me in the same manner as the Christians glorify Jesus, son of Mary, but say: 'He is a servant of God and His Messenger.'"

A religion who views even the Messenger of God in such a light is one of such moderation that it cannot tolerate the erecting of idol-like statues for some individuals, so that people may point to them with admiration and esteem. Many pretenders to greatness and self-proclaimed makers of history have slipped into the hall of fame through this open door, since those who are able to do so erects statues or monuments to themselves, or let their admirers do so, so that people do not appreciate those who are truly great.

Children's Toys

Children's toys in the form of human beings, animals, and the like are allowed in Islam.

Keeping Dogs without Necessity

Keeping dogs inside the house as pets was forbidden by the Messenger. Dogs kept for a purpose (e.g., hunting or guarding cattle or crops) are allowed.

Condemned Industries and Professions

Islam has forbidden certain professions and industries because they are harmful to society's beliefs, morals, honor, or good manners. Some of these are prostitution, erotic arts, and manufacturing intoxicants and drugs.

Trade

The Qur'an and the Hadith urge Muslims to engage in trade and commerce, and to travel in order to "seek God's bounty."

Forbidden Trades

Islam forbids all trade that involves injustice, cheating, making exorbitant profits, or promoting that which is *haram*. Examples of such trades are doing business in alcoholic beverages, intoxicants, drugs, pigs, idols, or anything whose consumption and use has been forbidden. Any related earnings are considered sinful.

Even if the trading is in entirely *halal* things, merchants must still adhere to many moral considerations, such as not lying and cheating, for those who cheat are considered to be outside the Islamic community; not tampering with the scales when weighing; not hoarding, lest they forfeit the protection of God and His Messenger; and not dealing in usury or interest (*riba*), for God has forbidden it.

The Prohibition of a Sale Involving Uncertainty

The Messenger forbade any kind of transaction that could lead to a quarrel or litigation due to some uncertainty.

Price Manipulation

In Islam, the market is to be free and allowed to respond to the natural laws of supply and demand. Unnecessary interference in the freedom of individuals is unjust. However, if any artificial forces (e.g., hoarding and price manipulation) interfere in the free market, public interest takes precedence over the individual's freedom. In such a situation, price control becomes permissible in order to meet society's needs and to protect it from greedy opportunists by thwarting their schemes. Researchers have concluded that, depending upon the nature of the circumstances, price controls may be either unjust and forbidden or just and permissible, depending upon the relevant circumstances.

Hoarding

Freedom for individual and natural competition in the marketplace is guaranteed by Islam. Nevertheless, it severely condemns those who, driven by ambition and greed, accumulate wealth at the expense of others and become rich by manipulating the price of food and other necessities.

Interfering in the Free Market

The Messenger forbade another practice related to hoarding: allowing a person in the town to sell on behalf of a person from the desert. Scholars have explained this as follows: A stranger would bring some goods to be sold in town at the current market price. A townsman would approach him, saying: "Leave them with me for a while. I will sell them for you when the price is better." If the stranger had sold his own goods, the price would have been lower, the people would have benefited, and he would have made a reasonable profit.

Brokerage

With the exception of such unlawful cases as mentioned above, brokerage is permissible, since it is a kind of mediation and connection between the buyer and the seller, which in many cases facilitates a profitable transaction for at least one of them or for both. In modern times, brokers have become far more necessary than before due to the complexities of trade and commerce, which involve all types of exports and imports, and wholesale and retail sales and purchases. Brokers play an important role in keeping things moving. There is nothing wrong, therefore, if they charge a commission for their services. The commission may be a fixed amount, proportional to the volume of sales, or whatever is agreed upon among the parties involved.

Exploitation and Fraud

In order to prevent the market's manipulation, the Messenger forbade *najash*. Ibn 'Umar explained that *najash* signifies someone's bidding for an item in excess of its price without having any intention of actually buying it, but merely in order to induce others to bid still higher. Many times this is prearranged for the purpose of deceiving others.

"He Who Deceives Us Is Not of Us."

Islam prohibits every type of fraud and deception, whether in buying and selling or in any other matter between people. In all situations, Muslims must be honest and truthful, holding their faith to be dearer than any worldly gain.

Frequent Swearing

The sin of deceiving becomes greater when a seller supports it by swearing in God's name that something is true. God's Messenger told merchants to avoid swearing in general and, in particular, in support of a lie: "Swearing produces a ready sale but blots out the blessing."

He disapproved of frequent swearing in business transactions because it is probably done to deceive people, and because it reduces respect for God's Name.

Withholding Full Measure

One way of defrauding customers is to measure or weigh inaccurately. The Qur'an orders full measure and full weight (6:52) and severely warns against any fraud in this aspect of business transactions:

> Woe to those that deal in fraud, those who, when they have to receive by measure from people, exact full measure, but when they have to give by measure or weight to people, give less than (what is) due. Do they not think that they will be called to account? On a Mighty Day – A Day when (all) humanity will stand before the Lord of the Worlds? (83:1-6)

Buying Stolen Property

In order to combat crime and to confine criminals within a very narrow sphere of activity, Islam has forbidden Muslims to buy any article that they know to be usurped, stolen, or taken unjustly from its owner. Anyone who does so abets the usurper, the thief, or the one committing injustice.

Interest

Islam permits an increase in capital through trade. At the same time, it blocks the way for anyone who tries to increase his or her capital through lending on usury or interest (*riba*), whether at a low or a high rate.

Sale for Deferred Payment (Credit)

While it is best to buy an article with cash, it is also permissible to buy on credit by mutual consent. Some jurists opine that if the seller increases his or her price and if the buyer asks for deferred payments, as is common in installment buying, the price differential due to the time delay resembles interest, which is likewise a price for time. Accordingly, they declare such sales to be *haram*. However, most scholars permit it because there is, on the whole, no resemblance to interest in such a transaction, since the seller is free to increase the price as he or she considers proper, as long as it does not cause blatant exploitation or clear injustice. If it does, it becomes *haram*. In order for such trade to be lawful, there should be mutual consent and the amount and the duration should be fixed and known to both sides.

Bribery

Taking a bribe is one way of consuming someone else's wealth wrongfully. A bribe refers to any kind of property offered to a judge or public servant in order to obtain a favorable decision favor of oneself or against a rival, to expedite one's own affair, or to delay any competition, and so on.

Wasteful Spending

Just as the wealth of others is sacred and any violation of it, whether secret or open, is forbidden, a person's wealth is sacred with respect to oneself. Thus, one should not waste it by extravagant or other wasteful spending.

Salaried Employment

Muslims are free to seek employment with a government, an organization, or an individual, as long as they can do their job satisfactorily and carry out their duties. However, they cannot seek a job for which they are unfit, especially if the job carries judicial or executive authority.

Forbidden Types of Employment

Muslims cannot take jobs that are injurious to the cause of Islam or harm Muslims. Accordingly, they cannot work for companies that manufacture *haram* items. Similarly, any service rendered in support of injustice or in promoting what is *haram* is itself *haram*.

For example, Muslims cannot work in organizations that deal with interest, in bars or liquor shops, nightclubs, and the like.

A General Rule in Earning a Living

When it comes to making a living, Islam differentiates between lawful and unlawful methods. One of the rules is that any transaction in which one person's gain results in another's loss is unlawful, while any transaction that is fair and beneficial to all the parties concerned, and that is transacted by mutual consent is, lawful.
The verses:

> O you who believe, do not devour one another's wealth in legally non-valid, wrongful ways, except it be a trade by mutual consent; and do not cause your own and community's perishing. (Do not forget that) God has deep, special compassion (toward you as believers). Whoever acts wrongfully through enmity (toward others) and by way of deliberate transgression and wronging (both himself and others), We shall surely land him in a Fire to roast there. That indeed is quite easy for God (4:29-30),

lay down two conditions for a transaction: mutual consent of the parties involved, and the benefit to one party should not be a loss to the other.

Other Activities

Illicit Sexual Intercourse

All revealed religions have forbidden and fought against fornication and adultery (*zina*). Islam, the last of the Divinely revealed religions, is very strict in prohibiting *zina*, for it leads to confusion of lineage, child abuse, family break-ups, bitterness in relationships, the spread of venereal diseases, and a general laxity in morals. Moreover, it opens the door to a flood of lusts and self-gratifications.

When Islam prohibits something, it closes all the avenues of approach to it. This is achieved by prohibiting every step and every means leading to what is *haram*. Accordingly, whatever excites passions, opens ways for illicit sexual relations between a man and a woman, and promotes indecency and obscenity is *haram*.

Superstitions and Myths

Soothsayers or diviners existed in Arab society during the Messenger's time. They deceived people by pretending to reveal information about past and future events through their contact with jinn or other secret sources. The Messenger struggled against this deception, which had no basis in knowledge, Divine guidance, or a revealed Scripture. For the same reason, divination with arrows and making decisions based upon what is observed in sand, seashells, tea leaves, cards, and palms, as well as fortune-telling by cards and similar methods, are all forbidden.

Magic

Islam also condemns magic and those who practice it. God's Messenger, upon him be peace and blessings, counted the practice of magic among those major deadly sins that destroy nations before destroying individuals, and that degrade those who practice them. Some jurists consider magic as unbelief (*kufr*) or as leading toward unbelief.

Omens

Drawing evil omens from certain articles, places, times, individuals, and the like was, and still is, a current superstition.

Relaxing the Mind

Following the Messenger's example, his noble and pure Companions relaxed their bodies and minds. 'Ali ibn Abi Talib said: "Minds get tired, as do bodies, so treat them with humor," and "Refresh your minds from time to time, for a tired mind becomes blind." Abu al-Darda said: "I entertain my heart with something trivial in order to make it stronger in the service of the truth."

Thus, there is no harm if Muslims entertain themselves to relax their mind or refresh themselves with some permissible sport or activity. However, the pursuit of pleasure should not become the goal of their life so that they devote themselves to it, forgetting one's religious obligations. Nor should one joke about serious matters. It has been aptly said: "Season your conversation with humor in the same proportion as you season your food with salt."

Muslims are forbidden to joke and laugh about other people's values and honor. Such sports and games as foot racing, archery, spear play, and swimming are permissible.

Singing and Music

Among the entertainments that may comfort the soul, please the heart, and refresh the ear is singing. Islam permits singing. In order to create an atmosphere of joy and happiness, it is recommended on such festive occasions as the 'Iyd days, weddings and wedding feasts, births, and *'aqiqat* (thanksgiving to God for the birth of a baby by sacrificing sheep). However, there are some limitations placed upon singing:

- The song's subject matter should not be against Islam's teachings. For example, if the song praises wine and invites people to drink, singing or listening to it is *haram*. It also must not stir up pessimism and despair.
- Although the subject matter may not be against Islamic teachings, the way of singing (e.g., bodily movements that stir up lust or impulses to commit *haram* acts) may render it *haram*.
- Islam opposes excess and extravagance in anything, so it cannot tolerate excessive involvement with entertainment. Too much time should not be wasted in such activities.
- Each individual is the best judge of oneself. If a certain type of singing arouses one's passions, leads one toward sin, excites the animal instincts, and dulls spirituality, one must avoid it so that he or she will not cave into temptation.
- There is unanimous agreement that if singing is done in conjunction with *haram* activities like attending a drinking party, or if it is mixed with obscenity and sin, it is *haram*.

Gambling, the Companion of Drinking

While permitting a variety of games and sports, Islam prohibits any game that involves betting (e.g., has an element of gambling). Muslims cannot seek relaxation and recreation in, or acquire money by, gambling.

The Qur'an mentions drinking and gambling together (5:90-91), since their harmful effects on the individual, family, and society are very similar. What is more like alcoholism than an addiction to gambling? This is why one usually is not found without the other. The Qur'an is absolutely right when it teaches us that both drinking and gambling are inspired by Satan, that they are akin to idolatry and divining by arrows, and that they are abominable habits that must be shunned.

The Lottery

Lotteries and raffles are also forms of gambling. There should be no laxity or permissiveness toward them in the name of "charitable institutions" or "humanitarian causes."

Movies

Movies may be regarded as permissible if the following conditions are met:

- The content must be free of sin and immorality – indeed, of anything that is against Islamic beliefs, morals, and manners. Portrayals that excite sexual desire or greed, glorify crime, or propagate deviant ideas, false beliefs, and the like are not permissible, and Muslims cannot watch or encourage them.
- Watching movies should not result in the neglect of religious obligations or worldly responsibilities.
- Physical intermingling and free mixing among men and women in movie theatres must be avoided in order to prevent sexual undertones and temptation.

Social Relationships

Relations among the members of an Islamic society are based upon two fundamental principles: awareness of the strong bond of brotherhood and sisterhood that links one individual to another, and protecting the individual's rights and the sanctity of his or her life, honor, and property, as guaranteed by Islam. Any words, deeds, or behavior that contravene or threaten these two principles are forbidden, the degree of prohibition depending upon the magnitude of material or moral injury that might result from it.

Severing Ties with a Fellow Muslim

It is *haram* for Muslims to shun, break ties, or turn away from a fellow Muslim. If two Muslims quarrel with each other, they may be allowed a cooling-off period of 3 days at the most, after which they must seek reconciliation and peace, overcoming their pride, anger, and hatred.

Settling Disputes

While it is incumbent upon disputants to settle their differences in an Islamic fashion, the Muslim community also has a responsibility in this regard. As it is based upon mutual caring and cooperation, it cannot stand by passively and watch its members dispute and quarrel with each other, and thereby permit the conflict to grow larger. Those who command respect and authority in the community are obliged to come forward to set things right with absolute impartiality and without allowing themselves to become emotionally involved with either side.

"Let Not Some People Mock Other People."

In 49:10-12, God prescribes several things related to preserving Muslim brotherhood and sisterhood and what this implies with regard to that which people consider sacred. The first of these is the prohibition of mocking, deriding, and scoffing at others.

"Do Not Slander."

The second prohibition is against lamz, which literally means "piercing and stabbing." Here it is used to mean finding faults, as the person who finds faults in others is doing something similar to piercing them with a sword or stabbing them with a dagger – and perhaps the wound inflicted by the tongue is more lasting. The form of prohibition expressed in 49:11 *(Do not slander yourselves)* is very subtle, for it means not to slander each other. This meaning is derived from the Qur'an's viewing the Muslim community as one body in its mutual concerns and responsibilities, so that whoever slanders a fellow Muslim in effect slanders himself or herself.

Suspicion

Islam seeks to establish its society on a clearn conscience and mutual trust, not on doubt, suspicion, accusation, and mistrust. Hence it mentions the fourth prohibition designed to safeguard what people hold sacred: *O you who believe, avoid (indulging in) much suspicion. Truly some suspicion is a sin* (49:12).

Sinful suspicion is defined as ascribing evil motives to others. Muslims cannot impute such motives to fellow Muslims without justification and clear evidence. Given that the basic assumption that people are innocent, mere suspicion should not be allowed to cause an innocent person to be accused.

Spying

Mistrust of others produces evil thoughts in the mind, while outwardly it leads a person toward spying. But since Islam establishes its society upon inner and outer purity, just as spying follows suspicion, the prohibition of spying comes immediately after that of suspicion. Prying into other peoples' private affairs and spying on their secrets is not permitted, even if they are engaged in sin, as long as they do it privately.

Backbiting

The sixth evil forbidden in the verses cited above is backbiting *(ghiyba): And do not ... backbite one another* (49:12). The verse likens it to eating of one's dead brother's (sister's) flesh. The Messenger, upon him be peace and blessings, wanted to drive home the meaning of backbiting to his Companions through questions and answers. He asked them: "Do you know what backbiting is?" They replied: "God and His Messenger know best." He said: "It is saying something about your brother (sister) which he (she) would dislike." Someone asked: "What if I say something about my brother (sister) that is true?" The Messenger replied: "If what you say of him (her) is true, it is backbiting; if it is not true, you have slandered him (her)." (Muslim, "Birr," 70; Abu Dawud, "Adab," 40)

Spreading Gossip

Another evil, which usually accompanies backbiting and is strictly forbidden by Islam, is gossiping. This is defined as passing on to others what you hear from someone in such a way that will cause dissension among people, sour their relationships, or increase already-existing bitterness between them.

The Sacredness of Honor

Islamic teachings safeguard human dignity and honor, and, in fact, regard them as inviolable and sacred. Once while looking at the Ka'ba, 'Abdullah ibn 'Umar remarked: "How great and sacred you are! But the sanctity of a believer is greater than yours." A Muslim's sanctity includes the sanctity of his or her life, honor, and property.

The Sacredness of Life

Islam has made human life sacred and has safeguarded its preservation. According to its teachings, aggression against human life is one of the greatest sins, second only to denying God. The Qur'an regards killing a person unjustly as equivalent to killing all people (5:22). Since the human race constitutes a single family, an offense against one member is an offense against all of humanity. The crime is more serious if the killed person was a believer in God:

> And for the one who kills a believer intentionally, his recompense is Hell, to abide therein. And the wrath of God is upon him and His curse, and a tremendous punishment has been prepared for him. (4:93)

The Messenger said: "The passing away of the world would mean less to God than the murder of a Muslim" and: "God may forgive every sin, except for one who dies as an idolater (and an unbeliever) or who kills a believer intentionally." (Nasa'i, "Tahrim," 1:2) On the basis of these verses and Traditions, Ibn 'Abbas deduced that God will not accept any repentance done by the murderer.

The Sanctity of the Lives of Allies and Non-Muslim Residents

Thus far we have quoted texts that warn Muslims against killing or fighting fellow Muslims. But let no one think that the life of a non-Muslim is not safe in a Muslim society, for God has declared the life of every person to be sacred, and He has safeguarded it.

This applies as long as the non-Muslims do not fight the Muslims. If they fight the Muslims, the Muslims can fight them in retaliation for their deeds. However, if the non-Muslims have a treaty with the Muslims or are *dhimmis* (non-Muslim residents of an Islamic state), their life is sacred and the Muslims cannot attack them.

Suicide

Whatever applies to murder also applies to suicide. Whoever takes his or her own life, regardless of the method used, has unjustly taken a life that God has made sacred. Since people did not create themselves, not even one single cell, their life does not belong to them but is a trust given to them by God Almighty. They are not allowed to diminish it, let alone to harm or destroy it.

Islam requires Muslims to be resolute in facing hardships. They are not permitted to give up and run away from life's vicissitudes when a tragedy befalls them or some of their hopes are dashed. Indeed, they are created to strive, not to sit idle; for combat, not for escape. Their faith and character do not permit them to run away from the battlefield of life, and they possess a weapon that never fails and ammunition that is never exhausted: the weapon of unshakable faith and the ammunition of moral steadfastness.

The Sanctity of Property

Muslims are permitted to earn as much as they desire, as long as they do so through lawful means and increase their wealth through lawful investments. However, Islam warns against attachment to wealth and the world and leading a luxurious, dissipated life, and exhorts believers to spend in God's way for the needy and God's cause.

Since Islam sanctions the right to personal property, it protects it, through moral exhortation and legislation, from robbery, theft, and fraud. The Messenger mentioned its sanctity in the same sentence with the sanctity of life and honor, and considered stealing as contradictory to faith: "A thief is not a believer while he (she) is engaged in stealing" (Bukhari, "Ashriba," 1; Muslim, "Iman," 24) and: "It is *haram* for a Muslim to take (so much as) a stick without its owner's consent."

Racial and Color Discrimination

There is no special distinction for people with a certain skin color or who belong to a particular "race" of humanity. Muslims cannot be a partisan of one race against another, and of one people against another.

Islam's Universal Mercy to Animals

Islam's universal mercy embraces not only human beings, whether believers, People of the Book, or non-Muslims, but all other living creatures. Accordingly, Islam prohibits cruelty to animals. Thirteen centuries before any societies for the prevention of cruelty to animals were established, Islam made kindness to animals a part of its faith, and cruelty to them a sufficient reason for a person to be thrown into the Fire.

God's Messenger, upon him be peace and blessings, once related to his Companions that a prostitute found a dog panting with thirst. She descended into a well, filled her shoes with water, and gave it to the dog. She continued to do so until the dog's thirst was quenched. The Messenger said: "Then God was pleased with her, forgave her sins, and led her to the way of Paradise." (Bukhari, "Anbiya," 54; Muslim, "Salam," 153) He also mentioned a woman who left a cat without food and drink to die; she was led to the way of Hell.

Respect for God's living creatures reached such an extent that when the Messenger saw a donkey with a branded face, he denounced such a practice: "I would brand an animal only on the part of its body farthest from its face." (Canan, *ibid.*, 6:306) When Ibn 'Umar saw some people practicing archery using a hen as a target, he said: "The Messenger, upon him be peace and blessings, cursed anyone who made a living thing into a target." Ibn 'Abbas said: "The Messenger forbade making animals fight each other, since people would goad animals into fighting each other until one of them was pecked or gored to death, or close to it." He also reported that the Messenger strongly condemned the castration of animals.

As regards slaughtering animals, Islam insists that it be done in the way that is least painful to the animal and that the knife be sharpened – but not in front of the animal. Islam also prohibits the slaughtering of one animal in front of another.

Sin

What Is Sin?

Sin is committing something that God and His Messenger have forbidden and not doing what they ordered to do. Since a believer's heart and conscience are sensitive to sin and obedience to God, God's Messenger said: "Righteousness is good morality, and sin is that which causes discomfort (or pinches) within your soul and which you dislike people to become informed of." (Tirmidhi, "Zuhd," 52) In other words, sin is what Muslims try to abstain from at all costs.

The Major Sins (al-Kaba'ir)

The major sins are those acts that God Has forbidden and threatened to punish severely if they are committed. God wills that they be avoided:

> If you avoid the major (part) of what you have been forbidden
> (to do), We will cancel out for you your (other) evil deeds and
> will admit you (to Paradise) with a noble entry. (4:31)

Scholars differ in this regard. Some say there are seven major sins, and support themselves with the following *hadith*: "Avoid the seven noxious things" – and after having said this, the Messenger mentioned them: "Associating anything with God as a partner, magic, killing one whom God has declared inviolate without a just case, consuming an orphan's property, devouring usury, turning back when the army advances, and slandering chaste women who are believers but indiscreet."

However, this *hadith* does not limit the major sins only to those mentioned. Rather, it points to the type of sins that fall into the category of "major" without excluding others, such as violating the parents' rights, adultery and fornication, consuming alcohol, gambling, and theft, all of which are also included in this category.

The scholars have established sins and listed them, as follows:
- Unbelief in any of the essentials requiring belief
- Hypocrisy
- Associating partners with God (*shirk*)
- Neglecting any pillar of Islam (i.e., the prescribed prayers, paying *zakat*, fasting Ramadan, and *Hajj*)
- Violating the parents' rights
- Murder
- Practicing magic
- Adultery, fornication, and homosexuality
- Theft and usurpation
- Consuming alcohol
- Gambling
- Dealing with usury and interest
- Slandering innocent people, especially chaste women
- Fleeing the battlefield
- Wrongfully consuming an orphan's property
- Lying
- Backbiting
- Gossiping
- Mocking others
- Spying and ill-suspicion
- Abandoning relatives
- Wrongdoing and injustice
- Fraud and cheating
- Violating other people's rights
- Pride and arrogance
- Bearing false witness and taking a false oath
- Oppression

- Consuming wealth acquired unlawfully
- Giving short weight or measure
- Committing suicide
- Giving and accepting bribes
- Showing-off
- Learning about Islam for the sake of this world
- Betraying a trust
- Recounting favors
- Listening to private conversations
- Breaking one's promise
- Fortune-telling and believing in fortune-tellers
- Making idols and engaging in idolatrous practices
- Trading in unlawful things
- Displaying overbearing conduct toward one's spouse, servant, children, weak people, and animals
- Offending neighbors
- Offending and abusing Muslims
- Wearing silk and gold (men only)
- Sacrificing an animal in the name of that which is not God
- Knowingly ascribing one's paternity to one who is not his or her real father.

Muslims must try not to commit any sins. Moreover, when they do so, they must repent immediately and seek God's forgiveness. Scholars say that any sin, no matter how small, is great so long as it is committed with ease and indifference, without repentance, and without seeking God's forgiveness, while any major sin, no matter how great, is not great so long as it is avoided as much as possible and the one who commits it repents and seeks God's forgiveness.

PRAYERS, SUPPLICATIONS, AND REMEMBRANCE OF GOD[12]

Belief requires prayer as a means of attainment and perfection, and our essence desperately needs it. God Almighty decrees: *Say (O Muhammad): "My Lord would not concern Himself with you but for your prayer"* (25:77), *and: Pray to Me and I will answer your (prayer)* (40:60).

If people say that they pray so many times but that their prayers are unanswered, despite the assurance given in the above verse, we should point out that an answered prayer does not necessarily mean its acceptance. There is an answer for every prayer. However, accepting the prayer and giving what is requested depends upon the All-Mighty's Wisdom. Suppose a sick child asks a doctor for a certain medicine. The doctor will give what is asked for, something better, or nothing. It all depends upon how the medicine will affect the child. Similarly the All-Mighty, Who is All-Hearing and All-Seeing, answers His servant's prayer and changes loneliness into the pleasure of His company. But His answer does not depend on the individual's fancies; rather, according to His Wisdom, He gives what is requested, what is better, or nothing at all.

Moreover, prayer is a form of worship and worship is rewarded mainly in the Hereafter. In essence, prayer is not done for worldly purposes, because worldly purposes are causes for the prayer. For example, praying for rain is a kind of worship occasioned by the lack of rain. If rain is the prayer's only aim, the prayer is unacceptable, for it is not sincere or intended to please God and obtain His approval.

Sunset determines the time for the evening prayer, while solar and lunar eclipses occasion two particular kinds of worship. Since such eclipses are two means of manifesting Divine Majesty, the All-Mighty calls His servants to perform a form of worship particular to these occasions. The prayer said has nothing to do with causing the eclipse to end, for this is known already through astronomical calculations. The same argument applies to drought and other calamities, for all such events occasion certain kinds of prayer. At such times, we best realize our impotence and so feel the need to take refuge in the high Presence of the Absolutely Powerful One through prayer and supplication. If a calamity is not lifted despite many prayers, we should not say that our prayer has not been accepted. Rather, we should say that the time for prayer has not yet ended. God removes the calamity because of His endless Grace and Munificence. The end of that event marks the end of that special occasion for prayer.

We must pursue God's good pleasure through worship, affirm our poverty and weakness in our prayer, and seek refuge with Him through prayer. We must not interfere in His Lordship, but rather let God do as He wills and rely on His Wisdom. In addition, we should not accuse His Mercy.

Every creature offers its own kind of praise and worship to God. What reaches the Court of God from the universe is a kind of prayer. Some creatures, like plants and animals, pray through the tongue of their potential to achieve a full form and then display and show certain Divine Names (e.g., a plant's seeds grow naturally into plants, and the joined semen and eggs of animals grow naturally into animals. Since they have this potential, their natural disposition to mature is, in essence, a prayer. By doing so they affirm the manifestation of such Divine Names as the All-Sustaining and All-Forming.).

Another kind of prayer is done in the tongue of natural needs. All living beings ask the Absolutely Generous One to meet their vital needs, as they cannot do so. Yet another kind of prayer is done in the tongue of complete helplessness. A living creature in straitened circumstances takes refuge in its Unseen Protector with a genuine supplication and turns to its All-Compassionate Lord. These three kinds of prayer are always acceptable, unless somehow impeded.

The fourth type of prayer is the one engaged in by humanity. This type falls into two categories: active and by disposition, and verbal and with the heart. For example, acting in accordance with causes is an active prayer. We try to gain God's approval by complying with causes, for causes alone cannot produce the result – only God can do that. Another type of active prayer is plowing the soil, for this is nothing other than knocking at the door of the treasury of God's Compassion. Such a prayer is usually acceptable, for it is an application to the Divine Name the All-Generous.

The second type of prayer, done with the tongue and the heart, is the ordinary one. This means that we ask God from the heart for something we cannot reach. Its most important aspect and finest and sweetest fruit is that we know that God hears us, is aware of our heart's contents, that His power extends everywhere, that He can satisfy every desire, and that He comes to our aid out of mercy for our weakness and inadequacy.

We should never abandon prayer, for it is the key to the Treasury of Compassion and the means of obtaining access to the Infinite Power. We should hold on to it and ascend to the highest rank of humanity and, as creation's most favored and superior member, include the whole universe's prayer in our prayer. We should say, on behalf of all beings: *From You alone do we seek help* (1:5), and become a beautiful pattern for all of creation.

Supplications and Remembrance of God

All words of praise and glorification of God, extolling His Perfect Attributes of Power and Majesty, Beauty and Sublimity, whether one utters them by tongue or says them silently in one's heart, are known as *dhikr* (remembrance of God). He has commanded us to remember Him always and forever: *O you who believe, celebrate the praises of God, and do so often; and glorify Him morning and evening* (33:41)

In a *hadith qudsi* (a Tradition whose meaning God inspired in the heart of the Messenger) the Messenger narrated: "God says: 'I am to My servant as he expects of Me, I am with him when he remembers Me. If he remembers Me in his heart, I remember him to Myself; if he remembers Me in an assembly, I mention him in an assembly better than his; if he draws nearer to Me a hand's span, I draw nearer to him an arm's length; if he draws nearer to Me an arm's length, I draw nearer to him a fathom length; and if he comes to me walking, I rush to him with [great] speed'" (Bukhari, "Tawhid," 50; Muslim, "Dhikr," 2).

God has bestowed a special distinction upon those who remember Him. The Messenger, upon him be peace and blessings, said: "The devotees have surpassed all." They asked: "Who are these exceptional people, O Messenger of God?" He replied: "Those men and women who remember God unceasingly" (Muslim). These are the people who are really alive. Abu Musa reported from the Messenger: "The likeness of the house where God is mentioned and the one where He is not is like that of a living to a dead person." (Bukhari, Da'awat," 66)

How Much Dhikr Is Required?

God, the Exalted, ordered that He should be remembered a great deal. Describing the wise men and women who ponder His signs, the Qur'an mentions: *those who remember God standing, sitting, and on their sides* (3:191) and: *those men and women who engage much in God's praise. For them has God prepared forgiveness and a great reward* (33:35). Mujahid, one of the earliest interpreters of the Qur'an, explained: "A person cannot be one of 'those men and women who remember God much' as mentioned in the above verse of the Qur'an, unless he or she remembers God at all times, standing, sitting, or lying in bed."

The Excellence of Dhikr Assemblies

Joining the assemblies or circles of *dhikr* is commendable, as shown by the following *hadith*: Ibn 'Umar reported: "The Prophet, peace be upon him, said: 'When you pass by a garden of Paradise, avail yourselves of it.' The Companions asked: 'What are the gardens of Paradise, O Messenger of God?' The Prophet, upon him be peace and blessings, replied: 'The assemblies or circles of dhikr. There are some angels of God who go about looking for such assemblies of *dhikr*, and when they find them they surround them.'" (Muslim, "Dhikr," 39)

The Excellence of Istighfar

Asking God's forgiveness for one's sins is also of great importance. Said Nursi says that we should take prayer in one of our hands and seeking God's forgiveness in the other. Prayer urges and reinforces one to do good deeds, while seeking His forgiveness discourages one to commit sins. 'Abdullah ibn 'Abbas said: "If one asks without fail for forgiveness from God, He shows him (her) a way out to get out of every distress and difficulty, and gives him (her) sustenance through ways utterly unthought of."

Supplicating at the Most Opportune Times and Locations

These are, for instance, the day of 'Arafat, Ramadan, Friday, the last part of the night, dawn, after the prescribed prayers, while prostration, while it is raining, between the *adhan* and the *iqama*, when armies meet each other, times of strain and great need, and when one's heart is soft and tender.

Praying for a Fellow Muslim in His or Her Absence

Safwan ibn 'Abdullah reported: "I visited Abu Darda's house in Syria. I did not find him there, but Umm Darda (his wife) was home. She asked: 'Do you intend to perform *Hajj* this year?' I replied: 'Yes.' She said: 'Please supplicate to God for us, for God's Messenger, upon him be peace and blessings, used to say: A Muslim's supplication for his or her fellow Muslim in his (her) absence is accepted. When he (she) asks for blessings for his (her) brother (sister), the commissioned angel says: Amen, may it be for you too!'"

Beginning a Supplication

It is highly recommended that one should begin the prayer and supplication with praises of God, seeking His forgiveness for sins, calling God's blessings and peace upon His Messenger, as well as on his Family and Companions, and reciting some of His Names.

Examples of God's Messenger's Prayers and Supplications

God's Messenger, upon him be peace and blessings, always prayed to God before any action. The books of Tradition (*hadith*) record no case in which he did not pray. As mentioned earlier, prayer is a mystery of servanthood to God, and the Messenger is the foremost in servanthood. This is made clear with every repetition of the declaration of faith: "I bear witness there is no deity but God; I also bear witness that Muhammad is His servant and Messenger." Note that he is called servant before Messenger. Whatever he intended to do, he referred it to God through prayer.

God created us and our actions. Although we should take the necessary precautions and follow precedents to accomplish things in this world, where cause and effect have a special place, we should never forget that everything ultimately depends upon God for its existence. Therefore, we must combine action and prayer. This is also required by our belief in God's Unity.

The Messenger's knowledge of God can never be equaled. As a result, he was the foremost in love of, and paradoxically, in fear of Him. He was perfectly conscious that everything depends upon God for its existence and subsistence. Whatever God wills, happens: *When He wills a thing, His command is to say to it "Be," and it is* (36:82). Things exist and the universe operates according to the laws established by God and the fulfillment of prerequisites. Fully aware of this, the Messenger did what he had to do and then, combining action with prayer, left the result to God with absolute confidence.

His supplications have been transmitted to us. When we read them, we see that they have deep meaning and accord exactly with the surrounding circumstances. They reflect profound belief, deep sincerity, absolute submission, and complete confidence. Some examples are given below:

In the Morning and Evening

- He used to recite *Surat al-Ikhlas, Surat al-Falaq*, and *Surat al-Nas* three times every morning and night before going to bed.
- We have reached evening and the whole creation, which is God's property, also has reached evening. All praise is due to God. There is no deity but God, the One Who has no partner with Him. His is the Sovereignty, and all Praise is due to Him. He has power over all things. O God, I ask You for the good of this night, and seek refuge in You from the evil of this night and the evil that follows it. O God, I seek refuge in You from sloth and from the evil of vanity. O God, I seek refuge in You from the torment of Hell-Fire and from the torment of the grave.
- God, with Your help we have reached evening, and with Your help we will reach morning. With Your help we live and by Your command we die. To You is our return.
- God, You are my Lord. There is no deity but You. You have created me, and I am Your servant. I try my best to keep my covenant with You and to live in the hope of Your promise. I seek refuge in You from the evil I have done. I acknowledge

Your favors upon me and acknowledge my sins. So forgive me, for none forgives sins but You.

- God, Creator of the heavens and Earth, Who knows the unseen and the seen, Lord and Possessor of everything. I testify that there is no deity but You. I seek refuge in You from the evil within myself, from the evil of Satan, and from his inciting one to attribute partners to God.
- In the Name of God, by Whose Name nothing in Earth or in the heaven can do any harm, and He is the All-Hearing, the All-Knowing.
- I am pleased with God as Lord, with Islam as religion, and with Muhammad as Prophet.
- God, I have reached morning and call You to bear witness, and the bearers of Your Throne, Your angels, and all Your creatures to bear witness, that You are God, other than Whom there is no deity, and that Muhammad is Your servant and Messenger.
- God, whatever favor has come to me has come from You alone, Who has no partner. To You all praise is due and all thanksgiving.
- God, I ask You for security in this world and in the Hereafter. O God, I ask You for forgiveness and security in my religion and my worldly affairs, in my family and my property. O God, cover my faults and keep me safe from the things I fear. O God, guard me from the front and the behind, from the right and the left, and from above. I seek in Your greatness the protection from unexpected harm from beneath.
- God, grant me sound health. O God, grant me sound hearing. O God, grant me sound eyesight. There is no deity but You.
- God, I have risen with Your help, blessings, security, and protection, so complete Your blessings upon me, Your security for me, and your protection in this world and in the Hereafter.
- God suffices me. There is no deity but He. In Him is my trust, and He is the Lord of the Mighty Throne. (seven times)
- God, You are my Lord. There is no deity but You. I put my trust in You. You are the Lord of the Mighty Throne. Whatever God wills happens, and whatever He does not will does not happen.

There is neither power nor strength save with You, the Exalted, the Mighty. I know that God has power over all things, and God comprehends all things in knowledge. O God, I seek refuge with You from the evil of myself and from the evil of all creatures under Your control. Surely the straight way is my Sustainer's way.

At Bed-Time

- God, by Your Name I live and die. Praise be to God, Who gave us life after death. To Him is the return. O God, save me from Your punishment on the day when You will raise Your creatures.

- God, Lord of the heavens, Earth, and the Mighty Throne, our Lord and the Lord of everything, Who causes the seed to grow and the date-stone to split and sprout, Who sent down the Torah and the Gospel and the Qur'an. I seek refuge in You from the evil of all evil-mongers under Your Control. You are the First and there is nothing before You, and You are the Last and there is nothing after You. You are the Outward and there is nothing beyond You, and You are the Inward and there is nothing more inward than You. Relieve us of our debt and poverty.

- Every night when he went to bed, the Messenger would hold out his hands together imploringly and blow over them after reciting *Surat al-Ikhlas, Surat al-Falaq*, and *Surat al-Nas*. Then he would rub his hands three times over whichever parts of his body he was able to rub, starting with his head, face, and front of his body.

- In Your name, O Lord, I lay myself down to sleep, and by Your permission I raise myself up. So if You take away my soul during sleep, forgive it. If You keep it alive after sleep, protect it just as You protect Your pious servants.

- (in bed:) *Allahu akbar* (God is the Greatest) 34 times, *Subhana'llah* (Glory be to God) 33 times, *al-hamdu li'llah* (All praise be to God) 33 times.

- God, hoping for Your Mercy and fearing Your wrath, I submit myself to You, refer my affairs to You, and take refuge in You.

There is no refuge or source of safety from Your wrath except You. I believe in the Book You sent down, and the Prophet whom you raised.

Upon Waking Up

- Thanks be to God, Who returned my soul, made my body sound, and permitted me to remember Him.
- There is no deity but You. Glory be to You. O God, I seek Your forgiveness for my sins and ask for Your mercy. O God, increase me in knowledge and let not my heart swerve after You have guided me on the right path. Grant me mercy from You, for You are the Grantor of bounties without measure.
- There is no deity but God. He is One and has no partner. To Him belongs all praise and all authority, and He has power over all things. Praise be to God, glory be to God, there is no deity but God. God is the Greatest. There is neither power nor strength save with God.

Upon Wearing Clothes

- All thanks and praise be to God, Who has clothed me and given me sustenance, whereas I have no power, nor strength.
- All praise and thanks be to God, Who has clothed me to cover my nakedness and made it a means of adornment for me.

Upon Seeing Another Muslim Wearing Some New Clothes

- May you live so long that you will wear out many garments.
- May you live so long that you wear out this garment, and may God replace it with a better one.

Upon Leaving One's House

- In the Name of God. I put my trust in God. There is neither power nor strength save with God.
- In the name of God. I believe in God and seek His protection. There is neither power nor strength save with God.
- God, I seek Your refuge against going astray or leading others astray, slipping or causing others to slip, doing wrong or

being wronged by others, and behaving arrogantly or being treated arrogantly by others.

Upon Entering One's House

- One enters one's house saying: "In the Name of God, the All-Merciful, the All-Compassionate," "Peace be upon you," and then: "O God. I seek of You the best of entrance and the best of departure. In the Name of God we enter and in the Name of God we go out, and we put our trust in God, our Lord."

When the Wind Blows

- God, I ask You for its good, and the good that is in it, and the good with which it is sent. I seek Your refuge against its evil, and the evil with which it is sent.

Upon Hearing Thunder

- God, do not destroy us with Your wrath or let us perish with Your punishment. Give us good health before it comes to pass.

During Sorrow, Grief, and Difficulties

- There is no deity but God, the Mighty, the Forbearing. There is no deity but God, the Lord of the Mighty Throne. There is no deity but God, the Lord of the heavens and Earth, and the Lord of the Throne of Honor.
- The Ever-Living, O the Eternal, I seek Your help by Your Grace.
- God, I hope for Your Mercy, so do not entrust me to myself even for a twinkle of eye. Set right all my affairs. There is no deity but You.
- There is no deity but You. All glory be to You. I have indeed been one of the wrongdoers.
- God, I am Your servant, son of Your servant, son of your maidservant. My rein is in Your hand. Your command concerning me prevails, and Your decision concerning me is just. I call upon You by every one of the All-Beautiful Names by which You have described Yourself, or which You have revealed in Your Book, or have taught anyone of Your creatures, or which You have chosen to keep in the knowledge of the unseen with

You, to make the Qur'an the delight of my heart, the light of my breast, and the remover of my griefs, sorrows, and afflictions.

Upon Encountering the Enemy, and When One is Afraid of the Ruler

- Master of the Day of Judgment. I worship You alone and seek only Your help.
- There is no deity but God, the Forbearing, the Gracious. Glory be to God, my Lord. Glory be to God, the Lord of the seven heavens and of the Mighty Throne. There is no deity but You. Strong is your protection, and great is Your praise.
- God suffices us for everything, and an excellent Guardian is He.

When in Debt

- God, make Your lawful bounties sufficient for me so as to save me from what is unlawful. From Your grace, grant me sufficient abundance to free me from the need of all except You.
- God, I seek refuge in You from all worry and grief. I seek refuge in You from incapacity and slackness. I seek refuge in You from cowardice and miserliness. I seek refuge in You from being overcome by debt and being subjected to people.

Comprehensive Prayers That Can Be Said at Any Time

- God, put between me and errors a distance as great as that which you have put between East and West. O God, cleanse me of my errors, just as a white garment is cleansed of dirt.
- God, I ask You for all good, including what is at hand and what is deferred, what I already know and what I do not know. I take refuge in You from every evil, including what is at hand and what is deferred, what I already know and what I do not know.
- God, nothing hinders what You grant, nor is anything granted that You hinder. A wealthy person cannot do us good, as wealth belongs to You.
- God, I have not told anything, taken an oath, made a vow, or done anything that You did not previously will. Whatever You

willed is, and whatever You did not will is not. There is neither power nor strength save with You. You are indeed All-Powerful over everything.

- God, I ask You for contentment after misfortune, a peaceful life after death, the pleasure of observing Your Face, and a desire to meet You. I take refuge in You from wronging others and from being wronged, from showing animosity and being subject to animosity, and from erring or committing unforgivable sins. If You leave me to myself, you leave me in weakness, need, sinfulness, and error. I depend only upon Your Mercy, so forgive all my sins, for only You can do so. Accept my repentance, for You are the Oft-Relenting, All-Compassionate.

- God, You deserve most to be mentioned, and none but You deserve to be worshipped. You are more helpful than anyone whose help may be sought, more affectionate than any ruler, more generous than anyone who may be asked for something, and more generous than anyone who gives. You are the Sovereign without partners, the Unique One without like. Everything is perishable except You.

- You are obeyed only by Your permission, and disobeyed only within Your knowledge. When somebody obeys You, You reward them; when someone disobeys You, You forgive them. You witness everything, being nearer to it than any other witness; and protect everything, being nearer to it than any other protector. You ordained the acts of all people and determined their time of death. You know what is in every mind, and all secrets are manifest to You.

- The lawful is what You have made lawful; the forbidden is what You have forbidden. Religion is what You have laid down; the command is what You have decreed. The creation is Your creation; the servants are Your servants. You are God, the All-Clement, All-Compassionate. I ask You, for the sake of the light of Your Face, by which the Heavens and Earth were illuminated, for the sake of every right belonging to You and for the sake of those who ask of You, to forgive me just in this morning and just in this evening, and to protect me, by Your Power, from Hellfire.

- God, I seek refuge in You from all knowledge that gives no benefit, from a heart that does not fear You, from an unsatisfied soul, and from a prayer that cannot be answered.

- God, I ask You for steadfastness in my affairs, resolution in guidance, gratitude for Your bounties and acceptable service to You, and a truthful tongue and a sound heart. I seek refuge in You from the evil of what You know. I ask You for the good of what You know, and Your forgiveness for what You already know. Surely You are the Knower of the Unseen.

- God, I ask You to enable me to do good, refrain from vice, and love the poor. Forgive me and have mercy upon me. When You will people's deviation, dissension, and disorder in public life, make me die before taking part in that disorder. I ask You for Your love and for the love of those whom You love, and for the love of the acts that will bring me closer to Your love.

- God, I ask You for the good in the beginning and in the end, in its most comprehensive form with its beginning and result, its manifest and secret kinds, and for the highest rank in Paradise.

- God, help me remember and mention You, thank You, and worship You most properly.

- God, I ask You for guidance, fear of You, chastity, and independence of others.

- God, bring all of our affairs to a good conclusion. Protect us from disgrace and ignominy in the world, and from being tormented in the Hereafter.

- God, we ask You for all of the good for which Your Prophet Muhammad asked You, and seek refuge in You from every evil from which Your Prophet Muhammad sought refuge in You.

Invoking God's Blessings and Peace upon God's Messenger, His Family, and Companions

God says: "God and His angels send blessings to the Prophet. O you who believe, send blessings to him, and salute him with all respect." God's sending blessings to the Prophet, peace be upon him, means that He praises him in front of the angels and has mercy upon him, and the blessings of angels mean their supplications invoking blessings upon the Prophet.

The Messenger himself said: "If anyone invokes blessings upon me once, God will bestow blessings upon him 10 times over" (Nasa'i, "Sahw," 55); and "Whoever desires to be given (his or her reward) in full measure, should send salutations to us – the members of my family – and should say: 'O God, shower blessings upon Muhammad the Prophet, his wives, the mothers of the believers, his descendants, and the members of his family, as you showered blessings upon the family of Ibrahim. You are the Praiseworthy and Glorious." (Bukhari, "Da'awat," 33)

Some Muslim scholars hold that it is obligatory to invoke God's blessings and peace upon the Messenger whenever his name is mentioned. They base their argument upon the *hadith*: "May the nose of the person in whose presence I am mentioned be covered with dirt if he (she) does not invoke blessings upon me. Let the nose of that person be smeared with dust who finds Ramadan but lets it come to an end without securing pardon for himself (or herself). May the nose of the person be smeared with dust whose aged parents, either one or both of them are still living, and who fails to enter Paradise (i.e., by serving them)."

Other scholars opine that this *hadith* means that urging and therefore invoking God's blessings and peace upon the Messenger, peace be upon him, only once during a gathering is obligatory. After that it is no longer necessary, although it is preferred and better to do so. In addition, it is preferred to invoke God's peace upon other Prophets and angels separately.

CHAPTER FOUR

Islamic Morality

ISLAMIC MORALITY

God's Messenger, upon him be peace and blessings, says: "I have been sent only to perfect good character (or morality)." Thus perfection (i.e., perfected morality or character) is the fruit and evidence of Islamic teachings and life, and signifies that one is moving from the status of being a potential human being to that of being a true human being. For this reason, both the Qur'an and the Messenger attach great importance to morality.

When asked about the Messenger's morality or character, his wife 'A'isha answered that it was the Qur'an. In other words, the Messenger embodied the Qur'an or, as some have described, was a moving or walking Qur'an. So, we will follow the Islamic morality from the Messenger's virtues as described in *The Messenger of God: Muhammad - An Analysis of the Prophet's Life*, by M. Fethullah Gülen.[1]

THE PROPHET OF UNIVERSAL MERCY

The beginning of existence was an act of mercy and compassion without which the universe would be in chaos. Everything came into existence through compassion, and by compassion it continues to exist in harmony. Muslim sages say that the universe is the All-Compassionate One's breath. In other words, the universe was created to manifest the Divine Name the All-Compassionate. Its subsistence depends upon the same Name. This Name manifests itself first as the All-Provider, so that all living creatures can receive the food or nourishment they need to survive.

Life is God Almighty's foremost and most manifest blessing, and the true and everlasting life is that of the Hereafter. Since we can deserve this life by pleasing God, He sent Prophets and revealed Scriptures out of His compassion for humanity. For this reason, while mentioning His blessings upon humanity in *Surat al-Rahman* (the All-Merciful), He begins: *Al-Rahman. He taught the Qur'an, created humanity, and taught it speech* (55:1-4).

All aspects of this life are a rehearsal for the afterlife, and every creature is engaged in action toward this end. Order is evident in every effort, and compassion resides in every achievement. Some "natural" events or social convulsions may seem disagreeable at first, but we should not regard them as incompatible with compassion. They are like dark clouds or lightning and thunder that, although frightening, nevertheless bring us good tidings of rain. Thus the whole universe praises the All-Compassionate.

Prophet Muhammad is like a spring of pure water in the heart of a desert, a source of light in an all-enveloping darkness. Whoever appeals to this spring can take as much water as needed to quench their thirst, to become purified of all their sins, and to become illumined with the light of belief. Mercy was like a magic key in his hands, for with it he opened hearts that were so hardened and rusty that no one thought they could be opened. But he did even more: he lit a torch of belief in them.

The Messenger preached Islam, the religion of universal mercy. His compassion encompassed every creature. He desired, of course, that everyone be guided. In fact, this was his greatest concern: *Yet it may be, if they believe not in this Message, you will consume yourself, following after them, with grief* (18:6). But how should he deal with those who persisted in unbelief and fought him to destroy both him and his Message? He had to fight such people. But when they wounded him severely at Uhud, he raised his hands and prayed: "O God, forgive my people, for they do not know" (Bukhari, "Anbiya'," 54; Muslim, "Jihad," 104).

The Makkans, his own people, inflicted so much suffering on him that he finally emigrated to Madina. Even after that, the next 5 years were far from peaceful. However, when he conquered Makka without bloodshed in the twenty-first year of his Prophethood, he asked the Makkan unbelievers: "How do you expect me to treat you?" They responded unanimously: "You are a noble one, the son of a noble one." He then told them his decision: "You may leave, for no reproach this day shall be on you. May God forgive you. He is the Most Compassionate of the Compassionate" (Ibn Hisham, *Sira*, 4:55; Ibn Kathir, *Al-Bidaya*, 4:344). Sultan Mehmed the Conqueror said the same thing to the defeated Byzantines after conquering Istanbul 825 years later. Such is the universal compassion of Islam.

The Messenger displayed the highest degree of compassion toward the believers:

> There has come to you a Messenger from among yourselves; grievous to him is your suffering; anxious is he over you, full of concern for you, for the believers full of pity, compassionate. (9:128)

He lowered unto believers his wing of tenderness through mercy (15:88), and was the guardian of believers and nearer to them than their selves (33:6). When a Companion died, he asked those at the funeral if the deceased had left any debts. On learning that he had, the Prophet mentioned the above verse and announced that the creditors should come to him for repayment (Muslim, "Fara'iz,' 14; Bukhari, "Istiqraz," 11).

God did not send a collective destruction upon the unbelievers during his time, although He had eradicated many such people in the past: *But God would never chastise them while you were among them; God would never chastise them as they begged forgiveness* (8:33). This verse refers to unbelievers of whatever time. God will not destroy peoples altogether as long as those who follow the Messenger are alive. Besides, He has left the door of repentance open until the Last Day. Anyone can accept Islam or ask God's forgiveness, regardless of how sinful they consider themselves to be.

For this reason, a Muslim's enmity toward unbelievers is a form of pity. When 'Umar saw an 80-year-old man, he sat down and sobbed. When asked why he did so, he replied: "God assigned him so long a life span, but he has not been able to find the true path." 'Umar was a disciple of the Messenger, who said: "I was not sent to call down curses upon people, but as a mercy" (Muslim, "Birr," 87) and "I am Muhammad, and Ahmad (praised one), and

Muqaffi (the Last Prophet); I am Hashir (the final Prophet in whose presence the dead will be resurrected); the Prophet of repentance (the Prophet for whom the door of repentance will always remain open), and the Prophet of mercy." (Ibn Hanbal, 4:395; Muslim, "Fada'il," 126.) When Ma'iz was punished for fornication, a Companion verbally abused him. The Messenger frowned at him and said: "You have backbitten your friend. His repentance and asking God's pardon for his sin would be enough to forgive all the sinners in the world" (Muslim, "Hudud," 17-23; Bukhari, "Hudud," 28).

The Messenger was particularly compassionate toward children. Whenever he saw a child crying, he sat beside him or her and shared his or her feelings. He felt a mother's pain for her child more than the mother herself. Once he said: "I stand in prayer and wish to prolong it. However, I hear a child cry and shorten the prayer to lessen the mother's anxiety" (Bukhari, "Adhan," 65; Muslim, "Salat," 192).

He took children in his arms and hugged them. Once when hugging his beloved grandsons Hasan and Husayn, Aqra ibn Habis told him: "I have 10 children, and have never kissed any of them." The Messenger responded: "One without pity for others is not pitied. What can I do for you if God has removed compassion from you?" (Bukhari, "Adab," 18). He said: "Pity those on Earth so that those in the Heavens will pity you" (Tirmidhi, "Birr," 16). When Sa'd ibn 'Ubada became ill, the Messenger visited him at home and, seeing his faithful Companion in a pitiful state, began to cry. He said: "God does not punish because of tears or grief, but He punishes because of this," and he pointed to his tongue (Bukhari, "Jana'iz," 45; Muslim, "Jana'iz," 12).

A member of the Banu Muqarrin clan once beat his maid-servant. She informed the Messenger, who sent for the master. He said: "You have beaten her without any justifiable right. Free her" (Muslim, "Ayman," 31, 33; Ibn Hanbal, 3:447). Freeing a slave was far better for the master than being punished in the Hereafter because of that act. The Messenger always protected and supported widows, orphans, the poor and disabled even before announcing his Prophethood. When he returned home in excitement from

Mount Hira after the first Revelation, his wife Khadija told him: "I hope you will be the Prophet of this Umma, for you always tell the truth, fulfill your trust, support your relatives, help the poor and weak, and feed guests" (Ibn Sa'd, *Tabaqat*, 1:195).

His compassion encompassed animals as well. He said: "God guided a prostitute to truth and ultimately to Paradise because she gave water to a dog dying of thirst. Another woman was sent to Hell because she left a cat to die of hunger" (Bukhari, "Anbiya'," 54; "Musaqat," 9; Muslim, "Salam," 153; Ibn Hanbal, 2:507). While returning from a battle, a few Companions removed some young birds from their nest to stroke them. The mother bird came back and, not finding its babies, began to fly around screeching. When told of this, the Messenger became angry and ordered the birds to be put back in the nest (Abu Dawud, "Adab," 164; "Jihad," 112; Ibn Hanbal, 1:404). Ibn 'Abbas reported that when the Messenger saw a man sharpening his knife directly before the sheep to be slaughtered, he asked: "Do you want to kill it many times?" (Hakim, *Mustadrak*, 4:231, 233).

The Messenger lived for others, and was a mercy for all the worlds, a manifestation of Compassion.

HIS MILDNESS AND FORBEARANCE

Mildness is another dimension of the Messenger's character. He was a bright mirror in which God reflected His Mercy. Mildness is a reflection of compassion. God made His Messenger mild and gentle, thereby allowing him to gain many converts to Islam and overcome numerous obstacles.

After the victory of Badr, the Battle of Uhud was a severe trial for the young Muslim community. Although the Messenger wanted to fight on the outskirts of Madina, most Muslims desired to fight on an open battlefield. When the two armies met at the foot of Mount Uhud, the Messenger positioned 50 archers in 'Aynayn pass and ordered them not to move without his permission, even if they saw that the Muslims had won a decisive victory.

The Muslim army, having only one-third of the men and equipment of the enemy, almost defeated the Makkan polytheists in the initial stage. Seeing the enemy fleeing, these archers forgot the Prophet's command and left their post. Khalid ibn Walid, the Makkan cavalry's commander, saw this and, riding round the mountain, attacked the Muslims from behind. The fleeing enemy soldiers turned back and caught the Muslims in a crossfire. They began to lose, more than 70 were martyred, and the Messenger was wounded.

He might have reproached those who had urged him to pursue their desires as well as the archers who had abandoned their post, but he did not. Instead, he showed leniency:

> It was by the mercy of God that you were gentle to them; if you had been harsh and hard of heart, they would have dispersed from about you. So pardon them and ask forgiveness for them and consult with them in the affair. And when you are resolved, then put your trust in God; surely God loves those who put their trust (in Him). (3:159)

This verse shows two prerequisites for leadership: mildness and leniency toward those who make well-intentioned mistakes, and the importance of consultation in public administration.

This mildness and forgiveness was a reflection of God's Names the All-Mild, All-Clement, and All-Forgiving. God does not stop providing for people despite their rebellion or unbelief. While most people disobey Him by indulging in unbelief, by explicitly or implicitly associating partners with Him, or transgressing His Commands, the sun continues to send them its heat and light, clouds full of rain come to their aid, and the soil never stops feeding them with its fruits and plants. God's Clemency and Forgiveness are reflected through the Messenger's compassion, mildness, and forgiveness.

The Messenger was never angry with anybody because of what they did to him. When his wife 'A'isha was slandered, he did not consider punishing the slanderers even after she was cleared by the Qur'an. Bedouins often behaved impolitely with him, but he did not even frown at them. Although extremely sensitive, he always showed forbearance toward both friend and foe.

For example, while he was distributing the spoils of war after the Battle of Hunayn, Dhu al-Huwaysira objected: "Be just, O Muhammad." This was an unforgivable insult, for the Prophet had been sent to establish justice. Unable to endure such offences, 'Umar demanded permission to kill "that hypocrite" on the spot. But the Messenger only replied: "Who else will show justice if I am not just? If I don't show justice, then I am lost and brought to naught" (Muslim, "Zakat," 142, 148; Bukhari, "Adab," 95; "Manaqib," 25).

Once when the Prophet was going home after talking to his Companions in the mosque, a bedouin pulled him by the collar and said rudely: "O Muhammad! Give me my due! Load up my two camels! For you will load them up with neither your own wealth nor that of your father!" Without showing any sign of being offended, he told others: "Give him what he wants" (Abu Dawud, "Adab," 1; Nasa'i, "Qasama," 24).

Zayd ibn San'an narrates:

> Before I embraced Islam, the Messenger borrowed some money from me. I went to him to collect my debt before its due time, and insulted him: "O you children of 'Abd al-Muttalib, you are very reluctant to pay your debts!" 'Umar became very angry with me and shouted: "O enemy of God! Were it not for the treaty between us and the Jewish community, I would cut off your head! Speak to the Messenger politely!" However, the Messenger smiled at me and, turning to 'Umar, said: "Pay him, and add 20 gallons to it, because you frightened him."

'Umar relates the rest of the story:

> We went together. On the way, Zayd said unexpectedly: "O 'Umar, you were angry with me. But I find in him all the features of the Last Prophet recorded in the Torah, the Old Testament. It contains this verse: *His mildness surpasses his anger. The severity of impudence to him increases him only in mildness and forbearance.* To test his forbearance, I provoked him deliberately. Now I am convinced that he is the Prophet whose coming the Torah predicted. So, I believe and bear witness that he is the Last Prophet." (Suyuti, *Al-Khasa'is*, 1:26; Ibn Hajar, *Al-Isaba*, 1:566.)

This mildness and forbearance was enough for the conversion of Zayd ibn San'an, a Jewish scholar.

The Messenger's mildness and forbearance captured hearts and preserved Muslim unity. As stated in the Qur'an (3:159), if he had been harsh and hard-hearted, people would have abandoned him. But those who saw him and listened to him were so endowed with Divine manifestations that they became saints. For example, Khalid ibn Walid was the Qurayshi general who caused the Muslims to experience a reverse at Uhud. However, when he was not included in the army that set out on the day after his conversion, he was so upset that he wept.

Like Khalid, Ikrima and 'Amr ibn al-'As were among those who did great harm to the Messenger and the Muslims. After their conversions, each became a sword of Islam drawn against wrongdoing unbelievers. Ibn Hisham, Abu Jahl's brother, converted to Islam shortly before the Messenger passed away. He was such a sincere Muslim that just before he was martyred at Yarmuk, he did not drink the water that Hudayfa al-'Adawi offered him. Rather, he asked that it be given to nearby wounded fellow Muslim groaning for water. He died, having preferred a fellow Muslim over himself (Hakim, *Mustadrak*, 3:242).

The Messenger brought up the Companions. Their greatness is shown in the fact that despite their small numbers, they successfully conveyed Islam to the furthest reaches of Asia and Africa within a few decades. In those areas, Islam became so deeply rooted that despite the concerted efforts by the superpowers of each era to extinguish Islam, it continues to gain new momentum and represents the only realistic alternative for human salvation. The Companions were transformed from their wretched pre-Islamic state to being guides and teachers of a considerable part of humanity until the Last Day, the vanguard of the most magnificent civilization in history.

In addition, the Messenger was absolutely balanced. His universal compassion did not prevent him from executing Divine justice, and his mildness and forbearance kept him from breaching any Islamic rule or humiliating himself. For example, during a military campaign Usama ibn Zayd threw an enemy soldier to the ground. When he was about to kill him, the man declared his belief in Islam. Judging this to be the result of a fear of imminent death, Usama killed him. When told of the incident, the Messenger reprimanded Usama severely: "Did you cleave his heart open and see (if what you suspected is true)?" He repeated this so many times that Usama said later: "I wished I had not yet become a Muslim on the day I was scolded so severely" (Muslim, "Iman," 158; Ibn Maja, "Fitan," 1).

Likewise, once Abu Dharr got so angry with Bilal that he insulted him: "You son of a black woman!" Bilal came to the Messenger and reported the incident in tears. The Messenger reproached Abu Dharr: "Do you still have a sign of Jahiliya?" Full of repentance, Abu Dharr lay on the ground and said: "I won't raise my head (meaning he wouldn't get up) unless Bilal put his foot on it to pass over it." Bilal forgave him, and they were reconciled (Bukhari, "Iman," 22). Such was the brotherhood and humanity Islam created between once-savage people.

HIS GENEROSITY

The Messenger is the most polished mirror in which God's Names and Attributes are reflected to the highest degree. As the perfect manifestation of these Names and Attributes, an embodiment of the Qur'an and Islam, he is the greatest and most decisive and comprehensive proof of God's Existence and Unity, and of the truth of Islam and the Qur'an. Those who saw him remembered God automatically. Each of his virtues reflected a Name or Attribute of God, and is a proof of his Prophethood. Like his mildness and forbearance, his generosity is another dimension of his excellent, matchless personality, a reflection and proof of his Prophethood.

The people of Arabia were renowned for their generosity even in pre-Islamic times. When we look at that era's poetry, we see that the Arabs were proud of their generosity. However, their generosity was not for the sake of God or for an altruistic motive; rather, it was the cause of self-pride. But the Messenger's generosity was purely for God's sake. He never mentioned it, and did not like to have it mentioned. When a poet praised him for his generosity, he attributed whatever good he had or did to God. He never attributed his virtues and good deeds to himself.

The Messenger liked to distribute whatever he had. He engaged in trade until his Prophethood, and had considerable wealth. Afterwards, he and his wealthy wife Khadija spent everything in the way of God. When Khadija died, there was no money for her burial shroud. The Messenger had to borrow money to bury his own wife, the first person to embrace Islam and its first supporter (Ibn Kathir, *Al-Bidaya*, 3:158-59).

If the Messenger had desired, he could have been the richest man in Makka. But he rejected such offers without a second thought. Although God mandated that one-fifth of all war spoils should be at the Messenger's free disposal, he never spent it on himself or his family. He and his family lived austerely and survived on scanty provisions, for he always gave preference to others.

The Messenger regarded himself a traveler in this world. Once he said: "What connection do I have with this world? I am like a traveler who takes shade under a tree and then continues on his way" (Bukhari, "Riqaq," 3). According to him, the world is like a tree under which people are shaded. No one can live forever, so people must prepare here for the second part of the journey, which will end either in Paradise or Hell.

The Messenger was sent to guide people to truth, and so spent his life and possessions to this end. Once 'Umar saw him lying on a rough mat and wept. When the Messenger asked him why he was weeping, 'Umar replied: "O Messenger of God, while kings sleep in soft feather beds, you lie on a rough mat. You are the Messenger of God, and as such deserve an easy life more than anyone else." He answered: "Don't you agree that the luxuries of the world should be theirs, and that those of the Hereafter should be ours?" (Bukhari, "Tafsir," 2; Muslim, "Talaq," 31).

The Messenger was, in the words of Anas, "the most comely and generous person" (Muslim, "Fada'il," 48; Bukhari, "Manaqib," 23). Jabir ibn Samura reports: "Once we were sitting in the mosque, and a full moon was shining above us. The Messenger entered. I looked first at the moon and then at his face. I swear by God that his face was brighter than the moon" (Suyuti, *Al-Khasa'is*, 1:123; Hindi, *Kanz al-'Ummal*, 7:168).

The Messenger never refused anyone and, as Farazdak said, only said "no" when reciting the profession of faith while praying. Once, a bedouin came and asked the Messenger for something. The Messenger complied with his request. The bedouin continued to ask, and the Messenger continued to give until he had nothing left. When the bedouin asked again, he promised that he would give it to him when he had it. Angered by such rudeness, 'Umar said to the Messenger: "You were asked and you gave. Again you were asked and you gave, until you were asked once more and you promised!" 'Umar meant that the Messenger should not make things so difficult for himself. The Messenger did not approve of 'Umar's words. 'Abdullah ibn Hudafa al-Sahmi stood up and said: "O Messenger, give without fear that the Owner of the Seat of Honor will make you poor!" Pleased with such words, the Messenger declared: "I was commanded to do so" (Ibn Kathir, 6:63).

He never refused a request, for it was he who said: "The generous are near to God, Paradise, and people, but distant from the Fire. The miserly are distant from God, Paradise, and people, but near to the Fire" (Tirmidhi, "Birr," 40) and: "O people! Surely God has chosen for you Islam as religion. Improve your practice of it through generosity and good manners" (Hindi, 6:571).

HIS MODESTY

In society, each person has a window (status) through which he or she looks out to see others and be seen. If the window is built higher than their real stature, people try to make themselves appear taller through vanity and assumed airs. If the window is set lower than their real stature, they must bow in humility in order to look out, see, and be seen. Humility is the measure of one's greatness, just as vanity or conceit is the measure of low character.[2]

The Messenger had a stature so high that it could be said to touch the "roof of the Heavens." Therefore, he had no need to be seen. Whoever travels in the realm of virtues sees him before every created being, including angels. Since he is the greatest of humanity, he is the greatest in modesty. This follows the well-knowing adage: "The greater one is, the more modest one is."

He never regarded himself as greater than anybody else. Only his radiant face and attractive person distinguished him from his Companions. He lived and dressed like the poorest people and sat and ate with them, just as he did with slaves and servants. Once a woman saw him eating and remarked: "He eats like a slave." The Messenger replied: "Could there be a better slave than me? I am a slave of God" (Haythami, Majma', 9:21).

One time when he was serving his friends, a bedouin came in and shouted: "Who is the master of this people?" The Messenger answered in such a way that he introduced himself while expressing a substantial principle of Islamic leadership and public administration: "The people's master is the one who serves them." Ali says that among people the Messenger was one of them. While the Muslims were building their mosque in Madina, the Prophet carried two sun-dried bricks; everyone else carried one (Bukhari, 1:111; Muslim, 2:65; Ibn Sa'd, Tabaqat, 1: 240).

While digging the trench to defend Madina, the Companions bound a stone around their stomachs to quell their hunger; the Messenger bound two (Tirmidhi, "Zuhd," 39). When a man seeing him for the first time began trembling out of fear, because he found the Prophet's appearance so awe-inspiring, the Messenger calmed him: "Brother, don't be afraid. I am a man, like you, whose mother used to eat dry bread" (Ibn Maja, "At'ima," 30; Haythami, 9:20). Another time, an insane woman pulled him by the hand and said: "Come with me and do my housework." He did so (Qadi 'Iyad, Al-Shifa', 1:131, 133). 'A'isha reported that the Messenger patched his clothes, repaired his shoes, and helped his wives with the housework (Tirmidhi, Shama'il, 78; Ibn Hanbal, 6:256).

Although his modesty elevated him to the highest rank, he saw himself as an ordinary servant of God: "No one enters Paradise because of his or her deeds." When asked if this was true for him as well, he said that he could enter Paradise only through the Mercy of

God (Bukhari, "Riqaq," 18). Humility is the most important aspect of the Messenger's servanthood. He declared: "God exalts the humble and abases the haughty" (Hindi, *Kanz al-ʿUmmal*, 3:113; Haythami, 10:325). ʿAli describes the Messenger as:

> He was the most generous person in giving, and the mildest and the foremost in patience and perseverance. He was the most truthful in speech, the most amiable and congenial in companionship, and the noblest of them in family. Whoever sees him first is stricken by awe, but whoever knows him closely is deeply attracted to him. Whoever attempts to describe him says: "I have never seen the like of him." (Tirmidhi, Hadith No. 3880.)

Chapter Five

Other Aspects of Islam

OTHER ASPECTS OF ISLAM

ISLAMIC SOCIAL LIFE

I slam provides complete guidance for all aspects of human life. Islamic law is not confined to civil and criminal matters, but also deals with administrative, socioeconomic, national, and international affairs.

In general terms, Islamic law is the knowledge, discipline, and science of humanity's rights and obligations and of what is good and bad for humanity on the individual and collective levels. Thus the Islamic view of life consists of a set of rights and obligations by which Muslims are expected to live. Broadly speaking, Islamic law deals with our life in terms of our relationship with our Creator, ourselves (our rights upon ourselves), other people, and our natural environment (the rights of the resources that God has given to us for our benefit).

Each person is an instinctive worshipper; only the nature of the deity worshipped or the way worship is offered differ. God's love abides in every person's heart. By the nature of their being created, all creatures have to submit to their Creator. Thus all creatures, including humanity in its biological life, are *muslim* and have to obey the rules of creation. The Qur'an both establishes that God is the natural Deity for our worship and explains the right way to worship Him. It stipulates the uniformity of worship just as it stresses God's Unity, the unity of the Worshipped, and the unity of worship.

There must be unity between our worship and our attitude toward life. The Deity to Whom we pray is the same One we address while studying, earning a living, and improving conditions on Earth; the same One we remember while eating, drinking, interacting with family members and all other individuals or societies, regardless of time or place: Say: *"Lo, my worship and my service and behavior, my living and my dying are for God, the Lord of the Worlds"* (6:162). Our constant reiteration of God's Name in our hearts makes us recall His Commands and our individual and social responsibilities.

When this happens, something very significant occurs in our life: Our regular worship gives us an extraordinary spirit. For example, the prescribed daily prayers (*salat*) allow us to repeat and refresh our faith five times a day. The prayer times – dawn, noon, afternoon, evening, and night – correspond with the five periods of our life: childhood and youth, maturity, old age, death, and life after death until the Resurrection. The next day's dawn signifies the Resurrection, so each day is a complete cycle of our life in parallel with that of the world.

While praying, Muslims dissociate themselves from their worldly engagements, even from all the world, and turn to God with all their being. Reciting the Qur'an elevates us to a state as if we were receiving it directly from the Lord of the Worlds. We request Divine help to enable us to follow His Chosen Way, refresh our belief, remind ourselves that one day we will have to account for our deeds, unburden ourselves, and ask Him to help us throughout our lives.

Thus the daily prayers strengthen our faith, prepare us for a life of virtue and obedience to God, and refresh our belief, from which spring courage, sincerity, purposefulness, spiritual purity, and moral enrichment. The Qur'an states that: *Daily prayers prevent a Muslim from committing vices of every kind* (29:45), and God's Messenger considers it the Muslims' (spiritual) ascension to God's holy presence.

Muslims are urged to perform their daily prayers in congregation, and must do so for the Friday (noon) congregational prayer. This creates a bond of love and mutual understanding, arouses a sense of collective unity, fosters a collective purpose, and inculcates a deep feeling of brotherhood and sisterhood. Prayers are a symbol of equality, for poor and rich, low and high, rulers and ruled, educated and uneducated, black and white all stand in rows and prostrate before their Lord. Furthermore, this gives a strong sense of collective discipline. Prayers train Muslims in those virtues that engender the development of a rich individual and collective life.

Islam regards human beings as God's vicegerents and cannot tolerate the degradation brought on by their submission to humiliation or oppression, for Islam is the real way to freedom and liberation. It invites people to struggle against oppression and tyranny for their freedom and dignity. By prostrating before God, Muslims declare that they bow to no other power. Islam forbids serfdom; promises universal freedom, independence in thought, action, property, and religion; and safeguards a person's integrity, honor, and dignity.

Islam frees people from their lusts so that sensual pleasure does not tempt and corrupt them. Consuming intoxicants and engaging in sexual and moral permissiveness, gambling, nightclubs, mixed social activities, immoral movies, fornication, adultery, extramarital sex, pornography, overspending, conspicuous consumption, arrogance, greed, and so on are all humiliating factors that destroy a person's honor and dignity. The daily prayer and other forms of worship, such as prescribed alms-giving (*zakat*), inculcate the will to struggle against self-degradation.

Dr. Laura Vaglieri, a well-known Orientalist, writes that:

> The spirit was liberated [through Islam] from prejudice, man's will was set free from the ties which had kept it bound to the will of other men, or other so-called hidden powers, priests, false guardians of mysteries, brokers of salvation; all those who pretended to be mediators between God and man, and consequently believed that they had authority over other people's wills, fell from their pedestals.
>
> Because the Unity of God embraces all other unities, this religion was born with the unique feature of amalgamating the secular with the religious, the worldly with the other-worldly, and with a clear approach to socio-economic affairs and with a well-defined administrative system.
>
> Man became the servant of God alone and towards other men he had only the obligations of one free man towards another. While

> hitherto men had suffered from the injustices of social differences, Islam proclaimed equality among human beings. Each Muslim was distinguished from other Muslims only by his greater fear of God, his good deeds, and his moral and intellectual qualities.[1]

Islam's most important principle is monotheism. This is not only a theological principle, but the actual cornerstone of Islamic epistemology and the fundamental principle of Islamic methodology and of all Islamic studies. In short, it states that authority, judgment, and power belong to God. This liberates humanity from domination, intermediation, and subjugation, and provides Muslims with a strong sense of independence.

When joined with the principle of *'amr bi al-ma'ruf wa al-nahy 'an al-munkar* (spreading and encouraging good and preventing evil), Muslims are provided with the legal, spiritual, social, theological, and ethical justification for erecting a Divine social order. Moreover, Islam condemns dictatorship, colonialism, oppression, tyranny, power politics, authoritarianism, totalitarianism, theocracy, oligarchy, and monarchy.

ISLAMIC ADMINISTRATION

The foremost feature of Islamic administration is twofold: All people are God's creatures and therefore no one enjoys any superiority coming from birth (race, family, and color, etc); and the government's power is neither absolute nor designed to enslave them. Rather, its main objective is to establish and promote the virtues approved of by God and to prevent and suppress vice. This is why all rulers should display righteousness and respect for God in their character, words, and actions. Government employees, judges, and military officers should imbibe this spirit and infuse it into society.

The rule of law is indispensable to an Islamic social order. The Prophet was sent with the Book (the Qur'an, the Islamic community's constitution) and the Balance (the Divine standard by which rulers must implement the Qur'an in order to rule the community according to absolute justice). No Muslim is above the law or can transgress its limits. The law is to be enforced without discrimination, and courts are to be free of outside pressure. History shows that most caliphs set the best examples by adhering to these principles. Even though they enjoyed greater power than past kings and present presidents and prime ministers, they adhered strictly to the law. Friendship and nepotism did not annul prescribed rules and regulations, and personal displeasure did not cause them to violate the legal code.

As justice and the rule of law are an Islamic constitution's foremost articles, people are to obey the government so that anarchy and social disorder can be avoided. But disobedience is allowed, for the Messenger is reported to have said: "There is no obedience in sin." This does not mean that people can revolt against the government, but that individual Muslims are responsible for their own felicity and salvation, for: *God does not change the state of a people unless they change themselves* (13:11). People make their own history and are responsible for their own individual and social conditions. Given this, advice and preaching should always come before revolt.

Another important article is the advisory system of government. Learned and pious people who possess sound judgment and expert knowledge, as well as enjoy the people's confidence, must be located and clarify their opinions based on the dictates of their conscience. This advisory system is so important that God praises the first, exemplary Muslim community as a community *whose affair is by counsel between them* (42:38).

This becomes even more explicit when we realize that this first community was led by the Prophet, who never spoke out of caprice or on his own authority, but only spoke what was revealed to him by God (53:2-3), and that God considers consultation so important that He orders His Messenger to practice it with his Companions (3:159). Even after the Muslims' reverse at the Battle of Uhud (625), due to some of the Companions' disobedience to the Prophet, God told him to engage in consultation. The Prophet and his rightly-guided successors always consulted among themselves whenever necessary.

Consultation settles many affairs among Muslims. Judges who cannot decide cases use it to reach a verdict based on the Qur'an and the Sunna, thus making it similar to *ijtihad* and *qiyas* (analogy). Furthermore, any punishment of a secondary nature that is not explicitly mentioned in the Qur'an and the Sunna can be pronounced after consulting authoritative Muslim jurists.

Another basic principle is that the government should be formed with the people's free consent – not through the use of force – only after they have been consulted. The people should entrust power to the best candidate after consulting among themselves, for this was how each true successor to the Prophet came to power.

Although this system was replaced by a sultanate after Hasan ibn 'Ali ibn Abi Talib resigned in 661, most Muslim rulers remained faithful to and obeyed the Islamic constitutional system's law and dictates. When rulers deviate from the Right Way, the people or their scholarly representatives should use consultation to bring about their abdication or reform.

The constitution also provides for the freedom of opinion. Promoting virtue and preventing vice is more than just a right for Muslims – it is their essential duty. Freedom of conscience and speech is the pivot that ensures the correct functioning of an Islamic society and administration. The people are free to criticize even the most prominent Muslims when they go astray and to speak their minds on all matters.

The final article of an Islamic constitution to be mentioned here is the public treasury, which is God's property and a trust. Everything should be received through lawful sources and spent only for lawful purposes. Rulers have no more control of the public treasury than trustees have over the property of minor orphans in their custody: *If he is rich, let him abstain altogether; if poor, let him consume it reasonably* (4:6). Rulers must account for the public treasury's income and expenditure, and Muslims have the right to demand a full account of these.

HUMAN RIGHTS IN ISLAM

Islam gave humanity an ideal code of human rights 14 centuries ago. These rights seek to confer honor and dignity on humanity and to eliminate exploitation, oppression, and injustice.

These human rights are rooted firmly in the belief that God, and God alone, is the Source of all human rights. Due to their Divine origin, no ruler, government, assembly, or authority can curtail or violate in any way the human rights conferred by God, nor can they be surrendered, if they are to remain Muslims.

Human rights are an integral part of the overall Islamic order, and all Muslim governments and organs of society must implement them in letter and in spirit within that order's framework. These rights, as compiled by eminent Muslim scholars based on the Qur'an and the Sunna, can be enumerated as follows:

- All people are equal, and no one shall enjoy a privilege or suffer a disadvantage or discrimination due to his or her race, color, sex, origin, or language.
- All people are born free.
- Slavery and forced labor are abhorrent.
- Conditions shall be established to preserve, protect, and honor the institution of family as the basis of all social life.
- Both the rulers and the ruled are subject to, and equal before, the law.
- Only those commands that conform to the law must be obeyed.
- All worldly power is considered a sacred trust to be exercised within the limits prescribed by the law, in a manner approved by it, and with due regard for its priorities.
- All economic resources shall be treated as Divine blessings bestowed upon humanity and shall be enjoyed by all, in accordance with the rules and values set out in the Qur'an and the Sunna.
- All public affairs shall be determined and conducted by mutual consultation, and the authority to administer them shall be exercised according to this consensus.
- Everyone shall undertake obligations proportionate to one's capacity and shall be held responsible *pro rata* for one's deeds.
- If a person's rights are infringed upon, he or she shall be assured of appropriate remedial measures in accordance with the law.
- No one shall be deprived of his or her rights guaranteed by the law, except by its authority and to the extent permitted by it.

- Every individual shall have the right to bring legal action against anyone who commits a crime against society as a whole or against any of its members.
- Every legally permitted effort shall be made to secure humanity's deliverance from every type of exploitation, injustice, and oppression, and to ensure humanity's security, dignity, and liberty as set out in the law.

Right to Belief and Practicing One's Belief

- Every person is free to prefer a belief and practice it, although Islam has a right to be communicated to everyone in accordance with God's rules and the Messenger's practice. No one can be coerced to believe, not believe, or choose a certain belief.
- No one shall insult or ridicule the religious beliefs of others or incite public hostility against them, for all Muslims are obligated to respect the religious feelings of others.

Right to Life

- As human life is sacred and inviolable, every effort must be made to protect it. No one can be exposed to injury or death, unless the law permits it.
- Just as in life, so also after death the sanctity of a person's corpse shall be inviolable. Muslims must ensure that a deceased person's corpse is handled with due solemnity.

Right to Freedom

- Every person is born free. No inroads can be made upon his or her right to liberty, except under law's authority and due process.
- Every individual and people has the inalienable right to physical, cultural, economic, political, and all other types of freedom, and are entitled to struggle by all available means against any infringement or abrogation of this right. In addition, every oppressed individual or people has a legitimate claim upon the support of other individuals and/or peoples in such a struggle.

Right to Equality and Prohibition of Impermissible Discrimination

- All persons are equal before the law and are entitled to equal opportunity and its protection.
- All persons are entitled to equal wage for equal work.
- No person can be denied the opportunity to work, be discriminated against, or exposed to greater physical risk due to religious belief, color, race, origin, sex, or language.

Right to Justice

- Every person has the right to be treated in accordance with the law, and only in accordance with the law.
- Every person has the right and the obligation to protest injustice, to use any recourse to provided by the law to remedy any unwarranted personal injury or loss, to self-defense against any charges laid against him or her, and to obtain fair adjudication before an independent judicial tribunal in any dispute with public authorities or with another person.
- Every person has the right and duty to defend the rights of any other person and the community in general (*hisba*).
- No person can be discriminated against while seeking to defend private and public rights.
- Every Muslim has the right to refuse to obey any command that is contrary to the law, no matter by whom it may be issued.

Right to a Fair Trial

- No person can be judged guilty of an offence and made liable to punishment before his or her guilt has been proven an independent judicial tribunal.
- No person can be judged guilty before a fair trial and a reasonable opportunity for self-defense.
- Punishment shall be meted out in accordance with the law in proportion to the seriousness of the offence, and with due consideration of the surrounding circumstances.
- No act can be considered a crime, unless the law clearly stipulates it as such.

• Every individual is responsible for his or her actions. Responsibility for a crime cannot be placed upon other members of the family or group, who are not directly or indirectly involved in the crime in question.

Right to Protection against the Abuse of Power

• Every person has the right to protection against harassment by official agencies. A person is liable to account for himself or herself only when defending himself or herself against specific charges when there exists a reasonable suspicion of involvement.

Right to Protection against Torture

• No person can be subjected to physical or mental torture; degraded; threatened either with personal injury or injury to his or her relatives or loved ones; made to confess to a crime; or forced to do something against his or her own will.

Right to Protection of Honor and Reputation

• Every person has the right to protect his or her honor and reputation against calumny, groundless charges, or defamation and blackmail.

Right to Asylum

• Every persecuted or oppressed person has the right to seek refuge and asylum, irrespective of his or her race, religion, color, and sex.

• The Sacred Mosque (al-Masjid al-Haram) in Makka is a sanctuary for all Muslims.

Rights of Minorities

• The Qur'anic principle of no compulsion in religion governs the religious rights of non-Muslim minorities.

• In a Muslim country, religious minorities have the choice to have their civil and personal matters governed by Islamic law or their own law.

Right and Obligation to Participate in Managing Public Affairs

- Subject to the law, every individual in the community is entitled to assume public office.
- Free consultation (*shura*) is the basis of the administrative relationship between the government and the people, and people can remove their rulers in accordance with it.

Right to the Freedom of Belief, Thought, and Speech

- Every person has the right to express his or her thoughts and beliefs so long as he or she remains within the law's limits. However, no one is entitled to disseminate falsehood, circulate reports that may outrage public decency, indulge in slander or innuendo, or cast defamatory aspersions on others.
- The pursuit of knowledge and truth is a right and a duty of every Muslim.
- Every Muslim has the right and duty to protest and strive (within the law's limits) against oppression, even if it involves challenging the state's highest authority.
- There is no bar on disseminating information, provided it does not endanger the security of the society or the state, and is confined within the law's limits.

Right to Free Association

- Every person is entitled to participate, individually and collectively, in the community's religious, social, cultural, and political life, and to establish institutions and agencies that promote good and prevent evil.
- Every person is entitled to work for establishing institutions that will allow these rights to be enjoyed. Collectively, the community is obliged to establish the conditions that will allow its members to fully develop their personalities.

The Economic Order and Related Rights

- All persons are entitled to the full benefits of nature and its resources to pursue their economic interests. These are blessings bestowed by God to benefit humanity as a whole.

- All people are entitled to earn their living according to the law.
- Every person is entitled to own property individually or in association with others. State ownership of certain economic resources in the public interest is legitimate.
- The poor have the right to a prescribed share in the wealth of the rich, as fixed by *zakat* and levied and collected in accordance with the law.
- All means of production shall be used to benefit the community as a whole, and may not be neglected or misused.
- In order to promote the development of a balanced economy and to protect society from exploitation, Islamic law forbids monopolies, unreasonable restrictive trade practices, usury, coerced contracts, and publishing misleading advertisements.
- All economic activities are permitted, provided they do not harm the community's interests or violate Islamic laws and values.

Right to Protection of Property

- No property may be expropriated, except by the law, in the public interest and on payment of fair and adequate compensation.

Status and Dignity of Workers

- Islam honors work and the worker, and enjoins Muslims to treat workers justly and generously. They must be paid what they have earned promptly, and also entitled to adequate rest and leisure.

Right to Social Security

- Every person has the right to food, shelter, clothing, education, and medical care consistent with the community's resources. This communal obligation extends in particular to all individuals who cannot take care of themselves due to some temporary or permanent disability.

Right to Establish a Family and Related Matters

- Every person is entitled to marry, establish a family, and bring up children in conformity with his or her religion, traditions, and culture. Every spouse is entitled to such rights and privileges, and carries such obligations as stipulated by the law.
- Each spouse is entitled to respect and consideration from the other spouse.
- Every husband is obligated to maintain his wife and children according to his means.
- Every child has the right to be maintained and properly brought up by his or her parents. Children cannot be made to work at an early age or bear any burden that might arrest or harm their natural development.
- If parents cannot discharge their obligations toward their children, the community must fulfill these obligations at public expense.
- Every person is entitled to material support, care, and protection from his or her family during childhood, old age, or incapacity. Parents are entitled to material support, care, and protection from their children.
- Motherhood is entitled to special respect, care, and assistance from the family and the community's public agencies.
- Within the family, men and women are to share in their obligations and responsibilities according to their gender, natural endowments, talents, and inclinations, bearing in mind their common responsibilities toward their progeny and relatives.
- No person may be married against his or her will, lose, or suffer a diminished legal personality on account of marriage.

Rights of Married Women Every married woman is entitled to

- live in the house in which her husband lives;
- receive what she needs to maintain a standard of living that is not inferior to that of her spouse, and, in the event of divorce, receive during her waiting period (*'idda*) support commensu-

rate with her husband's resources both for herself and the children she nurses or keeps, irrespective of her own financial status, earnings, or property held in her own right;

- seek and obtain a dissolution of marriage in accordance with the law, as well as to seek a divorce through the courts;

- inherit from her husband, parents, children, and other relatives according to the law;

- strict confidentiality from her spouse, or ex-spouse if divorced, with regard to any personal information that, if made public, could harm her interests. Her husband or ex-husband also has similar rights over her.

Right to Education

- Every person is entitled to receive an education in accordance with his or her natural capability.

- Every person is entitled to freely choose his or her profession and career, and to the opportunity for full personal development.

Right of Privacy

- Every person is entitled to the protection of privacy. Suspicion, spying, slandering, and backbiting are all forbidden.

Right to Freedom of Movement and Residence

- Every Muslim has the right to freely move in and out of Muslim lands.

- No one shall be forced to leave his or her country of residence or be deported arbitrarily without recourse to due process.

SUFISM: THE PATH TO INDIVIDUAL PERFECTION OR SPIRITUALITY[2]

Sufism (*tasawwuf*) is the path followed by Sufis to reach the Truth – God. While this term usually expresses the theoretical or philosophical aspect of this search, its practical aspect is usually referred to as "being a dervish."

What Is Sufism?

Sufism has been defined in many ways. Some see it as God's annihilating the individual's ego, will, and self-centeredness and then reviving him or her spiritually with the lights of His Essence. Such a transformation results in God's directing the individual's will in accordance with His Will. Others view it as a continuous striving to cleanse one's self of all that is bad or evil in order to acquire virtue. Shibli summarizes it as always being together with God or in His presence, so that no worldly or other-worldly aim is even entertained. Abu Muhammad Jarir describes it as resisting the temptations of the carnal self and bad qualities, and acquiring laudable moral qualities.

There are some who describe Sufism as seeing behind the "outer" or surface appearance of things and events and interpreting whatever happens in the world in relation to God. This means that a person regards every act of God as a window to "see" Him, lives his or her life as a continuous effort to view or "see" Him with a profound, spiritual "seeing" indescribable in physical terms, and with a profound awareness of being continually overseen by Him.

All of these definitions can be summarized as follows: Sufism is the path followed by an individual who, having been able to free himself or herself from human vices and weaknesses in order to acquire angelic qualities and conduct pleasing to God, lives in accordance with the requirements of God's knowledge and love, and in the resulting spiritual delight that ensues.

Sufism is based on observing even the most "trivial" rules of the Islamic law in order to penetrate their inner meaning. An initiate or traveler on the path (*salik*) never separates the outer observance of the Law from its inner dimension, and therefore observes all of the requirements of both the outer and the inner dimensions of Islam. Through such observance, he or she travels toward the goal in utmost humility and submission.

Sufism, being a demanding path leading to knowledge of God, has no room for negligence or frivolity. It requires the initiate to strive continuously, like a honeybee flying from the hive to flowers and from flowers to the hive, to acquire this knowledge. The initiate should purify his or her heart from all other attachments; resist all carnal inclinations, desires, and appetites; and live in a manner reflecting the knowledge with which God has revived and illumined his or her heart, always ready to receive Divine blessing and inspiration, as well as in strict observance of the Prophet's example. Convinced that attachment and adherence to God is the greatest merit and honor, the initiate should renounce his or her own desires for the demands of God, the Truth.

After these [preliminary] definitions, we should discuss the aim, benefits, and principles of Sufism.

Sufism requires the strict observance of all religious obligations, an austere lifestyle, and the renunciation of carnal desires. Through this method of spiritual self-discipline, the individual's heart is purified and his or her senses and faculties are employed in the way of God, which means that the traveler can now begin to live on a spiritual level.

Sufism also enables individuals, through the constant worship of God, to deepen their awareness of themselves as devotees of God. Through the renunciation of this transient, material world, as well as the desires and emotions it engenders, they awaken to the reality of the other world. Sufism allows individuals to develop the moral dimension of one's existence, and enables the acquisition of a strong, heartfelt, and personally experienced conviction of the articles of faith that before had been accepted only superficially.

The principles of Sufism may be listed as follows:

- Reaching true belief in God's Divine Oneness and living in accordance with its demands.
- Heeding the Divine Speech (the Qur'an), discerning and then obeying the commands of the Divine Power and Will as they relate to the universe (the laws of creation and life).
- Overflowing with Divine Love and getting along with all other beings in the realization (originating from Divine Love) that the universe is a cradle of brotherhood and sisterhood.

- Giving preference or precedence to the well-being and happiness of others.
- Acting in accord with the demands of the Divine Will – not with the demands of our own will.
- Being open to love, and spiritual yearning and delight.
- Being able to discern the meanings in facial expressions and the inner, Divine mysteries and meanings of surface events.
- Visiting and associating with people who encourage the avoidance of sin and striving in the way of God.
- Being content with permitted pleasures, and not taking even a single step toward that which is not permitted.
- Struggling continuously against worldly ambitions and illusions, which lead us to suppose that this world is eternal.
- Never forgetting that salvation is possible only through certainty or conviction of the truth of religious beliefs and conduct, sincerity or purity of intention, and the sole desire to please God.
- Two other elements may be added here: acquiring knowledge and understanding of the religious sciences and principles of Sufism, and following a perfected, spiritual master's guidance.

THE MAIN DYNAMICS BEHIND THE RAPID SPREAD OF ISLAM[3]

During the tenth century, Islam was the predominant religion of an area covering more than half of the then-known world. Its adherents inhabited three continents: from the Pyrenees and Siberia up to China and New Guinea, and from Morocco to the southern tip of Africa.

One of history's most striking facts is that Islam spread over such a vast area within 3 centuries. Most striking of all, within 50 years after the Hijra, all of North Africa (from Egypt to Morocco) and the Middle East (from Yemen to Caucasia, and from Egypt to the lands beyond Transoxiana) had come under the sway of Islam. During 'Uthman's reign (644-56), Muslim envoys reached the Chinese royal court and were welcomed enthusiastically. According to historians, this important event marks the beginning of Islam's presence in China.

How Islam Spread

Peoples of all eras have been ready to embrace Islam for a wide variety of reasons. But perhaps the foremost one, as pointed out by Muhammad Asad, a Jewish convert to Islam, is that:

> Islam appears to me like a perfect work of architecture. All its parts are harmoniously conceived to complement and support each other, nothing lacking, with the result of an absolute balance and solid composure. Everything in the teaching and postulate of Islam is in its proper place. (Muhammad Asad, *Islam at the Crossroads* [New Era Pubs.: 1982], 5.)

Most Western writers continue to accuse Islam of spreading by the sword. One major cause of this prejudice is that Islam often spread at the expense of Christianity. Some unbiased Western writers have admitted this:

> Muslims, according to the principles of their faith, are under an obligation to use force for the purpose of bringing other religions to ruin [probably he means Jihad, which is unfortunately misinterpreted and not for the purpose he claims, as will be explained later]; yet, in spite of that, they have been tolerating other religions for some centuries past. The Christians have not been given orders to do anything but preach and instruct, yet, despite this, from time immemorial they have been exterminating by fire and sword all those who are not of their religion. . . We may feel certain that if Western Christians, instead of the Saracens and the Turks, had won the dominion over Asia, there would be today not a trace left of the Greek Church, and that they would never have tolerated Muhammadanism as the "infidels" have tolerated Christianity there. (P. Bayle, *Dictionary*, "Mahomed," 1850.)

Islam's rapid expansion, unequalled by any other religion, was due to its religious content and values, as many unbiased Western intellectuals state:

> Many have sought to answer the questions of why the triumph of Islam was so speedy and complete? Why have so many mil-

lions embraced the religion of Islam and scarcely a hundred ever recanted? . . . Some have attempted to explain the first overwhelming success of Islam by the argument of the Sword. They forget Carlyle's laconic reply. First get your sword. You must win men's hearts before you can induce them to imperil their lives for you; and the first conquerors of Islam must have been made Muslims before they were made fighters on the Path of God. Others allege the low morality of the religion and the sensual paradise it promises as a sufficient cause for the zeal of its followers: but even were these admitted to the full, no religion has ever gained a lasting hold upon the souls of men by the force of its sensual permissions and fleshy promises. . .

In all these explanations the religion itself is left out of the question. Decidedly, Islam itself was the main cause for its triumph. Islam not only was at once accepted (by many peoples and races) by Arabia, Syria, Persia, Egypt, Northern Africa and Spain, at its first outburst; but, with the exception of Spain, it has never lost its vantage ground; it has been spreading ever since it came into being. Admitting the mixed causes that contributed to the rapidity of the first swift spread of Islam, they do not account for the duration of Islam. There must be something in the religion itself to explain its persistence and spread, and to account for its present hold over so large of a proportion of the dwellers on the earth... Islam has stirred an enthusiasm that has never been surpassed. Islam has had its martyrs, its recluses, who have renounced all that life offered and have accepted death with a smile for the sake of the faith that was in them. (Stanley Lane-Poole, *Studies in a Mosque* (Beirut: Khayats, 1966), 86-89.)

A. J. Arberry holds the same view:

The rapidity of the spread of Islam is a crucial fact of history ... The sublime rhetoric of the Qur'an, that inimitable symphony, the very sounds of which move men to tears and ecstasy". (M. Pickthall, The Meaning of the Glorious Qur'an, p.vii.) ...

This, and the urgency of the simple message carried, holds the key to the mystery of one of the greatest cataclysms in the history of religion. When all military, political and economic factors have been exhausted, the religious impulse must still be recognized as the most vital and enduring." (A. J. Arberry, Aspects of Islamic Civilization [Westport, CN: Greenwood Press, 1977], 12.)

Brockelman, usually very unsympathetic and partial, also recognizes Islam's religious values as the main factor for its spread
(Carl Brockelman, *History of the Islamic Peoples* [London: Routledge &
K. Paul, 1949]). Rosenthal writes: "The more important factor for
the spread of Islam is religious law of Islam (Shari'a which is an
inclusive, all-embracing, all-comprehensive way of thinking and
living) which was designed to cover all manifestations of life"
(Franz Rosenthal, *Political Thought in Medieval Islam* [Cambridge, UK:
Cambridge Univ. Press, 1958], 21).

Along with many other reasons, Islam spread because of its
followers' exemplary lifestyle and unceasing effort to transmit its
message throughout the world. These lie at the root of Islam's
conquest of hearts. Islamic universalism is closely associated
with the principle of *amr bi al-ma'ruf* (spreading and encouraging the good), for this is how Muslims are to spread Islam. This
principle seeks to convey Islam's message to everyone, without
exception, and to establish a model community that displays
Islam to the world: *Thus We have made of you a community justly
balanced, that you might be witnesses (models) for the peoples, and
the Messenger has been a witness for you* (2:143).

Islam's moral and ethical values usually have played an important part in its spread. One nineteenth-century European writer
recorded his impressions on how Islamic ethics influenced native
tribes as follows:

> As to the effects of Islam when first embraced by a tribe, can
> there, when viewed as a whole, be any reasonable doubt?
> Polytheism disappears almost instantaneously; sorcery, with its
> attendant evils, gradually dies away; human sacrifice becomes a
> thing of the past. The general moral elevation is most marked;
> the natives begin for the first time in their history to dress, and
> that neatly. Squalid filth is replaced by some approach to per-
> sonal cleanliness; hospitality becomes a religious duty; drunk-
> enness, instead of the rule, becomes a comparatively rare excep-
> tion... chastity is looked upon as one of the highest, and becomes,
> in fact, one of the commoner virtues. It is idleness that hence-
> forward degrades, and industry that elevates, instead of the
> reverse. Offences are henceforward measured by a written code

instead of the arbitrary caprice of a chieftain – a step, as every-one will admit, of vast importance in the progress of a tribe. The Mosque gives an idea of architecture at all events higher than any the Negro has yet had. A thirst for literature is creat-ed and that for works of science and philosophy as well as for commentaries on the Qur'an. (Quoted from Waitz by B. Smith, *Muhammad and Muhammadanism*, 42-43.)

Islam also spread rapidly because of its tolerance. Toynbee praises the Muslims' tolerance toward the Peoples of the Book after comparing it with the Christians' attitude toward Muslims in their lands (Arnold Toynbee, *A Historian's Approach to Religion* [New York: Oxford Univ. Press, 1956], 246). Link attributes Islam's spread to its credible principles and tolerance, persuasion, and other attractions (T. Link, *A History of Religion,* quoted in *Yabancilara Göre Eski Türkler,* "The Turks According to the Foreigners," Bedir Yayinevi, Ist.). Makarios, a seventeenth-century Orthodox Patriarch of Antioch, compared the Poles' harsh treatment of the Russian Orthodox to the Ottomans' tolerant attitude toward Orthodox Christians and prayed for the sultans (*ibid.*).

This is not the only example of non-Muslims' preference for Muslim rule over that of their own coreligionists. Byzantium's Orthodox Christians openly expressed their preference for the Ottoman turban in Istanbul to the hats of the Catholic cardinals. Elisee Reclus, a nineteenth-century French traveler, wrote that the Muslim Turks allowed all non-Muslims to observe their reli-gious duties and rituals, and that the sultan's Christian subjects were freer to live their own lives than those Christians whose lands were ruled by a member of a rival Christian sect (Elisee Reclus, *Nouvelle Geographie Universelle,* vol. 9; quoted in *Yabancilara Göre Eski Türkler. . .*). Popescu Ciocanel pays tribute to the Muslim Turks by stating that the Romanians were lucky to have Turkish, instead of Russian and Austrian, rulers. Otherwise, he points out, "no trace of the Romanian nation would have remained" (Popescu Ciocanel, *La Crise de l'Orient,* quoted in *Yabancilara Göre Eski Türkler. . .*).

The Muslims' attitude toward the people they conquered is quite clear in the instructions given by the Rightly-Guided Caliphs:

Always keep fear of God in your mind; remember that you cannot afford to do anything without His grace. Do not forget that Islam is a mission of peace and love. Keep the Holy Prophet (upon him be peace and blessings) before you as a model of bravery and piety. Do not destroy fruit trees or fertile fields in your paths. Be just, and spare the feelings of the vanquished. Respect all religious persons who live in hermitages or convents and spare their edifices. Do not kill civilians. Do not outrage the chastity of women and the honor of the conquered. Do not harm old people and children. Do not accept any gifts from the civil population of any place. Do not billet your soldiers or officers in the houses of civilians. Do not forget to perform your daily prayers. Fear God. Remember that death will inevitably come to everyone of you at some time or other, even if you are thousands of miles away from a battlefield; therefore be always ready to face death. (Andrew Miller, *Church History*; 'Ali ibn Abi Talib, *Nahj al-Balagha*.)

An historical episode, recorded by the famous Muslim historian Baladhuri in his *Futuh al-Buldan*, tells how pleased the indigenous peoples were with their Muslim conquerors and is of great significance:

When Heraclius, Emperor of the Eastern Roman Empire (610-41), massed his troops against the Muslims, and the Muslims heard that they were coming to meet them, they refunded the tribute they had taken from the inhabitants of Hims, saying: "We are too busy to support and protect you. Take care of yourselves." But the people of Hims replied: "We like your rule and justice far better than our former state of oppression and tyranny. We shall indeed, with your help, repulse Heraclius' army from the city." The Jews rose and said: "We swear by the Torah, no governor of Heraclius shall enter Hims unless we are first vanquished and exhausted." Saying this, they closed and guarded the city gates. The Christians and Jews of cities that had capitulated did the same. When, by God's help, Heraclius' army was defeated and the Muslims won, they opened the gates of their cities, went out with singers and musicians, and paid the tribute.

ISLAM: FROM PAST TO FUTURE

The most striking point of Islam and its history is that Islam completely changes those who accept it, no matter how ignorant, rude, and ill-mannered they were before, into embodiments of almost all virtues and human values. The intellectual, religious, cultural, and socioeconomic decadence of the pre-Islamic nomadic Arabs is known. Islam alone elevated them to be humanity's guides and teachers for centuries, and models for every age. The manner displayed by the Muslim envoy and his speech to the Sassanid commander-in-chief at the Battle of Qadisiya (636) shows how Islam changed "stones" into "gold" or "diamonds," a point that by itself proves Islam's Divine origin.

What Islam Has Brought to People

Rabiʿ ibn ʿAmir was brought up in pre-Islamic Arabia's dark polytheistic climate, where life was considered to consist of killing and plundering to eat. However, his embrace of Islam transformed him into one of humanity's "immortal" guides. During the War of Qadisiya (636), he entered the Sassanid commander's richly ornamented tent, dressed in a loose white garment, wearing a turban and holding a spear. Dismounting from his horse in the tent, he seized the pillow upon which the enemy commander was reclining, tore a hole in it, and tied his horse's reins to it. Not bowing before the commander, he rolled up the carpet and then sat cross-legged on the ground to show Islam's dignity and superiority over all other religions and how Muslims renounce their lives for the sake of their sublime cause.

When the bewildered commander asked about their cause, he replied:

> Our cause is to raise humanity from the dark pits of worldly life to the high, boundless realm of the spirit; from the humiliation of worshipping false and usually human-made divinities to the honor and dignity of worshipping the One God, the universe's sole Creator and Sustainer; and to free humanity from the oppression and depressions brought about by false religions into the luminous and peaceful climate of Islam.

This is the testimony of one who experienced Islam's beauties and how high Islam elevates its adherents culturally, intellectually, and spiritually.

Islam alone is responsible for major human developments, among them the following:

- Turning human thought away from superstition, love for the unnatural and inexplicable, and monasticism and toward a rational approach, a love for reality, and a pious and balanced worldly life.

- Inspiring the urge for rational and scientific research and proofs to verify the truth of established convictions.

- Opening the eyes of those accustomed to identifying God with natural phenomena.

- Leading people away from the path of baseless speculation and toward that of a rational understanding and sound reasoning based on observation, experimentation, and research.

- Defining the limits and functions of sense-perception, reason, intuition, and spiritual experience.

- Engendering a rapprochement between spiritual and material values.

- Harmonizing faith with knowledge and action.

- Replacing idolatry, the worship of human beings, and polytheism with a firm faith in God's Unity.

- Showing the path of spiritual evolution, moral emancipation, and salvation through active participation in this world's daily affairs.

- Bringing home to each and every people their true worth and position. Those who acknowledged only a "God-incarnate" or a "son of God" as their moral preceptor or spiritual guide were told that a human being like themselves, one who has no pretensions to God, actually can become God's vicegerent on Earth. Those who proclaimed and worshipped powerful personages realized that their false deities were people just like themselves.

- Emphasizing that no person could claim holiness, authority, or overlordship as a birthright, and that no one was born with the stigma of untouchability, slavery, or serfdom.

- Inspiring the thoughts of humanity's unity, human equality, and real freedom. Many principles of good behavior, culture and civilization, purity of thought and deed owe their origin to Islam. For example, Islam's social laws have infiltrated deep into human social life, its economic principles have ushered in many movements and continue to do so, its laws of governance continue to exert their influence, and its fundamental principles of law and justice continue to form a perpetual source of guidance for humanity.

- Establishing a practical framework for all aspects of international relations and regulating the laws of war and peace. This framework, the first of its kind in history, established an ethical code of war and foreign relations based on the ground of common humanity. Islam, as Arthur Leonard says, has left such an indelible mark on the pages of human history that it can never be effaced ... that only when the world grows will it be acknowledged in full.

- Founding one of the most brilliant civilizations in history. This should come as no surprise, since the first revealed verse of the Qur'an was: *Read: In the Name of your Lord Who created* (96:1). But why does the Qur'an order "read" when the local people have almost nothing to read? Because they – and humanity – are to "read" the universe itself as the Book of Creation, of which the Qur'an is the counterpart in letters or words. We are to observe the universe and perceive its meaning and content so that we can gain a deeper knowledge of the beauty and splendor of the Creator's system and the infinitude of His might. Thus we must penetrate the universe's manifold meanings, discover the Divine laws of nature, and establish a world in which science and faith complement each other so that humanity can attain true bliss in both worlds. Otherwise, as Bertrand Russell says, "unless man increases in wisdom (and faith) as much as in knowledge, increase of knowledge will be increase of sorrow" (Bertrand Russell, The *Impact of Science on Society* [New York: Columbia Univ. Press, 1951], 121) and "Science teaches man to fly in the air like birds, and to swim in the water like fishes, but man, without faith, cannot know how to live on the earth" (Quoted by C. E. M. Joad in *Counter Attack from the East*, 28).

The Qur'an's Purposes and Sciences

The Qur'an contains everything that the Creator deems necessary for us to make material and spiritual progress. Its most important aims are to make God known to us, open the way to faith and worship, and organize our individual and social life in such a way that we can realize perfect happiness in both worlds. Thus it mentions things in proportion to their significance and uses them to achieve these aims. Such matters as the pillars of faith, which are the fundamentals of Islam as well as the foundations of human life and essentials of worship, are explained elaborately, while other things are only hinted at briefly. The meaning of a verse may be compared to a rosebud: It is hidden by successive layers of petals, and a new meaning is perceived as each petal unfolds.

For example, the Qur'an hints at technological advances and marks their final development by mentioning the Prophets' miracles. It encourages us to fly by alluding implicitly to spaceships and aircrafts: *And to Solomon the wind; its morning course was a month's journey, and its evening course was a month's journey* (34:12). It invites us to search for cures to all illnesses: *(Jesus said:) I also heal the blind and the leper, and bring to life the dead, by the leave of God* (3:49), and hints that one day we will reach this goal and thus come to imagine that somehow we are immune to death. The verse: *Said he who possessed knowledge of the Book: "I will bring it (the Queen of Yemen's throne) to you (Solomon in Jerusalem) before your glance returns to you,"* (27:40) foretells that one day images or even actual things will be transmitted in a moment through knowledge of the Divine Book of the Universe, just as one with knowledge of the Book of Divine Revelation brings things from a great distance before one's glance returns to him.

The Qur'an also symbolically informs us that a killer can be identified by some cells taken from the victim's corpse. Such a case took place during the time of Moses. As recounted in 2:71-73, God told the Children of Israel to slaughter a cow and then place part of it on a murdered man's corpse. These are just some of the examples of Qur'anic allusions to future scientific and technological advances.

The Qur'an, being the book for every age and person, has great depths of meaning. It is an infinite ocean into which all people with knowledge and ability can dive deeply and, according to their capacity, find its pearls and coral. The passage of time only rejuvenates its scientific wisdom. Every generation discovers its wisdom anew, and its secrets continue to be revealed over time.

In: *Then He turned to Heaven when it was smoke, and said to it and to Earth: "Come willingly or unwillingly." They said: "We come willingly"* (40:11), the Qur'an indicates that there is some difficulty in such cooperation. We know that the atmosphere's molecules and atoms try to escape into space, while Earth tries to attract and capture them. But for there to be an atmosphere, the motions leading to the molecules' escape must be counterbalanced by the Earth's gravitational attraction.

This is an almost impossible condition to fulfill. From the standpoint of geophysics, these conditions require that three important balances be preserved: atmospheric temperature, Earth's proportionate gravitational attraction, and the nonviolation of this balance by various radiant energies arriving from space. The Qur'an expresses these facts in the verse mentioned above. That the almost impossible conditions are fulfilled only by God's power is indicated in: They said: "We come willingly."

Scientists interpret: *No, I swear by the positions of stars; and if you but knew, that is indeed a mighty oath* (56:75-76) as alluding to star locations, black holes, and white holes (quasars). The verse: *Glory be to Him, Who created in pairs all things that the earth produces, as well as their own selves, and many other things of which they know nothing* (36:36), after beginning by proclaiming that God duplicates nothing and that He has no likeness or equal, proceeds to say that all things were created in pairs. This type of existence indicates opposition simultaneously with similarity. The scientific definition of creation in pairs implies "similar opposites." The Qur'an gives three examples:

- Pairs produced by Earth (positron-electron, antiproton-proton, antineutron-neutron), those with different physical and chemical characteristics (metals and nonmetals); biologically opposed pairs (male and female plants and animals), and physically opposed pairs.

- Pairs of their selves (man and woman; such personality traits as cruel-compassionate, generous-mean; and traits that are similar but subject to opposed value judgments, such as hypocrisy-consideration).

- Pairs about which we do not know. The discovery of the positron and "parity" (creation in pairs), mentioned by the Qur'an 14 centuries ago, may be regarded as a turning point in contemporary physics.

The planets' spherical shape and rotations are indicated in: *He is the Lord of the heavens and Earth, and all that lies between them; He is the Lord of the easts* (37:15), for the concept of the "easts" introduces infinite dimensions and differs for each location on Earth. A point on Earth is in the east with respect to its western regions. Therefore the concept of east differs at every point on Earth, and these form an ensemble of easts. Besides, there are 180 points of sunrise, which means that the sun rises at one place for only 2 days in the year and thus there are 180 easts. And so this verse also indicates meridians, infinite dimensions, space's relativity, the planets' spherical shape, and Earth's rotation.

French scientist Jacques Cousteau discovered that the Atlantic Ocean and the Mediterranean Sea have different chemical and biological constitutions. After conducting undersea investigations at the Straits of Gibraltar to explain this phenomenon, he concluded that "unexpected fresh water springs issue from the southern and northern coasts of Gibraltar. These water sprouts gush forth towards each other at angle of 45°, forming a reciprocal dam like the teeth of a comb. Due to this fact, the Mediterranean and the Atlantic Ocean cannot intermingle." Afterwards, when shown the verse: *He has let forth the two seas, that meet together. Between them a barrier, they do not overpass* (55:19-20), Cousteau was amazed.

This verse further draws our attention to the plankton composition of the seas, and to the flora and fish distributions that change with variations in temperature. Many other Qur'anic verses shed light upon scientific facts, and every person is invited to study them: *We made the Qur'an easy for reflection and study. Will anybody study and reflect?* (54:17).

The Two Books and Islamic Civilization

Islam founded a most brilliant civilization. This should not be considered surprising, for, as mentioned above, the Qur'an begins with the injunction: *Read: In the Name of Your Lord Who created*(96:1). This order, which came at a when there was very little to read and most people were illiterate, means that we should "read" the universe, which is the "Book of Creation." Its counterpart is the Qur'an, a book of letters and words. We are obliged to penetrate into the universe's manifold meanings, discover the Divine laws of nature, and establish a world in which science and faith complement each other, for all of this will enable us to attain true bliss in both worlds.

Obeying the Qur'an's injunctions, Muslims studied both the Book of Divine Revelation (the Qur'an) and the Book of Creation (the universe), and founded a magnificent civilization. Scholars from all over Europe and elsewhere benefited from the great Muslim centers of higher learning at Damascus, Bukhara, Baghdad, Cairo, Fez, Qayrawan, Zaytuna, Cordoba, Sicily, Isfahan, and Delhi. Historians liken this Muslim golden age, in full flower when Europe was enduring its dark Middle Ages, to a beehive. Roads were full of students, scientists, and scholars traveling from one center of learning to another. Such "Renaissance" men and women as Jabir ibn Hayyan, Ibn Ishaq al-Kindi, Muhammad ibn Musa al-Kharizmi, al-Farabi, Avicenna, Abu al-Hasan al-Mas'udi, Ibn al-Haytham, al-Biruni, al-Ghazzali, Nasir al-Din al-Tusi, and Abu Bakr al-Razi were shining like stars in the high sky of science.

Islam has maintained an intimate connection between science and Islamic studies. Thus the traditional education of Islamic scientists, particularly in the early centuries, comprised most of contemporary sciences. In later life, each scientist's aptitude and interest would cause him or her to become an expert and specialist in one or more sciences.

Universities, libraries, observatories, and other scientific institutions played a major role in the continuing vitality of Islamic science. These, together with students who would travel hundreds of miles to study under acknowledged scholars, ensured that the whole corpus of knowledge was kept intact and transmitted from one place to another and from one generation to the next. This knowledge did not remain static; rather, it continued to expand and enrich itself. Today, there are hundreds of thousands of Islamic (mainly in Arabic) manuscripts in the world's libraries, a large number of which deal with scientific subjects.

Abu Yusuf Ya'qub al-Kindi (the "Philosopher of the Arabs") wrote on philosophy, mineralogy, metallurgy, geology, physics, and medicine, among other subjects, and was an accomplished physician. Ibn al-Haytham was a leading Muslim mathematician and, without doubt, the greatest physicist. We know the names of over 100 of his works. Some 19 of them, dealing with mathematics, astronomy, and physics, have been studied by modern scholars. His work exercised a profound influence on later scholars, both in the Muslim world and in the West, where he was known Alhazen. One of his works on optics was translated into Latin in 1572.

Abu al-Rayhan al-Biruni was one of the greatest scholars of medieval Islam, and certainly the most original and profound. He was equally well-versed in mathematics, astronomy, the physical and natural sciences, and also distinguished himself as a geographer and historian, a chronologist and linguist, and as an impartial observer of customs and creeds. Such figures as al-Kharizmi (mathematics), Ibn Shatir (astronomy), al-Khazini (physics), Jabir ibn Hayyan (medicine) are remembered even today. Andalusia (Muslim Spain) was the main center from which the West acquired knowledge and enlightenment for centuries.

In his monumental *Introduction to the History of Science*, George Sarton divided time into chronological chapters and named each chapter after that period's most eminent scientist. From the mid-eighth century to the mid-eleventh century, each of the seven 50-year period carries the name of a Muslim scientist: "The

Time of al-Khwarizmi," "The Time of al-Biruni," and so on. Within these chapters we have the names of about 100 important Islamic scientists and their main works.

John Davenport, a leading scientist observed:

> It must be owned that all the knowledge whether of Physics, Astronomy, Philosophy or Mathematics, which flourished in Europe from the 10th century was originally derived from the Arabian schools, and the Spanish Saracen may be looked upon as the father of European philosophy. (Quoted by A. Karim in *Islamic Contribution to Science and Civilization*.)

Bertrand Russell, the famous British philosopher, writes:

> The supremacy of the East was not only military. Science, philosophy, poetry, and the arts, all flourished... in the Muhammadan world at a time when Europe was sunk in barbarism. Europeans, with unpardonable insularity, call this period 'The Dark Ages': but it was only in Europe that it was dark – indeed only in Christian Europe, for Spain, which was Mohammedan, had a brilliant culture." (*Pakistan Quarterly*, vol. 4, no. 3.)

Robert Briffault, the renowned historian, acknowledges in his *The Making of Humanity*:

> It is highly probable that but for the Muslims, modern European civilization would have never assumed that character which has enabled it to transcend all previous phases of evolution. For although there is not a single aspect of human growth in which the decisive influence of Islamic culture is not traceable, nowhere is it so clear and momentous as in the genesis of that power which constitutes the paramount distinctive force of the modern world and the supreme course of its victory – natural sciences and the scientific spirit. . . . What we call science arose in Europe as a result of a new spirit of inquiry; of new methods of investigation, of the method of experiment, observation, measurement, of the development of Mathematics in a form unknown to the Greeks. That spirit and those methods were introduced into the European world by the Muslim Arabs.[4]

During the tenth-century, Muslim Cordoba was Europe's most civilized city, the wonder and admiration of the time. Travelers from the north heard with something like fear of the city that contained 900 public baths and 70 libraries with hundreds of thousands of volumes. Yet whenever the rulers of Leon and Navarre needed surgeons, architects, dressmakers, or musicians, they applied to Cordoba.[5] The Muslims' literary influence was so vast that, for example, the Bible and liturgy had to be translated into Arabic for the Christian community's use. Even non-Muslim Spaniards were vividly attracted to Muslim literature.

For the first 5 centuries of its existence, the realm of Islam was a most civilized and progressive area. Studded with splendid cities, gracious mosques, and quiet universities, the Muslim East offered a striking contrast to the Christian West, which was sunk in the Dark Ages. Even after the disastrous Mongol invasions and Crusades of the thirteenth century and onwards, it displayed vigor and remained for ahead of the West.

The Ethos Brought about by the Messenger

It is difficult for us to understand Prophet Muhammad, upon him be peace and blessings, fully. As we tend to compartmentalize the universe, life, and humanity itself, we have no unitary vision. However, Prophet Muhammad perfectly combined a philosopher's intellect, a commander's valor, a scientist's genius, a sage's wisdom, a statesman's insight and administrative ability, a Sufi master's spiritual profundity, and a scholar's knowledge in his own person.

Philosophers produce students, not followers; social or revolutionary leaders make followers, not complete people; Sufi masters make "lords of submission," not active fighters or intellectuals. But in Prophet Muhammad we find the characteristics of a philosopher, a revolutionary leader, a warrior and statesman, and a Sufi master. His school is one of the intellect and thought; revolution, submission and discipline; and goodness, beauty, ecstasy, and movement.

Prophet Muhammad transformed crude, ignorant, savage, and obstinate desert Arabs into an army of skilled fighters, a community of sincere devotees of a sublime cause, a society of gentleness and compassion, an assembly of sainthood, and a host of intellectuals and scholars. Nowhere else do we see such fervor and ardor combined with gentleness, kindness, sincerity, and compassion. This is a characteristic unique to the Muslim community, one that has been visible since its earliest days.

The "Garden" of Muhammad. Islam, the school of Prophet Muhammad, has been a "garden" rich in every kind of "flower." Like cascading water, God has brought forth from it such majestic people as Abu Bakr, 'Umar, 'Uthman, 'Ali, 'Umar ibn 'Abd al-'Aziz, Mahdi al-'Abbasi, Harun al-Rashid, Alp Arslan, Mehmed the Conqueror, Selim, and Sulayman. These were not only statesmen of the highest caliber and invincible commanders, but also men of profound spirituality, deep knowledge, oration, and literature.

The Messenger's blessed, pure climate produced invincible generals. Among the first generation we see such military geniuses as Khalid, Sa'd ibn Abi Waqqas, Abu 'Ubayda, Shurahbil ibn Hasana, and A'la al-Khadrami. They were succeeded by such brilliant generals as Tariq ibn Ziyad and 'Uqba ibn Nafi', both of whom combined military genius with human tenderness and religious conviction and devotion.

When 'Uqba, the conqueror of North Africa, reached the Atlantic Ocean, 2,000 miles away from Arabia, he cried out: "And now, God, take my soul! If this sea didn't stretch out before me, I would convey Your holy Name across it to other lands!" We can hardly imagine Alexander "the Great" thinking such thoughts as he set out for Persia. Yet as conquerors, the two men achieved comparable feats.

'Uqba's idealism and his "possibility" with respect to the Divine Will would be transmuted into irresistible action in this world. Alexander's empire crashed after his death; the lands 'Uqba conquered still retain Islam as their dominant worldview, creed, and lifestyle 14 centuries later, despite attempts to change this reality.

Tariq was a victorious commander, not only when he defeated the 90,000-man Spanish army with a handful of self-sacrificing, valiant men, but also when he stood before the king's treasure and said: "Be careful, Tariq! You were a slave yesterday. Today you are a victorious commander. And tomorrow you will be under the earth."

Yavuz Selim, an Ottoman Sultan who regarded the world as too small for two rulers, was truly victorious when he crowned some kings and dethroned others, and also when he silently entered Istanbul at bedtime, after conquering Syria and Egypt, to avoid the people's enthusiastic welcome. He also was victorious when he ordered that the robe muddied by his teacher's horse be placed over his coffin because of its sanctity-it had been "muddied" by the horse of a scholar.

During the rapid conquests after the Prophet, many conquered people were distributed among the Muslim families. Those emancipated slaves eventually became the foremost religious scholars: Hasan ibn Hasan al-Basri (Basra); 'Ata' ibn Rabah, Mujahid, Sa'id ibn Jubayr, and Sulayman ibn Yasar (Makka); Zayd ibn Aslam, Muhammad ibn al-Munkadir, and Nafi' ibn Abi Nujayh (Madina); 'Alqama ibn Qays al-Nakha'i, Aswad ibn Yazid, Hammad, and Abu Hanifa Nu'man ibn Thabit (Kufa); Tawus and ibn Munabbih (Yemen); 'Ata ibn 'Abdullah al-Khorasani (Khorasan); and Maqhul (Damascus). They all opened as splendid, sweet-smelling flowers in the garden of Muhammad. They established the Islamic legal code and brought up thousands of jurists, who wrote and complied volumes that are still valued as legal references.

One of these jurists, Imam Abu Hanifa, founded the Hanafi legal school, which has hundreds of millions of followers today. He brought up such great scholars as Imam Abu Yusuf, Imam Zufar, and Imam Muhammad Hasan al-Shaybani, who taught Imam Muhammad Idris al-Shafi'i. The notes Abu Hanifa dictated to Imam al-Shaybani were expounded centuries later by Imam Sarakhsi (the "Sun of Imams") in the 30-volume work *Al-Mabsut*.

Imam Shafi'i, who established the methodological principles of Islamic law, is regarded as a reviver or renewer of religious sciences. However, when his students told Imam Sarakhsi that Imam Shafi'i had memorized 300 fascicles of the Prophetic Traditions, the latter answered: "He had the *zakat* (one-fortieth) of the Traditions in my memory." Imam Shafi'i, Abu Hanifa,

Imam Malik, or Ahmad ibn Hanbal, and so many others, were brought up in the school of Prophet Muhammad.

And then there are such Qur'anic interpreters as Ibn Jarir al-Tabari, Fakhr al-Din al-Razi, Ibn Kathir, Imam Suyuti, Allama Hamdi Yazir, and Sayyid Qutb. In addition, there are such famous *hadith* collectors as Imam Bukhari, Muslim, Tirmidhi, Abu Dawud, Ibn Maja, Nasa'i, Ibn Hanbal, Bayhaqi, Darimi, Daraqutni, Sayf al-Din al-'Iraqi, Ibn Hajar al-Asqalani, and many others. They are all ever-shining stars in the luminous sky of Islamic sciences. All received their light from Prophet Muhammad.

According to Islam, God created humanity on the best pattern, as the most universal and all-embracing theater of Divine Names and Attributes. But people, because of their heedlessness, can fall to the lowest levels. Sufism, the inner dimension of Islam, leads people to perfection or enables them to reacquire their primordial angelic state. Islam has produced countless saints. As it never separated our metaphysical quest or gnosis from the study of nature, many practicing Sufis were also scientists. Such leading saints as 'Abd al Qadir al-Jilani, Shah Naqshband, Ma'ruf al-Karkhi, Hasan Shazili, Ahmad Badawi, Shaykh al-Harrani, Ja'far al-Sadiq, Junayd al-Baghdadi, Bayazid al-Bistami, Muhy al-Din al-'Arabi, and Mawlana Jalal al-Din al-Rumi have illumined the way to truth and trained others to purify their selves.

Being embodiments of sincerity, Divine love, and pure intention, Sufi masters became the motivating factor and the source of power behind the Islamic conquests and the subsequent Islamization of those lands. Figures like Imam al-Ghazzali, Imam Rabbani, and Bediüzzaman Said Nursi are revivers or renewers of the highest degree, and combined in themselves the enlightenment of sages, the knowledge of religious scholars, and the spirituality of great saints.

Islam is the middle way. Its elaborate hierarchy of knowledge is integrated by the principle of Divine Unity. There are juridical, social, and theological sciences, as well as metaphysical ones, all deriving their principles from the Qur'an. Over time, Muslims developed elaborate philosophical, natural, and mathematical sciences, each of which has its source in a Beautiful Name of God. For example, medicine depends on the Name the All-Healing; geometry and engineering on the Names the All-Just and All-Determiner, and All-Shaper and All-Harmonizing; and philosophy reflects the Name the All-Wise.

Each level of knowledge views nature in a particular light. Jurists and theologians see it as the background for human action; philosophers and scientists see it as a domain to be analyzed and understood; and metaphysicians consider it the object of contemplation and the mirror reflecting suprasensible realities. The Author of Nature has inscribed His Wisdom upon every leaf and stone, upon every atom and particle, and has created the world of nature in such a way that every phenomenon is a sign singing the glory of His Oneness.

Conclusion

Although Islam ruled two-thirds of the known civilized world for at least 11 centuries, laziness and negligence of what was going on beyond its borders caused it to decay. However, it must be pointed out clearly that only Islamic civilization decayed – not Islam. Military victories and superiority, which continued into the eighteenth century, encouraged Muslims to rest on their laurels and neglect further scientific research. They abandoned themselves to living their own lives, and recited the Qur'an without studying its deeper meanings. Meanwhile, Europe made great advances in sciences, which they had borrowed from the Muslims.

What we call "sciences" are, in reality, languages of the Divine Book of Creation (another aspect of Islam). Those who ignore this book are doomed to failure in this world. When the Muslims began to ignore it, it was only a matter of time before they would be dominated by some external force. In this case, that external force was Europe. European cruelty, oppression, and imperialism also contributed greatly to this result.

A civilization, which is far from satisfying humanity's perennial needs, cannot last for long. Such Western sociologists as Oswald Spengler and many others have predicted the collapse of modern civilization on the same grounds. Whether these predictions are true or false, we believe that the world's people will soon be awakened to the perennial values brought by the Divinely revealed Religion. These values were preached during history by all the Prophets and Messengers, and represented by them and their followers. Islam, which God sent through Muhammad as the last and perfected form of the religion He appointed for humanity during its history, is the last or perfected form of these religions to meet the needs of all peoples until the Day of Judgment, and the Prophet Muhammad is the last of the Prophets and Messengers. The world's people will be awakened to these values inherent in the Divine Religion, in which the world and the Hereafter, matter and spirit, mind and heart, and faith and science exist in a united and harmonious form. In addition, the bright world of the future will be established on the firm foundation of Islam's creed, ethics, spirituality, and morality, as well as its legal, social, and economic structures.

HOW DO I BECOME A MUSLIM?

Becoming a Muslim requires no special ceremony, because it is a personal commitment. It is enough for one to believe and declare: "I bear witness that there is no deity but God, and I bear witness that Muhammad is His servant and Messenger" (*Ashhadu an la ilaha illa'llah wa ashhadu anna Muhammadan 'abduhu wa Rasuluh*). This declaration of faith should be made before two or more Muslim witnesses in order that one who makes it may be known as a Muslim, but the absence of such witnesses must not cause one to delay becoming a Muslim.

After becoming a Muslim, one should perform the major ablution (*ghusl*), begin to acquire knowledge about Islam's principles and beliefs, as well as how to conduct one's life, and how to perform the lesser ablution (*wudu'*) and pray. After this, the new Muslim must do his or her best to learn other individual responsibilities. One of the best ways to do this is to seek out the company of Muslims who actively practice their faith and can explain its underlying principles and ultimate goals.

NOTES

432

CHAPTER ONE

1.   Said Nursi, *The Letters* [trans.], Kaynak, Izmir, 1998, 2:1-2. Said Nursi (1876-1960): One of the greatest contemporary Muslim scholars; credited with preserving Islam in Turkey during a time of enforced secularization.

CHAPTER TWO

1.   *An Apology for Muhammed and the Qur'an*, London, 1869.

2.   'Ali ibn Abi Talib (600-61): Son-in-law of Prophet Muhammad, fourth caliph (ruled: 656-61), one of the most outstanding figures of early Islam, and considered to be a model of virtue, courage, and wisdom. (*Nahj al-Balagha*, [trans: Ja'far Husayn], Qum, 120)

3.   This section is summarized from Said Nursi, *The Words 2* [trans.], Kaynak, Izmir, 1997.

4.   This section is summarized from M. Fethullah Gülen, *Essentials of the Islamic Faith* (trans.,) The Fountain, NJ, 2000, 41-103.

5.   Summarized from M. Fethullah Gülen, *Essentials of the Islamic Faith* [trans.] The Fountain, NJ, 2000, and Said Nursi, *The Words 1* [trans.], Kaynak, Izmir, 1997, "The 26th Word."

6.   The Traditions concerning the Last Things quoted here can be found in the sections of "Kitab al-Fitan" or "Kitab Ashrat al-Sa'a" in Hadith collections. See especially: Ibn Maja, "Fitan," 33; Ibn Hanbal, *Musnad*, 3:367, 5:13, 6:75; Ibn Abi Shayba, *Al-Musannaf*, 7:490; Hakim, *Mustadrak*, 4:575.

7.   Summarized from M. Fethullah Gülen, *Ölüm Ötesi Hayat* (Life after Death), chapter 2, and *Essentials of the Islamic Faith* [trans.], The Fountain, 2000, chapter 3.

8.   Said Nursi, *The Letters* [trans.], Kaynak, Izmir, 1998, 1:2-3.

9.   M. F. Gülen, *Essentials of the Islamic Faith*.

10.   This section is summarized from Said Nursi, *The Words* [trans.], Kaynak, Izmir, 1997, "The 28th Word."

11.   Summarized mostly from M. Fethullah Gülen, *Essentials of the Islamic Faith* [trans.], The Fountain, NJ, 2000, and Said Nursi, *The Words 2*, "The 25th Word," Kaynak, İzmir, 1997.

12.   Said Nursi, *The Words* [trans.], Kaynak, Izmir, 1997, 2:2-4.

13.   Ibid, 2:10-11, 44.

14.   Some may ask why the Almighty did not preserve other Scriptures. First, He has pre-knowledge of everything and thus knew and predetermined that human well-being and happiness would require a final Prophet. He chose Prophet Muhammad for this position. Through him, He perfected Islam so that it would address all levels of knowledge

of understanding and solve all human problems until the Last Day. As this would obviate the need for another Prophet to revive or restore the religion, He preserved the Qur'an. Second, it is not a sign of God's favor to Muslims to preserve the Qur'an. Rather, as His predetermination includes human free will, He knew that Muslims would be devoted to their Book more than any other people would be devoted to their own. He has preserved the Qur'an by creating the means for its preservation.

15 Prof. Suat Yildirim, *Kur'an-i Kerim ve Kur'an Ilimlerine Giris* ([The Holy Qur'an and An Introduction to the Qur'anic Sciences] Istanbul: 1983, 43, 62-63.

16 Suphi al-Salih, *Kur'an Ilimleri* [trans.], Konya, 57.

17 *Ibid.*, 61.

18 M. M. Puye, *Genuineness of the Holy Qur'an,* Karachi, 1974, 95-98 (reporting from al-Suyuti's *Al-Itqan,* and from Tabarani and Ibn al-Asakir).

19 Yildirim, *ibid.,* 62-66; al-Salih, *ibid.,* 62-65.

20 Yildirim, *ibid.,* 66-70; al-Salih, *ibid.,* 65-73.

21 *Isharat al-I'jaz* (Signs of the Qur'an's Miraculousness), Istanbul, 9.

22 Joseph Hell, *The Arab Civilization*, 10.

23 Mostly edited and summarized from *Towards Understanding Islam* by al-Mawdudi, I.I.F.S.O., 1970, 59-60.

24 Ibn Hisham, *Sirat al-Nabawiya*, 1:282.

25 Sir William Muir, *Life of Muhammad* (Osnabrück: Biblio, 1988).

26 Lamartine, *Historie de la Turquie*, 2:26-27.

27 Ibn Kathir, *al-Bidaya wal-Nihaya*, 4:76; Ibn Hisham, *Sira*, 3:182.

28 M. Mutahhari, *Jaziba wa Dafi'a-i Ali*, Tehran.

29 M. Hamidullah, *Islam Peygamberi* [trans.], Istanbul, 1972, 1:145-146.

30 Summarized from Said Nursi, *The Words 1* [trans.], Kaynak, Izmir, 1997, "The 23rd Word."

CHAPTER THREE

1 This section is quoted from Said Nursi, *The Words* [trans.], Kaynak, Izmir, 1997, 1:23-25; "The 4th Word."

2 Ibid, 1:49-59; "The 9th Word."

3 From Bediuzzaman Said Nursi, *The Letters* [trans.], Kaynak, Izmir, 1998, "The 29th Letter."

4 This section is taken (edited and summarized) from Muhammad Hamidullah, *Introduction to Islam* and from Ahmad Shafa'at and Asghar Qureshi, *Hamdard Islamicus* 20, no. 3 [Jul-Sept 1997]).

5 Abu'l-Fazl Ezzati, *An Introduction to the History of the Spread of Islam*, London 1978, 199-200.

6 This section is taken from various parts (edited and summarized) of Yusuf al-Qaradawi, *The Lawful and Prohibited in Islam,* trans. Muhammad Siddiqi (ASIN: 1999).

7 This section is taken (and partly edited) from Hammuda Abdul-Ati, *Islam in Focus* (Kuwait: IIFSO, 1990), 184-91.

[8] Prof. Suat Yildirim, "Kur'an-i Hakim ve Aciklamali Meali" ("The Wise Qur'an Interpreted with Explanatory Notes"), *Zaman newspaper*, Istanbul, 1998, 77.

[9] This section is summarized from M. Fethullah Gülen, *The Messenger of God: Muhammad - An Analysis of the Prophet's Life* [trans.], 337-349.

[10] This section is taken from Said Nursi, *The Letters 2* [trans.], Kaynak, Izmir, 1998, "The 21st Letter."

[11] This section is taken (partly edited) from Yusuf al-Qaradawi, *The Lawful and Prohibited in Islam*, trans. Muhammad Siddiqi (ASIN: 1999).

[12] This section is taken (edited and summarized) from Said Nursi, *The Words 1*, Kaynak, Izmir, 1997, "The 23rd Word"; Sayyid Sabiq, *Fiqh al-Sunna* [trans.], Ist., 1:445-480; and M. Fethullah Gülen, *The Messenger of God: Muhammad - An Analysis of the Prophet's Life*, [trans.], 279-283.

CHAPTER FOUR

[1] M. Fethullah Gülen, *The Messenger of God: Muhammad - An Analysis of the Prophet's Life* [trans.], 283-300.

[2] Said Nursi, *The Letters 2* [trans.], Kaynak, Izmir, 1998.

CHAPTER FIVE

[1] Vaglieri, Laura Veccia, *Apologia dell Islamismo,* Washington, American Fazl Mosque; trans.; Aldo Caselli, *An Interpretation of Islam,* Beirut: Laila Khalidy Memorial Foundation, 1957, 30-33.

[2] This section is taken from M. Fethullah Gülen, *Key Concepts in the Practice of Sufism* [trans.], The Fountain, NJ, 1999.

[3] This section is mostly summarized from Abu'l-Fazl Ezzati, *An Introduction to the History of the Spread of Islam*, London, 1978.

[4] For the last three quotations, see: Abu'l-A'la al-Mawdudi, *Towards Under-standing Islam*, I.I.F.S.O., 1970, 69.

[5] Thomas Arnold, *The Legacy of Islam*, Oxford, 1931, 9.

INDEX